...MPORARY SOC...

...l Editor: ANTHONY GIDDENS

...s aims to create a forum for debate between different ...l and philosophical traditions in the social sciences. As ...overing broad schools of thought, the series will also ...ate upon the work of particular thinkers whose ideas have ...jor impact on social science (these books appear under the ...es title of 'Theoretical Traditions in the Social Sciences'). ...ries is not limited to abstract theoretical discussion – it will ...clude more substantive works on contemporary capitalism, ...ate, politics and other subject areas.

...hed titles

...Bilton, Kevin Bonnett, Philip Jones, Ken Sheard, Michelle Stanworth and ...rew Webster, *Introductory Sociology*
...Clarke, *Marx, Marginalism and Modern Sociology*
...Durkheim, *The Division of Labour in Society* (trans. W. D. Halls)
...Durkheim, *The Rules of Sociological Method* (ed. Steven Lukes, trans. W. D. ...s)
...rankel, *Beyond the State?*
...y Giddens, *A Contemporary Critique of Historical Materialism*
...v Giddens, *Central Problems in Social Theory*
...Giddens, *Profiles and Critiques in Social Theory*
...Giddens and David Held (eds), *Classes, Power and Conflict: Classical and ...porary Debates*
...gham, *Capitalism Divided?*
...so... Christopher Dandeker and Clive Ashworth, *The Structure of Social ...*
..., *Herbert Marcuse and the Crisis of Marxism*
..., *Marxism and Ideology*
..., *...x and the Division of Labour*
Gerry Rose, *Deciphering Sociological Research*
John Scott, *The Upper Classes: Property and Privilege in Britain*
Steve Taylor, *Durkheim and the Study of Suicide*
John B. Thompson and David Held (eds), *Habermas: Critical Debates*
John Urry, *The Anatomy of Capitalist Societies*

Forthcoming titles

Martin Albrow, *Max Weber and the Construction of Social Theory*
Ali Rattansi and Dominic Strinati, *Marx and the Sociology of Class*

CONTEMPORARY SOCIAL THEORY

General Editor: ANTHONY GIDDENS

Theoretical Traditions in the Social Sciences

This new series introduces the work of major figures in social science to students beyond their immediate specialisms.

Published titles

Barry Barnes, *T. S. Kuhn and Social Science*
Ted Benton, *The Rise and Fall of Structural Marxism*
David Bloor, *Wittgenstein: A Social Theory of Knowledge*
Christopher G. A. Bryant, *Positivism in Social Theory and Research*
Mark Cousins and Athar Hussain, *Michel Foucault*
Bob Jessop, *Nicos Poulantzas: Marxist Theory and Political Strategy*
Julian Roberts, *Walter Benjamin*
Rick Roderick, *Habermas and the Foundations of Critical Theory*
James Schmidt, *Maurice Merleau-Ponty: Between Phenomenology and Structuralism*
Dennis Smith, *Barrington Moore: Violence, Morality and Political Change*
Piotr Sztompka, *Robert K. Merton: An Intellectual Profile*

Forthcoming titles

Ira Cohen, *Structuration Theory*
John Forrester, *Jacques Lacan*
William Outhwaite, *Realist Philosophy in the Social Sciences*
Dennis Smith, *The Chicago School*
Robin Williams, *Erving Goffman*

Other books by Piotr Sztompka

System and Function: Toward a Theory of Society
Sociological Dilemmas: Toward a Dialectic Paradigm
Masters of Polish Sociology (editor and contributor)

Robert K. Merton

An intellectual profile

Piotr Sztompka

Professor of Sociology
Jagiellonian University at Krakow, Poland

© Piotr Sztompka 1986

All rights reserved. No reproduction, copy or transmission of this publication may be made without written permission.

No paragraph of this publication may be reproduced, copied or transmitted save with written permission or in accordance with the provisions of the Copyright Act 1956 (as amended).

Any person who does any unauthorised act in relation to this publication may be liable to criminal prosecution and civil claims for damages.

First published 1986

Published by
MACMILLAN EDUCATION LTD
Houndmills, Basingstoke, Hampshire RG21 2XS
and London
Companies and representatives
throughout the world

Typeset by
Wessex Typesetters
Frome, Somerset

Printed in Hong Kong

British Library Cataloguing in Publication Data
Sztompka, Piotr
Robert K. Merton: an intellectual profile.
1. Merton, R. K.
I. Title
310'.092'4   HM22.U52M4
ISBN 0-333-37210-7
ISBN 0-333-37211-5 Pbk

Stock No.	209236
Class No.	301(092) MER
Checked	S2T

To Robert K. Merton,
my master-at-a-distance turned friend—
on his seventy-fifth birthday

'He has attempted to arrive at a synthesis of many of the traditions in the shadow of which he stands and so to transcend every particular influence. Putting them to use, he rose above them all while remaining deeply in their debt.'—Lewis A. Coser (1975, p. 99)

Contents

Preface ix
Acknowledgements xii
Robert K. Merton: Selected Biographical Moments xiii

1 Analysing Merton   **1**
   Assumptions   1
   Directives   5
   The logic   7

2 The Scholar   **9**
   Self-image   10
   As seen by others   14
   The academic role-set   17
   Intellectual genealogy   20
   Scientific contribution   30

3 On Science   **34**
   Sociological approach to science   34
   From sociology of knowledge to sociology of science   37
   Science as a system   45
   Scientific ethos and scientific mind   49
   Scientific community   60
   Science as process   66
   Toward a sociological epistemology   75

4 On Sociological Method   **80**
   Poverty of sociology   81
   Canons of science   86
   Problem-formulation   93
   Concept-formation   98
   Research 'versus' theory   102
   Theory of the middle range   107

	Paradigms	113
	Disciplined eclecticism	115
5	**On Sociological Orientation**	**119**
	The crisis of sociology	120
	The focus of sociology	123
	Functional analysis	126
	Neo-functionalism	136
	Structural analysis	143
	Combining functional and structural analysis	150
	The third dimension: temporal analysis	152
6	**On Social Structure**	**158**
	Anatomy of social structure	159
	Varieties of consensus and dissensus	173
	Modalities of behavioural adaptations	182
	Moulding personality	192
7	**On Social Processes**	**199**
	Structure, conflict and change	200
	Adaptive processes	202
	Structure-building	210
	Behind the stage; action and agent	227
8	**A Modern Sociological Classic**	**240**
	The classicist theme	241
	The cognitivist theme	246
	The structuralist theme	248
	The theme of irony	252
	The classicist synthesis of classical sociology	257
Notes and References		262
Bibliography		301
Name Index		315
Subject Index		319

Preface

Like thousands of sociologists all over the world I have made indirect acquaintance with Robert K. Merton via his books, and particularly the seminal *Social Theory and Social Structure*.[1] My initiation in sociology, and my growing fascination with the field, owed much to the twenty-and-one essays contained in that volume. At that time I already had a vague intuition that Merton's work somehow differed from many other volumes I was reading. Other authors attracted me by their erudition, or deductive precision, or systematic coherence, or insightfulness, or originality. But none of those virtues *per se* seemed a fitting characterisation for Merton. And then I hit upon the term 'wisdom', defined by *Webster's New World Dictionary* as 'the quality of being wise; the power of judging rightly and following the soundest course of action, based on knowledge, experience, understanding, etc.; good judgement; discretion; sagacity'.[2] Up to now Merton has remained for me the embodiment of *sociological wisdom*: the modern sage of social science.

Fifteen years ago I met the sage in person, in his open-neck shirt and colourful scarf, at a party for visiting professors at Columbia University, and soon after, at his book-packed study on Riverside Drive in New York. Immediately friendly, open, sympathetic, concerned with the work and fate of a young apprentice from a far-away country. To my admiration for the work, the admiration for a man was added.

And then, several other meetings and innumerable hours of involved debates followed, both in New York, and at international congresses. There were also many letters, but I will never forget one little postcard signed Bob, that I received at perhaps the most difficult time for me and my country, bringing encouragement, friendship and solidarity.

Thus when Anthony Giddens approached me with the offer of writing a book on Merton's social theory for his series at Macmillan

Publishers, I could not be more enthusiastic – for both scientific and personal reasons. Now that my intellectual adventure with Merton's work is over, though certainly encoded deeply and permanently in my sociological thinking as one of the most challenging and educative experiences, I have to make a record of my indebtedness and gratitude.

The largest share of that goes, naturally enough, to my proper subject-matter, Robert Merton himself. After all, had he not been writing so profusely and so well on so many topics, my reading and re-reading of his voluminous work would not have been as exciting, rewarding and enriching. But my deep gratitude is also due for more direct help – his generosity in giving me full access to otherwise unobtainable resources and files: to minor publications, reprints, manuscripts, proofs, conference papers, outlines of future work, as well as unique samples of his scientific correspondence with other scholars and intellectuals. I have also had the privilege and benefit of his thorough and insightful comments, criticisms and suggestions at the stage of conceiving the book, as well as constant, though discreet encouragement at the time of actual writing. Wasn't it wonderful for example to receive those 'Twenty-five suggestions [on writing] to ladies and gentlemen who have completed an American college education and are now pursuing graduate studies as candidates for higher degrees', given to his students some seventy years ago by Franklin H. Giddings? Or Merton's own 'Memorandum to whom it should concern from one who is concerned about the singular use of plurality and other such assaults on the English language',[3] summing up some egregious practices he observed as editor. Thus, briefly and formally, for the record, had it not been for Robert K. Merton, this book would not have been possible – *literally and figuratively*, in all senses of this statement.

To Professor Anthony Giddens from the University of Cambridge I am deeply indebted for the idea of my taking up this challenging endeavour, as well as for many insightful and important editorial suggestions.

Mary Wilson Miles served as an intermediary between Merton and myself and provided immense help in many practical matters, especially in the collection of bibliographical sources. For her efforts, heartfelt thanks.

And Steven Kennedy, the social science editor at Macmillan Publishers, remained poised and accommodating, in spite of technical problems created by the geographical distance separating author and publisher. He also displayed in abundance the virtue crucial for publishers – patience.

The final version of the manuscript was prepared in the stimulating and friendly environment of the University of Michigan at Ann Arbor, where I stayed as a Fellow of the American Council of Learned Societies in 1984–5.

Krakow/Ann Arbor   Piotr Sztompka

Acknowledgements

The author and publishers wish to thank the following who have kindly given permission for the use of copyright material: F. Barbano and Universitetsforlaget, Oslo, for extract, 'Social Structures and Social Functions: The Emancipation of Structural Analysis in Sociology' in *Inquiry* 11/1968; R. Bierstedt and Academic Press, Florida, for extract from, *American Sociological Theory: A Critical History*, Academic Press, New York (1981); C. Campbell and the American Sociological Association for extract, 'A Dubious Distinction? An Inquiry into the Value and Use of Merton's Concepts of Manifest and Latent Function', in *ASR*, Vol. 47 (1) (1982); Z. K. and C. P. Loomis for extract, *Modern Social Theories: Selected American Writers*, Princeton (1961) Van Norstrand; R. K. Merton and Howard Fertig Inc. for extract from *Science, Technology and Society in Seventeenth-Century England*, Howard Fertig, New York (1970); R. K. Merton and the University of Chicago Press for extract, *The Sociology of Science: Theoretical and Empirical Investigations*, ed. N. W. Storer, Chicago 1973, University of Chicago Press; R. K. Merton for extract, *Sociological Ambivalence and Other Essays*, The Free Press, New York (1976); R. K. Merton and ABT Books for extract, *Social Research and the Practicing Professions*, ed. A. Rosenblatt and T. F. Gieryn, Cambridge (1982); R. K. Merton for extract, *On The Shoulders of Giants: A Shandean Postscript* (1965), The Free Press, a division of Macmillan Inc., New York; R. K. Merton for extract, 'Anomie, Anomia and Social Interaction: Contexts of Deviant Behavior', in M. Clinard (ed.), *Anomie and Deviant Behavior: A Discussion and Critique*, 1964, The Free Press, a division of Macmillan Inc., New York; R. K. Merton for extract, *Social Theory and Social Structure*, enlarged edition, New York (1968), The Free Press, a division of Macmillan Inc., New York; R. K. Merton and P. F. Lazarsfeld for extract, 'Friendship as Social Process: A Substantive and Methodological Analysis', in *Freedom and Control in Modern Society*, ed. M. Berger *et al.*, New York (1954), Van Nostrand; A. Stinchcombe for extract, 'Merton's Theory of Social Structure' in *The Idea of Social Structure: Papers in Honor of R. K. Merton*, ed. Lewis A. Coser, Academic Press, New York (1975).

Every effort has been made to trace all the copyright-holders but if any have been inadvertently overlooked the publishers will be pleased to make the necessary arrangement at the first opportunity.

Robert K. Merton: Selected Biographical Moments

1910	Born into working-class family in Philadelphia
1031	Receives A.B. from Temple University
1936	Receives Ph.D. from Harvard University
	Publishes 'The Unanticipated Consequences of Purposive Social action'
1936–9	Tutor and instructor at Harvard
1937	Publishes (with P. A. Sorokin) 'Social Time: A Functional and Methodological Analysis'
1938	Publishes first book, *Science, Technology and Society in Seventeenth-century England*
	Publishes 'Social Structure and Anomie'
1939	Publishes 'Bureaucratic Structure and Personality'
1939–41	Associate Professor, then Professor and Chairman, Department of Sociology at Tulane University in New Orleans
1941–79	Assistant Professor to Professor; Giddings Professor of Sociology
1942	Publishes 'A Note on Science and Democracy (The Normative Structure of Science)'
1946	Publishes *Mass Persuasion*
1948	Publishes 'The Self-fulfilling Prophecy'
1949	Publishes *Social Theory and Social Structure*
1950	Publishes (with Alice Kitt Rossi) 'Contributions to the Theory of Reference Group Behavior'
1954	Publishes (with P. F. Lazarsfeld) 'Friendship as a Social Process: A Substantive and Methodological Analysis'
1956	Publishes (with M. Fiske and P. Kendall) *The Focused Interview*
1957	Publishes (with G. L. Reader, P. L. Kendall *et al.*) *The Student-physician*

	Publishes 'The Role-set: Problems in Sociological Theory'
	Publishes 'Priorities in Scientific Discovery: A Chapter in the Sociology of Science'
	Elected President of American Sociological Association*
1964	Publishes 'Anomie, Anomia and Social Interaction: Contexts of Deviant Behavior'
1965	Publishes *On the Shoulders of Giants*
1968	Publishes 'The Matthew-effect in Science: the Reward and Communication Systems of Science'
1968	Receives honorary degrees from Yale University and the University of Chicago**
1971	Publishes (with Harriet Zuckerman) 'Patterns of Evaluation in Science: Institutionalization, Structure, and Functions of the Referee System'
1972	Publishes 'Insiders and Outsiders: A Chapter in the Sociology of Knowledge'
1973	Publishes *The Sociology of Science*
1975	Elected first President of Society for Social Studies of Science
1976	Publishes *Sociological Ambivalence*
1979	Publishes *The Sociology of Science: An Episodic Memoir*
	Edits (with T. J. Trenn) Ludwik Fleck, *Genesis and Development of a Scientific Fact* (translation from the German)
1980	Receives honorary degree from Harvard University
1982	Publishes *Social Research and the Practicing Professions*
1983	Publishes (with Vanessa Merton and Elinor Barber) 'Client Ambivalences in Professional Relationships'
	MacArthur Prize Fellow
1984	Publishes 'Socially Expected Durations I: A Case Study of Concept Formation in Sociology'
	Publishes 'The Fallacy of the Latest Word: The Case of Pietism and Science'
1979–84	University Professor Emeritus and Special Service Professor at Columbia University
1984	University Professor Emeritus at Columbia University

* He has served as President of several other academic societies and is an honorary member in a dozen academies and learned societies.

** He has received some twenty honorary degrees from universities in the United States and abroad.

1

Analysing Merton

My task is to draw a portrait. A special portrait; not artistic but scientific, not of a person but of a mind. The pieces are all here: some twenty books written and edited, many articles, unpublished papers, reviews, outlines of lectures, personal letters, the record and traces of more than fifty years of intellectual creativity. How to turn this heap of precious stones into a mosaic – with a shape, a structure, a meaning, an impact?

Here Merton himself provides a clue. On page 70 of *Social Theory and Social Structure* he observes: 'If true art consists in concealing all signs of art, true science consists in revealing its scaffolding as well as its finished structure.'[1] Adapting this to my purpose of presenting a *scholarly portrait of a scholar*, I begin by revealing scaffolding; my assumptions, the directives guiding my efforts, the logic of reconstruction. As one of Merton's teachers, L. J. Henderson, liked to counsel his attentive students 'It's a good thing to know what you are doing'.[2] This chapter explains what I intend to do in this book.

Assumptions

Four central ideas underly my interpretation of Merton's work. At this stage they are here stipulated only as tentative assumptions or interpretative hypotheses which will be given increasingly firm foundation as the analysis proceeds, and one trusts will be amply confirmed by the close.

The first assumption says: Merton's work constitutes a *coherent system of thought*, not a scattered set of contributions. This is by no means obvious, owing to his rather unorthodox strategy of doing social science.[3] He evidently prefers writing essays and articles to the writing of fat books. As Daniel Bell observes: 'Writers, like runners, develop "natural" length. The man who runs the 100-yard dash will rarely be a good half-miler; wind capacity and the sense of pace are necessarily different'.[4] In terms of this metaphor Merton is certainly like a middle-distance runner. Most of his formidable output is in the form of extended essays, long articles, introductions, reviews, discussions – sometimes getting so long as to turn imperceptibly into a book, as that 'Shandean postscript' of 290 pages just published in its third, Vicennial Edition,[5] or that 'Episodic Memoir' of 150 pages tracing the development of the sociology of science;[6] but most often gathered up in numerous collections among which *Social Theory and Social Structure* (in its three major editions), *The Sociology of Science*, *Sociological Ambivalence* and *Social Research and the Practicing Professions* are most significant. The true 'book', in the sense so dear to the humanists and so alien to the natural scientists, he has written only one and only when he had to – his doctoral dissertation on *Science, Technology and Society in Seventeenth-Century England*.[7]

Moreover, the thematic range of his interests is very wide: from drug-addicts to professionals, from anomie and structurally induced deviation to social time, from friendship-formation to role-conflicts, from functional analysis to scientific ethos, from medical education to multiple discoveries, from bureaucratic structure to the origins of medieval aphorisms etc. In the poetic idiom of one recent appraisal, 'He is moving with the speed and grace of a humming bird from one blossom to the next, never still but always seeming in flight'.[8]

It is easy to be misled by all this, to mix form with content, appearances with substance, the criteria important for bookbinders and booksellers with those significant for the analyst, and then to claim with Bierstedt that 'Merton alone among our American sociologists has made no effort to construct a system of sociology', and therefore, supposedly, 'he has given us no systematic work, no theory of the social order, no system of sociology'.[9] It is true only in the sense that Merton always opposed the practice of building his own system *from scratch*, attempting instead to put himself firmly on the shoulders of sociological giants of the past. But it is grossly mistaken if intended to mean that there are no systemic interlinks between Merton's contributions. If I read Merton correctly, there is precisely a system of sociological thought emerging from his persistent and disciplined inquiry. The building blocks of the system are given by means of disparate solutions to the many problems he finds puzzling. The unity and coherence of the whole is provided by the common frame of mind of the architect; Merton's characteristic sociological orientation. Several observers agree that there is a striking 'consistence of viewpoint which marks not only his major work *Social Theory and Social Structure* but the many miscellaneous works which have come from this seminal scholar'.[10] Thus, result is a coherent intellectual system.

I perceive that system as a two-tier edifice. The first level is made up of ideas about reality, particularly the social reality. In a word, ideas about society. It may be called the *sociological system*. The second level is made up of ideas about science, and particularly social science. In a word, ideas about sociology. It may be called the *meta-scientific system*. The most striking feature of the construction is the close fit of both levels, bound strongly together by reciprocal links. On the one hand, science is itself conceived as a social phenomenon, and scientific cognition as a social process. Thus, the sociological ideas inform the meta-sociological analyses. And, on the other hand, the ideas about science, its functioning and organisation are seen as applying with appropriate modification to other social institutions. The realm of science becomes a sort of micro-model for social reality as such; the realm of society a sort of macro-model for the study of science. In my reading, Merton's various scientific contributions at both levels of analysis are mutually interrelated and make up a coherent whole. This is what I understand by a system of thought.

The second assumption to be examined in this book holds that Merton has not stopped at the level of concrete or middle-range propositions, but has produced a *full-fledged general theory*. Again one is easily misled on this point, and the fault is partly Merton's, for two reasons. First, in his opposition to scholastic, formalistic 'grand theory',[11] he seems to confuse the *manner* of theorising with the *level* of theorising. Opting for empirically grounded and empirically consequential theory, he seems to imply that it can *only* be attained at a middle level of generality, as a 'theory of the middle range'. But as Stinchcombe aptly observes: 'in the dialectic between Parsons and Merton, generality has been confused with woolliness. Merton, in taking up the correct position on woolliness, has tricked himself into taking up the incorrect position on general theory. The true situation is precisely the opposite. It is because Merton has a better general theory than Parsons that his work has been more empirically fruitful'.[12] And second, in his own theoretical research he has chosen to stay at the middle level, producing numerous middle range theories – of deviance, of role conflicts, of reference-groups, of sociological ambivalence, of bureaucratic structure, of scientific communities and many others – instead of general accounts of social order and social change. Thus, if one sticks close to the surface of occasional declarations of preference, one can readily overlook the general theoretical implications of the actual work and conclude that 'with Durkheim as [his] "role model", [we do not] find a general theory of society in Merton'.[13]

But if one digs further into the matter, searching for the structure of Merton's thought, one is immediately faced with the conclusion that 'many of Merton's papers deal, on a deeper level, with the same theme, even when the titles and the apparent subject matter seem quite different',[14] and that 'the great variety of Merton's empirical theories is generated from a small set of common elements, organised around a core theory'.[15] This *core theory*, or common theme is most general; it crowns the system of Merton's more specific contributions. Since that system consists of two major parts – sociological and meta-scientific – two general theories are to be found there: *a general theory of society* and a *general theory of science*, these being interlinked and sharing a common logic.

The third assumption holds that Merton's intellectual development over a period of some fifty years has been marked by *continuity and coherence*. To be sure, he often returns to previously stated ideas, modifying them, enriching them, following them up with new evidence.[16] But I have not found a single instance when he would be made to reject or revoke any of them in full. It seems as if he were slowly and persistently uncovering and polishing pieces of some matrix of sociological knowledge.[17] Of his works generally he could perhaps say much the same that he remarked in the preface to a new edition of his doctoral dissertation, appearing thirty-two years after its first printing: 'Even now, I am led to subscribe to the subdued concluding sentence of this aged but perhaps not obsolete essay'.[18] For a scholar as self-critical and anti-dogmatic as Merton, this is quite a strong assertion.

The fourth assumption of this analysis maintains that Merton's work has a set of pervasive leitmotifs – central ideas – which can be described as the classicist theme, the cognitivist theme, the structuralist theme and the ironic theme. These cut across the several levels of his system of thought, the various substantive areas of his interest and the various kinds of research he has undertaken. These themes provide the key to the understanding and interpretation of Merton's intellectual identity.[19]

Before the usefulness of these themes for understanding can be demonstrated in detailed analysis, a rough summary of them must suffice. By the *classicist theme*, I mean the observed tendency to search for the golden mean, to reconcile seeming contradictions and to formulate intermediate solutions to basic meta-theoretical and theoretical problems; it is further to strive for simplicity, parsimony, coherence, harmony and elegance of exposition. By the *cognitivist theme*, I mean the belief that the goal of science is better understanding, or explanation of problems, utilising restrictive criteria of evidence which are more or less common to the various scientific disciplines, and demanding empirical confirmation, objectivity, detachment – with practical utility as an ultimate but not necessarily immediate corelate. By the *structuralist theme*, I mean a focus on structural constraints and facilitations, social situations, social configurations and social contexts as that which explains or is to-be-explained by sociological theory. Finally, by the *ironic theme*, I mean the recognition of complexities, contradictions and paradoxes of the human condition, circular processes and unanticipated effects in society, a far from unilinear course of history, the intricacy and relativity of all things social. It is the composite of these four themes that characterises Merton's work and gives it an unmistakable stamp. I shall return to the systematic reappraisal of these themes toward the end of the book.

Directives

Several more specific interpretative directives will be applied in the following analysis. To some extent, they are entailed by the basic assumptions, to some extent derive from my analytical preferences. Taken together, they define my approach to Merton's work.

To begin with, I treat Merton's ideas as a self-contained, even though still developing, body of thought, in abstraction both from biographical context – the phase of his life in which they were formulated, the concrete sequence of their development, and the psychological circumstances of their emergence.[20] I also abstract these ideas from the historical, political, social and economic contexts which may have influenced the author. Irrespective of the moment and circumstances of their origin, the ideas are examined as a unified whole, a distinctive Mertonian enclave in Popper's 'World 3',[21] as building blocks from which Merton's system of thought is reconstructed. Thus, this intellectual portrait more nearly resembles a snapshot rather than a motion picture; an academic study or ivory tower, rather than a barricade provides the setting.

Throughout, I adopt a generalising, interpretative approach, trying to reconstruct the general theory which is for the most part implicit, and sometimes deeply hidden in Merton's sociological contributions. For that reason I shall dig below the surface of particular results and literal pronouncements. In this respect, the actual portrait will be somewhat like a police identi-kit, outlining the main features of the subject, rather than a realistic canvas in elaborate detail.

I also adopt a detached and *immanent approach*, seeking to avoid infusing that portrait with my sympathies and antipathies, as well as with my own theoretical predilections and commitments. After all, this is to be a scholarly portrait; a possibly true representation, and not a caricature. The merits and deficiencies of Merton's work should derive from analysis, reconstruction and interpretation, rather than being insinuated by high-sounding adjectives. The merits and limitations of ideas are to be judged on their own terms by means of immanent criteria, rather than in terms of external, transcendental frames of reference, taken from other systems of thought. The ultimate expression of this approach will be the attempt to treat Merton's sociological theory as a *self-exemplifying case*; to appraise it in terms of his own conceptions of science and sociology.

Finally, I take a prospective approach, attempting to identify the *future-oriented potentials* of Merton's work. Tracing its potentials of elaboration, I shall try to show by examples how it stimulates further conceptual, typological and theoretical research, by producing sociological puzzles, specifying sociological ignorance, and identifying lacunae in current theoretical knowledge.[22] By tracing its potentials of application, I shall try to show, again with fitting examples of actual research, how it can provide a rationale for further empirical inquiry in various fields of sociology. And tracing its potentials of relevance,[23] I shall try to indicate, or at least to hint at its possible direct or indirect implications for social practice.

The logic

Two complementary and cross-cutting principles organise this analysis of Merton's work. The first focuses on its deep-structure and leads to the unravelling of the four themes, which constitute the pervasive and distinguishing features of Merton's contributions, *the unique style or grammar of his thinking*. To repeat, these are the classicist theme, the cognitivist theme, the structuralist theme and the ironic theme. The elements of each theme will be identified as we proceed, with their being brought together in the last, synthesising chapter.

In order to proceed systematically with the analysis, another organising principle is needed. That one focuses on the surface-structure of Merton's work and leads to the identifying of the chief substantive areas and topics with which he deals. In a first approximation, I have earlier referred to his scientific (sociological) ideas, his image of society; and to his meta-scientific (metasociological) ideas, his image of scientific cognition. But we now need a more fine-grained distinction. In a further approximation, we must distinguish Merton's ideas that refer to science as such; those belonging to meta-science, and representing his image of science from those ideas that refer exclusively to the social sciences, most particularly sociology; these belonging to meta-sociology and representing his image of sociology. It seems reasonable to examine them separately.

But of course, the intellectual portrait would be empty were one to forget that ideas have their creator, the scholar. Precisely because I confine myself to an intellectual portrait, only one aspect of the entire person can be included; his abstracted, one-sided, almost Picasso-like profile, of the man solely as scholar and not as father, citizen, adopted New Yorker, political man, tennis-player, concert- and theatre-goer, prestidigitator.[24] To put it otherwise, I shall focus wholly on his role as a scholar, neglecting the many other roles he plays. The characterisation of that role, prescribed and realised as seen by others and also by himself must find its place, too.

As can be seen, then, my discussion follows a logical sequence. It begins by characterising Merton as scholar, following with his ideas on science, moving next to his ideas on sociology, to arrive at his ideas on society. In the last, synthesising chapter, I try to define his intellectual identity in terms of the four underlying themes.

2

The Scholar

Behind the bibliography that runs to some thirty pages of print,[1] there is a man, 'a man of knowledge' – to use Znaniecki's apt phrase,[2] who has been creating all that for half a century. My aim in this chapter is to outline his profile. Not in full but only in the form of a one-dimensional sketch, derived from looking through the prism of his social role as a man of knowledge, as a scholar.

Like other roles, academic roles involve a basic duality. On the one hand, they consist of *normative expectations*, to adopt Merton's '4Ps formula' they consist of prescriptions, preferences, permissions and proscriptions. On the other hand, they consist of *actual performance*, the contingent and variable implementation of norms and values in actual conduct. Expectations and realities may of course diverge, subject to underlying circumstances.

Each academic role, again like any other, is played in front of an audience, 'significant others', 'reference groups', 'the social circle' – and also in front of oneself. The definition of normative expectations as well as the evaluation of the performance are provided by the audience and also by the scholar himself. His conduct is prescribed and judged by the community of peers, but he can also set his own standards and appraise his own performance. And again, the self-definitions and self-appraisals may diverge from the definitions and appraisals given by others.

The social roles performed by scholars take various forms. Numerous typologies have been suggested in the sociological literature to give order to that variety. Merton himself makes use of three typologies. First, in an early review of Znaniecki's *The Social Role of the Man of Knowledge*, in 1941, he endorses the typology provided by the co-author of *The Polish Peasant*: 'Technological Advisers', 'Sages', 'Scholars' and 'Explorers'.[3] He goes on to make the pointed observation that 'this is a classification of social roles and not of persons, and that individual men [and he would no doubt now write: and women] of knowledge may incorporate several of these analytically distinguishable roles'.[4]

Then, in a paper written in the mid-1950s with Lazarsfeld, Merton introduces two further distinctions about what he describes as 'styles of intellectual life'. The one is between 'the generalizers and the empiricists, between the sociologists primarily concerned with developing substantive doctrines which go well beyond presently available data and the sociologists primarily concerned with extending the range of certified facts in hand'.[5] The other distinction is between substantive theorists, producing concepts and propositions about social behaviour, and formal methodologists whose statements deal with the logic of inquiry.[6]

Finally, in a paper written in 1972, Zuckerman and Merton apply the intervening idea of a role-set to the social structure of science and observe that 'the status of scientist involves not a single role but, in varying mixtures, a complement of roles. These are of four principal kinds: research, teaching, administrative, and gatekeeper roles'.[7] The fact that those components of the role-set appear in 'varying mixtures' and with varying emphases allows one to distinguish *researchers*, primarily concerned with inquiry; *teachers*, primarily concerned with the dissemination of knowledge; *administrators*, primarily concerned with the organisation of science; and *gatekeepers*, doing much to set and apply the criteria and to control entrance into the scientific community as well as mobility within it.[8]

These considerations and distinctions help us organise the characterisation of Merton as scholar. I begin by reconstructing his normative image of his social role; briefly what he wants to do in his work and how he wants to do it, to use his favourite expression 'what he is up to'. I then report the expressed opinions as well as the implicit cues through which other scientists indicate their perception of his actual work. From both perspectives, I apply the typologies of scientific roles which Merton has himself endorsed or proposed, and go on to venture my own hypothesis concerning Merton's scientific role, and the basis and evidence of his intellectual influence. Finally, I try to locate his place in the history of sociology: how he relates himself to the sociological tradition and what I take to be his lasting contribution to the evolving discipline.

Self-image

A crucial component of a normative social role is the goal or goals that a person sets for himself. What is the ultimate goal of Merton's sociology? Is there one dominant goal or a hierarchy of goals?

One point seems evident at the outset: in Merton's case the goal is cognitive rather than critical or practical. Merton wants to know the truth, and he evidently believes that nothing is more practical than the truth. He apparently shares the creed of those philosophers who claim that 'knowledge is power' or, in paraphrase of an earlier source, that 'knowledge makes one free'. But what kind of knowledge is clearly of primary importance: is it the *descriptive account* of concrete facts, *deductive explanation* by means of general laws, the *understanding* of human meanings assigned to social phenomena? And what should this knowledge be about: isolated events, 'iron regularities', 'laws of motion', 'meaningful symbols'?

None of those answers by itself seems to fit. If I read Merton correctly, his ultimate goal is attaining a specific form of sociological knowledge that I would describe as the *nomological understanding of social patterns*. That is to say, his main preoccupation is to introduce a measure of intellectual order into human perceptions of social life. Such intellectual order is produced by generalised concepts, taxonomies, typologies, classifications, and law-like formulas; in a word, by nomological postulates. And its consequence is a higher level of enlightenment, a more thorough understanding of social experience, sometimes punctuated by the 'Eureka elation' that comes with having achieved a significant finding or idea. The attainment of nomological knowledge is possible precisely because social life is not chaotic, haphazard, atomistic, but is *patterned or structured*.[9] The goal of sociology is to unravel those patterns, reconstruct those structures, particularly those which have not been identified in everyday social life. Thus, it is the objectively real nature of social life that makes social knowledge possible, and also goes far to determine the type of social knowledge that is possible and should be sought – namely, the generalised account of patterned social phenomena.

To this ultimate goal, more specific, lower-level goals are logically related. There are five of them, and as their designations all happen to begin with 'c', I shall refer to them as *Merton's 'five Cs formula'*. Those specific goals include: consolidation, codification, clarification, continuity and cumulation of sociological knowledge. As early as the introduction to *Social Theory and Social Structure* in 1949, he defines his pervasive preoccupations: 'the consolidation of theory and research and the codification of theory and method are the concerns threaded through the chapters of this book'.[10] On many pages of the same volume, as well as in other works, he declares and exemplifies the crucial importance of the clarification of ideas, of 'unmuddling the muddle' so typical of sociological discourse. And finally, he is constantly emphasising the continuity and *selectively cumulative* character of scientific growth, attempting to place his ideas in the mainstream of valid sociological tradition, to point the directions in which these ideas can in turn be superseded; to stand 'on the shoulders of giants' in order to look further than them.

Goals are one thing, the means chosen to attain them quite another. Within the complex normative role of a scholar, those means can be conceived in most diverse ways. What is Merton's strategy of achieving his self-defined goals? To my mind the answer is to be found in the expressions used almost obsessively throughout the whole of Merton's work: 'disciplined inquiry' and 'systematic research'. By way of illustration, this one of the many phrasings of the idea: 'the great difference between social science and sociological dilettantism resides in the systematic and serious, that is to say, the intellectually responsible and austere, pursuit of what is first entertained as an interesting idea'.[11] To me this signifies two things. First, that research should be *systematic*, *orderly*, observing a patterned sequence, though this does not require a fixed tidy set of steps like that outlined in textbooks on the 'scientific method'. And second, it means that research should be *persistent*, not stopping before reaching the actual, but always temporary limits of cognitive possibilities, either of the researcher, or of the scientific community of the time. To borrow a phrase from the title of Popper's autobiography, it must be an 'unended quest'.[12]

The norm of systematic, disciplined and persistent inquiry is most general. Other, lower-level norms can be discovered in Merton's work, all of them clearly related to the master imperative. One is the demand of *methodological self-consciousness* of the scholar. Merton is fond of quoting the adage of one of his teachers L. J. Henderson, which, once quoted is worth repeating: 'It is a good thing to know what you are doing'.[13] To maintain control of inquiry, one must be aware of how one is going about it. This must be made as explicit as possible. In Merton's succinct phrasing which merits repeated quotation: 'If true art consists in concealing all signs of art, true science consists in revealing its scaffolding as well as its finished structure'.[14] Another lower-level norm of scholarship exacts a high degree of *self-criticism*. This is crucial for persistently pursuing the inquiry, rather than resting content with the results achieved thus far. In Merton's words: 'To suspect the full measure of one's ignorance is a first step toward supplanting ignorance with knowledge'.[15] This is later developed in the concept of 'specified ignorance'. Another specific norm postulates the complementarity of various forms of inquiry, particularly of empirical and theoretical research. It is a call for theoretically significant and at the same time empirically founded study. This is taken as necessary for achieving consolidated, multi-dimensional knowledge. This has been stated ironically: 'each of us is perpetually vulnerable to pharasaism. We thank whatever powers that be that we are not like other sociologists who merely talk rather than observe, or merely observe rather than think, or merely think rather than put their thoughts to the test of systematic empirical investigation'.[16]

Formulating those norms, Merton does not forget that science is after all (or before all) a creative enterprise, and there are no rules for creativity. This is a theme pervading his discussions of science from the doctoral dissertation of 1938, up to the recent introduction to the Vicennial (1985) edition of *On the Shoulders of Giants*. His latest formulation of the requirement of creativity is most compact: 'the difficult trick in the art and craft of science is to exercise discipline while still obeying one's daimon'.[17]

Returning to the typology of scholarly roles, we can say that in these terms, Merton would fit the category of 'secular scholar' and 'explorer' (particularly the 'systemiser' and 'discoverer of problems') in Znaniecki's terms; the 'generaliser' and 'substantive theorist' in the Merton–Lazarsfeld scheme and a scholar primarily committed to research among the four components in the Zuckerman–Merton image of the scientific role-set.

In defining a normative social role, the scholar also has a postulative idea of the audience for whom the role is being performed, some notion of the 'significant others', 'reference groups', and 'the social circle'. For a scholar emphasising research, theorising, generalising, the crucial audience is constituted by his peers, the scientific community of like-oriented, competent or outstanding scholars.[18] Yet the question remains: which scientific community? Here a distinction between types of influentials introduced by Merton in quite a different context proves useful. He defines the basic types in this way: 'By a local, I mean one who is largely oriented to his organization or immediate community that dominates his interests, concerns, and values. By a cosmopolitan, I mean one who is oriented toward the larger social world beyond his immediate organization or community, with extended interests, concerns and values'.[19] Merton's reference groups are clearly seen in cosmopolitan terms. That is so in a double sense: he is concerned with having his ideas noted, assessed and utilised beyond the discipline of sociology, while within the discipline itself, he speaks to the widest, international audience.[20] Writing of others, he makes relevant observations which can be treated as a self-characterisation as well: 'Scientists live and work in larger social and cultural environments than those comprised by their local milieux. And this seems to be true particularly of the most creative among them. Outstanding scientists tend to be "cosmopolitan", oriented to the wider national and trans-national environments, rather than "locals" oriented primarily to their immediate band of associates'.[21]

This self-diagnosis of Merton's role as a scholar can now be compared with the perspective of the scientific community on him and his work; his peers' account of what he is up to, and their appraisal of what he has done.

As seen by others

The sociological community perceives Merton as a man of the Academy, primarily the scholar involved in the disinterested search for truth, with reason as his major tool. Bierstedt expresses a widely held opinion: 'Merton is not engaged in a "critique of society", major or minor. . . . Merton is a sociologist, not a moralist. The "function" of the functional analyst is not to criticize society but only to understand it'.[22]

The understanding conveyed by Merton's work is perceived in quite definite terms. It is not the understanding provided by detailed, factual accounts nor that given by the rigorous deductive subsumption of the facts under general laws nor that which results from the hermeneutical analysis of meanings. Rather, it is a sociological understanding produced by *the uncovering of objective, latent patterns inherent in social life*, which appear as obvious and self-evident only *after* analysis has made them manifest. Turner believes that the appeal of Merton's work 'lies in the substantive imagery that it depicts and the "feeling" among many sociologists that it points to an important set of social processes. This is where Merton's genius lies.'[23] And Garfield seems to follow the same thread when he observes: 'So much of what he says is so beautifully obvious – so transparently true – that one can't imagine why no one else has bothered to point it out'.[24]

The ultimate, overall influence of Merton's sociology derives from his efforts as a theorist. In effect, his scholarly role is perceived as pre-eminently or even exclusively that of a theorist. Manis and Meltzer make it explicit: 'He has produced some empirical studies, but his major works in the field have been as a theorist, especially in the areas of the sociology of knowledge, mass communications, bureaucracy and the professions.'[25] The analysis of citations to Merton's work shows on more systematic grounds, that this perception is widespread and prevailing. A study of more than 2500 articles in which Merton was quoted in the eight-year period, 1970–77, leads Garfield to conclude: 'the strength of his influence is derived primarily from his theoretical contributions. . . . In both the natural and social sciences, then, at least two-thirds of the citations are for concepts rather than findings. This confirms the impression that Merton's major contribution has been that of a theorist.'[26]

More specifically, among the various kinds of theoretical achievements assigned to Merton, the *formulation, clarification and elaboration of concepts* seems to rank highest. Blau's appraisal is typical: 'Merton's own work illustrates the great contributions to theoretical understanding that can be made by introducing new concepts, refining old ones, devising simple conceptual schemes, and constructing complex paradigms.'[27] Similarly, Lazarsfeld conceives what he calls a 'conceptual ramification' as one of Merton's greatest talents.[28] Bierstedt makes the same point, in more symbolic idiom: 'Ideas are toys for Merton, coloured balls to be conjured out of nowhere, thrown in the air, and caught again with a magician's flair and finesse.'[29] Again, this portrait is confirmed by citation studies. Garfield found that 83 per cent of the citations in the social-science journals and 63 per cent of the citations in the natural-science journals refer to Merton's conceptual contributions. He concludes: 'The data also show that the main strength of his influence rests on his prolific production of unique sociological concepts that are widely accepted and used.'[30]

Besides the conceptual analysis, the *systematisation, codification and synthesis of knowledge* are also considered as kinds of theoretical efforts characteristic of Merton's scholarly role. As Manis and Meltzer express this often repeated observation: 'in his theorizing and his research, his performance as a systematizer of knowledge is most notable. The paradigm is a characteristic feature of Merton's output and an illustration of his role as systematizer. . . . Most frequent, and equally relevant, is Merton's emphasis upon codification.'[31] And Coser makes much of Merton's 'capacity to draw from many sources and, in a grand synthesizing effort to rise above all of them.'[32]

Finally, numerous authors notice another of Merton's special abilities: the *formulation of new problems*, puzzles, questions and hypotheses, in ways conducive to empirical testing. Due to such heuristic insights and hunches, Stinchcombe writes that 'of all contemporary theorists of social structure, Merton has had the greatest impact on empirical research.'[33]

In terms of the various typologies of scholarly roles, then, the perception of Merton by the scientific community seems to approximate his self-definition. Again, it is the roles of 'systematiser', 'discoverer of problems', 'generaliser', 'substantive theorist' and 'researcher' that are most heavily emphasised. And there is little doubt about the cosmopolitan reception of his ideas. His contributions are both trans-disciplinary and trans-national. Garfield amply documents the observation that 'Merton's impact certainly ranges well beyond the social sciences.'[34] He quotes the evidence from his citation-studies which show that Merton's work is referred to by physicians, psychiatrists, information-scientists, physicists, biologists, biochemists, as well as by social scientists. His works are drawn upon profusely: 'Merton's citation record is almost 400 per cent greater than that of the average cited author in the natural sciences.'[35] Garfield concludes: 'the data emphatically confirm my intuitive judgement that the influence of Robert K. Merton ranges far beyond his home discipline of sociology. Not only is he highly cited throughout the social sciences, but the pattern of citations to his work reveals that he has had a considerable impact on the natural sciences as well.'[36] Oromaner finds that as a sociologist Merton belongs to the number of scholars 'who make fundamental trans-national contributions to that discipline'.[37] His data on the most influential foreign authors in British sociology for the period between 1958 and 1967 put Merton (along with Durkheim and Parsons) at the top of the list.[38] A similar picture would no doubt appear were such studies carried out in other countries. The fact that *Social Theory and Social Structure* has been translated into a dozen or so languages – and has had several editions in some of them, speaks for its cosmopolitanism.[39]

The academic role-set

So far, our attention has been focused on what Merton and others *take him to be doing*. His self-definition of a scholarly role, as reconstructed from explicit statements or implicit hints, has been found to coincide with the perceptions of his role by the scientific community. I now shift the perspective to focus on deeds rather than opinions, on what Merton *is in fact doing* rather than on what he is believed to be doing.

It seems that the ascription to Merton – by himself and others – of the role of 'systematiser', 'generaliser', and 'researcher' and defining his audiences and domains of influence as cosmopolitan holds true, but only partly so. A one-sidedness must be corrected and qualified. The trouble with Merton, and one of the secrets of his influence is that he does not easily fit into ordinary categories. 'The prior distinctions, between teaching–research, oral–written communications, breadth–narrowness, individual–team activities etc. have not seemed useful as ways of distinguishing Merton's roles as a man of knowledge. Merton has involved himself in all of these and performed each of them admirably.'[40] This observation by Manis and Meltzer requires expansion.

Is Merton a theorist? Of course. Yet in the preface to *Social Theory and Social Structure* he remarks: 'It is evident that the theoretical sociologist who is remote from all research, who learns of it only by hearsay as it were, runs the risk of being insulated from the very experience most likely to turn his attention to new and fruitful directions. His mind has not been prepared by experience.'[41] Bierstedt's appraisal is entirely in point: 'he is devoted to bringing theory and research more closely together in a field where a conspicuous gap obtains between them.'[42] He devotes extensive methodological considerations to the necessary interplay and complementary relationship between theory development and *empirical research*, undertaking a powerful criticism of *both* narrow empiricism and scholastic 'grand theory', and suggesting the fruitful idea of 'middle-range theory' as an antidote to both extremes. He roots his theoretical constructions in empirical data and derives the empirical consequences of his theoretical ideas. Finally, he carries out or directs empirical studies. Does all this closely fit the image of the 'pure theoretician'?

Is Merton a substantive theorist? Of course, much of his work deals with substantive matters or, putting it simply, with human society in its various aspects and manifestations. But there is also much explicit methodological reflection on scientific and sociological procedures. In fact, as I shall argue later, there is an entire *system of methodology* dealing with the various phases of scientific work, ranging from problem-formation to theory-construction.

Is Merton a researcher? Of course, the research is central in his role-complex. But he also seems to attach much attention to the dissemination of knowledge, to *teaching others*. In a recent interview he admits: 'I've always enjoyed teaching . . . But I am sure that I wouldn't have been motivated to continue all those years had it not been a very rewarding experience. Among other things, it forced me to do the preparatory work which again had this quality, of course, of leading me to work some things out that I would probably not have done otherwise. But the ultimate reinforcement was through the rewards which came from the unexpected but interesting, the unexpected but relevant, developments taking place right there in the classroom. I came to count on that. . . . As I think back on the papers I've published over the years, the ones that engaged me most deeply derived from the lectures I developed for courses.'[43] He has also advanced a strong case for the 'oral transmission of knowledge' as a permanent and indispensable task of the university: 'oral publication in the form of lectures, seminars, teaching laboratories, workshops and kindred arrangements remains central to them'.[44] Merton's students provide rich testimony to his masterful teaching: 'Though formal and distant to most students, Merton's classroom performance has been a source of their admiration, envy, and emulation. His lectures would be articulated systematically and gracefully. Specificity and clarity have characterized his theoretical presentations. A wealth of illustrations derived from historical, scientific and media sources has supported his abstract analyses'.[45] Another of his students recalls: 'I was utterly bowled over by Merton's lectures. He hardly ever consulted his notes, yet his sentences built into paragraphs and his paragraphs into blocks of ideas with a precision and logical clarity that amazed me no end. Each lecture seemed a publishable and finished work of art. He was a master of persuasion.'[46] Is this the picture of a researcher enclosed within the walls of the laboratory, or the library, or out observing in the larger society?

Another component of a role-set, the gate-keeping role, has also been far from neglected by Merton. Some 120 published reviews, some twenty introductions and forewords to books by other authors, innumerable referee reports for book publishers, academic journals, scholarly foundations – this is a formidable record of a life-long activity, which in this case should perhaps be labelled *gate-opening* rather than gate-keeping, for as the unpublished materials also show, he is often enthusiastically supportive of scholarly promise and achievement while maintaining strict academic standards.

A distinct and considerable part of his work time has been taken up by the *editing of manuscripts*. Caplovitz estimates that 'Merton has spent from a third to a half of his professional life reading and commenting on the works of others. . . . For the past thirty-five years, Merton, the editor, has written hundreds of lengthy and detailed memos to would-be authors explaining the flaws in their manuscripts, and suggesting means of correcting them.'[47] Merton himself refers to editing as his 'hobby-horse'[48] and in another place muses: 'Why I take pleasure in editing is not altogether clear to me. But as long as I do, I'll continue, in the convenient belief that this is the Lord's work which, in its way, contributes to one's sense and sensibility.'[49]

It is the administrative role that he fulfils only when he is forced to. During a third of a century he was associated with Paul Lazarsfeld as his deputy in the Columbia Bureau of Applied Social Research, refusing to take the position of Director, even during the years when Lazarsfeld was out of the country. His close co-workers testify that 'he does not find these [administrative] activities congenial. He does not like to organize things or to run them.'[50] It is not a big loss; there are many members in each scientific community who find administrative work to their liking. It is only to the good of science that Merton leaves the field to them.

Finally, is Merton really a 'cosmopolitan influential'? Yes, clearly so, but for anyone who has visited the Department of Sociology at

Columbia University, where Merton has been teaching for the last forty-four years, or attended the meetings of American Sociological Association in which Merton has served as President, or meetings of learned societies, academic councils, committees, commissions, boards of foundations and the like of which he is a member – it becomes obvious what measure of 'local influence' he has also acquired and is able to exert.

In this balanced combination of numerous social roles, in the avoidance of one-sided, exclusive commitments to a single role, I find the manifestation of a more fundamental trait, the specific orientation typical of his life and work. As he defines the concept himself: 'The social orientation differs from the social role as here conceived, refers to the theme underlying the complex of social roles performed by an individual. It is the (tacit or explicit) theme which finds expression in each of the complex of social roles in which the individual is implicated.'[51] The specific orientation expressed in Merton's role-set comes down to the search for the Aristotelian 'golden-mean' – an attempt to bridge the extremes, to fill in the gaps, to overcome one-sided biases. It is an aspect of what I have labelled as the classicist theme, one which shall be encountered many times more in the discussion to come.

Intellectual genealogy

Science is a historical phenomenon. What is scientifically known at a particular time is just a phase in a process linking what *has become known* in the past with what *will be known* in the future. A proper recognition of the processual and historical nature of science invites an attitude of humility on the part of scholars, as they realise that their ideas are neither absolutely new nor absolutely final, that what they know derives largely from the work of predecessors, and will in turn be modified by their successors. I begin by focusing on the first half of that statement: the relation of the scholar to the traditions of the discipline, to see how Merton relates himself to the sociological heritage, and how that relationship is perceived by contemporaries.

The general question happens to be one of Merton's pervasive concerns. The history of science has been of prime interest to him – an interest to which he returns time and again ever since his 1935 doctoral dissertation *Science, Technology, and Society in*

Seventeenth Century England. We shall have ample occasion to discuss his image of the history of science in the next chapter. But for our purposes here, for the sake of understanding Merton's perspective on scientific ancestors, one book is crucial: *On the Shoulders of Giants*. In this essay, least scholarly in its epistolary and Shandean form and most scholarly (even ironically scholastic) in content – as Denis Donoghue puts it 'an eccentric and yet concentric work of art'[52] – Merton traces through the centuries the origins and correlates of the metaphor commonly attributed to Newton: 'If I have seen further, it is by standing on the shoulders of Giants'.[53] Having explored the connotations of two dozen or so versions of the idea appearing before Newton, and even more after Newton, he locates the source in the twelfth century as formulated by Bernard of Chartres: 'We are like dwarfs [standing] upon the shoulders of giants, and so able to see more and see farther than the ancients'.[54] This metaphorical idea provides the key to Merton's perspective on sociology of an earlier time and his own place in the chain of sociological tradition.

The metaphor can be easily misunderstood, for it involves a certain ambiguity. In Merton's opinion that ambiguity was at least implied as early as 1616, when 'the irascible chaplain Goodman alerts us to the double-edged character of the giant-and-dwarf figure. It now appears that it can be used as effectively to extol the dwarfs who are raised high on the giants' shoulders as to extol the giants without whom there would be no eminence from which the little men could see far and wide'.[55] An exclusive emphasis on one side of the metaphor leads to a double possible pathology of scientists' attitudes toward the masters long before them. One is what I propose to call the *fallacy of compulsive novelty*, so dear to the sociological 'Now-generation', in which scholars come to believe that their ideas are totally and completely original, without significant continuity with the past. Another is the *fallacy of dogmatic reiteration*, committed so often by the exegets of sociological wisdom, when old ideas are taken as the ultimate and final truth and the role of a scholar is restricted to their faithful reproduction and commentary on them.

Merton is strongly opposed to both extremes. In science, he reasons, there is no *creatio ex nihilo* or absolute novelty. Scholars seek to shape, reshape and enrich the stock of knowledge existing in their epoch. Scientists should not, therefore, isolate themselves from the intellectual tradition of their discipline. 'My intent', Merton explains, 'is to indicate metaphorically that any one of us scholars or scientists are merely dwarfs as we draw upon the gigantic intellectual legacy which provides our points of departure'.[56] And because of that, he adds in another context 'I have long argued that the writings of classical authors in every field of learning can be read with profit time and again, additional ideas and intimations coming freshly into view with each re-reading'.[57] This is particularly relevant for the adept of a young science like sociology: 'the sociologist *qua* sociologist rather than as historian of sociology, has ample reason to study the works of a Weber, Durkheim, and Simmel and, for that matter, to turn back on occasion to the works of a Hobbes, Rousseau, Condorcet or Saint-Simon'.[58]

On the other hand, without *creatio*, there is no science. Science limited to the knowledge of the past, refusing to push ahead in new directions, is science in name only. Merton subscribes to this part of his favourite Whitehead's adage which says: 'A science which hesitates to forget its founders is lost'.[59] And he invokes Galileo: 'a man will never become a philosopher by worrying forever about the writings of other men, without ever raising his own eyes to nature's works.'[60] His opposition to dogmatism, scholasticism, 'sterile exegesis', or 'zealous repetition' is encountered time and again in various contexts. By way of illustration his criticism of once widespread attitudes of American scholars toward Cooley and Mead is worth quoting at length: 'because the words of the forefathers became final words, little was built upon their insightful suggestions. They were honoured, not in the manner in which men of science do honour to their predecessors, by extending and elaborating their formulations on the basis of cumulatively developed problems and systematic researches bearing on these problems, but in the manner in which *littérateurs* honour their predecessors, by repeatedly quoting "definitive" passages from the masters' works'.[61]

In this passage, Merton's solution to the dilemma of dogmatism versus absolute novelty becomes visible. Once again, it is the attempt to find the Aristotelian golden-mean, to resolve the dilemma by rejecting the extremes, to synthesise the core of component ideas. It is another aspect of the classicist theme, the orientation I find pervading the whole of Merton's work. Thus, he advises: 'Draw upon the wisdom of the past, to be sure, or else the implicitly arrogant claim to knowledge beginning with yourself will stand self-condemned. But do not confuse this dependence upon the corporate giants of the past with a merely learned repetition of what they have taught you. Instead follow your bent where it leads.'[62]

More specifically, Merton's policy of relating to the masters seems to imply three directives. First, a *selective approach*, it means the constant effort to derive from the masters of the past the core of their ideas and to sift it from the inevitable marginal contributions, blind alleys or outright mistakes.[63] The ancient giants must be recognised *not because they are ancient but because they are giants*. Second, the precept of *reading anew* means entering into a sort of critical dialogue with the masters, interpreting their ideas in the light of new perspectives and approaches, later discoveries, experiences, newly gathered data. In Merton's words: 'What is to be found in writings of the past is anything but fixed, once and for all. It changes as our own intellectual sensitivities change; the more we learn on our account, the more we can learn by re-reading from our freshly gained perspective'.[64] Third, the injunction to critically enrich, partly supplant, or reject past ideas, if found incomplete, deficient or obsolete: 'the founding fathers are honoured, not by zealous repetition of their early findings, but by extensions, modifications and, often enough, by rejection of some of their ideas and findings'.[65]

Merton is quite faithful to this professed policy in his own scientific conduct. Various commentators have noted that he was among the first in his generation of American soiologists to turn their attention to the heritage of European sociology, to have mastered it in depth, to have 'assimilated European thought patterns more thoroughly than most of his predecessors'.[66] But his attitude toward European masters has not been exegetic or dogmatic. Rather, it has been self-consciously critical, with an emphasis on possible continuities. He has not wanted to talk about them, but to draw upon them:[67] 'He has been led to eliminate from European theories weaknesses that were rooted in overgeneral or overconfident formulations and to recast, refine, and systematise these theories in tune with the empirical exigencies of his research in an American setting'.[68] As Stinchcombe perceptively observes further on, Merton follows his own directives through a critically selective approach to the work of the masters: 'He refuses to adopt dogmatisms while adopting their virtues. . . . What we find repeatedly is a free willingness to borrow and a free willingness to shear off from the borrowings the grandiosity and sectarianism of the originals'.[69] An almost identical appraisal is given by Coser: 'By stripping evaluative dross and time-and-place-bound elements from the intellectual productions of the past, it becomes possible for Merton to incorporate past contributions into the body of current paradigms which can become springboards for future advances'.[70] In taking such an attitude toward the masters 'Merton pays them the type of homage that alone befits one's ancestors in the world of science: he shows how by profiting from their vision a later generation can, from its vantage point, afford to correct and extend it'.[71]

Who are those giants whose work Merton picks out for critical continuation? Attributions of intellectual influences are obviously risky. The self-consciousness of the author may sometimes mislead; either because, as Merton himself warns 'No one knows fully what has shaped his thinking',[72] or because there may be extraneous reasons for manifesting attachment to one scientific tradition, and distancing oneself from another. Similarly, the appraisals of peers may be equally biased, owing to the theoretical (and sometimes also extratheoretical) commitments of the commentator. But with all these reservations, some points concerning Merton's intellectual ancestry are relatively secure.

To begin with, there is his pre-eminent indebtedness to Emile Durkheim. Were he required to choose the most significant piece of sociological research, he 'would nominate Durkheim's *Suicide* for that lofty position'.[73] In the lists of his recognised masters, he unfailingly places Durkheim in the forefront,[74] indicatively, Durkheim is quoted more often than any other author in Merton's major volume, *Social Theory and Social Structure*. Perhaps it is also symptomatic that Merton devoted his first printed paper to tracing the influences of Durkheim in contemporary French sociology.[75] Several commentators have observed that 'one can trace a continuous line from Durkheim to Merton, which places these two authors on the same plane',[76] or again, 'Emile Durkheim became his consciously chosen role model'.[77] The French editor of Merton's volume *On Theoretical Sociology* gave it the characteristic title *Éléments de theorie et de methode sociologique*, and advertised it as a work of 'un Durkheim americain'.[78]

All that is not without reason. In our later discussion we shall discover how close various ideas of Merton come to the thought of the French giant, both on the metascientific or methodological level and on the level of substantive propositions. Here I point only to the most obvious continuities. To begin with, there is a striking similarity of the dominant orientation of their sociologies. Of the four themes or leitmotifs I have singled out as characterising Merton's sociology, two clearly fit Durkheim as well: the cognitivist theme and the structuralist theme. In brief: their common attempt to have sociology develop into a reasonably rigorous, 'hard' science of a specifically social subject-matter, with explanations in terms of identified social factors. Both authors combine a passion for abstract conceptual and theoretical considerations with empirical analyses. Merton's sociology is in continuity with Durkheim's in terms of common theoretical and methodological orientations, functional and structural. This is widely recognised by present day observers. Giddens refers to functionalism: 'Durkheim's works have been without doubt the most important single influence upon the development of functionalism in the present century'.[79] And Barbano focuses on structuralism: 'There is no doubt that Merton's work is a continuation of Durkheim's type of cognitive interest and social optics, and that he has renewed the latter's phenomenology within the framework of an image of society as social structure'.[80] There are also obvious substantive continuities: from Durkheim's study of suicide to Merton's analyses of anomie and deviance; from Durkheim's sociological analysis of religion to Merton's sociological study of science; and others as well.

Next in line of Merton's intellectual ancestors I would put Karl Marx. In fact, Merton's attitude toward the author of *Das Kapital* is perhaps the most telling illustration of his general approach to the sociological giants of the past. In the case of Marx, it is especially easy to fall into the trap of dogmatism – of both the apologetic and the negativistic sort. As Merton puts it: 'Like attitudes toward most revolutionary ideas, attitudes toward Marxism have long been polarized; they have typically called for total acceptance or total rejection. Sociologists who have come to reject the Marxist conceptions out of hand have not uncommonly rejected also the subject-matters to which they pertained. . . . At the other pole, those who regard themselves as disciples of Marxist theory seem to act as disciples merely, content to reiterate what the masters have said or to illustrate old conclusions with newly selected examples'.[81] Merton rejects both dogmatisms, and takes his typical golden-mean approach: 'I have long since abandoned the struggle to determine what "Marxism" is or is not. Instead, I have taken all that I find good in Marxian thought – and that is a considerable amount – and neglected conceptions which do not seem to me to meet tests of validity'.[82] Such an approach allows him to follow some Marxian ideas, while remaining far removed from Marxism in the political or ideological sense. Abstracting the *intellectual substance of Marxism* from its political message makes possible the situation in which 'Marx transcends more than national boundaries. He is claimed as an ancestral influence by many sociologists who can truly say: nous ne sommes pas Marxistes'.[83] This comment can surely be applied to Merton himself.

Several contemporary observers have noticed Merton's significant indebtedness to Marx. They emphasise his 'profound knowledge of the Marxian canon',[84] or even claim with Gouldner that 'Merton was always much more Marxist than his silences on that question may make it seem'.[85] A notable and puzzling exception is Bierstedt who asserts that Marxism plays no role in Merton's theory, and that no Marxist influence can be detected in his work. This leads to a more extended thesis as strong as it is doubtful: 'there is no Marx in the history of American sociological theory'.[86]

To my mind, Merton was strongly influenced by Marx's approach as well as by some of his substantive ideas. Again, I allude only to the more important continuities. To begin with, many components of the structuralist theme and ironic theme that I attribute to Merton's work also characterise Marxian theory: the emphasis on sociological, and particularly structural, factors in the explanation of human phenomena; the focus on contradictions, conflicts, and circularity of social processes. Then, the idea of the social-structural determination of knowledge, turned into the idea of the social-structural determination of science, have uncontestable Marxian roots. Merton calls Marx 'a progenitor of the sociology of knowledge as of much else in social thought'[87] and emphasises his contribution to the emergence of the sociology of scientific knowledge: 'It is appropriate to refer to Marx in the "of-course-mood" because few, if any, would contest his basic influence upon widespread ways of construing the interaction between society and scientific thought'.[88]

Third in line of ancestry comes Georg Simmel. Merton goes to some pains to acknowledge this influence, including Simmel among his recognised 'masters-at-a-distance',[89] and paying tribute to him in connection with several detailed analyses. Those elements in Merton's sociology which I describe by the term 'structuralist theme' and 'classicist theme' can readily be traced back to Simmel, among them, the focus on relationships and structures and the search for balanced, precise, elegant, intermediate solutions. Merton's indebtedness to Simmel becomes all the more apparent in the context of conceptual analyses. He takes a quite similar approach to conceptual ramifications and also reaches quite similar substantive results. For example, Merton starts from Simmel's hunches in his analysis of patterned interactions,[90] social visibility and observability,[91] in-group integration and inter-group conflicts,[92] the completeness, openness and closedness of groups,[93] and several others.

In speaking of sociological masters, one must sooner or later come to Max Weber. In this case, it is *later* rather than *sooner*, as there is relative neglect of the German giant in Merton's work.[94] To be sure, Merton explicitly identifies Weber as one of his 'masters-at-a-distance',[95] but this amounts to little more than lip-service. Except for the doctoral dissertation on the Puritan ethic and the genesis of modern science, and the discussion of bureaucratic structure – it is hard to discover Weberian themes in Merton's work. Perhaps it is due to the fact that their substantive interests and foci of attention do not coincide. Merton's structuralist approach implies the relative neglect of the theory of action, human motivation or forms of rationality. His preference for the study of interactional and group phenomena entails the neglect of political macrostructures and the phenomenon of power. And on the rare occasions when Merton enters the world of Weber's sociology, he mostly accepts Weber's results as given. This is the case with the theory of action,[96] the idea of 'value-free' sociology, or the model of bureaucratic organisation.[97]

So much for the classics of an earlier time. Among the later 20th-century masters, some of whom were Merton's contemporaries or even immediate teachers, six names should be mentioned. One is Florian Znaniecki. Merton reports: 'I was a 'self-selected student-at-a-distance of Znaniecki',[98] and points to the influence exerted by the idea of 'human documents' in shaping his own uses of 'content analysis' as well as the impact of the theory of social organisation underlying the Thomas and Znaniecki classic *The Polish Peasant in Europe and America*. Further recognition is given to the early formulations in the sociology of science found in Znaniecki's *The Social Role of the Men of Knowledge*.[99]

Another 20th-century master is Bronislaw Malinowski. In the introduction to the Polish edition of *Social Theory and Social Structure*, Merton emphasises the crucial significance of Malinowski's functional anthropology for the development of his own ideas on functional analysis. Obviously it has been a sort of negative influence; by rejection of certain of Malinowski's tenets, Merton reached his sophisticated version of 'neo-functionalism' or 'dynamic functionalism'.[100] This seems to happen quite often in the history of science. As Merton observes: 'it was not necessary to agree with Malinowski, in order to learn from him'.[101]

An important influence on Merton's ideas, particularly in the field of sociology of science was exerted by George Sarton, at the time of his graduate studies undoubtedly 'the acknowledged world dean among historians of science'.[102] Merton himself refers to his relationship with Sarton as 'short, incompleat and sometimes unruly apprenticeship followed by an intermittent epistolary friendship that continued until George Sarton's death a quarter-century later'.[103] The main influence of Sarton can be found at the level of general interests and particular qualifications; interest in science, its development, operation of scientific communities and specific techniques of studying historical sources. Apart from that, at a recent centennial of Sarton's birth held at the University of Ghent, Merton acknowledged numerous 'gifts' tangible and intangible that he had received from his mentor; including the conducive micro-environment for the work on his doctoral dissertation, opening the pages of the newly established journal *Isis* for Merton's first publications, and publishing *Science, Technology, and Society in Seventeenth-Century England* in another of Sarton's periodicals, *Osiris*.[104]

Then come the two most influential teachers, under whom, and later with whom, Merton learned and worked: Pitirim Sorokin and Talcott Parsons. It was not entirely a direct and solely positive influence. Merton was apparently not an easy pupil. Admiring his teachers he did not hesitate to criticise them and to build his own intellectual system partly in opposition to theirs. The case of Sorokin is particularly telling. Having the young Merton collaborate with him on one important part of his treatise *Social and Cultural Dynamics* (1937),[105] and on an article on 'Social Time' (1937), and some thirty years later publicly praising *On the Shoulders of Giants* as a masterpiece, Sorokin also went so far as to label Merton's paradigm of functional analysis as 'a modern variation on Alexandrian or medieval scholasticism in its decaying period. [It is] heuristically sterile, empirically useless, and [a] logically cumbersome table of contents'.[106] Here Merton apparently did not follow the letter of his master's teachings. The same was true of the theory of reference groups of which Sorokin wryly remarked: 'a multitude of Merton's propositions, especially in his theory of the reference groups represent a codification of trivialities dressed up as scientific generalizations'.[107] The ambivalence of Sorokin's attitude is beautifully rendered by the inscription in one of his books: 'To my darned enemy and dearest friend – Robert – from Pitirim'.[108]

Another of Merton's teachers is Talcott Parsons. Speaking for his entire generation of Harvard sociologists Merton remarks: 'Talcott was both cause and occasion for our taking sociological theory seriously'.[109] His influence on steering Merton's interest towards theoretical considerations was certainly immense. But at the same time for almost forty years, since the memorable meeting of the ASA in the 1940s Parsons' abstract manner of theorising has been a subject of Merton's persistent challenge leading him to propose the notion of a 'middle-range theory'.[110] Similarly, the static and ahistoric 'structural-functionalism' proposed by Parsons was a subject of Merton's strong critique contributing to the birth of his own dynamic 'functional analysis'. But their theoretical debate always stayed within the borders of exemplary civility. As Merton recollects: 'I remember the grace with which, some thirty years ago, he responded in a forum of this same Association to my mild mannered but determined criticism of certain aspects of his theoretical orientation'.[111] Years later Parsons came to acknowledge Merton's 'major contribution to the understanding and clarification of the theoretical methodology of what he, I think quite appropriately, called "functional analysis" ',[112] and then saluted him 'for his highly creative role in developing the foundations of this challenging intellectual situation'.[113]

Finally, one must recognise Merton's decades-long collaboration with Paul Lazarsfeld, producing fruit in several co-authored works as well as in numerous research projects at the Columbia Bureau of Applied Social Research. It is a rare case of basically different styles of research and theorising supplementing and enriching each other, coming as close to real complementarity as could be expected in case of two strong, independent individualities, with divergent backgrounds, thought styles and scholarly goals.[114]

Scientific contribution

The social role of a scholar is not played out in a vacuum; rather it is performed within the context of an ongoing process of scientific development. Related in some way to past achievements, it also opens to the future; one is asked to contribute something to an expanding stock of human knowledge.

The scholar's orientation toward the past is not without consequences for his orientation toward the future. The more firmly his thinking is rooted in sound achievements of the past, the better his own chances of contributing in significant ways to the permanent progress of knowledge. As Coser puts it: 'By standing in the line of great ancestors, and by acknowledging the shadow they cast, one enhances the chance that he, in his turn, will later be reckoned among the ancestors himself'.[115]

We have inspected a formidable company of giants on whose shoulders Merton has explicitly placed himself. Now it is high time to inquire into his own contribution to the stock of sociological knowledge. Of course, this question can be answered conclusively only by the end of this book, after Merton's substantive work has been examined in detail. Now I identify only the types of results, areas, or disciplines in which the impact of his work is most marked.

To begin with, he has formulated and codified the canons of two theoretical and methodological orientations which, particularly in combination, have proved to be fruitful in studying the social world. Starting with a critical reformulation and extension of selected ideas of social anthropology, he has come to the specification of *functional analysis* – the research-oriented, open and liberal version of functionalism, which later became described as 'neo-functionalism', 'dynamic functionalism', or 'empirical functionalism'. And synthesising core ideas of the sociologists who have been oriented to the patterned, repetitive, hidden 'form' or organisation of social life, he has proposed an approach known as 'structural analysis', or *sociological structuralism*, which as a result of its empirical bent, openness and liberal formulation, proves to be quite distinct from the orthodox and doctrinaire 'structuralist schools' of ethnology or linguistics. What is most in point, he has shown the way to a fruitful synthesis of both approaches.

Then, Merton has introduced a wealth of fruitful and enlightening concepts or in Herbert Blumer's term, 'sensitising ideas' into the sociological discourse. As he identifies new aspects of social life which he finds sociologically significant, he coins neologisms to designate them.[116] A number of these have entered the vocabularies not only of social science but the vernacular of everyday life.[117] Some have already become cases of the process in the history of thought which Merton has identified as 'obliteration by incorporation (OBI)' in which the sources of an idea, finding or concept become obliterated by incorporation in canonical knowledge, so that only a few are still aware of their parentage.[118] Merton has also highlighted earlier concepts-and-terms which had gone largely unregarded, performing what he calls a 'cognitive conduit'.[119] A brief sample of Mertonian coinages and adaptations must suffice. With regard to the institution of science and the behaviour of scientists, he introduced into sociological usage the earlier existing terms-and-concepts of serendipity and eponymy. He originated the terms-and-concepts of the self-fulfilling prophecy, specified ignorance, potentials of relevance, disciplined eclecticism, the Matthew effect, the Eureka syndrome, the Phoenix phenomenon, strategic research site, patterned misunderstandings, self-exemplifying ideas and practices, the fallacy of the last word, coterie-science, organised scepticism, oral publication and so on. Merton's other often utilised terms-and-concepts referring to the structure and functioning of society include role-set and status-set, manifest and latent functions, pseudo-Gemeinschaft, institutionalised evasions, local and cosmopolitan influentials, juvenocracy, observability, sociological ambivalence, the '4 Ps' of social norms (prescribed, preferred, permitted, prohibited), institutionalised altruism, social dysfunctions, homophily and heterophily, and many others.[120] As our discussion proceeds, I shall be choosing items from this large menu, which are especially attractive to my sociological taste. Recalling the simple truth that human beings can only think of those objects or ideas which they identify and designate,[121] we see the ways in which the horizons of sociological thinking have been expanded by giving precise and pointed names to previously latent, unrecognised or unexamined aspects of social experience.

A final component of Merton's work is found in his substantive – empirical and theoretical – work in specialised fields of sociology. There is, in the language of Paul Lazarsfeld 'his first love'[122] – the sociology of science. His pioneering work in this specialty has been widely recognised. Thus, according to Robert Bierstedt: 'To ask what Merton has contributed to this area of inquiry is almost to ask the wrong question. The sociology of science is a sea over which he exercises an admiral's suzerainty. It was he who explored it, surveyed it, and drew its charts'.[123] Or from another perspective, this appraisal given by Barry Barnes and Robert Dolby: 'The earliest papers of any importance in the field are probably those of Robert Merton, written in the late 1930s and early 1940s; Merton's ideas have been extremely influential with all subsequent contributors and it is probably no exaggeration to state that the literature of the subject has been overwhelmingly concerned with the development and extension of Merton's original insights'.[124]

Another of Merton's early fields of interest, though not as sustained, was the sociology of the professions, particularly the medical profession, where with a group of colleagues he initiated the sociological study of medical education.[125] That interest is in accord with his belief that 'occupations in general and the professions in particular have come to be recognized as one of the more significant nuclei in the organization of society'.[126] Some of his papers in this field have been republished in the volume *Social Research and the Practicing Professions*.

In the sociology of deviance, Merton's article 'Social Structure and Anomie' has become a truly classical contribution; it 'has probably been more frequently cited and reprinted than any paper in sociology'.[127] During the last half-century it has led to fundamental theoretical discussions, conceptual and taxonomic elaborations, and empirical application.

Another early substantive interest, clearly indebted to Paul

Lazarsfeld, is the sociology of mass communications. Although not at all as consequential as Lazarsfeld who virtually founded this special field,[128] Merton contributed numerous empirical analyses, conceptual innovations (e.g. local and cosmopolitan influentials), theoretical ideas (e.g. differences in the problematics and analytical techniques of the sociology of knowledge and mass communications), and methods (e.g. the focused interview, devised with Patricia Kendall; and recently adapted in the extended research use of 'focus groups').

Finally, one must consider the field of microsociology, where Merton's analyses of interactions, *roles*, *role-sets*, *status-sets*, group properties and *reference groups* have also become classical. Of Merton's theory of reference groups, for example, Herbert Hyman – the originator of the idea and the term – has this to say: 'It is a monument, and one that has not crumbled in the quarter-century now passed since it was built'.[129]

The list is certainly incomplete, since I focus only on the outstanding contributions. But it must suffice for the moment, as *prima facie* evidence of the range, variety and significance of Merton's scholarly achievements.

3
On Science

I now leave the man, and embark on the study of his ideas. The corpus of thought produced by a scientist always contains some, at least, implicit image of science.[1] It provides the general framework of assumptions within which his efforts acquire meaning and on the basis of which the scientist produces his substantive contributions. In the case of Merton, this image is quite explicit, developed and elucidated. This may derive from his lifelong preoccupation with the analysis of science, this being his hallmark from the doctoral dissertation of 1935 tracing the origins of modern Western science to the article published in 1984 which states his current position on that question in the wake of a debate which has been going on for fifty years.[2]

It is therefore both for reasons of a systematic nature – a scientist's image of science being logically prior to his work in science – and for reasons of a biographical nature – the especial significance given to the analysis of science in Merton's lifelong work – that the study of his scientific ideas begins with a study of his ideas about science.

Sociological approach to science

Merton is a sociologist *par exellence*. With some exaggeration his creed could perhaps be put in the equation: *everything significantly and specifically human is social*. It is understandable, then, that in his approach to such an exclusively and purely human phenomenon as science he will focus on its social nature.

Nothing is more alien to Merton than an ivory-tower view of science, conceiving of it as a completely self-contained and isolated domain, made up only of abstract intellectual or cognitive substance: 'Even the most artless and single-minded of scientists, living out their work-lives within the confines of the laboratory, must now know, to adopt a remark by Butterfield, that they are "not autonomous, god-like creatures acting in a world of unconditioned freedom" '.[3] He puts his idea even more strongly in another context: 'Vestiges of any tendency to regard the development of science and technology as wholly self-contained and advancing irrespective of the social structure are being dissipated by the actual course of historical events'.[4]

If I read Merton correctly, his conception of the social character of science includes three related claims. First, science is always located within some *social context*. That context consists of social phenomena and processes that influence the course and cognitive character of science, and social phenomena and processes that are, in turn, being influenced by science. As he notes, that perspective was adopted from the time of his first study of science: 'The orientation was simple enough: various institutions in the society are variously interdependent so that what happens in the economic or religious realm is apt to have some perceptible connections with some of what happens in the realm of science, and conversely'.[5] He goes on to specify: 'A principal sociological idea governing this empirical inquiry holds that the socially patterned interests, motivations and behavior established in one institutional sphere – say, that of religion or economy – are interdependent with the socially patterned interests, motivations and behavior obtaining in other institutional spheres – say, that of science'.[6]

Depending on the character of the phenomena and processes providing the context for science, one may speak of the *macro-environments of science*, made up of large-scale systems in society as the political, economic, the class system, social consciousness – and the *micro-environments of science*, made up of intellectual milieux, schools of thought, 'invisible colleges', universities or academies with their local traditions. Thus, Merton observes that there are 'diverse and still poorly understood ways in which interpersonal milieux influences cognitive orientations and formations of specific ideas'.[7] Normally, though not unexceptionally or necessarily, the macro-environments are less immediately and closely related to science than the micro-environments. Exceptions occur either in such societies or historical epochs where science becomes subjugated by economy, polity, religion; or in conceivable societies, whose economic, political, ideological, religious structures are significantly shaped by the development of science.

Second, science is also *social in its internal structure*. It consists of a set of individuals (scientists), carrying out certain activities (research), and achieving types of results (knowledge). Those individuals are brought together, or get together to form groups, collectivities and communities of scientists. They enter into complex networks of interactions, conforming to or departing from certain kinds of norms and values, and receiving various kinds of rewards and punishments from others in the social system. Their products are evaluated, distributed, applied, suppressed or destroyed by others, in each case bringing about definite consequences for both society and culture. It is enough to note these well-recognised patterns in order to see that science is in its tacit and explicit organisation a social enterprise.

To repeat: it is social in a double sense; one, because it is interrelated with other aspects of society, built into the wider social context; and two, because it is itself a significant social structure, endowed with identifiable social dimensions. *Science is social both as a part of the wider society and as a social world in itself.*

Third, the changes occurring in the domain of science are significantly *influenced by social changes*. The history of science must include the 'externalist approach'.[8] For Merton, 'externalist' is one part of the 'social'; it signifies an approach that takes into account other elements besides the purely cognitive, and examines their interplay. These changes occur in both the external social context of science (macro- and micro-environments), and in the internal social make-up of science. An exclusively 'internalist' approach treats scientific ideas either as independent of social contexts and evolving according to their own logic or even as crucial primary determinants of social development. A modern historian provides an illustration of such an idealistic perspective in his study of early science: 'During these times of decisive change in rational procedures it was the mind itself, not economic institutions nor economic development, which called the new tunes and composed most of the variations which the greatest scientists were playing on them'.[9] Hall sums up his view: 'Social forms do not dominate mind; rather, in the long run, mind dominates social forms',[10] and makes a strong case for the 'internalist' history of science: 'The intellectual change is one whose explanation must be sought in the history of the intellect'.[11] Nothing could be further from Merton's perspective.

From sociology of knowledge to sociology of science

Merton's focus on the social aspects of science culminates in founding a separate scientific discipline – *the sociology of science* (including a sociological history of science) – which has become a flourishing subfield of sociological studies. The logic of Merton's intellectual development leading him inevitably toward the sociology of science may be conceived in terms of two stages. The first covers his rediscovery of the sociology of knowledge, as founded much earlier by Marx, Mannheim and Scheler. The second covers his drift away from the sociology of knowledge toward the sociology of science; his own, original contribution.

It seems that Merton was driven toward the sociology of knowledge by his general theoretical and methodological orientation. Anticipating the detailed analysis that will be taken up in later chapters, I must single out certain crucial assumptions of this orientation here. One is a systemic model of society: conceiving of human phenomena and processes as interrelated in patterned ways. Knowledge as an aspect or component of the human world cannot therefore be treated *in isolation* from its other aspects or components or from the social system as a whole. Another assumption in Merton's orientation is the structural and functional perspective: conceiving the properties of each human phenomenon or process, each component of the social system, as shaped (constrained or facilitated) by its location within the network of intrasystemic relationships (structural position), and by the part it plays in the social system as a whole (social function). Again, knowledge as an element of the human world must be seen as *depending on its structural location* within the system and its functional or dysfunctional role for the system. Thought must be rooted in social structure and functionalised.

Finally, a third assumption of Merton's orientation involves a *pluralistic and conflict-ridden image of society*. Society is seen as composed of multiple and varied elements which are in potential conflict, fulfilling contradictory roles in the system as a whole. Contradictions within the social structure and mutually contradictory functions are the rule rather than the exception in the social system. Knowledge, a component of the human world shares this eternal predicament; its rootedness in a particular sector of the social structure and its commitment to particular functions in that structure lead it inevitably to be pluralistic and conflictual itself. Each particular component of knowledge must therefore be treated as 'perspectivistic', as related to its structural base and diverse functions. Depending on such social relativisation, some claims to knowledge acquire the quality of truth, while other claims appear as falsification of reality. In Merton's own words: 'The "Copernican revolution" in this area of inquiry consisted in the hypothesis that not only error or illusion or unauthenticated belief but also the discovery of truth was socially (historically) conditioned. . . . The sociology of knowledge came into being with the signal hypothesis that even truths were to be held socially accountable, were to be related to the historical society in which they emerged'.[12]

In this way Merton was led to embrace the crucial idea of the sociology of knowledge: 'the social relations in which a man is involved will somehow be reflected in his ideas'.[13] Or more precisely: knowledge is related to the existential (structural and/or functional) location in the social system; the truth and falsity of knowledge depend on its existential location, and existential locations are variably conducive to knowledge or falsehood. The last element of this conception Merton describes as 'the problem of patterned differentials among social groups and strata in access to knowledge'.[14]

It should be noted that the sociology of knowledge, in spite of the reference to sociology, was largely a *doctrine of philosophy* rather than a *scientific theory*. This was the case not only because of the philosophical style of analysis adopted by its founders but mainly because of its problematic focus: it was an epistemological search for the preconditions of truth. It could less misleadingly be called 'sociological epistemology' since it searched for these preconditions in the social domain. Its epistemological nature resulted from its focus being on the content, the substance of ideas; it is obviously only the content of ideas that can be qualified as true or false.

There is not much more than a skilful systematic summary of the Marxian and Mannheimian sociology of knowledge in Merton's early articles devoted to that topic including his well known 'Paradigm for the Sociology of Knowledge'.[15] His original and creative contribution starts only when he turns from the sociology of knowledge in the particular sense of a philosophical focus on the content of ideas and their truthfulness or falsity. In the course of this intellectual evolution, the sociology of science slowly emerges in its modern shape.

Several shifts of foci seem to be involved in the transition. To begin with, Merton rejects the philosophical bias of the sociology of knowledge and attempts to reclaim the subject for sociology, to turn it into an *empirical, scientific discipline*. He expresses his dissatisfaction with the fact that 'the sociology of knowledge remains largely a subject for meditation rather than a field of sustained and methodical investigation'.[16] And in a letter to Znaniecki he praises *The Social Role of the Men of Knowledge*: 'It provides a much needed corrective to the largely epistemological bias of much of what passes as the sociology of knowledge'.[17]

Merton shifts his attention from knowledge *tout court* to systematically achieved empirical and theoretical knowledge – in brief, to *scientific results*: 'At the core of the discipline . . . is a sociological interest in the social contexts of that knowledge which is more or less certified by systematic evidence. . . . The sociology of knowledge is most directly concerned with the intellectual products of experts, whether in science or philosophy, in economic or political thought'.[18]

Most significantly, Merton shifts the focus from scientific knowledge alone to the whole of *science in operation* including the structure and operation of the specific social subsystem. There is no longer a place for considering the truthfulness or falsity of scientific beliefs, of the content of knowledge. The one aspect of knowledge (the scientific results) that remains within the scope of Merton's interest is the 'cognitive structure' – a patterned style, form, theme, orientation, climate – pervading scientific thought in a given society at a given time. It is not *what* is believed, but rather *how* the beliefs – of whatever cognitive sort – are conceived and stated, that becomes relevant for the new approach. Along with that fragile residuum of the traditional (cognitive) concept of knowledge, a whole array of previously neglected phenomena crucial for the new concept of science comes to the fore: the normative system of science, the behavioural patterns of scientists, the organisation of scientific communities in relation to scientific knowledge. Instead of searching for the epistemological conditions of truth or falsity, the study of the social conditions making for the operation of scientific enterprise, and conversely, the conditions producing the pathologies of science, begins in earnest. This can no longer be called the sociology of knowledge. A new discipline, the sociology of science has emerged, proclaiming as its main goal 'understanding the social dynamics of science and of its place in society'.[19]

Finally and crucially, Merton basically extends the focus of attention of the sociology of science. He departs explicitly from the tradition of the sociology of knowledge with its implied focus on the social sciences, ideology and philosophy, to include the whole of science, the social and *also the natural-science disciplines*. He comments: 'Had Mannheim systematically and explicitly clarified his position in this respect, he would have been less disposed to assume that the physical sciences are wholly immune from extra-theoretical influences, and, correlatively, less inclined to urge that the social sciences are peculiarly subject to such influences'.[20] In this significant formulation he dots the 'i': 'The role of extra-scientific factors in determining the direction of natural and of social science development differs rather in degree than in kind. . . . There is no basis for assuming that the validity of empirical judgment is necessarily any more affected by these extra-scientific influences in the one case than in the other'.[21] This encompassing persuasion leads him eventually to focus mainly on the natural sciences, where he finds the mechanisms and processes of science operating in their most developed forms. He turns to the study of the social sciences, and in particular to the sociology of sociology, only in a supplementary manner; to search for the peculiarities of young, underdeveloped, 'pre-paradigmatic' fields.

Through this intellectual evolution, Merton laid the foundations of a sociology of science: *the empirical sociology of scientific communities as producing, selecting and distributing scientific knowledge*. In his own terms: 'the subject-matter of the sociology of science is the dynamic interdependence between science, as an ongoing social activity giving rise to cultural and civilizational products, and the environing social structure. [It focuses] on the reciprocal relations between science and society'.[22] In establishing the foundations of the sociology of science Merton moves toward correcting the surprising imbalance in sociology as such which he noticed at the beginning of his own scientific work: 'An abundance of monographs dealt with the juvenile delinquent, the hobo and saleslady, the professional thief and the professional beggar but not one dealt with the professional scientist'.[23]

The new discipline slowly acquires full academic identity. To achieve what Merton later described as 'cognitive and professional identity', it is crucial to delimit its own, specific problematics. Merton contributes to that goal in considerable measure, taking up and investigating various concrete problems of the sociology of science in his numerous influential studies. Put in metaphorical terms: he charts the various areas of the emerging discipline, and in effect, the topography of its previous *terra incognita* appears in clear relief. That effort is obviously informed by Merton's wider intellectual orientation. There are, in fact, numerous striking parallelisms between his study *of* science and his study of society, *by means* of science. As soon as he made the intellectual decision to treat science in social terms, as an aspect of society, his more general theoretical and methodological orientations and even particular theories dealing with other aspects of society became immediately relevant. Cole and Zuckerman correctly observe: 'Merton's analysis of science and scientists did not develop independently of his other theoretical efforts. On the contrary, the problems he has selected and the mode of attack he has used are clearly related to his general interest in applying structural and functional analysis to social patterns in various institutional spheres'.[24] In fact, Merton himself criticises early research in the sociology of science as being *ad hoc*, as empiricist, 'not of the . . . theoretical kind that linked up systematically with doctrines in the wider discipline of sociology'.[25] The interaction of sociological ideas also moves in the other direction. The study of science as a social system may inform the wider theory of society. Science becomes a sort of laboratory for studying or testing more general social regularities.[26] I shall point to those parallelisms between Merton's theory of science and his general theory of society as we proceed.

Merton seems to assume three fundamental distinctions in his delimitation of the problem-areas central to the sociological study of science. The first is the distinction between the external structure of science – the social environments of science, both micro and macro – and the internal structure of science, the interrelated components of the social system of science, treated as an empirical phenomenon, temporarily in abstraction from its semantic, cognitive content. To repeat: in this conception, the truth-value, it means the semantic relationship of what scientists say to some underlying reality about which it is being said, does not interest the sociologist of science. What is of interest is the complex network of empirical phenomena and processes involved in doing science.

The second distinction refers to that network of empirical phenomena and processes which constitutes the internal structure of science. It counterposes the cognitive structure of science and the *social structure of science*. The cognitive structure covers all the residual aspects of scientific ideas that remain after abstracting from questions about their truth or falsity ('bracketing' their substantive content). It centres on the forms, styles, shapes of scientific beliefs; for example on their being quantitative or qualitative, formalised or loosely arranged, empirically oriented or scholastic, precise or vague and the like. Notice that those are aspects of scientific ideas which can be approached in an empirical way, so to say from the outside, temporarily disregarding their semantic meaning. The social structure of science, on the other hand, covers all those social aspects of scientific enterprise involving the behaviour and social organisation of people producing, selecting and distributing scientific knowledge. By their very nature, these aspects of science can be empirically investigated.

The third distinction specifies in more fine-grained detail the internal make-up of the social structure of science. It includes the normative structure of science (or the cultural structure of science), counterposed to the group structure of science (or the social organisation of science). The former is composed of the norms and values, roles and institutions characteristic for the specific domain of the human world known as science. The latter is composed of groups, collectivities and communities of scholars in their differentiation, interrelations and activities. As Merton recalls the intellectual evolution leading him to that distinction: 'In order to investigate the character of those reciprocal influences between science and society and how they came about, it was therefore essential to enlarge my earlier effort to find a methodical way of thinking about science as institutionalized ethos (its normative aspect) and science as social organization (its patterns of interaction among scientists)'.[27]

Those distinctions allow one to reconstruct the typology of problems clearly conceived by Merton as central to the developing field of the sociology of science. One set of problems deals with the *external relationship* of science to its social environments. Both the cognitive structure of science and its social structure, may be so related. And the relationship itself must be conceived as mutual, reciprocal, operating both ways. This was emphasised already in Merton's earliest approaches to the problems of the sociology of science: 'The study takes seriously the notion of institutional interchange as it abandons the easy assumption of exclusively one-sided impact'.[28] Specific types of problems thus emerge:

(a) Impact of external social environment on the internal social structure of science – its normative ethos and its social organisation. Evidence of Merton's keen interest in this issue is found in this studies of the origins of science as significantly influenced by the environing social and cultural atmosphere – particularly the normative ethos expressed in a particular form of religious creed as well as in his studies of the decay and degradation of science under the rule of totalitarian ideologies. As he puts it: 'The sociologist of science is specifically concerned with the types of influence involved (facilitative and obstructive), the extent to which these types prove effective in different social structures and the processes through which they operate'.[29]

(b) Impact of the internal social structure of science on the external social environment. Merton himself does not attach much attention to this problem but it is taken up by followers of his work. It is suggested that the ethos of science and its internal particular organisational forms may provide a sort of pattern or model for the wider polity, economy, and supposedly become reflected in the democratic forms of social organisation. This is emphasised by Ezrahi: 'As a simpler exemplification of the principles of discourse in which open criticism and diverse positions are resolved in authoritative consensus, science becomes an ideal for politics – an ideal toward which politics can only aspire. . . . It is this constructive dimension of criticism in the internal life of science which lends special force to science as a cultural example relevant to the liberal–democratic response to the problem of authority'.[30]

(c) Impact of external social environment on the internal cognitive structure of science: the prevailing style of scientific discourse. This may involve the macroenvironments of science (examples: the general cultural atmosphere of the Middle Ages influencing

scholastic forms of thought or the case of bureaucratic and autocratic polity favouring narrowly-empirical, statistical bookkeeping research); or more obviously, its micro-environments (examples: the organisation of the university, or local intellectual traditions of certain scholarly community dictating specific thought-styles).
(d) Impact of the internal cognitive structure of science on the external social environment. Again, this is not in Merton's own focus, but it is conceivable as a distinct area of empirical study (example: the extent to which the element of rationality, almost definitionally involved in scientific thought, may become reflected in the rationality of social organisation, management, administration).

Another set of problems deals with the *internal relationships* of components within the social system of science. Utilising the basic distinctions between the cognitive and social structure of science as well as between the normative and the group structure of science leads to another typology of four central problems:

(a) Impact of the social structure of science on its cognitive structure; the dominant styles, forms of thinking (examples: how the bureaucratisation of science limits non-standard forms of scientific expression; how the reward system of science advantages certain forms of scientific products; how the age structure of science becomes reflected in changing emphases on certain styles of discourse).
(b) Impact of the cognitive structure of science on its social structure: its ethos, organisation and behaviour patterns of scientists (example: scholastic or dogmatic forms of thinking vitiating the norm of 'organized scepticism' or the mechanism of 'institutionalized vigilance'[31]).

Both types of problems are relatively new in the sociology of science. As Cole has noted: 'It is only in the last few years that sociologists have made a serious attempt to put the study of scientists and their institutions together with the study of their ideas'.[32] The remaining two problems seem more obvious.
(c) Impact of the normative structure of science on its group structure: the character of scientific communities and actual behaviour of scholars (examples: processes of scientific

socialisation and social control in academic community, 'institutionalised evasions' and deviant patterns among scientists). Mulkay observes that the process of rule-application in science is by no means simple, and suggests an entire programme of research focused on it: 'we would have to try to describe the kinds of interpretative procedures and resources employed by scientists in using evaluative codes . . . , we would have to try to show how scientists' use of normative formulations is linked to various kinds of interactional context and, perhaps, to participants' interests.' In short he postulates the study of 'how such a complex repertoire of rules is put into practice'.[33]

(d) Impact of the group structure of science on its normative structure: ethos, institutions, roles (examples: how certain prevailing modes of scientific conduct become embedded in normative standards; how developing forms of research produce new scholarly roles; in short, the issues of normative morphogenesis as applying to the realm of science).

Science as a system

The study of science carried out in line with the foregoing directions produces an *image of science as a system*: a complex totality of variable and variously interrelated components. 'From this perspective, science appears as one of the great social institutions, coordinate with the other major institutions of society; the economy, education and religion, the family and the polity'.[34] Merton adopts specific emphases in treating the system of science. His own contributions focus on certain components: the scientific ethos, the scientific community and the scientific mind (a particular personality and character syndrome typical of scholars). He focuses mainly on a single aspect of the external environment: the political system. Finally, he considers science in dynamic, temporal perspective focusing on processes of change in science; in brief, the sociological history of science.

By treating science as a system, Merton commits himself on two counts. On the one hand, he must take its components as mutually interrelated to some significant degree. The principle of inter-relation is taken from a functional perspective: each component is assumed to fulfil functions for other components, as well as for the system as a whole. For example, the scientific ethos is seen as implemented in the operation of the scientific community as well as in the occupational personalities of scientists. The operation of the scientific community is treated as indispensable to the development of those occupational personality traits which fall in line with the requirements of the scientific ethos. Those traits are in turn perceived as conducive both to the operation of the scientific community and to the legitimation of the scientific ethos. But it is essential to note, no concrete degree of integration is assumed in a specific case. It is not established by definition or treated as given, but rather as *contingent and problematic*, to be empirically observed. Merton allows for conditions leading to dysfunctional consequences of certain components with respect to others and to the system as a whole; and correspondingly – for the potential disintegration of the system, due to the mutual incongruence of its elements or subsystems.

On the other hand, in treating science as a system Merton must conceive it as dissociated, at least to some degree, from the environment. Or to put it otherwise, he must attribute a *degree of autonomy* to science. That quasi-autonomy can pertain to each of the major components of the system. The autonomy of the scientific ethos means that its constitutive norms, values and roles comprise a sort of peculiar enclave within the wider normative system. The autonomy of the scientific mind means that its constitutive complex of attitudes, orientations, occupational personality traits is in some way distinct from that typically prevailing in the larger society. The autonomy of the scientific community is a more complex matter; it seems to involve a double process. In the dissociative process scholars separate themselves to a degree in their scientific roles from the wider society, sever links to the social structure, emancipate themselves from particularistic loyalties, detach themselves from the other social positions they occupy, whether of class, nationality, ethnicity, religion, and so on. In effect, they become unattached, free-floating individuals, somewhat akin to Mannheim's 'intelligentsia'. But such atomistic, individualistic autonomy represents only a half-way point in the social process that produces the distinctive quasi-autonomy of science. Merton goes beyond Mannheim, by adding a related associative process in which scholars, individually insulated from the wider society, develop alternative attachments, affiliations, links and loyalties, thus becoming rooted in a new social structure, as members of particular communities of scholars, with their own, distinct principles of integration. As Merton puts it: 'The margin of autonomy in the culture and institution of science means that the intellectual criteria, as distinct from the social ones, for judging the validity and worth of that work transcend extraneous group allegiances. The acceptance of criteria of craftsmanship and integrity in science and learning cuts across differences in the social affiliations and loyalties of scientists and scholars. Commitment to the intellectual values dampens group-induced pressures to advance the interests of groups at the expense of these values and of the intellectual product'.[35] Only at this moment is their collective autonomy safeguarded, and through it the individual autonomy of each member.

Like internal integration, external autonomy is treated as problematic and contingent. Its degree is also an empirical matter: 'The circumstances and processes making for the fragility or resiliency of that autonomy constitute one of the great questions in the sociology of knowledge'.[36] Basically, that autonomy is never complete. It is always *partial and relative* since the system of science is related in manifold ways to the environment: 'As science has become more institutionalized it has also become more intimately interrelated with the other institutions of society'.[37] But the scientific community becomes a sort of mediating filter, partially insulating the scientists – their behaviour, their ethos, their occupational personality – from the immediate and direct impact of extrascientific pressures. In Merton's words: 'No matter how the environing culture and society affect the development of scientific knowledge, and . . . no matter how scientific knowledge ultimately affects culture and society, these influences are mediated by the changing institutional and organizational structure of science itself'.[38]

Among the manifold aspects of the institutional environment that can impinge on the autonomy of science, Merton selects only one for detailed consideration. It seems that for him a crucial context defining the limits of possible autonomy for science is the political context. Beginning with observations on Nazi Germany, he goes on to draw more general conclusions on the disastrous impacts of the totalitarian state on the system of science. Such an impact occurs on all three major components: the scientific ethos, the scientific mind and the scientific community.

Merton attends primarily to the normative system of science and its decay under totalitarianism: 'The conflict between the totalitarian state and the scientist derives in part, then, from an incompatibility between the ethic of science and the new political code which is imposed upon all, irrespective of occupational creed. The ethos of science involves the functionally necessary demand that theories or generalizations be evaluated in terms of their logical consistency and consonance with facts. The political ethic would introduce the hitherto irrelevant criteria of the race or political creed of the theorist'.[39]

The scientific mind, with its disinterested, Faustian quest for truth as the central attitude, is also endangered when instrumental, utilitarian, practical considerations are taken as alone compelling: 'One sentiment which is assimilated by the scientist from the very outset of his training pertains to the purity of science. Science must not suffer itself to become the handmaiden of theology or economy or state. . . . As the pure science sentiment is eliminated, science becomes subject to the direct control of other institutional agencies and its place in society becomes increasingly uncertain'.[40] Equally dangerous to the scientific mind is the abdication of the sceptical, critical spirit, and its replacement by dogmatism and blind conformism to extra-scientific authorities. The scientific mind is the antithesis of the 'captive mind' – to use Czeslaw Milosz's apt phrase.[41] As Merton explains: 'whether it be the sacred sphere of political convictions or religious faith or economic rights, the scientific investigator does not conduct himself in the prescribed uncritical and ritualistic fashion. He does not preserve the cleavage between the sacred and the profane, between that which required uncritical respect and that which can be objectively analyzed. . . . Science . . . comes into psychological, not logical conflict, with other attitudes toward the same data which have been crystallized and frequently ritualized by other institutions'.[42]

Finally, although Merton gives relatively little attention to that aspect, there is obviously the impact of the totalitarian state on the dissolution of the scientific community. It is just a special case of the more general attempt to destroy the 'civil society' – all forms of communities, associations, collectivities which, not subordinated to the all-powerful state, are integrated on other than political bases. The concentrated demands of political allegiances, loyalties and commitments upon scholars weakens or even eliminates the internal cohesion and solidarity of scientific communities: 'As long as scientists themselves are uncertain of their primary loyalty [to science], their position becomes tenuous and uncertain'.[43] The foundations of their autonomy are undercut.

The implication of the foregoing analysis is that 'the persistent development of science occurs only in societies of a certain order'.[44] There is no doubt that, for Merton, the context functionally indispensable for the proper operation of the system of science is the *liberal–democratic order*. Dewey observed long ago that 'the future of democracy is allied with the spread of the scientific attitude'.[45] Merton's emphasis can be expressed by reversing Dewey's statement: *the future of science is allied with the spread of the democratic attitude and institutions*. The reason given is precisely the compatibility of the liberal–democratic order with the scientific ethos, the scientific mind and the scientific community, thus allowing the system of science to safeguard its indispensable relative autonomy. In Merton's words: 'science is afforded opportunity for development in a democratic order which is integrated with the ethos of science'.[46] It is only in such an order that a functional prerequisite for science is met: 'Science flourishes and scientists make progress in an atmosphere of free inquiry and free interchange of ideas, with the continued mutual stimulation of active minds working in the same or related fields'.[47]

Now, one can wonder to what extent Merton's strong liberal–democratic creed *shapes* his image of science, and to what extent his apology of liberal–democratic order *derives* from his commitment to science conceived in a specific way. Does he find in liberal–democratic institutions the indispensable context for science, defined independently of any political considerations, or rather does he derive the properties of a scientific system by implicit analogy to liberal–democratic institutions? As we proceed it will become obvious that Merton's concrete characterisation of the components of scientific system, makes it an almost perfect *micro-model of liberal–democratic polity*. This seems far from accidental.

Scientific ethos and scientific mind

Merton's analysis of the scientific ethos introduced in the early 1940s, remains a focus of discussion and inquiry. Mulkay expresses what seems to be the common opinion: 'Merton provided the first systematic and the most influential attempt by a sociologist to identify the main norms operative among scientists and to show how these norms contribute to the advance of scientific knowledge'.[48]

The definition of the scientific ethos runs as follows: 'The ethos of science is that affectively toned complex of values and norms which is held to be binding on scientists. The norms are expressed in the form of prescriptions, preferences, permissions, and proscriptions. They are legitimatized in terms of institutional values'.[49] There is no explicit definition of a correlative, individual concept of scientific mind, scientific personality, or to use Merton's occasional term 'scientific conscience'.[50] Nevertheless it seems useful to conceive of that as a complex of typical attitudes, orientations, occupational personality traits of scientists. The scientific mind is therefore an individual reflection of an extra-individual (objective), and inter-individual (shared) scientific ethos. In the ideal, limiting case there is a perfect correspondence of the social norms and values and the personal tendencies of individual scientists; the full internalisation of the scientific ethos by members of the scientific community. In actuality, there is of course only an approximate correspondence; various degrees or levels of internalisation, ranging from superficial, opportunistic compliance to deep acceptance, both rational and emotional. In any case, it will be instructive to discuss the components of the scientific ethos along with their counterparts in the scientific mind.

Merton's definition of the scientific ethos invites several comments. Perhaps the most important is the observation that scientific ethos is conceived as *normative*; morally binding and not only technically useful. It must be distinguished from scientific methodology which has only a technical rationale: 'The mores of science possess a methodological rationale but they are binding, not only because they are procedurally efficient, but because they are believed right and good. They are moral as well as technical prescriptions'.[51]

Then, the ethos is conceived as regulatory with respect to the conduct of scientists. The distinction of norms and values as components of the ethos is based on the distinction of the two phases of conduct being regulated. Merton obviously assumes that actions of the scientists may be conceived of in terms of a voluntaristic, means-ends scheme, as goal-oriented, rational actions. Therefore values simply mean the proper (prescribed, preferred or permitted) goals of action, and norms, the proper means for seeking those goals.[52]

Finally, some level of integration is assumed to exist within the 'complex' of norms and values; both in the hierarchical, vertical sense whereby norms are 'legitimised' by values and in the horizontal sense whereby each norm and value is coordinated or made congruent with other norms and values. The logic of that integration is again functional: the norms are functional for the attainment of values, various norms and values are functionally interlinked, mutually enforcing. But of course this is only the limiting case. Empirically, *integration is never perfect*. In reality, there are historically varying degrees of integration with various contradictions or ambivalences appearing or even becoming built into or institutionalised in the scientific ethos. In the extreme case, counter-norms and counter-values accompany each norm and value, a situation which can perhaps be described as 'scientific anomie', producing various kinds of deviant or 'anomic' responses of scientists.

The structure of the scientific ethos as Merton conceives it can be considered first in terms of its components, and then modes of their interrelations. In this conception, what are taken as the ultimate goals of the scientific enterprise, as defined by legitimising values? I believe Merton would agree with this simple formula: science as activity is the ongoing search for empirically founded truth, ergo the frequent practical utility of the true knowledge. His case for science is primarily cognitivistic, intrinsic, but accompanied by a derived, pragmatic, 'utilitarian' corollary. It seems founded on the assumption common among scientists that what is true is at least potentially useful, whereas the reverse does not necessarily hold. Anyway, *truth comes first*. Merton describes that widespread belief as having 'a double confidence: that fundamental scientific knowledge is a self-contained good and that, in any case, it will in due course lead to all manner of useful consequences serving varied interests in society'.[53]

Two values compose Merton's cognitivistic creed. The one is *objectivity*: the commitment to the pursuit of knowledge, as adequate and as complete as possible. 'Objectivity', says Merton, 'is the central value in the ethos of science'.[54] And if internalised, it turns into corresponding attitudes of objectivism, rationality, open-mindedness, antidogmatism, avoidance of prejudices. The other value is *originality*: the commitment to the pursuit of new knowledge. 'Originality can be said to be a major institutional goal of modern science, at times the paramount one'.[55] It has its own corresponding set of attitudes and occupational personality traits: driving curiosity, even inquisitiveness, intrinsic joy in discovery, creativity, innovativeness, compulsive quest for understanding. Whereas objectivity is a value which works to safeguard the *truth* of science, originality is a value that works to safeguard it from stagnation: 'the emphasis on the value of originality has a self-evident rationale, for it is originality that does much to advance science'.[56] Both values are complementary, mutually reinforcing, and mutually constraining. For example, the value of objectivity bridles the search for novelty for novelty's sake, makes originality count only if it is, to paraphrase Merton's favourite qualifier, 'disciplined originality'. As he puts it: 'the institution of science actually calls for variants that will better meet the goal of new knowledge. Each variant must be shown to satisfy the norms of evidence'.[57] On the other hand, the value of originality prevents the futile repetitions in the guise of science of well-known, trivial results. It directs the efforts of scientists toward really enlightening truths.

To the cognitive values of science Merton adds a third value, which in some periods constitutes the additional, pragmatic case for science by defining its 'utilitarian' rationale. This is the value of *relevance*: the pursuit of knowledge that can 'help society achieve objectives other than knowledge itself; power, comfort or pecuniary gain, health, repute, efficiency, or almost anything other than the advancement of knowledge for its own sake'.[58] The corresponding syndrome of the individual scientific personality or character would presumably involve compassion for the human fate, sensitivity to poverty, injustice, evil, melioristic or activistic attitude. Relevance, is a background value to safeguard the potential utility of science for good or evil, for this or that social group. Already in his earliest articles Merton was aware of this double relativisation of the notion of relevance, often put into questions such as those raised by Robert Lynd: Knowledge *for what*? and Knowledge *for whom*? But he opposed the tendency to make scientists responsible for the directions in which their results are applied by extra-scientific agencies: 'Since the scientist does not or cannot control the direction in which his discoveries are applied, he becomes the subject of reproach and of more violent reactions in so far as these applications are disapproved by the agents of authority or by pressure groups. The antipathy toward the technological products is projected toward science itself'.[59] This he believes to be a fundamentally misguided challenge. Like all other values relevance is never autonomous, but rather interlinked with the whole ethos of science. Utility of scientific results can derive only from the exercise of the other two values. The cognitive values of objectivity and originality bridle the fallacy of relevance for the sake of relevance, just as the value of relevance constrains the search for esoteric, wholly impractical knowledge.

To those overriding, legitimising values – objectivity, originality and relevance – Merton subordinates numerous norms, 'institutional imperatives', defining the acceptable or preferred means for realising those values. A first norm is described as 'universalism'. It requires science to be *impersonal*: 'truth claims, whatever their source, are to be subjected to pre-established impersonal criteria: consonant with observation and with previously confirmed knowledge. The acceptance or rejection of claims entering the lists of science is not to depend on the personal or social attributes of their protagonist; his race, nationality, religion, class and personal qualities are as such irrelevant'.[60] It is wholly opposed to 'the engagingly simple formula of moral alchemy [which holds that] the same behaviour must be differently evaluated according to the person who exhibits it'.[61] Again, objectivity, impartiality, detachment, tolerance – seem to constitute the corresponding, prerequisite attitudes expected of individual practitioners of science.

A second norm is described as 'communism', or better, to avoid ready misunderstandings, 'communalism'.[62] It requires that scientific knowledge be treated not as private property of its creator, but rather as a common good, to be *freely communicated* and distributed. Merton says: 'The substantive findings of science are a product of social collaboration and are assigned to the community. They constitute a common heritage in which the equity of the individual producer is severely limited'.[63] The pro-social, altruistic orientations would presumably correspond to this norm at the level of the individual occupational personality.

A third norm is called 'disinterestedness', one I suggest that can be combined, in a somewhat paradoxical fashion, with another

Merton described later as 'recognition'. Both specify the prescribed reasons or acceptable motives for scholarly endeavours. Disinterestedness demands the subordination of extrinsic interests to the *intrinsic satisfaction* of finding the truth. Recognition allows for one type of supplementary reward which, though seemingly extrinsic to the search for truth is only partly so, for it refers primarily to the scientific community. Normatively, the recognition that should count for a scholar is that which comes from scholarly peers, the recognition of the academic quality of the work, its excellence, its priority as significant discovery. It can become generalised into prestige within scholarly circles and then, derivatively, into fame, even beyond those circles. As Merton reflects: 'outstanding scientists . . . labor hard to have their names inscribed in the golden book of firsts'.[64] This particular type of interestedness is normatively acceptable since it does not endanger the achievement of scientific goals. Quite the reverse; if it is kept short of the abuses of megalomania or the lust for acclaim, it provides legitimate supporting motivation for authentic scholarly achievements: 'In providing apt recognition for accomplishment, the institution of science serves several functions, both for scientists and for maintenance of the institution itself'.[65] In thinking of psychological counterparts of the foregoing, traits such as ambitiousness, extrovertism, other-directedness immediately come to mind.

A fourth norm is described as 'organised scepticism', more recently amplified by the kindred notion of 'organised criticism'. Again, these terms seem to signify aspects of the same norm. One sub-norm requires the scientist to doubt; the other to check whether the doubt is well founded. Organised scepticism is basically a *negative proscription*. It requires 'the suspension of judgment until the facts are at hand',[66] abstention from accepting knowledge claims before they are adequately confirmed, empirically or theoretically, 'in accordance with the rules of evidence current at the time'.[67] Organised criticism is a *positive prescription* of active effort to collect requisite evidence, by subjecting knowledge claims to hard tests: 'This norm calls for public criticism by scientists of claimed contributions to scientific knowledge, both their own contributions and, more easily perhaps, those of others'.[68] The demand of self-criticism is perhaps the most exacting. Merton refers to 'that most difficult aspect of organised scepticism which calls for being at least as critical of one's own work as of the work being put forward by one's peers', but he is quite emphatic about its importance: 'the credo of the authentic scholar and scientist requires it: we must be prepared to reject our brain-children, no matter how dear they are to us, or else they will die of too much love'.[69] This normative expectation is extended to apply to the critic who 'should be critical of his criticism'.[70] Organised scepticism and organised criticism are associated with a complement of requisite psychological tendencies: a sceptical frame of mind, responsibility and restraint in coming to conclusions, thoroughness in examining the evidence, awareness of one's beliefs and prejudices, institutionally exacted humility and modesty with respect to one's knowledge claims, intellectual honesty in abandoning ideas found invalid.

This image of the scientific ethos is of course highly simplified and idealised.[71] Merton is quite aware of that. To bring the image closer to actuality, he introduces several correctives. The notion of *normative ambivalence* corrects what may be called 'the overintegrated image of science'. As Merton observes analysing the sociological ambivalence of scientists: 'Potentially contradictory norms develop in every social institution'.[72] For example the norm of organised scepticism demands that 'the scientist should not allow himself to be victimised by intellectual fads, those modish ideas that rise for a time and are doomed to disappear', but at the same time the value placed on originality requires that 'he must remain flexible, receptive to the promising new ideas and avoid becoming ossified under the guise of responsibly maintaining intellectual traditions'.[73] As can be seen, this type of contradiction is intrinsic to the scientific ethos.

Another type of contradiction derives from the emergence of specific *counter-norms* within the social role of a scholar. 'Role-behavior is alternatively oriented to dominant norms and to subsidiary counter-norms in the role. . . . The major norms and the minor counter-norms alternatively govern role-behavior to produce ambivalence'.[74] For example: in an empirical study of the elite group of 'Apollo-project' scientists, Mitroff traces the emergence of the norm of strong emotional involvement and stubborn commitment to one's own ideas – clearly contradictory to disinterestedness and organised scepticism. He also discovers the emerging counter-norm of 'particularism', giving *a priori* preference and a surplus of credibility to results achieved by recognised authorities, so patently contrary to the norm of universalism. The responses of his subjects 'indicate a deep ambivalence. They reflect not a simple either/or choice between complete impartiality or complete bias but a complex tug-of-war between two opposing norms operating simultaneously'.[75]

Further corrective of the ideal, simplified image of the scientific ethos is the allowance Merton provides for the active, interpretative, selective attitude of scientists who must cope with the ambivalent normative expectations comprising the ethos. 'Since these norms cannot be simultaneously expressed in behavior, they come to be expressed in an oscilation of behaviors. . . . Alternation of subroles evolves as a social device for helping people in designated statuses to cope with the contingencies they face in trying to fulfill their functions'.[76] Mulkay follows this lead and claims that the mediation of interpretative considerations results not only from the ambivalent nature of the normative system but from the essential properties of each of the constitutive norms and values: 'All rule-like formulations employed by scientists acquire their meaning through the interpretative work carried out by individuals in the course of social interaction in specific contexts'.[77]

All the foregoing correctives have to do with the complexities of the ethos of science itself, or of its applications to specific cases. The final corrective focuses on the *actual behavioural deviations* from the scientific ethos. It is a complete mistake to attribute a naive, idealised, Arcadian image of scientists to Merton.[78] Witness this typical reminder of the notorious gap between norms and behaviour: 'the painful contrast between the actual behavior of scientists and the behavior ideally prescribed for them'.[79] The norms and values *embedded* in the scientific ethos, the norms and values *recognised* or professed by scientists, and the norms and values actually *enacted* in their conduct may be quite different. What scientists are expected to do, what they say they do, and what they in fact do, do not necessarily coincide. In this respect, at least, scientists do not differ from other people. This corrects for the possible 'oversocialized image of a scholar'[80] and opens the way for the empirical study of scientific rules-in-use rather than rules-in-books. Such studies have in fact been undertaken and show significant discrepancies between Merton's account of scientific ethos and prevailing realities. Barnes and Dolby find that 'Scientists typically stress such terms as rationality and scepticism in situations of celebration, justification or conflict: they are addressed to outsiders as well as to other scientists, and in the latter case . . . are too nebulous to influence behavior'.[81] Mitroff emphasises that every one of the scientists interviewed 'indicated that they thought the notion of the objective, emotionally disinterested scientist naive'.[82]

The departures from the ethos of science seem to derive either from the failures of socialisation and social control, or from the impact of alternative counter-norms effectively socialised and sanctioned. The behaviour is deviant (relative to the ethos of science) because either scholars have not internalised the ethos or have internalised an alternative one. Here, the sources of deviance lie outside of the ethos itself, in the wider social environment. But *the ethos itself may, under some circumstances, become pathogenic*, originating pressures toward deviant behaviour. To investigate this most interesting type of case, Merton applies his theory of anomie: 'a culture giving emphasis to aspirations for all, aspirations which cannot be realized by many, exerts a pressure for devant behavior and for cynicism, for rejection of the reigning moralities and the rules of the game. We see here the possibility that the same pressures may in some degree be at work in the institution of science'.[83] Here, as elsewhere, the gap between heavily stressed aspirations and actual possibilities gives rise to all sorts of deviant adaptations. 'The absolutization of aspirations can, in its way, be just as damaging as the decay of aspirations to life in civil society'.[84]

To be more specific, *anomic behaviour in science* derives primarily from the great value placed upon originality, and uniformly so for all working scientists, whereas the opportunities and possibilities of achieving original results are most variable, owing to personal constraints (restricted abilities, talents, competences) and to structural constraints (limited resources, means of scientific production, available technology). Deviant behaviour originates 'in response to a discrepancy between the enormous emphasis in the culture of science upon original discovery and the actual difficulty many scientists experience in making an original discovery. In this situation of stress, all manner of adaptive behaviors are called into play, some of these being far beyond the mores of science'.[85] This is indeed one of the paradoxes of social life: 'that same premium on originality which has reinforced intrinsic motives for advancing the frontiers of scientific knowledge also contains pathogenic components'.[86] Among the typical deviant responses Merton examines are: outright fraud, the fabrication of 'data', aggressive self-assertion, the denouncing of rivals, plagiary and charges of plagiary. All these are active adaptations to anomic conditions. There are also passive adaptations: the withdrawal from inquiry in favour of administrative or teaching roles, apathy imbued with fantasy, or 'secret megalomania'.[87] The temptation to use deviant means to establish one's claims to priority and originality does not escape even the greatest. Recalling the controversy between Newton and Leibniz over the invention of the calculus, Merton emphasises the deep, structural roots of their departures from the ethos of science: 'We can gauge the immense pressures for self-vindication that must have operated for such a man as Newton to have adopted these [deceptive] means for defence of his claims. It was not because Newton was so weak but because the institutionalized values were so strong that he was driven to such lengths'.[88]

An extensive follow-up of these hypotheses is to be found in the study by Zuckerman. On the basis of a detailed scrutiny of cases of extreme deviance in science, she arrives at a list of typical violations of scientific norms. Cognitive norms (methodological and technical criteria of scientific work) are violated in the form of 'reputable errors' when errors occur although methodological rules were followed and proper precautions taken, while 'disreputable errors' involve the inadvertent neglect of methodological canons and procedural precautions, or at the extreme, deliberate but concealed departures from them.[89] The moral norms of science are violated in three types of cases. A first is fraud, which takes the form of 'the fabrication, fudging, and suppression of data',[90] or in the more picturesque terminology of Charles Babbage: 'forging', 'trimming', and 'cooking' of data.[91] This type of deviance violates norms of both disinterestedness and organised scepticism. A second type is plagiarism in its various forms, this violating the norm of communism in science.[92] And third is the suppression of innovative ideas in science, which operates in the form of 'disciplinary dogmatism' or 'disciplinary monopoly' and violates the norms of organised scepticism and universalism.[93] Finally, norms of less consequential nature which constitute 'the etiquette of science' are breached in the under-acknowledgment of collaborators' contributions to joint research, *ad hominem* attacks in scientific discourse, publicity seeking by scientists, and occasionally self-eponymysing (the inventor or discoverer assigning an eponymy to himself).[94]

Zuckerman concurs with Merton's observation that deviance – or at least detected deviance – in science is comparatively rare, relative to other institutional domains: 'Taking the various forms of seriously deviant behavior together, that is, forgery, data manipulation, data suppression, and plagiarism – willful acts of deceit – the known cases number perhaps several hundred in a cumulative population of research scientists which, over the generations, number something on the order of more than a million, each at work over a span of years'.[95]

The hypothetical explanation of that striking circumstance is found – in truly Durkheimian style – in the fact that the same normative and social conditions are pressing for deviant behaviour as for its disclosure: 'the greater the socially induced pressure for deviant behavior, the greater the likelihood that it will be detected'.[96] And more specifically: 'The intense competition for making original scientific contributions – the "race for priority" – and the peer recognition that comes with it created pressures for deviant behavior. . . . But that same intense competition as a system property also focuses the attention of scientists on [the same] particular problems, intensifies their critical review of others' work in the field, and encourages efforts to check important new truth claims through replication'.[97] Thus pathogenic tendencies in science, produced by the characteristic strains in the scientific system are countered, to some extent, by mechanisms of social control built into the same scientific enterprise.

Closing the discussion of the scientific ethos one cannot but register a certain nagging doubt. Is it not a little inconsistent to treat science pre-eminently as a social, and therefore changing, historical phenomenon – and at the same time define the core part of the institution of science, the scientific ethos, in clearly ahistorical terms? For Merton, the values and norms that he includes in the ethos of science are *constant*, unchanging, equally valid for Newton and Einstein, for science in 17th-century England and 20th-century United States. What warrant is there for excluding that fragment of social reality from the principle of historical relativisation of all things social? Empirical studies seem to indicate the evolving character of the scientific ethos coordinated with the changing model of science.[98] It is true that Merton's account is relevant for the traditional model of academic science.[99] The question worth investigating is how far the modern, complex scientific enterprise – in part almost industrial in nature – departs from this model, and how the divergences bear on the transformations of the scientific ethos.

Scientific community

The system of science, conceived of as a comprehensive totality is both *an institution* made up of norms and sanctions and a *social organisation* made up of individuals in their role behaviour and mutual, interactive relationships. The latter may be described as the scientific community. Coordinated with the scientific ethos and scientific mind, it provides the arena in which scientific norms and values are implemented in practice, and scientific attitudes and motivations are expressed and affirmed. Much of Merton's contributions to the sociology of science deal with the detailed analysis of internal mechanisms and processes operating within the scientific community, and it is to this part of his work I now turn, albeit rather sketchily.

In line with his general orientation, Merton treats the scientific community as a *system*, within which he distinguishes at least six subsystems. The first he describes as 'the system of institutionalized vigilance'.[100] Almost from the start of his studies in the sociology of science Merton emphasises that *science is public, not private* in nature.[101] This is most obviously the case for the results of science, but is also often the case with aspects of the research-process, even including problem-selection. These are subject, often without such explicit design, to examination, appraisal, criticism and verification by other scientists as they make use of these results or methods: 'Scientific research is typically, if not always, under the exacting scrutiny of fellow experts, involving, as it usually though not always does, the verifiability of results by others. Scientific inquiry is in effect subject to rigorous policing, to a degree unparalleled in any other field of human activity. Personal honesty is supported by the public and testable character of science. . . . The unending exchange of critical judgment, of praise and punishment, is developed in science to a degree that makes the monitoring of children's behavior by their parents seem little more than child's play'.[102] This is of course crucial for safeguarding the objectivity of scientific claims, their authentic originality and relevance: 'Continuous appraisal of work and recognition for work judged well done by the standards of the time constitute a mechanism for maintaining the processes of falsification and confirmation of ideas that are required for the cognitive development of science'.[103] This mechanism, when it operates adequately, realises and affirms the norms of universalism and organised scepticism; it converts non-particularistic standards and critical attitudes into organisational principles, making them independent of the good will or personal integrity of this or that scholar. In fact, the relationship between the norms and their organisational implementation is so close that Merton uses the alternative designation, 'a system of organized scepticism' for this aspect of the scientific community.[104]

Closely interlinked with the system of institutionalised vigilance is the communication system of science. To be checked, verified, corrected, rejected, or incorporated in the stock of public knowledge, the results of science and in principle the process of investigation must be made *visible* to other scholars. 'For science to be advanced it is not enough that fruitful ideas be originated or new experiments developed or new problems formulated or new methods instituted. The innovations must be effectively communicated to others. . . . For the development of science, only work that is effectively perceived and utlized by other scholars, then and there, matters.'[105] It is the rationale underlying the emphasis so commonly put in science on publication – both written and oral – just as it is for the various methods of registering priority-claims to ideas, discoveries or inventions, once they are communicated to others. Merton pays particular attention to the conditions determining the visibility of scientific results, focusing especially on an aspect of the phenomenon of visibility called 'the Matthew effect'.[106] The term derives from the biblical adage to the effect that those who already have will have even more. In the present context it means that the works published by recognised scholars have much better chances of visibility in the scientific community than equally significant or original contributions by scholars of less renown.

Merton maintains a persistent interest, although one still expressed only in the form of 'oral publication' in the mechanism of 'cognitive conduits', through which selected ideas are picked up, diffused, amplified, modified or their source 'obliterated by incorporation' in the stock of knowledge, thus often living beyond the intentions of their creators. 'Scholars can, along with their own work, provide conduits for the transmission of knowledge long overlooked by others, including the originating authors of that knowledge themselves who introduce it briefly and never again revert to it'.[107] He quotes the examples of the 'Thomas theorem', the Veblenian concept of 'trained incapacity', the 'Burke theorem', the Allport–Schanck concept of 'pluralistic ignorance' as cases in which he found himself engaged in the 'conduit function'. And of course his *On the Shoulders of Giants* (often referred to as OTSOG) is a masterpiece of tracing the 'conduits' through which that metaphor has been transmitted over the centuries.

Two special cases of the transmission of ideas are singled out by Merton for detailed consideration. One type, identified in OTSOG, is called the 'anatopic or palimpsestic syndrome' or simply a 'palimpsest' in which 'the altogether innocent transmitter becomes identified as the originator of the idea when his merit lies only in having kept it alive, or in having brought it back to life after it had long lain dormant or perhaps in having put it to new and instructive use'.[108] In the case of the palimpsest, the later usage covers over the original source, at times even though that source is explicitly mentioned. Thus, a fitting illustration of the palimpsest is the concept of 'trained incapacity' which has been mistakenly attributed to Merton by a good many authors.[109] Referring explicitly to Veblen's concept of 'trained incapacity' Merton proceeded, in 1940, to utilise that concept in his analysis of 'Bureaucratic Structure and Personality'. Nevertheless, the detailed application of the concept resulted in a palimpsest which often assigned invention of the concept to Merton.

The other special pattern is 'obliteration by incorporation' (OBI for short). It refers to the situation in which both the original source and the literal formulation of an idea are forgotten, owing to its long and widespread use: 'earlier and often much weightier scientific contributions tend to be obliterated (though not without occasional and sometimes significant exceptions) by incorporation into later work'.[110] This pattern is often found in the form of the canonical knowledge which is distilled in textbooks.[111] Those examples show that although the operation of the communication system ordinarily reflects and implements the norm of communism (or communalism) analysed earlier, it has its own set of potential errors and dysfunctions.

Another major component of the scientific community is the evaluation and reward system, a complex set of mechanisms for allocating rewards for scientific accomplishments. For scientists, the prizes acceptable in the ethos of science, the rewards that matter most are those received from their peers. These are embodied in various forms of *recognition*, ranging from references, citations, awards, medals, honorary degrees, fellowships in learned societies, to Nobel Prizes and scientific immortality in the form of eponymy (affixing the name of the scholar to his discovery).[112] 'Graded rewards in the realm of science are distributed principally in the coin of recognition accorded research by fellow scientists. . . . Both the self-image and the public image of scientists are largely shaped by the communally validating testimony of significant others that they have variously lived up to the exacting institutional requirements of their roles'.[113] Zuckerman emphasises that the institutionalised distribution of such rewards is one of the main mechanisms – apart from internalisation and the sanctioning of violations – that makes for conformity to the norms and values of the scientific ethos.[114]

In his extensive empirical analyses, Merton centres on institutionalised mechanisms of evaluation and reward-allocation, and particularly the referee-system, so typical of modern science. In that sphere he has focused on tracing processes in the operation of the system which lead to departures from the ideals of distributive justice and equity, producing appraisals which are biased or skewed; in short where recognition is disproportionate to achievement (the limiting case being the scholar whose only achievement is recognition). One of these processes, as has been noted in another context, is 'the Matthew effect', in its aspect of 'the accruing of greater increments of recognition for particular scientific contributions to scientists of considerable repute and the withholding of such recognition from scientists who have not yet made their mark'.[115] Or, to put it briefly – breeding fame by fame. Merton's testing grounds for identifying this pattern are found in collaborative, multi-authored contributions and multiple, independent discoveries. In both cases, the famous scholars (for example, Nobel laureates) tend to receive disproportionate or even exclusive credit. Another process of similar sort results in the 'phenomenon of the 41st chair'. As is the case of the French Academy with its numbers strictly confined to 40, the number of places at the top of every pyramid of scientific standing is limited. The limitation of rewards means in effect that some scholars are under-rewarded for their contributions. In the case of the Nobel Prizes for example 'a good number of scientists who have not received the prize and will not receive it have contributed as much to the advancement of science as some of the recipients, or more'.[116]

When the evaluation-and-reward system operates effectively, it affirms two norms: the norm of disinterestedness having scientific peers appraise scientific contributions and rewarding them in terms of their scientific merits, and the norm of universalism applying uniform, non-particularistic criteria in the evaluation and the corresponding allocation of rewards. Both the Matthew effect and the phenomenon of the 41st chair are processes and structural constraints that of course militate against those norms and represent *socially induced deviations* from the norms.

Merton goes on to examine the stratification system of the scientific community which results from these processes, the *patterned differentiation of scholars* according to identifiable criteria. He focuses on three criteria, distinguishing partly correlated and partly independent dimensions of stratification. The most important one is the hierarchical, or pyramidal status-prestige system — the ranking of scholars resulting from the variable measures of recognised achievement. The 'strategic research site' for Merton is the scientific elite, and particularly the group of Nobel laureates.[117] He focuses on another aspect of the Matthew effect, in this context disproportionate access to research resources, facilities and stimulating academic environments for the selected few. He also makes a new and revealing observation about upward mobility in science, discussed under the heading of 'the ratchet effect': 'once having achieved a particular degree of eminence, they [the scientists] do not later fall much below that level (although they may be outdistanced by newcomers and suffer a relative decline in prestige).'[118] Or, in other words: 'Although rank and authority in science are acquired through past performance, once acquired they tend to be ascribed (for an indeterminate duration)'.[119]

Another component of the differentiation system, the status-role system, is not hierarchical, but horizontal or functional, and is only derivatively correlated with the prestige hierarchy. It is produced by the division of labour among scientists as they select or at least pre-eminently emphasise one or another of four social roles in science: research, teaching, administration or gate-keeping.[120] There are also the connected parascientific or service roles such as technicians, assistants, librarians, secretaries. Although those roles are collectively indispensable for the functioning of the scientific enterprise, they are differently evaluated. 'Almost in a pattern of revealed preference, the working of the reward system in science testifies that the research role is the most highly valued. The heroes of science are acclaimed in their capacity as scientific investigators, seldom as teachers, administrators or referees and editors.[121] It must be noted that this conclusion of Zuckerman and Merton obviously refers to some ideal scientific community, where all the structural mechanisms are operating properly. There are known historical cases when the administrative role becomes exalted far above the research or teaching roles. There are others where the teaching role, especially when understood as close to indoctrination or political education, acquires pre-eminence. Thus, pathological developments must also be recognised as possible in the stratification system of science.

Zuckerman and Merton have also examined the age structure in the stratification of science. That thorough study includes various important observations, hypotheses and queries, which cannot be given even the semblance of justice here.[122]

Along with stratification, the scientific community involves systems of recruitment and instruction. These are of strategic importance for internalisation of the scientific ethos converting its norms and values into enduring tendencies of scientists' character and occupational personality. Scientific socialisation – the selection and training into scientific roles – is an intricate process, having some irreducible specificity in comparison with other types of socialisation. But this process has thus far been strangely neglected by Merton.

A final component of the scientific community requiring mention here is the informal influence system: the network of personal ties, acquaintanceships, friendships, loyalties, solidarities that cut across other systems and significantly modify their operation. In his recent work, Merton pays ever-growing attention to this elusive domain. In particular, he gives a new prominence to the 17th-century notion of 'the invisible college' as this has been redefined for modern usage by the historian of science Derek de Solla Price.[123] Merton notes sociologically relevant elements of the invisible college: 'clusters of geographically dispersed scientists who engage in more frequent cognitive interaction with one another than they do with others in the larger community of scientists. . . . Members of an emerging invisible college regard themselves as major reference individuals and regard themselves collectively as a reference group, whose opinions of their work matter deeply and whose standards of cognitive performance are taken as binding'.[124] He applies this differentiated concept in his account of the origins and development of the sociology of science as a sociological specialty.[125] Quite the same emphasis appears in Merton's fascination with the long-forgotten work of the Polish scientist and self-taught sociologist Ludwik Fleck,[126] whose concept of 'thought collective' he reintroduces in his analysis of the sociology and philosophy of science. The thought collective signifies in his account 'the community of people actively engaged in the exchange of ideas in particular domains'.[127] All this points to further promising avenues of inquiry into the informal structures of scientific communities. Again, one has to note that Merton paints a somewhat idealised picture of the system of informal influence. He seems to forget that this system is equally open to various forms of pathology as the ones discussed earlier. Suffice it to mention nepotism, academic cliques and factions, hidden networks of exchanging favours, to see other cases of departures from the ideal of science as prescribed by the scientific ethos.

Science as process

Thus far, the system of science has been largely discussed from a static, structural perspective. This does not mean of course that it is conceived of as inert and stable, devoid of change or internal functioning. Each component or subsystem was seen as operating in its own right with significant impact on the operation of others and on the functioning of a system as a whole. But all those processes were seen as internal to the system; they were seen as *changes in*, not *changes of* science as an institution. Nothing was said about the origins of that system and its transformation as a whole. Yet it is obvious that modern science did come into being at a particular moment, and that contemporary science differs from early modern science.

Merton does not neglect this problem. In fact, his interest in science began with the study of its origins, and his preoccupation with the history of science is so pervasive that some commentators have referred to it as obsessive.[128] As a result, the dimension of time was found in Merton's analysis from the start as the system of science was examined from a dynamic perspective. The questions, how modern science emerged and how it developed appear high on Merton's agenda.

The earlier question was approached in his first book.[129] The hypothesis concerning the birth of modern science is reached along two paths. The first one is inductive. His interest in the origins of modern, empirical science in 17th-century England led him to observe a *linkage between religious commitments and a sustained interest in science.* He noted that English scientists in that period were disproportionately ascetic Protestants or Puritans, although of course the reverse did not hold with only a minute minority of Puritans becoming scientists. As Merton testifies, this specific observation relates to the more general idea formulated by Weber: 'Only then, and almost as though he [Merton] had not been put through his paces during the course of graduate study, was he belatedly put in mind of that intellectual tradition, established by Max Weber, Troeltsch, Tawney and others, which centered on the interaction between the protestant ethic and the emergence of modern capitalism'.[130]

The second path is deductive. The hypothesis fits into Merton's general perspective, particularly the crucial idea of institutional interchange: 'A principal sociological idea governing this empirical inquiry holds that the socially patterned interests, motivations and behavior established in one institutional sphere – say, that of religion or economy – are interdependent with the socially patterned interests, motivations and behavior obtaining in other institutional spheres – say, that of science'.[131]

Following Weber's lead, Merton traces the links between Puritanism and empirical science. His general view of the causal mechanisms is much like Weber's. Religious beliefs imply certain values (or ethos); once internalised, these values help shape specific psychological motivations (or orientations); the motivations are expressed in actions of certain kinds; those actions are conducive to producing, sustaining, modifying or curbing social institutions other than religion itself; those institutions in turn then feed back on religion, either in a positive, supportive sense or in a negative, destructive sense.

To be more concrete, various phases of this chain of reciprocal influence must be specified. The ethos of Puritanism derived from ascetic Protestantism is taken to comprise the following values: 'a strong emphasis on everyday utilitarianism, intramundane interests and actions . . . the belief that scientific understanding of the world of nature serves to manifest the glory of God as "the great Author of Nature", the right and even the duty to challenge various forms of authority, a strong streak of traditionalism, all these coupled with the exaltation of both empiricism and rationality'.[132] Those values and attitudes are seen to have had the effects of stimulating scientific research by inviting the empirical and rational quest for identifying the God-given order in the world, and for practical applications; just as they legitimised scientific research through religious justification. Thus Puritanism, transformed from a theological, via an ethical into a psychological force, contributed to the emergence of science and then 'inadvertently contributed to the legitimacy of science as an emerging social institution'.[133] Once having obtained institutional legitimacy, and with it a degree of autonomy, science largely severed its link with religion, finally to become a counterforce, curbing the influence of religion, by putting some of its legitimacy into question. Here again Merton exhibits his predilection for discovering the circular processes that produce paradoxical effects: the *irony of history*.

What is the character of the link between various phases of the process? The Puritan persuasion is obviously not a sufficient condition for taking up scientific work. Only a small fraction of Puritans had chosen to become scientists. Is it, then, a necessary condition? What does seem necessary is a certain motivational constellation, canalising scientific activities and furnishing them with legitimacy.[134] But can this not derive from other than religious sources? Of course it can. It is only a matter of *historical contingency* that Puritanism proved to provide stimulus and justification for science in 17th-century England: 'Ascetic Protestantism helped motivate and canalize the activities of men in the direction of experimental science. This is the historical form of the hypothesis'.[135] And more precisely: 'As it happened, Puritanism provided major (not exclusive) support in that historical time and place'.[136] But this historical circumstance cannot be generalised: 'Other functionally equivalent ideological movements could have served to provide the emerging science with widely acknowledged claims to legitimacy'.[137] Thus Puritanism was by no means historically indispensable for the emergence of modern science. Moreover, even in the particular historical circumstances when it did play that role, it was definitely not an exclusive basis. Merton attaches great importance to the parallel role of concrete exigencies facing England at that time in the fields of *economy, technology, and warfare*. Unfortunately this part of Merton's book has been left in the shade by his followers and commentators, focusing on the more striking thesis on the impact of Protestant ethic. As Nelson observes: 'Surely . . . Merton would have to agree that it was the "Puritanism and science hypothesis" which constituted the distinctive feature of his effort in 1938 and which, indeed, constitute it even now'.[138] The more so it is necessary to emphasise that he did not restrict his field of vision to that main problem. His even-handed 'rejection of both simplisms', an exclusive focus on one factor, whether 'idealistic' or 'materialistic', leads him to an intermediate, synthesising position: 'The model of interpretation adduced in this study does provide for the mutual support and independent contribution to the legitimacy of science of both the value orientation supplied by Puritanism and the pervasive belief in, perhaps more than the occasional fact of, scientific solutions to pressing economic, military and technological problems'.[139]

A final theoretical interpretation holds that when religion proves to be a significant component in the set of causal factors producing or supporting science, its impact need not be treated as manifest, as intended and recognised by the true believers. Rather, this operates as an unintended and often unrecognised consequence: 'the hypothesized relation between ascetic Protestantism and the emergence of modern science was largely an unintended consequence of the religious ethic and related patterns of action (religiously derived practice) instead of being only the result of direct and deliberate support of science by religious leaders'.[140]

To recapitulate: Merton's conception of the origins of modern science is located on three levels of generality. At its most concrete level, 'the socio-historical hypothesis'[141] reads: in 17th-century England, ascetic Protestantism, along with other social and cultural elements, served the unintended and unrecognised function of encouraging and legitimising science. Almost the same weak interpretation of Merton's claim is given by Patel: 'he does not consider Protestantism as the cause of the growth of science in seventeenth-century England. His contention is modest. He considers that the growth of science at that particular time and place was the latent consequence of Protestantism. Thus, religion is neither a sufficient nor a necessary condition for the growth of science'.[142] On the 'middle-range level', the hypothesis reads: the emergence of modern science required, *among other things*, a specific attitudinal orientation reflecting a particular value-complex (ethos), which could have been unintentionally derived from other institutional sources as well as from a religious creed. Finally, at the most general and abstract level the hypothesis simply affirms 'the dynamic interdependence of social institutions',[143] including religion and science. At this level it becomes in fact an 'orienting hypothesis' indicating the viable directions of inquiry, rather than an empirical statement reporting the results of inquiry.

Merton's theory of the origins of experimental science in 17th-century England has evoked wide-ranging use and wide-ranging criticism, with the discussion seeming far from ended, to judge from current publications. In fact Merton himself treats that recurrent discussion as an example of the 'Phoenix phenomenon' which appears often 'in the history of systematic thought: the continuing resiliency of theories or theoretically derived hypotheses'.[144]

If the foregoing interpretation of Merton's thesis is correct, most of the critical challenges must be regarded as inconclusive, irrelevant or missing the mark. The dogmatic choice of an alternative approach provides a first type. When Hall opts for the 'internalist approach' in the history of science, emphasising the autonomous development of ideas, he may be justified as long as he keeps from treating it as the exclusive option. It is not enough, at least in science, to stipulate that some point of view is 'clear': 'Clearly, externalist explanations of the history of science have lost their interest as well as their interpretative capacity [and] it is clear that the trend towards intellectual history is strong and universal'.[145] It would be good *to demonstrate* this claim. Only then would Merton's explicitly externalist approach be seriously jeopardised. As matters stand, the challenge is empty and inconclusive.

The dogmatic choice of an alternative theory within the general externalist approach provides a second, kindred type. For example, it is hard to go along with Tenbruck who claims that Merton did not fulfil Weber's mandate: 'Weber had been contemplating a very different account of the rise of science where religion would have played a truly essential rather than a merely supportive role'.[146] It seems that this critic projects his own view into Weber's supposed intentions, while in fact proposing an alternative theory in which (a) religion not only instigates the birth and institutionalisation of modern science, but remains a permanent central motivational force of mature science, this because (b) science is the modern expression of the perennial, fundamentally religious quest for meaning in the world: 'In the last analysis the rise of modern science was a quest for Truth writ large, a search for meaningful cosmos and for the certainty of uncontroversial rules to tell us how we ought to act and to live'.[147] In the absence of convincing evidence that theory, patently different from Merton's, must be regarded as doubtful.

A third kind of challenge comes from authors who question Merton's interpretation of historical data. I do not undertake to discuss Kearney's claim, on historical grounds, that some crucial components of Merton's account of 17th-century England are open to debate; Kearney maintaining that the social structure was still aristocratic without significant bourgeois tendencies and that science was not yet a rational, forward-looking, empirically rooted enterprise but rather an exercise in 'natural history' or philosophy.[148] Even if this were the case, and this is far from having been established by the critic, it would undercut only the most concrete, historical formulation of Merton's thesis, leaving the two more general – and crucial – ideas unaffected.

A fourth kind of criticism rests on the assumption that Merton treated his hypothesis as a general, ahistorical law. In this version, historical evidence is adduced to show that the imputed law does not hold in some cases: 'Seeking to test the significance of the Puritan ethic, it will strike [the reader] that this is notably irrelevant to the efflorescence of medical science in sixteenth-century Italy, and no less to the successes of that brilliant group in France which preceded the Royal Society by a few years . . . . The link is obviously not essential to science as such, for counter-instances are too numerous'.[149] Merton himself warns against such a 'fallacy of misplaced concreteness' and goes to some pains to emphasise the *historical, non-general character of his hypothesis* in its first, concrete formulation. He is also quite explicit about possible *alternative ideological configurations* that provide requisite values and motivations for the emergence and spread of science. This type of challenge obviously misses the mark.

A fifth kind of criticism points to the insufficient specification of the explanandum in Merton's theory: 'we do not learn what seventeenth-century science was, nor does it serve to answer Merton's question: why were people more interested in physics than in biology? . . . Such inquiries tell us nothing about Boyle, or Hooke, or Newton, that is significant to consideration of their work as scientists'.[150] This is certainly a valid point, although its critical impact is rather muted by the fact that Merton is fully aware of it: 'the study might have taken further advantage of the strategic polar cases to isolate the role of rationality in affecting the kinds of science that became of prime interest, instead of confining the inquiry to the question of an interest in the sciences generally'.[151] This challenge institutes directions for further inquiry rather than invalidating the explanation of what was taken as problematic.

To summarise; Merton's thesis was an important pioneering step on the road 'toward the comparative historical sociology of sociocultural process in the spirit of Max Weber, Alfred Weber, Durkheim, Mauss, the Durkheimians, Joseph Needham, and a number of contemporary historians and philosophers of science'.[152] Its significance lies in opening certain directions of research, rather than in achieving ultimate results. To return to Nelson's appraisal: 'In their original form, the theses about the cultural and social background of the "institutionalization" of modern science . . . had the flavor of an adventure into largely unknown but highly contested ground, and in the opinion of many then, and even now, remain an area needing to be carefully studied against wider background than have so far been brought into focus'.[153]

To account for the origins of modern science, whatever the merit of such an exercise, is only half the story if one wants to perceive the system of science in dynamic perspective. The other half must deal with the course and direction of scientific development.

Merton provides some implicit clues, as well as explicit formulations which allow one to grasp his conception of this matter. His prescription of a *selective and critical continuity with earlier scientific tradition*, put in terms of the famous metaphor of a dwarf standing on the shoulders of giants, and conceived of as a component of the scientist's role makes sense only within an image of science as a *cumulative and progressing process*. In fact, the ideas of cumulation and progress appear explicitly in Merton's early works. In one of his first articles, he agrees with Alfred Weber in distinguishing civilisation (including science) from culture, and goes on to contrast 'the cumulative nature of civilization and the unique (noncumulative) character of culture'.[154] The same idea directly addressed to science appears several years later: 'Current systematic theory represents the selective accumulation of those parts of earlier theory which have survived the test of decades of research'.[155] This formulation introduces a distinct qualification. The cumulation of scientific knowledge is treated as *selective*. More recently it is even more expressly stated that cumulation of selective and *uneven in pace*. One must reject 'the naive belief in a steady unilinear rather than in a variously selective and uneven cumulation of scientific knowledge . . . [and to embrace the] hypothesis of fluctuations and oscillations in the historical development of science'.[156] But equally fallacious as a belief in unilinear progress is the opposite conception of complete relativism: 'When relativists deny a selective accumulation of scientific knowledge and science-based technology, they abandon more than common sense'.[157] Thus, *the overall process of development is the selective and uneven cumulation of scientific knowledge whereas its overall direction is ultimately progressive*: 'the beautiful Greek mythology could summon up no more scientific imagination than to endow the doomed Icarus with wings contrived from feathers and wax. And while we may not like the noisy Concorde, we must confess that this science-based piece of technology derives from a somewhat better knowledge of aerodynamics than that'.[158]

In more fine-grained terms, the cumulation of knowledge is seen as taking two forms: revision and replacement. Writing in 1959, Merton notes that 'As inquiry proceeds along these lines, it uncovers a gap in the theory: the set of ideas is found to be not discriminating enough to deal with aspects of phenomena to which it should in principle apply. In some cases it is proposed to fill the gap by further differentiation of concepts and propositions that are consistent with the earlier theory, which is regarded as demonstrably incomplete rather than fundamentally mistaken. In other cases, the new conceptions put in question some of the assumptions underlying the earlier theory which is then replaced rather than revised'.[159] In the one case, cumulation follows a course of *gradual incrementations* of knowledge; in the other something akin to a *revolution or mutation* occurs, introducing radical transformation of scientific views. Both types of cognitive change are covered by the generic idea of the selective cumulation of scientific knowledge: 'The theory provides for the growth, differentiation, and development of science just as it allows for the fact that new increments in science are in principle or in fact repeated increments. It allows also for occasional mutations in scientific theory which are significantly new even though they are introduced by more than one scientist'.[160] In a typical Mertonian fashion the proposed conception of scientific development is clearly intermediary to both the extreme incrementalist position and the radical version of 'scientific revolutions'.[161] He seems to take some elements from both standpoints and combine them in a synthetic manner.

As in Merton's inquiry into other cognitive and social processes in science, he identifies pathological or dysfunctional patterns in the process of progressive, selective cumulation. Obsessive fascination with past achievements leads to the belief that there is nothing new under the sun. The notion of cumulation is wholly forgotten. This then is the sin of 'adumbrationism': 'Adumbrationism . . . refers to the dedicated, deliberate search for all manner of earlier versions of scientific or scholarly ideas. At the extreme, the adumbrationist describes the faintest shadow of resemblance between earlier and later ideas as virtual identity'.[162] But as is put in one of Whitehead's aphorisms which Merton often reiterates: 'to come very near to a true theory, and to grasp its precise application, are two very different things'.[163]

The opposite assumption that the newest ideas are necessarily the best ideas leads to the mistaken identification of novelty with advance. This time it is the image that scientific development does not exhibit unilinear progress that is lost to view. This is the sin of the 'fallacy of the latest word', defined as the 'usually tacit belief that the latest word on a given subject or problem is necessarily the best word, at least *pro tem*, if indeed it is not the definitive, once-and-for-all word'.[164]

Finally, there is the well-known deviation from norms of science described as the phenomenon of plagiary in which others' ideas are presented as one's own. Parallel to this pattern, but not involving deliberate deception is the less-known phenomenon of 'cryptomnesia' or 'unconscious plagiary': 'seemingly creative thought in which ideas based upon unrecalled past experiences [of others' or one's own prior ideas] are taken to be new'.[165] All these processes significantly distort the selective cumulation of scientific knowledge.

Toward a sociological epistemology

Merton's road toward a sociology of science began with the rejection of the philosophical approach then typical for the sociology of knowledge. He wanted to turn the sociological study of science into an *empirical, scientific discipline*. The foregoing discussion has sketched the measure of his success. As one contemporary commentator puts it: 'there developed a unique area of specialization within sociology – the sociology of science – which was, in a way, predicated on the rejection of epistemological questions'.[166] Within the sociology of science numerous areas of research began to flourish, all retaining Merton's early anti-philosophical bias. 'As these fields have developed in following years, however, their practitioners have tended to ignore epistemological questions in favor of questions concerning such matters as the origin of scientific ideas, their communication to other scientists, scientific productivity, the reward system in science, and related matters'.[167] As Phillips summed it up: 'Today there exists a considerable literature in the sociology of science, but, with the exception of a small number of British sociologists, those working in the sociology of science have rejected epistemological concerns'.[168] The decade which passed since these words were written has brought decisive change in this respect.

This strong rejection of epistemological questions had to be an initial and provisional phase since the students of science could not but see that *science is, after all (or rather, before all), the search for knowledge*. Having studied the scholarly roles, the normative structure of science, social control in science, the operation of a scientific community, the development of science and related matters, one must ask how all those mechanisms and processes contribute to or deflect from the ultimate cognitive goal. The epistemological questions have to be brought back in. But the sociological understanding of science that had been gained in the meantime allows us to approach those questions in a new way. The basis has been laid for a *sociological epistemology*. This is the meaning of the significant developments in the sociology of science for the last ten years associated with such names as Mary Douglas, Barry Barnes, David Bloor, Michael Mulkay,[169] among others.

Significantly enough Merton himself embarked – although with some reluctance – on this road back from the sociology of science toward sociological epistemology. His contribution is not yet much developed or original; it is based mainly on the ideas of Ludwik Fleck, that forgotten microbiologist whose work has found in Merton, along with Thaddeus Trenn, an enthusiastic editor, translator and advocate.[170] But even from his brief discussions, Merton's own epistemological creed appears quite clearly. It can be reconstructed as a coda in closing my account of his ideas about science.

Science, as the search for knowledge, of course makes sense only if it is assumed that something *can be known*, that the world is knowable. On this point Merton has never expressed doubts. The assumption of intelligibility of the world is made explicit from his earliest work: 'the very notion of experiment is ruled out without the prior assumption that Nature constitutes an intelligible order, so that when appropriate questions are asked, she will answer, so to speak. Hence, this assumption is final and absolute'.[171] But the assumption of intelligibility is only the beginning of cognitive wisdom; it leaves open all the questions concerning the nature of the intelligible object, the relation between the object and subject, the limits of intelligibility, the ways and means of obtaining maximum knowledge. Merton approaches those questions step by step.

In accord with his sociological persuasion, he rejects from the outset 'the naive notion that the creation of new knowledge can be a purely individual phenomenon'.[172] In place of the traditional, individualistic approach he proposes a sociological epistemology, in which the knowing-subject is seen within a social context, and the cognition itself is constructed as *socially mediated*. Developing these ideas, he follows Fleck's insightful observations closely. In the case of science, the knowing subject, the scientist, is always a member of some collectivity of scientists. He is immersed in the 'thought collective': 'the community of people actively engaged in the exchange of ideas in particular domains'.[173] Thus, scientists tend to adopt a particular 'thought style': 'a socially generated and shared readiness for a particular way of perceiving and conceiving which exercises a definite constraint on the form and substance of thinking'.[174] Taking into account the notions of thought collective and thought style, one can conceive of the cognitive relation as triadic, involving the object-to-be-known, the social knowing-subject, and the resulting knowledge. Cognition, says Merton, 'must rather be conceived as a triadic relationship which includes also the stock of then-and-there legitimated knowledge. Since that stock of knowledge is shared by working members of a thought collective,[175] this does away with the artless notion that the creation of new knowledge is a purely individual phenomenon'.

Triadic sociological epistemology may easily degenerate in two directions, depending on whether extreme, one-sided positions are allowed. On the one hand, the constraints of the thought collective on the shape of scientific facts (what is taken to be true) may be neglected, and the facts construed as simply a *direct reflection* of external reality. On the other hand, the influence of the thought collective may be so exaggerated that the external reality may be wholly lost sight of, or even treated as non-existent. Here, scientific facts become treated as unrestricted, *free emanations* of the thought collective.

In line with his typical style of thinking, Merton rejects both extreme standpoints. An asocial theory of knowledge merely reflecting reality is only a return to the dualistic epistemology which he had already abandoned. He focuses therefore his criticism on the other extreme, that of radical cognitive relativism, which seems to forget that knowledge is about something: 'along with the social and cognitive interactions of scientists in collectives, there is also – to use his [Fleck's] words – the objective reality (that which is to be known)'.[176] As members of their thought communities, scientists approach something which is out there, the reality they study. The *active orientation* – the subjective or social-subjective frame – is superimposed upon the passive, *objectively existing world*: 'the unreified passive element of knowledge provides objective, rule-of-the-game, cognitive constraints upon what flows imaginatively from the thought style. . . . It is not the case, as a radical cognitive relativism would have it, that anything and everything goes – or transforming Bentham's almost forgotten phrase, that pushpin is as good as poetry'.[177] Thus, the content of scientific knowledge appears as a product of double, cross-cutting influences: of the objective reality (actually *existing world*) and the socially produced and shared way of perceiving (*thought style*). As Merton puts it: 'The work of the scientist is at every point influenced (not determined) by the intrinsic requirements of the phenomena with which he is dealing and perhaps just as directly by his reactions to the inferred critical attitudes or actual criticism of other scientists and by an adjustment of his behavior in accordance with these attitudes'.[178]

Abandoning the view which assumes cognition as an asocial, direct reflection of reality, as well as the view which assumes that reality is only a social construction, Merton formulates an epistemological position which affirms the *social mediation of reality*. It might perhaps be described as sociological neo-Kantianism.

This leads him directly to the problem of objectivity. If reality is taken as given, existing out there, the goal of science must be conceived as representing it adequately, though provisionally: 'The ethos of science involves the functionally necessary demand that theories or generalizations be evaluated in terms of their logical consistency and consonance with facts'.[179] But how is this type of objectivity to be attained if knowledge is always socially mediated, tempered by the assumptions of particular and variable thought-collectives? Merton seems to believe that the mechanism making for the progress of science toward a more adequate and more extensive knowledge (in a word, more objective knowledge) is to be found precisely in the *plurality of thought-collectives* and their respective thought-styles which inevitably produce *cognitive and social conflict*. Such conflict is seen to a degree as functional, beneficial, because the clash of perspectives makes for perspectives becoming offsetting or complementary approximations to an objective reality. This view is aptly summed up by Mitroff: 'the proliferation of contesting views on any subject is fundamental to the progress of science. . . . The fact that men differ greatly in the make-up and degree of their commitments and biases enables scientific objectivity to emerge from conflict and passion'.[180]

The dialectical notion of objectivity, gaining field in contemporary science is, to be sure, not explicitly phrased in Merton's works. But it is sufficiently consistent with his general orientation and formulations in many other contexts, that I feel justified in ascribing it to him as an element of his evolving epistemological standpoint.

The sociological epistemology of Merton is still in a rudimentary stage. The direction in which it is evolving opens up the opportunity of utilising his earlier achievements in the sociology of science to throw new light on the old puzzles of human cognition.

4
On Sociological Method

Sociology is a peculiar science. In many other disciplines, scholars are simply studying their subject-matter, leaving metascientific considerations to specialised methodologists or philosophers of science. But in sociology, most leading theorists, from Comte to Merton, with Durkheim, Weber, Znaniecki, Parsons and significant others on the way, are not only *doing* science but *thinking about* the ways of science. Their metasociological thinking takes two distinct forms. Some of it is critical, pointing out numerous weaknesses, fallacies and lacunae of the sociological enterprise. Some of it is constructive, outlining directives, proposals and suggestions for doing sociology better. These preoccupations are so pervasive that they breed their own critics. Such critics climb to a still higher level (one is tempted to say a meta-metasociological level) and generously assign blame; to the critics of sociology for their masochism; to the reformers of sociology for their utopianism and perfectionism. And strangely enough, from that elevated platform, most distant from facts, they sometimes advise everybody else to get down to earth and the facts.

Metasociological reflection, both in its critical and constructive forms, may focus on two distinct aspects of the discipline. One I call the aspect of method. It refers to the procedures utilised by sociologists in their research; ranging from problem-formation, through data-collection, conceptual elaboration, model-construction, interpretation to theory-building. It also refers to the shape of results attained in the process; scientific descriptions, explanations, prognoses and the like. These aspects of sociology are content-free; formal in the sense that they do not presuppose any particular image of society. This type of criticism is not undertaken from the perspective of a specific social theory but rather from the point of view of consensual, generic canons of scientific logic. The directives are not derived from particular beliefs about society, but rather from general assumptions concerning the proper operation of scientific inquiry. But another aspect or dimension of sociology has been gaining prominence in metasociological debates. This, I call the aspect of the approach. It refers to the orientation guiding sociologists in all phases of research and infusing the results attained with hidden, underlying assumptions about the nature of society. Such orientation is always content-bound or substantive in the sense that it is informed by a particular, presupposed *image of social reality*. It makes sense only within the framework of some assumed ontology. Here the criticism is rooted in the affirmation of one theoretical orientation, and the rejection of others. The directives for studying society are entailed and justified by the conception of what society is rather than what science is.

These two distinctions serve as organising principles for my discussion of Merton's views about sociology. He is no exception in the long line of eminent sociologists who have been preoccupied not only with *society* but also with *sociology*. In fact, that concern – both critical and prescriptive – with sociological methods and sociological approaches is so profound that for a recent commentator it evidently foreshadows Merton's substantive contributions. Defining 'metasociological theory' as 'theory whose subject is sociology rather than society', Bierstedt claims that 'indeed almost all of Merton's theoretical writings belong to this category'.[1] I shall have ample occasion to correct this restricting myopia in the chapters to come, but for a moment I focus precisely on Merton's metasociological ideas. This chapter examines his views on sociological method, and the next, on sociological approaches.

Poverty of sociology

There is a dominant theme in the criticism directed by sociologists against sociology. On the surface level, it focuses on the formal dimension of problems, procedures, results and applications. It manifests disenchantment with the actual state of sociology, particularly in comparison to the real or presumed achievements of other scientific disciplines. And it blames the situation mainly on the youthfulness of sociology in the family of sciences. I have chosen to call this type of criticism 'the-poverty-of-sociology-tradition'.[2] It is by no means alien to Merton. Much of his scepticism concerning sociology seems to derive from this source. Consider the main points at which Merton detects symptoms of retardedness and underdevelopment of contemporary sociology. Apart from its intrinsic interest, this exercise will throw light on Merton's positive methodological creed. To see what a man dislikes is often the best way of discovering his likes and tastes.

For Merton, the gravest fault of sociology seems to consist in the dissociation of theory and research, of reason and experience, of rational and empirical procedures. Exclusively one-sided emphasis on each produces equally worthless results. Thus, the exclusive concentration on conceptual schemes, brings the 'risk of producing twentieth-century equivalents of the large philosophical systems of the past, with all their suggestiveness, all their architectonic splendor and all their scientific sterility'.[3] The penchant for hypotheses, guesses, hunches unchecked by experience produces 'the danger of constructing shaky though towering edifices of deduction in the shape of long sorites in which each component is a product exclusively of reason rather than observation organized by reason'.[4]

These risks are not only hypothetical. In fact, as Merton maintained as early as 1948: 'a large part of what is now called "sociological theory" consists of general orientations towards data, suggesting types of variables which need somehow to be taken into account, rather than clear, verifiable statements of relationships between specified variables. We have many concepts but few confirmed theories; many points of view, but few theorems, many "approaches" but few conclusions. Perhaps a shift in emphasis would be all to the good'.[5] Almost two decades later, when – partly due to Merton's own efforts – the situation changes, and scholastic 'grand theory', as C. Wright Mills called it,[6] becomes widely discredited, he still perceives a typical lag of research behind theory. In 1964, Merton observes: 'sociological theory tends to outrun the inevitably slower pace of systematic empirical research in sociology, . . . theoretical ideas – more or less abstract imagery of how things are and operate – are often more swiftly developed than the considerable spate of empirical research required both to test these ideas and to clarify them'.[7]

Pure theorising, without sufficient validation in facts, is the source of unfounded claims to knowledge, as well as dilletantism in the guise of science. 'Amateur sociologising' displaces 'disciplined inquiry' and assumes that 'statements become authoritative simply by being put into the black and white magic of print'.[8] Similarly, 'frivolous ignorance' takes the place of 'specified ignorance', coupled with claims of having knowledge where it is in fact absent.[9] In this sort of 'sociologising', to use again Merton's inimitable prose, 'short impatient answers' substitute for 'long patient study'.[10] Sociology then comes close to unbridled speculation: 'sociologists . . . do not typically carry through operationally intelligible procedures, do not systematically assemble needed types of data, do not employ a common body of concepts and do not utilize the same criteria of validity'.[11]

Perhaps the limiting case of an anti-empirical fallacy is the practice of dogmatic exegesis, where the work of the masters is treated as the ultimate truth, exempted from requirements of empirical test. It is quite common that in sociology 'old quotations newly illustrated have been mistaken for research'.[12] Again, this is not only a hypothetical possibility. Quite a number of us sociologists are 'behaving like sociological barnacles, clinging desperately to the theories we have learned in our youth or that we may have helped develop at any age'.[13]

The opposite extreme, an exclusive narrowly empirical taste for theoretically unconnected data and low-level generalisations is equally disastrous. Merton clearly does not take to 'miscellanies of facts' and a 'plethora' of isolated correlations. He sees empirical generalisations, 'summarizing observed uniformities of relationships between two or more variables',[14] only as way-stations in the growth of knowledge. He notes that 'the sociological literature abounds with such generalizations which have not been assimilated to sociological theory', and as a result 'there tends to be a marked dispersion of empirical inquiries, oriented toward a concrete field of human behavior, but lacking a central theoretical orientation'.[15]

Apart from the original sin – the separation of theory and research – each in itself displays certain notable weaknesses. By way of examples I list a few of those which are identified in Merton's writings. To begin with, sociological theory, even when it is truly a theory, often suffers from the lack of unified technical language, with consequent ambiguities, ambivalences and the permanent risk of extra-sociological connotations being smuggled from common sense or from other scientific disciplines. As Merton makes the point: 'sociology . . . is still searching for its Lavoisier . . . to establish a standard nomenclature that keeps sociologists from ascribing varied meanings to many technical terms'.[16] Sociological theory also lacks a formalised, axiomatic structure, being confined most often to the traditional narrative form, with all its inherent frailties: 'Sociology has few formulae, in the sense of highly abbreviated symbolic expressions of relationships between sociological variables. Consequently, sociological interpretations come to be highly discursive. The logic of procedure, the key concepts, and the relationships between variables not uncommonly become lost in the avalanche of words. They are then obscured from the reader, and at times, from the author as well, and in these instances the critical reader must laboriously reach out for himself the implicit assumptions of the author'.[17]

On the empirical plane, research is often found to involve unspecified, imprecise or uncritically selected variables. Two typical sins are identified by Merton as the 'nothing-but fallacy', and the 'and-also fallacy'. The first signifies the neglect of variables other than those selected for analysis, coupled with the assumption that only the variables selected explain the studied case in all its concreteness. It is an expression of an excessive reductionism; it is of course, what Whitehead described as 'the fallacy of misplaced concreteness'. It is the rationale for the *ceteris paribus* clause, demanding 'other things' to be equal, whereas in fact they rarely are, if ever, equal, except provisionally in experimental situations. The second, opposite fallacy is to provide such a liberal allowance for possible 'other factors', that every hypothesis can be saved *ad hoc* from falsifying evidence, by arguing, *ex post facto*, that some additional variables are operating in the given case. As Merton puts it: 'The "nothing-but fallacy" is apparently most often exemplified by those who do precise work, but implicitly assume that the few factors taken into account tell the whole story; the "and-also fallacy" by those who allude to a long list of additionally relevant variables, without accepting the responsibility of actually incorporating these into the analysis'.[18]

Merton often seems to attribute these and kindred weaknesses of contemporary sociology to the youthfulness of that 'very new science dealing with a very ancient subject'.[19] Sociological analyses are still in a 'primitive stage',[20] sociologists are 'just beginning to acquire the knowledge needed to cope with the many social ills man has the inveterate capacity to contract',[21] the content of sociological journals resembles the content of the *Proceedings* in the early days of the Royal Society.[22] These sins, then, are the sins of youth, notorious perhaps but not eternal, pervasive but not perennial, widespread but not necessary, sad but not hopeless. In the long run they can be overcome, as sociology comes of age.

The standards that sociologists set for their scientific aspirations, the criteria which bring on pessimism if not despair, are ultimately correct but anachronistic. They derive from more mature disciplines, which are in radically different phases of development: 'We social scientists happen to live at a time in which some of the physical sciences have achieved comparatively great precision of theory and experiment, a great aggregate of instruments and tools, and an abundance of technological by-products. Looking about them, many social scientists take this as a standard for self-appraisal'.[23] It is a mistake because stages in the natural development of knowledge cannot be omitted: 'Perhaps sociology is not yet ready for its Einstein because it has not yet found its Kepler – to say nothing of its Newton, Laplace, Gibbs, Maxwell or Planck'.[24]

I wonder if Merton still believes in the youthfulness of sociology after spending a lifetime on helping its coming of age, and witnessing its dynamic development for the last half a century. But in the early texts quoted above, there is a characteristic tendency: the validity of the *general* methodological patterns of the natural sciences for the domain of social inquiry is not questioned. At most, it is qualified by the idea of divergent starting points in basically similar developmental sequences. In an evolutionist vein, Merton conceives it an error to assume that 'all cultural products existing at the same moment of history must have the same degree of intellectual maturity'.[25] Social sciences were born later, therefore they should not be compared with the natural sciences as they are today, with their much longer genealogy. But for the future of the social sciences, the *general standards*, as opposed to *specific methods and procedures*, of present-day natural sciences are appropriate. They can and they should be applied as guidelines for present efforts, and as criteria of achievement, when the social sciences do finally come of age.

Note again the characteristic tendency to search for balanced, intermediate solutions. Merton's version of the belief in the ultimate unity of sciences is far from the extreme of positivism, as it rejects the validity of copying natural-scientific methods and procedures. But it is also far from the opposite extreme of radical humanism, as it accepts the validity of general scientific standards for the domain of man, society, history. A science of society is a science, but very special science. It should strive to be more *scientific*, but in its *particular mode*.[26] Merton's methodological reflection focuses both at the general level of scientific canons, common to all branches of science, and at the specific level of sociological procedures and techniques, unique to the particular discipline.

Canons of science

Merton's positive image of the sociological method may be reconstructed as a two-tier edifice. The materials of the tiers are, figuratively speaking, of various sorts. The upper tier consists of general assumptions about the scientific logic. It is close to the philosophy of science. Merton's attention is not focused here. The assumptions he accepts often remain implicit, and I shall have to reconstruct them either from dispersed hunches or from the overall context of Merton's analysis. The lower tier consists of specific pronouncements about sociological method; the rules of sociological methodology, in Merton's account. Here his attention is clearly focused, and here he makes explicit, important contributions.

At both levels his analysis is sometimes descriptive, reporting what scientists in general or sociologists in particular actually *do*; and sometimes it is normative, prescribing what they *should do*. It is so, in spite of the fact that he often proclaims an antinormative attitude and concern with purely descriptive methodology. For example, in formulating a set of rules for functional analysis he claims: 'the elements of the paradigm have been mainly discovered, not invented',[27] and a little later: 'the paradigm does not represent a set of categories introduced *de novo*, but rather a codification of those concepts and problems which have been forced upon our attention by critical scrutiny of current research and theory'.[28] Analysing the research on friendship formation in methodological terms, he explicitly recognises the *ex-post-facto* character of the endeavour; providing a detailed, formalised account of what has been the actual practice of discursively oriented researchers.[29] But simple description of methodological ways is not enough. There is no escape from choice when actual research practice is as differentiated as it is in sociology. One must align oneself with certain ways of doing science and thus reject others. Defining what is wrong, one cannot avoid committing oneself to what one believes is right. Prescriptive, normative methodology is simply inescapable, as the logical supplement to descriptive methodology and methodological critique.

Merton is not only methodologically aware of what sociologists actually do, he also patently dislikes some of it, going on to state the types of procedures and results he prefers. As he is not only or mainly a methodologist, the best corroboration of his methodological creed can be found in his own substantive work. It is helpful that he happens to be quite consistent in putting his own blueprint to use. To reconstruct his sociological method I start from the general level of scientific logic and present this in the form of eight canons.

Canon one: science is a *disciplined inquiry*. There is a repeatable hint as to the way in which Merton proposes to distinguish science from non-scientific (philosophical) and extra-scientific (common-sense) cognition. His criterion of demarcation is revealed by such terms as 'disciplined inquiry', 'systematic investigation', 'methodical research' which appear times without number in various parts of his work. Two ideas seem involved. First, that science is a self-conscious endeavour; subject to clearly specified goals, with scientists generally aware of the procedures they follow toward those goals. 'Sociologists in company with all others who essay scientific work must be methodologically wise; they must be aware of the design of investigation, the nature of inference, the requirements of a theoretic system'.[30] Of course the foregoing is a prescription, a normative ideal toward which science should aim; the actual level of methodological self-consciousness on the part of the working scientists is tremendously varied. Second, the idea of 'disciplined inquiry' implies that scientific process follows some orderly sequence of steps. Again, it is important to emphasise that such a sequence is only an ideal, a methodological construct, often departing from the actual research practice. The naive positivistic belief in some preordained, *unilinear pattern* of scientific work was rejected by Merton as early as in his first published article on 'Recent French Sociology' (1934), where he referred ironically to 'the enlightened Boojum of Positivism'.[31] He often reiterates the distinction between the completed scientific work as reported in print and the actual road that is leading to that, the latter always full of false starts, unexpected leaps, outright mistakes, loose ends and happy accidents. But still the self-consciously entertained methodological ideal is necessary to introduce some measure of control into the process of scientific creation. 'In the end, the difference between plausible ideas and the systematic empirical investigation of those ideas represents a central difference between the literary observer of "the human condition" and the sociologist'.[32]

Canon two: science is a *detached inquiry*. There is no place for extra-scientific (ethical, moral, political) valuations in the internal analyses of science as distinct from the ground for selecting certain rather than other *problems* for investigation. Science is concerned with actuality, perhaps with potentiality (with what *is* and what *is possible*), but not with ethical rightness (what *should be*). Science is analytical and synthesising categorical investigation, not a normative one. Merton believes that 'the history of the sciences shows that the provisional emancipation from sentiment in order to investigate phenomena methodically has been a most difficult task and has occurred at different times in the various sciences'.[33] And he thoroughly approves of Maxwell's observation: 'It was a great step in science when men became convinced that, in order to understand the nature of things, they must begin by asking, not whether a thing is good or bad, noxious or beneficial, but of what kind it is and how much is there of it'.[34] All this sounds convincing enough, but the canon of detached inquiry is perhaps most difficult to apply in actual research. Merton makes an implicit distinction between extra-scientific valuations and intra-scientific valuations. The latter making up his notion of the scientific ethos are not only *admissible*, but *prescribed* guidelines of scientific work. But one can venture a suspicion that Merton's conception of the scientific ethos is itself informed by some of his extra-scientific, ethical beliefs, particularly by his strong liberal–democratic political creed. Is it accidental that, as was emphasised before, the institution of science as conceived by Merton is such a perfect micro-model of a liberal–democratic polity? Or is it rather the effect of smuggling the extra-scientific valuations into the domain of science already at the level of meta-scientific reflection? I am not blaming Merton for his axiological options reflected in his idea of science. In fact I share them to a large extent. The point I am making is that apart from problem-selection there is another area particularly sensitive to the impact of extra-scientific valuations, and that is the image of science accepted by a scientist. It can be doubted if at this level science can ever be really detached, or value-free.[35]

Canon three: science is a *nomological inquiry*. It aims to discover order, regularities, uniformities, patterns in the realm of experience, and then to embody them in scientific laws, abstract statements of invariance. A set of such statements makes up a scientific theory: 'the term sociological theory refers to logically interconnected sets of propositions from which empirical uniformities can be derived'.[36] Neither pure descriptions nor dispersed empirical generalisations are full-fledged science, even though they provide indispensable raw-materials for the formulation of laws. In his discussion of the problem of social roles, Merton makes this relevant observation: 'sociographic accounts are of course an indispensable phase of the movement toward the sociological analysis of social roles. . . . Nevertheless, this must be recognized as only a transient phase. Sociography is no permanent substitute for sociological analysis'.[37] And more explicitly: 'there are discoverable uniformities in social life and . . . modern sociology, for all its limitations, discovers some of them'.[38]

Canon four: science is *explanatory inquiry*. Precisely because it formulates laws, science can explain the phenomena and processes of experience, by treating them as instances of more general regularities, or to put it otherwise, by deductively subsuming the descriptions of events under general theory. The power of a theory is greater, the greater the range and variety of phenomena it can explain. The deductive–nomological model of explanation seems to underlie much of Merton's thinking. One of the characteristic explicit statements is the following: 'Such classes of mechanisms [he is referring here to attitudinal patterns characteristic of the processes of friendship-formation] are explanatory in the sense that they comprise relationships between variables which have been found, with great regularity, to have observable consequences for designated systems (in principle, the systems may vary greatly: a respiratory system, the organism, the self, partners in a social relationship, a social organization or a complex of related organizations or institutions). When they are applied to phenomena which are regarded as a special case in point, as another specimen of this regularity, they are said to explain'.[39]

Canon five: science is both *empirical and rational* inquiry. These two aspects or phases of scientific research are inherently combined. Science must go *beyond facts*, enlightening them with prior and subsequent reflection, but science must stop *short of pure speculation* by relating thought to experience. Merton maintains: 'Any sharp separation of reason and empirical data in contemporary science must therefore distort much of the operative reality. Work in the scientific laboratory rests upon both, with one or the other raising questions that must be resolved by a congruence between them'.[40]

Canon six: Science is both *inductive and deductive* inquiry. It either starts from observations and ends with laws, or starts from hypotheses and ends with their corroboration in data. Neither course is satisfactory if it stops half-way, before reason meets phenomena, or phenomena meet reason. Merton puts it in a nicely concise formula, defining 'the productive pattern of inquiry in which . . . men pursue facts until they uncover ideas or pursue ideas until they uncover facts'.[41]

Canon seven: scientific results have a double foundation, *empirical and theoretical*. Every result reached by science is tentative and revocable: 'After all, neither under the laws of logic nor under the laws of any other realm, must one become permanently wed to an hypothesis simply because one has tentatively embraced it'.[42] Whatever claim science puts forward, it must be firmly justified, carefully checked, extensively corroborated, repeatedly resisting falsification. One direction of testing is empirical. Scientific claims must be shown to be congruent with facts: some criterion of *adequacy* is involved in this case. The other direction is theoretical: scientific claims must be shown to follow from or to be consistent with other established, well-founded propositions. Here some criterion of *consistency* is invoked. Merton's early specification of both these criteria seems to bring him close to a sophisticated version of Popper's ideas. One could describe it as constructive falsificationism. First of all, Merton is aware of the inconclusive nature of empirical verification by means of supporting evidence, or confirming illustrations. As early as 1945 he notes that 'verification' actually involves the fallacy of affirming the consequent unless there are grounds for asserting the strong implication: 'if, and only if . . .'.[43] And he quotes Peirce: 'if we look over the phenomena to find agreements with the theory, it is a mere question of ingenuity and industry how many we shall find'.[44] It is only when repeated and persistent attempts to falsify the hypothesis fail that it acquires a successively higher level of plausibility, as Popper has persuasively argued. But, second, even if the theoretical hypothesis is empirically falsified, for Merton it is not sufficient ground for its rejection, as long as an alternative, better theory is not in sight. Precisely because any scientific idea is always rooted in both empirical facts and general theories, there is always the problem of decision: 'when are we to trust the governing idea; when the contravening "fact" '.[45] Merton observes: 'a generic critique, as distinct from certain specifics, that provides no alternative, theoretically grounded hypothesis covering the same ground (and preferably more) as the hypothesis being rejected is evidently still some distance from a compelling refutation'.[46] And, to dot the 'i', Merton proceeds to endorse the view of Lakatos: 'Contrary to naive falsificationism, no experiment, experimental report, observation statement or well-corroborated low-level falsifying hypothesis alone can lead to falsification. There is no falsification before the emergence of a better theory'.[47]

Canon eight: scientific results have a *potential* double value or function; *cognitive and practical*. Scientific knowledge serves both the quest for understanding and the quest for effectiveness; it provides enlightenment as well as resource (a conception with a distinct Baconian echo). Both are logically interlinked: 'There is then, this basic duality in science; it can provide greater understanding of how things happen to be as in fact they are, just as it can provide understanding that enables us to change things from what and where they are'.[48] On the one hand, scientific knowledge is *potentially* practical, insofar as it entails directives for eventual application, therefore it should never be put into the 'iron cage' of demands for immediate 'relevance'. 'Experience has shown that the most esoteric researches have found important applications'.[49] On the other hand, this does not mean that one may not evaluate the likelihood of potential application at any given moment. Here Merton introduces an important term-and-concept: 'The concept of the potentials of relevance directs attention to the obvious and important fact that different sectors of the spectrum of basic research have differing probabilities of being germane to certain kinds of practical outcomes'.[50] And of course, to look at it from the reverse side, all practical applications are ultimately reasonable only if backed by sound science; they have varying foundations of eventual scientific justification. When scientists come to assume this intimate relationship of science and practice uncritically, it results in 'a double confidence: that fundamental scientific knowledge is a self-contained good and that, as a surplus value, it will in due course lead to all manner of practical consequences serving the other varied interests of men'.[51]

There seems to be no doubt that Merton conceives of the eventual practical applicability of scientific knowledge in terms of a technological, or 'external' model, akin to Comte's old motto: 'Savoir, pour prevoir, pour prevenir'. The relationship of science and practice, though often close, is mediated by the crucial phase in which basic knowledge is translated into technological directives, and only then are manipulative actions taken by agents with respect to the given object with some change of the object in view. The 'internal' model of practical applications recognising the *direct, unmediated impact of knowledge* on the object described or explained (the phenomenon of reflexivity) is somehow beyond Merton's focus. It is surprising because his discussion of 'self-fulfilling prophecies' refers to the typical case of such direct impact of knowledge (in the form of predictions) on the social reality. There is only one step from the notion of 'self-fulfilling prophecy' to the concept of 'praxis' – the immanent unity of cognitive and practical action.[52] But Merton refuses to take this step, keeping to the traditional, 'technological' image.

The canons of scientific method, as reconstructed above, provide Merton with the general rationale for the more specific directives of sociological investigation. These concern the several phases of the research-process, from the specification of sociological problems, through conceptual and typological elaborations, theory construction and empirical testing, codification of theories to the selection among alternative theoretical accounts. Merton does not construct an all-embracing system of sociological methodology; instead, he selects strategic phases in the sequence of sociological inquiry and concentrates his focus on them. These will be examined seriatim.

Problem-formulation

The first phase of research which occupies much of Merton's attention is problem-finding or the formulation of problems. The complexity of this task is summarised in the adage attributed to Darwin: 'it is often more difficult to find and formulate a problem than to solve it'.[53] Merton emphasises the importance of this phase: 'whatever the worth of one or another tool of inquiry, it is the questions put into the inquiry that determine the significance of results. If the questions are trivial, then the answers will be trivial'.[54]

Sociology faces a set of particular difficulties since the questions posed by sociologists may often coincide with questions raised by members of society. There is an intricate relationship between *sociological* problems and *social* problems; those selected for research by sociologists and those of concern to members of society, the 'social problems' that involve a 'discrepancy, judged intolerable, between social standards and social actuality'.[55] Or put more precisely: 'Social problems have been identified as the substantial, unwanted discrepancies between what exists in a society and what a functionally significant collectivity within that society seriously (rather than in fantasy) wants to exist in it'.[56] When sociological problems happen to be identical with social problems, they are said to be socially relevant. But complicating matters, one must note with Merton, that the discrepancy between social values and reality may be readily visible or not, widely perceived or not; consequently, social problems are of two sorts: 'Apart from manifest social problems – those objective social conditions identified by problem-definers as at odds with the values of the society – are latent social problems'.[57] The latter category is defined in the following way: 'By latent social problems, I mean those unwanted social conditions that are at odds with some of the (often declared) values and interests of groups and strata in the society but are not generally recognized as being so'.[58] A good example appears in Merton's early work: 'Just as men for centuries neglected the problems of soil erosion, in part because they were unaware that erosion constituted a significant problem, so they are still neglecting the social erosion ascribable to present methods of introducing rapid technological changes'.[59]

The sociological problems that coincide with manifest social problems have manifest societal relevance and are therefore widely regarded as important and worthy of pursuit. But the sociological problems which coincide with latent social problems are generally not regarded as important and often judged as futile or sterile. Their relevance may be termed latent; in such cases sociologists adopt the role of defining social problems for otherwise unaware members of society, and in the process may help to convert latent social problems into manifest ones, meanwhile legitimising their own endeavours as a side-effect.[60]

Finally, both sociological problems and social problems may be provided with a *cognitive* rationale or a *practical* rationale. People – sociologists as well as 'laity' – may simply want to understand something better, just for the sake of enlarged knowledge and comprehension, or they may also want to change something for the better, to improve a condition or state of affairs. Sociological problems may represent Veblen's 'idle curiosity', the disinterested wish to know or 'practical curiosity', the interested wish to change.[61] Similarly, social problems may be experienced as inviting a quest for enlightenment (why things are not as they should be), or a quest for reform (what to do in order to change them for the better). Sociological problems which coincide with cognitively defined social problems are said to be cognitively relevant, and those coinciding with practical social problems, practically relevant. Merton refers to Whitehead's metaphor: 'Science is a river with two sources, the practical source and the theoretical source. The practical source is the desire to direct our actions to achieve predetermined ends. . . . The theoretical source is the desire to understand.'[62]

These diverse aspects and locations of sociological problems do not tell the whole story. Merton insightfully observes that the concept of practical relevance is doubly relativistic. First, one must ask: practical relevance *for whom*? In a complex, differentiated society, the value-standards used to define social problems are not homogeneous but diverse and the actual conditions of human life are not uniform but differentiated. 'Standards and their implementation', Merton observes, 'differ to a degree among the several social strata and social segments'.[63] Therefore 'one group's problem will be another group's asset. . . . The same social conditions will be defined by some as a social problem and by others as an agreeable and fitting state of affairs'.[64] This consideration implies that, whatever their particular form, the practical relevance of sociological problems will inevitably be group-relative. Recognition of the second relativistic aspect requires us to ask: relevant, but *when*? As soon as the time perspective is introduced, the relevance of sociological problems takes diverse forms: those problems may be actual, immediate and short-run; or potential, anticipated for the long run. Merton proposes the concept of 'potentials of relevance' to emphasise that certain kinds of research, seemingly without practical relevance – unrelated to actually experienced social problems – may be crucially relevant at some future time. 'The concept relates to a policy of research support for those lines of inquiry of basic research, which as far as can be judged, will have the greatest degree of relevance for the supporting enterprise. (This is distinct from the policy of only supporting applied and developmental research focused on the solution of specific problems.)'[65]

The foregoing analysis indicates that the selection of sociological problems inevitably presupposes valuations, explicit or tacit. Whether one chooses cognitively or practically relevant problems; whether one chooses problems relevant for this or that group; whether one chooses problems of immediate relevance or rather seemingly irrelevant problems with potentials of relevance for the future – all this rests on valuations. 'Moral issues inhere in the very formulation of problems for sociological research', says Merton, following Weber's well-known doctrine. And goes on: 'Scientists, like everyone else, have values. And of course, those values influence their selection of problems for investigation. In that sense, science in general and sociology in particular is not value-free. Far from it; with or without intent, the choice of problems has 'value-relevance' (*Wertbeziehung*)'.[66] As we shall see, this is the only phase in the research-process where Merton allows for extra-scientific valuations, treating them as legitimate and unavoidable. Fully in accord with Max Weber, he normatively rejects the penetration of valuations in the further stages of scientific inquiry. If the scientists allow such valuations to interfere in their research it must be considered as improper and illegitimate.

Along with the choice of sociological problems for investigation, Merton has devoted considerable attention to their structure, both internal, the kinds of components and their composition; and external, the location in the larger cognitive context. As to the earlier, Merton singles out as a crucial component so-called 'originating questions'. Some of these questions are addressed to analytically identified facts, some to relationships between facts – 'uniformities of relations between classes of sociological variables'.[67] Merton treats questions concerning facts as part of the task of description, ascertaining their properties in detail. He takes such questions to be quite significant for sociology, because sociological problems can easily be based on biased or false assumptions of a 'merely' factual sort. 'As a phase in instituting a problem', Merton argues, 'fact-finding seems to have a particular force in sociology. This is so because people are apt to assume that they know the facts about the workings of society without special investigation, because society is, after all, their native habitat'.[68] The questions concerning relationships between variables are conceived of as going beyond the establishment of facts, presumably aiming toward the explanation of social reality.[69] Merton seems to stop short of realising that what the question *refers to* – facts or relationships – and how one *approaches* them – with descriptive or explanatory intent, are two distinct matters. The accounts of facts may be descriptive, diagnostic, simply stating their properties or they may be explanatory, deriving their properties from more general knowledge, asking not only how something is, but why it is so. And, *mutatis mutandis*, the same is true for the statements of relationships. These may be approached with the descriptive intent of simply confirming their existence or the explanatory intent of finding out why they do hold.[70] Along with originating questions of these types, the internal structure of the problem includes its explicit or implicit rationale – the definition of cognitive or practical relevance, and finally the set of 'specifying questions', indicating the observations that may provide a solution to the problem.

As for the external structure of the problem, Merton points out that it cannot be isolated, *ad hoc*, hanging in the air, but must relate in some way to prior sociological knowledge. On the one hand, it derives not so much from an undisciplined, undirected curiosity but rather from scientists' 'specified ignorance': 'the express recognition of what is not yet known but needs to be known in order to lay the foundation for still more knowledge'.[71] On the other hand, its eventual solution must have more than self-contained, immanent interest; it must make some difference with respect to a larger body of actual knowledge. As Merton puts it: 'In science, the questions that matter are of a particular kind. They are questions so formulated that the answers to them will confirm, amplify, variously revise, or refute some part of what is currently taken as knowledge in the field'.[72]

To meet these requirements, it is helpful to focus on a particular, strategic range of problems, and to study them in selected 'strategic research sites'. Merton holds that strategic problems are formulated at a middle level of generality: 'It would be important to identify the strategic, intermediate range of problems, namely those which have generalized theoretical and practical significance, but which are not too large in scope to be subjected to disciplined research'.[73] He expands on that idea in another context: 'In short, questions initially restricted to a particular institutional sphere have a double objective. On the one hand, they direct attention to what may be distinctive to the particular class of institutions or organizations under study. These distinctive characteristics are not at once swallowed up in generalities that deliberately neglect them. On the other hand, these questions of restricted scope can often be extended to wider classes of situations'.[74] From the middle level, the opportunities for consequential research open up in two complementary directions, toward the particular and concrete and toward the general and abstract.

Apart from the question of level, it is also helpful to select the substantive research site in which the problem is to be investigated: 'The history of sociology has its own complement of cases in which long-dormant problems were brought to life and developed by investigating them in situations that strategically exhibit the nature of the problem'.[75]

The pursuit of scientifically significant problems is a never-ending quest. This is not merely because the number of potential problems is unlimited but also because attempts to solve any one problem often produce *new problems*, as a sort of paradoxical side-effect. Problems not only give birth to solutions but to new problems as well. Merton singles out two variants of that process. First, as we have seen is the working of 'specified ignorance'; the *more* one knows, the more one becomes aware how *little* òne knows. The solution to a particular problem pushes back the frontiers of rationalised curiosity or practical needs, and opens up new problematic areas of experience. Second is a particular type of 'serendipity pattern'; as during the pursuit of certain problems one hits upon some observations or ideas suggesting quite new problems. In introducing the general notion of 'serendipity' into sociology, Merton began with its long established definition: 'the discovery through chance by a prepared mind of new findings that were not looked for'.[76] As he developed the idea in more precise and formal terms, he went on to say: 'The serendipity pattern, then, involves the unanticipated, anomalous and strategic datum which exerts pressure upon the investigator for a new direction of inquiry which extends theory'.[77] In more recent years, the significant role of anomalies in scientific inquiry has of course been much developed in the philosophy of science.

Concept-formation

So much for the first phase of the research process, the formulation of problems. The next phase chosen by Merton for methodological discussion is that of concept-formation. Achieving clarity, precision and unambiguous meaning of sociological concepts seems to be an almost obsessive preoccupation. He begins by noting that 'The choice of concepts guiding the collection and analysis of data is, of course, crucial to empirical inquiry'.[78] At the same time he clearly realises a predicament of sociology resulting from its intimate link with everyday experience and common-sense accounts of that experience. That linkage is expressed both in the long-noticed infusion of words with established common-sense connotations into the sociological vocabulary and in the reciprocal flow of sociological words into the vocabulary of everyday life and thought, producing what Merton calls 'the sociological vernacular'.[79] Meanings from everyday language have drifted into sociology, and conversely 'a great variety of sociological terms have drifted into our everyday language'.[80] Within sociology, this makes for ambiguous, imprecise and dubious jargon; in the wider society it makes for superficial vogue-words. This does little good. 'Clarity of analysis and adequacy of communication are both victims of this frivolous use of words. At times the analysis suffers from the unwitting shift in the conceptual content of a given term, and communication with others breaks down when the essentially same content is obscured by a battery of diverse terms'.[81]

The way out of this predicament is to develop a technical language, as distinct from jargon. Merton calls upon the authority of Peirce: 'No study can become scientific . . . until it provides itself with a suitable technical nomenclature, whose every term has a single definite meaning universally accepted'.[82] And he expands on that idea: 'it is time to distinguish between jargon and that essential of all disciplined thought, technical language. Technical language is a more precise and condensed form of thought and communication than colloquial language. It is designed to fix definite meanings in which each word has ideally only one denotation and is deliberately deprived of connotations. Jargon, in contrast, is a muddled and wordy imitation of technical language'.[83]

The poles defining the evolution of concepts in sociology are Fleck-like 'proto-concepts' on the one hand, and full-fledged, precise concepts on the other. 'A proto-concept', Merton defines, 'is an early, rudimentary, particularized, and largely unexplicated idea (which is put to occasional use in empirical research and, indeed, often derives from it); a concept is a general idea which, once having been defined, tagged, substantially generalized and explicated can effectively guide inquiry into seemingly diverse phenomena'.[84]

He maps two roads from proto-concepts toward concepts with a corresponding more precise meaning. In other words – toward more unambiguous language for sociology. One is the couching of new, rigorously defined terms to grasp previously unrecognised, tacit concepts. As Merton observes: 'Men are not permanently imprisoned in the framework of the (often invented) concepts they use; they can not only break out of this framework but can create a new one, better suited to the needs of the occasion'.[85] Merton is, as we have seen, a profuse inventor of neologisms.

But he also repeatedly reminds us, in rejecting the old conception that each sociologist of substance should develop his own 'system of sociology', that one scholar obviously cannot build the language of science anew. Even more important, therefore, is the other road toward conceptual and terminological clarity: disciplined analysis and careful *elucidation and elaboration* of existing concepts. Merton is a true master in such an endeavour. His own practice and formulations allow us to distinguish several phases of conceptual analysis and elaboration. The first imperative for the scholar is to raise the concepts being used to a level of self-awareness, and thus to lay them open to critical scrutiny: 'As is well known, the first step in the search for sociological order amid apparent disorder is to re-examine, in theoretical terms, the concepts in terms of which data are reported'.[86] This is so important precisely because, as Merton repeatedly emphasises *'facts' do not speak for themselves*; they are always interpreted, couched in terms of some conceptual schemes. It is just an aspect of what I referred to earlier as his sociological 'neo-Kantianism'. Then comes the conceptual analysis proper; dissection of the dimensions, aspects, phases of the concept; defining each of them as precisely as possible and recombining them again, specifying the possible combinations, permutations, ramifications. The end-products of this are typically in the form of extensive classifications, typologies, taxonomies – identifying possible variants of the phenomenon or process under study. Referring to one of his most famous efforts of this sort, the analysis of the concept of social deviation and the resulting typology of deviant adaptations, Merton observes: 'After all, the principal purpose of the classification is not merely to identify forms of socially deviant behavior, for none of these is apt to have gone unnoticed through the millennia of recorded history. As with other classifications, the purpose is to derive these forms by combining a limited number of defined elements, and so to discover the relations of each form to all the rest'.[87]

The final stage of conceptual elaboration endows the concepts with operational meaning, by specifying observations ('indices'[88]) through which their referents can be recognised. The rephrasing of each concept in operational terms is important, of course, because it makes sociological propositions testable, open to confirmation or disconfirmation: 'Although this statement', Merton observes regarding operationalised formulations, 'apparently says no more than the statement which it replaces, it says it better – better in the sense that it facilitates analytic operations by the sociologist who would study this process empirically, and better in the sense that it raises productive questions'.[89] The ultimate goal is to specify the concepts as precisely as possible – when feasible in quantifiable manner by forming them into measurable 'variables'.[90] Concepts so specifiable are directly amenable to the most rigorous form of empirical verification, the most demanding empirical check for a theory, quantitative analysis. 'Independently collected, systematic and quantitative data', Merton states, 'supply the most demanding test called for by such an empirically-connected theory'.[91] In a more extensive characterisation he writes: 'The quantitative orientation is designed, so far as possible, to put interpretative ideas on trial by facing them with suitable compilations of statistical data, rather than relying wholly on selected bits and scraps of evidence that too often catch the scholar's eye simply because they are consistent with his ideas'.[92] The reservation 'so far as possible' must not go unnoticed. Merton is too critical a scholar to fall prey to the fetishisation of quantitative methods. He is fully aware that the worst sin against precision is pretended and therefore pretentious precision: 'A premature insistence on precision at all costs may sterilize imaginative hypotheses'.[93] He joins with David Sills and Stephen Stigler in the intellectual game of tracing the actual wording of Kelvin's dictum: 'when you cannot measure it, when you cannot express it in numbers, your knowledge is of a meagre and unsatisfactory kind', as well as a rebuttal by Jacob Viner: 'when you cannot measure it, when you cannot express it in numbers, your knowledge is of a meagre and unsatisfactory kind'.[94] The message of this epistolary exchange, almost in the Shandean fashion (reminding one of Merton's OTSOG) is simple: *put not your trust wholly in numbers*. As the authors put it: 'in the final analysis, our debt to non-numeric scholarship exceeds our debt to quantification, to the point where it might have made even the redoubtable Kelvin uncomfortable'.[95] In his own research practice, Merton often rests content with qualitative analysis, when quantification seems premature or downright impossible. But in his conception, qualitative analysis is far removed from loose, impressionistic narration; it involves a disciplined, systematic, self-conscious scrutiny of the meanings involved in sociological propositions. This is crucial, because 'Precision is an integral element of the criterion of testability'.[96] The road by which the relative precision is to be reached depends on the particular properties of the area under study. Sometimes, quantitative precision is possible, sometimes qualitative precision must suffice.

Research 'versus' theory

A third phase of sociological inquiry on which Merton has some important things to say is empirical research. The central idea is the *intimate linkage* of empirical research and theory. This works in two directions: empirical research is *informed by* theory, and empirical research significantly *influences* theory. As Merton puts it: 'there is two-way traffic between social theory and empirical research. Systematic empirical materials help advance social theory by imposing the task and by affording the opportunity for interpretation along lines often unpremeditated, and social theory, in turn, defines the scope and enlarges the predictive value of empirical findings by indicating the conditions under which they hold'.[97] In this conception, all empirical research presupposes theoretical context, whether the researchers are aware of that or not.

In the course of tracing the influence of sociological theory on empirical research, in his early article of the mid-1940s, Merton makes a variety of basic points, which since then have entered the textbooks of sociological methodology. First, he observes that the delimitation of facts for empirical study is carried out by means of concepts, which in turn derive from a theory: 'an explicit conceptual outfit, a part of theory, is necessary even for fruitful discoveries of fact'.[98] Second, that the selection of variables is always influenced by the underlying theoretical orientation: 'Such orientations involve broad postulates that indicate types of variables which are somehow to be taken into account'.[99] Third, that the use of certain *techniques or research procedures makes sense only in view of some theoretical assumptions*. To these hardly controversial points, Merton adds further observations on the less evident functions of a theory. Thus, fourth, he points out that theory provides a framework within which separate and disparate empirical findings are interrelated and consolidated. Fifth, such consolidation is seen as prerequisite to the cumulation of research, by establishing connections and implications of various results, achieved at various moments of time. Sixth, by providing a generalised framework within which the empirical findings are fitted, theory allows one to proceed beyond the concrete findings toward wider areas of similar phenomena, thus augmenting the heuristic power of the initial results. Seventh, theory provides stronger foundation for the extrapolation of observed empirical trends, thus augmenting the predictive power of attained results. Eighth and finally, by providing logical links between separate findings, theory facilitates their empirical validation, pooling the evidence that supports or refutes each of them. As Merton puts it: 'The integrated theory sustains a larger measure of confirmation that is the case with distinct and unrelated hypotheses, thus accumulating a greater weight of evidence'.[100] And elsewhere he adds: 'Confirmed by whatever relevant facts are available, our interpretation enjoys a measure of plausibility; consistent with a wider body of theory that in turn is supported by systematic empirical inquiry, it may lay claim to a further degree of validity'.[101]

Turning to the reverse side of the relationship and studying the impact of empirical research on sociological theory, in another article of the 1940s, Merton dismisses as obvious the first function of research, namely the testing (verifying or refuting) of hypotheses, and proposes to focus on less evident functions. 'It is my central thesis', he writes, 'that empirical research goes far beyond the passive role of verifying and testing theory: it does more than confirm or refute hypotheses. Research plays an active role'.[102] Thus, second, research exerts pressure for initiating theory; it fulfils an important heuristic function. Merton refers to that as another aspect of the 'serendipity pattern', the discovery of an 'unanticipated, anomalous and strategic datum'.[103] In this context, it is seen as 'the occasion for developing a new theory or for extending an existing theory'.[104] Third, research exerts pressure for elaborating the conceptual scheme inherent in the theory. If newly discovered facts resist attempts to squeeze them into the traditional conceptual scheme, this presses for this scheme to be reformulated or extended, and the encompassing theory recast. Fourth, research re-focuses theoretic interest toward new phenomena, or new aspects of known phenomena: 'This occurs chiefly through the invention of research procedures which tend to shift the foci of theoretic interest to the growing points of research'.[105] A prime example is the purposeful collection of sociologically relevant statistics. Fifth, research contributes to the clarification of concepts, demanding their clear definition, operationalisation or even quantification. Merton describes this function as follows: 'What often appears as a tendency in research for quantification . . . can thus be seen as a special case of attempting to clarify concepts sufficiently to permit the conduct of empirical investigation. The development of valid and observable indices becomes central to the use of concepts in the prosecution of research'.[106]

The message carried by this analysis of decades ago is clear: sociological theory cannot be divorced from sociological research and vice versa. Attempts to conduct empirical inquiry purged of theoretical bases and components are misguided and doomed to failure. Even though this point is now taken for granted by most sociologists, it is always worth repeating. And Merton's early formulation is particularly clear and persuasive.

Merton's strong belief in the unity of research and theory finds further expression as he moves to consider the next phase of the research process, namely theory-construction. Here it forms the backbone and rationale of a notion perhaps more widely discussed than any other in his methodological repertoire: theories of the middle range. Before coming to that, however, we require a sketch of what Merton means by a theory.

Surprisingly enough, the concept of theory proves to be among the most elusive and ambiguous in sociological methodology, enough so to trouble the sophisticated theorists. Merton does not present his idea of theory in clear and explicit form; rather that idea must be reconstructed from his writings. As usual, an instructive way of beginning is by considering his *counterimage of a theory*; what, in his view, a theory *is not*. That procedure provides clues to what he takes a theory to *be*.

First, Merton warns against the frequent confusion of the history of theory with systematic theory. Systematic theory is of course rooted in earlier theories but goes beyond them, representing the product of *selective and critical cumulation* of knowledge. As he puts it: 'the attractive but fatal confusion of current sociological theory with the history of sociological ideas ignores their decisively different functions'.[107] Thus a theory is a body of thought which, irrespective of its genealogy, meets the contemporary criteria of scientific value and validity. Second, Merton goes to some pains to delimit theory from methodology: or to put it otherwise, to distinguish substantive theory from meta-theory: 'At the outset we should distinguish clearly between sociological theory, which has for its subject matter certain aspects and results of the interaction of men and is therefore substantive, and methodology, or the logic of scientific procedure'.[108] Thus, a theory is a set of statements about society, not about sociology. Third, theory must be distinguished from a conceptual scheme: 'an array of concepts – status, role, Gemeinschaft, social interaction, social distance, anomie – does not constitute theory, though it may enter into a theoretic system'.[109] Statements constitutive of a theory are, then, propositional, not definitional; they affirm something about reality and not about the meanings of concepts. They can therefore be confronted with reality; confirmed or falsified. Fourth, it seems, although this is only an interpretative conjecture, that Merton does not regard the descriptive propositions identifying the values of single variables as theoretical, even when they are general, ascribing that variable to a wide class of cases. Rather, he reserves the characterisation 'theoretical' to *relational propositions*, asserting a relationship between variables. He refers to them variously as 'statements of invariance',[110] 'empirical relationships',[111] 'uniformities of relationships',[112] 'statements of social uniformities'.[113] Fifth, it also seems – again with the reservation of conjectural interpretation – that Merton does not regard as theoretical concrete statements of correlation or dependence between variables – 'those detailed orderly descriptions of particulars that are not generalized at all'[114] – reserving the term 'theoretical' for *general propositions*, covering open classes of cases, these being of varying and, as we shall see, not necessarily wide scope. Sixth, he expressly rejects the identification of a theory with a miscellany of isolated, dispersed propositions. Theory is a *system* of propositions. It is only 'when propositions are logically interrelated [that] a theory has been instituted'.[115] The task of the theorist is 'to develop specific, interrelated hypotheses'.[116]

By implication, Merton's positive definition of a theory would read: a theory is a system of logically interrelated, general propositions, positing relationships between variables in some domain of reality. His explicit statements come close to this account: 'the term sociological theory refers to logically interconnected sets of propositions from which empirical uniformities can be derived'.[117] Or in another context: 'a theory in the exacting sense [means] a set of logically connected assumptions giving rise to a continuous flow of hypotheses that can be confirmed or falsified by empirical research'.[118]

Those definitions also contain a hint concerning the internal structure of a theory. Coupled with other allusions found variously in Merton's work, they allow us to surmise that he conceives of a theory as a three-layered totality. The upper level consists of 'seminal ideas', 'an image that gives rise to inferences',[119] 'assumptions giving rise to a continuing flow of hypotheses'.[120] This can perhaps be referred to as the most general *conceptual model* of the given domain of reality. The intermediate level is made up of 'propositions', 'specific hypotheses', 'laws'.[121] The lowest level comprises the 'empirical uniformities',[122] empirically confirmable or falsifiable inferences.[123] It will be noted that in this account, the empirical implications of the theory, actually derived or potentially derivable, are treated as components of a theory. Logical relationships of a vertical sort obtain among the three layers, as contrasted with horizontal interrelations within each layer. Propositions or hypotheses 'flow' from assumptions or basic images; empirical uniformities or inferences are 'derived' from the propositions.

For Merton, theory so conceived seems to constitute the ultimate goal of the sociological enterprise: 'Each to his last, and the last of the sociologist is that of lucidly presenting claims to logically interconnected and empirically confirmed propositions about the structure of society and its changes, the behavior of man within that structure and the consequences of that behavior'.[124] But no theory is final; it is always just a successive link in a chain of theoretical development. It therefore not only has autonomous value, but also instrumental value for producing further and better theory. *It has a duty – so to say – to help achieve its own creative overcoming.* This is realised by instigating and channelling empirical research in directions conducive to its modification, extension or – at times – outright rejection of a theory. Such is the rationale of Merton's concern with the functions of theory for empirical research, recounted in the preceding paragraph.

In this case as well, I am inclined to believe that Bierstedt does not understand Merton's intentions. He maintains that 'Here Merton appears to be denigrating any theory that is not useful in research'. And goes on to comment: 'Surely it is an odd notion that theory somehow has to justify itself by being useful for research. The notion that sociological theory is 'an analytic tool', an instrument that helps to carry on research, is surely an erroneous or at least a wayward one. . . . Knowledge in the form of theory is the end of inquiry, in both senses of the word end, and it is a good in itself'.[125] What Merton says about 'the bearing of sociological theory on empirical research' of course has nothing to do with building an utilitarian case for sociological knowledge, denying that it is an end in itself. Quite the contrary, it is entirely within the borders of his cognitivist case for knowledge. Theory serves knowledge as it provides understanding, but it also stimulates the research that produces empirical knowledge, which in turn makes for better theory, and, therefore, deeper understanding. Merton does not at all reject the idea that theory is a *goal* of the research process (presumably the first sense of Bierstedt's 'end'), but he surely rejects the idea that any theory is *final* (a possible second sense of Bierstedt's 'end'). Theoretical inquiry, like any other scientific quest, is unending. And it moves forward precisely because of that 'two-way traffic' between theoretical considerations and empirical research. To ascribe an instrumental, research role to theory is not 'denigrating theory', but denigrating dogmatism.

Theory of the middle range

If sociological theory as such is treated as the ultimate (though never final) strategic goal of the sociological enterprise this does not mean that specific forms of theory cannot be singled out as tactical goals, suitable for certain phase in the development of a discipline. Merton's notion of theory of the middle range can best be understood in such a connection. It expresses his conviction that some otherwise commendable methodological and theoretical aspirations may be premature for sociology, because of its underdevelopment or simply, youthfulness. For the time being, to be productive, aspirations must be bridled and realistically based. Merton develops the notion of middle-range theory as the theoretical goal suitable for the contemporary epoch of sociology.

This notion serves him also as a tool of criticism of certain tendencies in sociological inquiry which he finds unacceptable. One is narrow empiricism or 'practical empiricism';[126] collection of data uninformed by (explicit) theory and not directed toward the further reformulation of theory. In a word, his first line of attack is against *sociology purged of theory*. But, for him, the opposite extreme is equally unacceptable. That extreme is the *abstract theorising* of those engaged in trying to construct a total theoretical system covering all aspects of social life. Thus his second and most persuasive line of criticism is directed against sociology which claims to attain a unified, all-comprehensive theory. Almost forty years ago at a meeting of the American Sociological Society Merton raised this kind of argument directly and publicly against Talcott Parsons. In the course of the famous (although civil and as Merton recollects even amiable) confrontation, he questioned the value of 'general theories of social systems which are too remote from particular classes of social behavior, organization and change to account for what is observed'.[127] Such theories turn out to be 'master conceptual schemes' which are 'architectonically splendid' but 'scientifically sterile'.[128] It cannot be otherwise since the attempt is misguided at the present stage of the discipline's development. In a word, it is anachronistic: 'Some sociologists still write as though they expect, here and now, formulation of the general sociological theory broad enough to encompass the vast ranges of precisely observed details of social behavior, organization and change and fruitful enough to direct the attention of the research workers to a flow of problems for empirical research. This I take to be a premature and apocalyptic belief. We are not ready. Not enough preparatory work has been done'.[129]

Against this critical background Merton framed his positive programme for sociology in the late 1940s: 'Sociology will advance in the degree that the major concern is with developing theories adequate to limited ranges of phenomena and it will be hampered if attention is centered on theory in the large. . . . I believe that our major task today is to develop special theories applicable to limited ranges of data . . . rather than to seek here and now the "single" conceptual structure adequate to derive all these and other theories'.[130] Almost like an echo, a similar policy is still being advocated by Goode some thirty years later: 'I believe that the best sociology for the next fifty years will be made up of numerous nodules of theory fragments, each constituted by precise descriptions and predictions that apply to only limited areas of social behavior; . . . little islands of valid knowledge'.[131]

In a later, significantly reworded formulation Merton calls for theories that will 'deal with limited aspects of social phenomena' or which will be 'applicable to limited conceptual ranges'.[132] Such a *tactical goal*, taken to be appropriate for present-day sociology, is defined as follows: 'Throughout we focus on what I have called theories of the middle range: theories that lie between the minor but necessary working hypotheses that evolve in abundance during day-to-day research and the all-inclusive systematic efforts to develop a unified theory that will explain all the observed uniformities of social behavior, social organization and social change'.[133] As typical examples of middle-range theory, Merton refers to the theory of role conflicts, of reference groups, of social mobility, of the formation of norms, of class dynamics, of conflicting group pressures, of the flow of power and interpersonal influence in communities, of deviant behaviour and social control, of social perception and various others.[134]

It is not held that the search for middle-range theories should pre-empt the entire attention of sociologists; there is ample room for the *consolidation* of those theories by means of more general sets of concepts and propositions. But this should be treated as a gradual process 'evolving, not suddenly revealing, a progressively more general conceptual scheme that is adequate to consolidate groups of special theories'.[135] Seen in this way, middle-range theory becomes – in Weick's apt description – 'a discrete confirmed theory that applies to limited ranges of data, consolidates segregated hypotheses and is itself available for consolidation with other middle-range theories'.[136]

The notion of middle-range theory, appealing and persuasive as it is, nevertheless has a certain ambiguity. This is revealed by Merton's terminological vacillations in the definiens where we find such expressions as 'limited ranges of phenomena', 'limited ranges of data',[137] 'limited aspects of phenomena', and 'limited conceptual ranges'.[138] The difficulty is that the term 'range' may mean either the range of *objects*, or the range of *properties* (predicates); it may refer either to *the scope* of the theory, or to *the level of generality* of the theory.[139] Like other theory, sociological theory ascribes certain properties (or more precisely: some relations between properties) to certain objects (or more formally: to some domain). The domain may be narrow or wide, delimited typologically (for example: families, groups, nations), or historically (for example: Polish society of the 1980s, 19th-century Europe, 17th-century England). A theory of families is narrower in scope than a theory of groups, and a theory of European society in the 19th century is wider than a theory of Polish society in that period. In turn, the relations predicated for a particular domain may be concrete or general; referring to properties of a less abstract or more abstract sort. A theory asserting that economically deprived people tend to be politically radical is less general than a theory maintaining that frustrated people tend to be aggressive, precisely because economic deprivation is treated as a less abstract property than frustration and political radicalism as less abstract than aggressive behaviour. The dimension of scope and the dimension of generality are separate, and not necessarily correlated. Thus, there may be a general theory of a (relatively) narrow scope: for example, Smelser's theory of collective behaviour, treating of crowds, mobs, social movements – which are, after all, only a limited class of human collectivities – in terms of an abstract 'value-added scheme'.[140] And conversely, there may be a concrete theory of very wide scope: for example, Allport's theory of prejudice – which is, after all, a particular type of human emotion – tracing its appearance in all sorts of collectivities and various situational contexts.[141]

If middle-range theory refers to theory of medium scope, the consolidation of this kind of theories would simply mean *extending the scope of objects*, by bringing together theories referring to similar objects (for instance, combining theories about workers with theories about clerks, drivers, teachers, shop assistants, carpenters etc., into a theory about employees). But if middle-range theory refers to the theory of medium generality, the consolidation of such theories would involve *raising the generality of predicates*, by introducing new, more embracing concepts (for instance, combining theories of rape, alcoholism, drug-addiction, murder, suicide, etc. into a theory of deviation).

In spite of occasional misleading terminological slips, Merton certainly has the second meaning in mind. Middle-range theory is a theory of *medium level of generality*, operating with predicates neither of the most concrete sort, bound to specific observations, nor of the most abstract sort, wholly divorced from observation. The consolidation, of both the ideas leading to a middle-range theory and of middle-range theories, is tantamount to the gradual elaboration of concepts to cover ever more aspects, properties, characteristics, and dimensions of a domain. This is the process that led Merton from the concept of criminality to that of social deviation, from the concept of socialisation to that of social control, from the everyday idea of 'keeping up with the Joneses' to the differentiated concept of reference-group behaviour, from the familiar observation of family quarrels to the differentiated concept of role-conflict in general; and so on. The consolidation does not stop but in principle continues toward ever more general theories of society.

Merton's middle-range strategy of theory construction has been widely discussed, lavishly praised, often misunderstood, sometimes abused, and even 'obliterated by incorporation'. Its applications have spread far beyond the field of sociology, to such disciplines as archeology, biology and others.[142] The assets of middle-range theory most often emphasised derive precisely from its being located in the 'middle'. It bridges some important gaps found in sociology from its beginnings. To begin with, it links theoretical inquiry with empirical research, being close enough to observables for empirical testing, and being far enough removed from facts for theoretical generalisation. Then, it links cognitive interest and practical interest. According to Eisenstadt, it is most conducive to preserving the unity of scholarly and critical orientation required of sociology. The emancipatory calling of sociology can easily degenerate into apologetic, sectarian tendencies or into seemingly neutral, pragmatic fact-finding. Middle-range theorising curbs both risks: 'The tendency to abdicate sociology "in favor" of ideological and political positions usually entailed a concentration on philosophical, epistemological–methodological discourses, while the abdication in a more technocratic direction has usually entailed the heavy, almost exclusive concentration on the purely methodological or survey type of research. Common to both types was the withdrawal from the type of research most closely related to the emancipatory dimension of sociology: middle-range theories concerned with the analysis of the workings of societies and of contemporary social reality in its diverse aspects'.[143] Next, such theorising is held to bridge the gap between various substantive foci which are traditionally taken as unrelated. A prime example is the distinction between macrosociology and microsociology: 'This type of theory cuts across the distinction between microsociological problems as evidenced in small group research, and macrosociological problems, as evidenced in comparative studies of social mobility and formal organization, and the interdependence of social institutions'.[144] Finally, middle-range theorising provides a meeting ground for various theoretical and methodological orientations in sociology, usually treated as competing or mutually exclusive. It can achieve that mediatory status, because it is relatively neutral with respect to the assumptions of each. As Merton puts it, theories of the middle range 'are frequently consistent with a variety of so-called systems of sociological theory. So far as one can tell, the theory of role-sets is not inconsistent with such broad theoretical orientations as Marxist theory, functional analysis, social behaviorism, Sorokin's integral sociology, or Parsons' theory of action'.[145]

So much for the assets. Now some words about supposed liabilities. Like other general ideas middle-range theory is subject to misunderstandings and misdirected challenges. One misunderstanding which Merton singles out himself for strong rebuttal is the charge that a middle-range strategy invites the lowering of theoretical aspirations.[146] The charge may be properly addressed only to those who abuse the concept, giving it an empiricist descriptive meaning. An example is the justification of limited scope of research – strictly local, provincial, unrepresentative – by invoking middle-range doctrine. Another is the justification of narrow-empirical, descriptive research (even if wide in scope) as presumably following Merton's prescriptions.

Another misunderstanding involves taking Merton's *methodological doctrine* as purporting to give an account of the *actual development of sociology*. When Opp invokes historical evidence to demonstrate that 'there is no simple progress from special, empirically confirmed theories to a unified "scientific system" ',[147] he confuses the *logical* level of analysis with the empirical (*historical*) level. Merton is proposing a logical sequence; he does not claim that it coincides with the historical development of sociology. It is, in fact, precisely to the extent that such developments *do not* coincide with the proposed strategy of consolidating middle-range theories that its articulation, as a critical and postulative tool, becomes required.

Finally, there is the misunderstanding, bordering on outright *naïveté*, which assumes that Merton is proposing an easy, instantly applicable, almost algorithmic recipe for developing significant sociological theory. When Opp states in a critical mood that 'there are no logical rules which permit the inference of a general sociological theory from theories of the middle range', and that 'there are no logical rules for proceeding to general theory',[148] he is, of course, only alluding to what is fundamental about the creative process, in or outside science. One does not expect simple, effective guidelines or algorithms for creative ideas. Unfortunately he then blames Merton for leading sociologists into a blind alley: 'He [the sociologist applying Merton's strategy] first tries to realize a partial goal (he constructs a certain number of theories of the middle range); if he has reached this goal, he does not know how to proceed further'.[149] Opp apparently would have one specify an actual number of middle-range theories required to consolidate into a unified theory: 'Now the sociologist would like to know how many theories of the middle range must be constructed until he can turn his attention to the construction of a general theory. On this point Merton is silent'.[150] It is certainly wishful thinking to expect that sort of methodological advice from a methodologist.

Paradigms

Having examined the interaction between empirical research and theory construction in sociological inquiry, Merton goes on to focus on their codification, on bringing them together in systematic fashion. In his view 'disciplined inquiry' requires a 'triple alliance' of theoretical statements, empirical data and methodology. With Paul Lazarsfeld he works out a detailed example – the social patterning of friendships – that exhibits 'the interlocking use of substantive conceptions (both theoretical and empirical) and of methodological or formal conceptions in the analysis of a particular type of sociological problem'.[151] To this general end, he has long made use of the analytical tool described as a 'paradigm'. In view of the widespread currency of the term in the sense given to it by Kuhn and his theory of scientific revolutions, it must be emphasised that Merton's usage is quite different.[152] For Merton, the paradigm is a *heuristic scheme* destined to introduce a measure of order and lucidity into qualitative and discursive sociological analysis by codifying the result of prior inquiry and specifying the directions for further research. He continues emphasising the heuristic nature of the paradigm: 'I believe', he writes, 'that such paradigms have great propaedeutic value'.[153] And goes on to say: 'Paradigms for sociological analysis are intended to help the sociologist to work at his trade'.[154]

Nevertheless, some commentators construe the Mertonian type of paradigm as a *product* rather than an *instrument* of research. For example, Martindale: 'Some statements suggest that the paradigm is a system of theory in which every concept is logically derivable, the paradigm being in fact a completed system of theory reduced to its most economic axiomatic structure, a calculus of concepts'.[155] But as has been indicated such paradigms are codifications of concepts, data, theories and methods; they do not refer to society but to sociology, specifying certain cognitive past developments and pointing to future developments. Put otherwise, paradigms are formulated on the metascientific rather than the substantive level. The concept of paradigm cannot therefore be taken as identical or similar to Weber's ideal type as Martindale suggests: 'It may be assumed that Merton's paradigms are, perhaps intentionally, a more loose version of what Weber intended by the ideal type'.[156] Ideal types, although they are also tools of inquiry, have a direct substantive reference, they *refer to society* and its various aspects, whereas Merton's paradigms are designed to guide sociological analysis, they are *metasociological* constructs.

This becomes evident from inspection of various of Merton's paradigms: for functional analysis (1938–49), for deviant social behaviour (1938), for the study of intermarriage (1940), for the sociology of knowledge (1945), for the study of prejudice and discrimination (1948), for structural analysis (1975). It is all more evident from his explicit formulation of the theoretical functions served by paradigms. Introducing one of the earliest – the 1945 paradigm for the sociology of knowledge – he describes its functions in these terms: 'it does provide a basis for taking an inventory of extant findings in the field; for indicating contradictory, contrary, and consistent results; setting forth the conceptual apparatus now in use; determining the nature of problems which have occupied workers in the field; assessing the character of the evidence which they have brought to bear upon these problems; ferreting out the characteristic lacunae and weaknesses in current types of interpretation'.[157] And as something of afterthought to the later, 1948 article on 'Discrimination and the American Creed', he explicates five functions of paradigms in more systematic way. First is the notational function: paradigms 'provide a compact parsimonious arrangement of the central concepts and their interrelations as these are utilized for description and analysis'.[158] Second is the control function: 'the explicit statement of analytic paradigms lessens the likelihood of inadvertently importing hidden assumptions and concepts, since each new assumption and each new concept must be either derivable from the previous terms of the paradigm or explicitly incorporated in it'.[159] Third, paradigms advance a cumulation of knowledge by making consecutive researches comparable; building on the same foundations, falling within the same niches, covering the same areas. Fourth, paradigms have a sensitising function by suggesting 'modes of systematic cross-tabulation of putatively significant concepts',[160] pointing to the lacunae of existing knowledge and to unknown aspects or dimensions of complex sociological problems. Fifth, paradigms codify qualitative analysis 'in a way that approximates the logical if not the empirical rigor of quantitative analysis'.[161] All this derives from identifying the logic often hidden in discursive presentations, and specifying the logical links between concepts, data, theories and methods utilised in a particular kind of inquiry.

The fruitfulness of paradigms can be best assessed by examining their actual fruit in Merton's own work, as this is done in the chapters to come. Here it is enough to emphasise the congruence of the idea of paradigms with two of Merton's preoccupations: contributing to methodological *self awareness* in sociology and to its being a collectively and selectively *cumulative* enterprise.

Disciplined eclecticism

The last phase of research at the focus of Merton's metatheoretical attention is the choice among theories. Sociological inquiry produces many diverse theories. 'Theoretical pluralism is a typical rather than accidental state, a normal rather than pathological condiction of every scientific discipline. As he puts it: 'The plurality of current theories, paradigms, and thought-styles is not a mere happenstance, simply incidental to the development of each field of inquiry. Rather, it appears to be integral to the socially patterned cognitive processes operating in the disciplines. With the institutionalization of science, the behavior of scientists oriented toward norms of organized scepticism and mutual criticism works to bring about such theoretical pluralism'.[162] In sociology, theoretical pluralism is even more pronounced in its still early state of development. Referring to one orientation to sociological studies, structural analysis, Merton observes: 'The plurality of partly overlapping, partly distinctive theories seems to reproduce in this one region of inquiry the actual and, to my mind, the cognitively appropriate state of sociology at large'.[163] As Blau aptly comments on Merton's conception: 'Far from considering the coexistence of these diverse and often conflicting theoretical perspectives as a sign of the pathology of sociological inquiry, Merton looks upon them as a sign of the discipline's vigor and emphasizes that complementary views are essential for a thorough understanding of social structure and that competing theories make vital contributions to the advancement of knowledge in a field'.[164]

Sociologists must choose from that plurality of theories, to commit themselves to some, and to by-pass others. The gravity of the predicament depends on the character of the various theories. Two distinct situations seem to require distinct policies. In one, the theories refer to different objects or to different aspects of the same object. One may say: they utilise *selective emphases, distinct foci* of interest. In such cases, the theories may be taken as complementary. Merton seems to have this situation in mind when he notes that 'The existence of many theories need not mean that they are in conflict and that we must choose among them. Often they are complementary, not contradictory'.[165] He expands this idea elsewhere: 'the idea central to theoretical pluralism: that though theoretical orientations may differ in their cogency when directed toward the same problems, their very difference of perspective typically leads them to focus on different rather than the same problems. As a result, the theories are often complementary or unconnected rather than contradictory'.[166]

In this type of situation the appropriate policy is described as 'disciplined eclecticism': 'the controlled and systematic use of complementary ideas drawn from differing orientations in the form of what can be called "disciplined eclecticism" characterizing much of social science today'.[167] The qualification 'disciplined' is not incidental; it is clearly intended to demarcate Merton's approach from eclecticism pure and simple, in the common pejorative meaning of superficial and unreflective fusion of miscellaneous ingredients. Merton is quite explicit about it: 'in describing and advocating a plurality of theoretical orientations in sociology in the form of a "disciplined eclecticism", I neither describe nor advocate a kind of theoretical anarchism in which anything goes'.[168] It may be conjectured from the context of Merton's work that 'disciplined eclecticism' refers first of all to self-awareness of procedures of inquiry, a clear recognition of the elements of diverse theoretical orientations that are being combined and a sense of the presuppositions and implications inherent in each of them. Second, it requires a critical and selective adaptation, utilising only those theories which meet the criteria of validity and guided by the goal of their ultimate mutual consistency and compatibility: 'The various theoretical perspectives can be brought together in a more comprehensive theory, of course, only if they adopt mutually consistent assumptions and give rise to compatible hypotheses'.[169] When theories are combined in this way, it opens the road to a more comprehensive, many-sided sociological knowledge.

The second type of situation confronting the investigator is more difficult and poses more pressing dilemmas. It is found when various theories refer to the same aspects of the same object but make *diverse knowledge claims* about them. In short, they deal with the same phenomena, but assert different things about them. Here theories can no longer be treated as complementary: they are contradictory and competing. Merton does not present a clear solution to this predicament. He seems to have an overriding faith in the relatively efficient operation of science, as a social institution and community of scholars. Through 'organised skepticism', open competition, public contest of ideas — the weaker theories eventually become eliminated and stronger ones gain the field. Whitehead's adage is another of Merton's favourites: 'The clash of doctrines is not a disaster but an opportunity'.[170] Very early in his career, in 1941, he had observed that 'Znaniecki shows how rivalry between schools of sacred thought leads to secularization. . . . Conflict, as a type of social interaction, leads to the partial secularization of sacred knowledge. . .'.[171] Finally, Merton sets forward his own position: 'when conflict is regulated by the community of peers, it has its uses for the advancement of the discipline. . . . Were it not for such conflict, the reign of orthodoxies would be even more marked than it sometimes is'.[172]

But Merton seems to forget that 'organized skepticism' must apply *criteria*. There must be guidelines to distinguishing better and worse theories. Merton is strangely silent on this topic. Is it because he takes it for granted that empirical criteria are decisive and conclusive; that the direct confrontation with facts will sooner or later show some theories to be true, and others false? I doubt it; his expressed position described earlier as sophisticated falsificationism would not allow for that. Or is it a pragmatic test that he has in mind, showing inevitably, even if in the long run, that some theories are useful and others useless? Again, I doubt this interpretation; he is too committed to the case for the intrinsic worth of scientific knowledge to dismiss out of hand such theories which have not (yet) proved their practical utility. The whole idea of the 'potentials of relevance' is introduced precisely to defend the validity of such theories. Thus, finally, he has to assume some autonomous, *theoretical criteria*, a distinct 'theoretical logic'[173] allowing scientists to decide among theories which otherwise seem equally valid and useful. After all, he makes such choices himself, opts for some theories or orientations, rejects others. But if this is the case, he leaves his criteria hidden and implicit, does not discuss them directly. Perhaps clues will emerge as we come to study his substantive theories and learn why he selects them rather than others. But the explicit methodological analysis of the research process remains open-ended and incomplete, leaving the sociologist somewhat at sea, faced with an overabundance of competing and seemingly incommensurable theories.

5
On Sociological Orientation

In this chapter I leave the formal, content-free plane of sociological method and embark on the study of the substantive plane of sociological orientations. Whereas the methodological directives outlined in the preceding chapter do not presuppose any definite image of the subject-matter, though obviously they rest on epistemological foundations, the sociological orientation involves clear ontological commitments. It presupposes a particular *image of society* and it makes sense only within the framework provided by that image.

The sociological orientation specifies the aspects, phases and domains of social life that are to be considered crucial. In Merton's retrospective words, as he reflected on his early distinction between 'theoretical orientations' and 'hypothetico-deductive theory', 'Such orientations involve broad postulates that indicate *types* of variables which are *somehow to be taken into account* rather than specifying determinate relationships between particular variables. Indispensable though these orientations are, they provide only the broadest framework for empirical inquiry'.[1] By the same token, each sociological orientation excludes some other aspects, phases or domains, as relatively insignificant. It commits itself to certain foci, and deliberately neglects other foci. In this way it determines the scope of theoretical results that can possibly be reached. As another of Merton's favourite adages – what he calls 'the Kenneth Burke theorem' – puts it: 'A way of seeing is also a way of not seeing – a focus upon object A involves a neglect of object B'.[2]

Merton devotes much attention to the concept of sociological orientations (or approaches[3]). His interest in it is expressed both negatively, through critiques of other orientations, and positively, through the explication and elaboration of orientations he finds most promising and fruitful. I follow the same sequence in my analysis.

The crisis of sociology

During the last decade and more, sociologists' criticisms of sociological thought has taken a new turn. The focus on the weaknesses of sociological method is replaced by a focus on the inadequacy of sociological orientations. The 'poverty-of-sociology' tradition is largely replaced by the 'crisis-of-sociology' debate.[4]

It is by no means accidental that the book most often quoted by participants in the debate is Kuhn's *The Structure of Scientific Revolutions*. Two ideas of Kuhn's influential account of the course taken by scientific development bear directly on the contemporary reappraisals of the state of sociology. One is the notion of paradigms (in a *different* sense than the Mertonian notion): universally accepted theoretical and methodological orientations dominating a scientific community in a historical period. When applied to sociology and other social sciences, it suggests that the discipline is still in a pre-paradigmatic stage. Kuhn reports: 'I was struck by the number and extent of the overt disagreements between social scientists about the nature of legitimate scientific problems and methods. Both history and acquaintance made me doubt that practitioners of the natural sciences possess firmer or more permanent answers to such questions than their colleagues in social science. Yet, somehow, the practice of astronomy, physics, chemistry, or biology normally fails to evoke the controversies over fundamentals that today [1958 – 1962; the dates of first and revised edition] often seem endemic among, say, psychologists or sociologists'.[5] The other of Kuhn's pertinent ideas is the notion of puzzles: the unsolved problems and questions that cannot be approached within the framework of a particular paradigm and whose accumulation presses for a fundamental change in the paradigm; the scientific revolution. The application of this notion to sociology suggests that it is in a pre-revolutionary stage, searching for a new paradigm, as the traditional ones had exhausted their potentials. A typical formulation of such a view is found in Birnbaum: 'A doctrinal or theoretical crisis in a system of thought occurs when either of two sets of abstract conditions obtains: (a) the possibilities of the internal development of the system exhaust themselves; the system's categories become incapable of transformation; the discussion generated by the system becomes scholastic, in the pejorative sense of the term, and (b) the realities apprehended by the system in its original form change, so much so that the categories are inapplicable to the new conditions'.[6]

In an anticipatory fashion (written in most cases well before Kuhn) Merton's critique of sociology seems to be informed by both of Kuhn's central ideas.[7] The lack of universally accepted paradigm is viewed as implying two distinct conditions: one that can be conceived as normal, and another as pathological. The normal condition is the *plurality* of orientations, or approaches. Merton claims: 'the plain fact is that no single all-embracing and tight-knit theoretical orientation has proved adequate to identify and to deal with the wide range of problems requiring investigation in detail'.[8] In this sense 'it can be argued, without paradox and with as much persuasiveness, that sociology has been in a condition of crisis throughout its history'.[9] In fact, the term 'crisis' with its pejorative connotation seems misapplied: 'It would be a curious reading of the history of thought to suggest that the absence of disagreement testifies to a developing discipline'.[10]

But as Merton indicates, a plurality of orientations can easily 'degenerate' into such pathological forms as fragmentation, *polarisation*, and rival dogmatisms. This is the danger in contemporary sociology, in the proper sense of the term 'crisis'. Fragmentation means that the theoretical orientations are isolated, becoming separate, self-contained bodies of thought, with no mutual openings, no heuristic interstimulation, no conceptual interpenetration, no theoretical interchange. Merton refers to 'the notorious tendency for theoretical pluralism to degenerate into theoretical fragmentation, in which the various theoretical orientations become mutually irrelevant'.[11] Polarisation means that theoretical orientations are placed in an antagonistic relationship; they are not only separated but hostile; the market-place of ideas is turned into a battlefield of ideas; the intellectual competition is transformed into social conflict. This situation is marked by the appearance of strongly defined sociological 'schools'. Writing in 1961, a decade or so before Alvin Gouldner announced 'the coming crisis of Western sociology', Merton observes: 'The very multiplicity of systems, each with its claim to being the genuine sociology, led naturally enough to the formation of schools, each with its masters, disciples, and epigoni. Sociology became internally differentiated not in terms of specialization but in the form of rival claims to intellectual legitimacy, claims typically held to be mutually exclusive and at odds'.[12] And in another context he emphasises the same tendency: 'sociologists are more apt [than others] to retreat into parochial enclaves of like-minded [scientists]. This kind of social differentiation is less in terms of specialized knowledge than in terms of competing school-allegiances'.[13]

Finally, is the ultimate pathology in which the *dogmatism* of certain sociological orientations involves the claim to a monopoly of a valid and fruitful set of ideas, and the uncritical, *a priori* rejection of all other orientations: 'To the extent that members of a thought-collective claim exclusive access to sound knowledge about a given region of phenomena they deny that there is truth in the ideas being advanced by cognitively opposed thought-collectives'.[14] In Merton's view, this constitutes a crisis *par excellence*: 'the chronic crisis of sociology, with its diversity, competition, and clash of doctrine, seems preferable to the therapy sometimes proposed for handling the acute crisis, namely, the prescription of a single theoretical perspective that promises to provide full and exclusive access to the sociological truth'.[15] He continues: 'it is not so much the plurality of paradigms as the collective acceptance by practicing sociologists of a single paradigm proposed as a panacea that would constitute a deep crisis with ensuing stasis'.[16] This, because such dogmatisms would effectively limit the perspective, produce sociological myopia or outright blindness: 'This sociologist or that one is anesthetized to inconvenient facts by his unremitting commitment to a theory. This becomes all the worse when the theory is implicit. For then it insistently dominates what we see, what we believe we see and what, though it is relevant and is there for the seeing, remains regrettably unseen'.[17]

Further accord with Kuhn's ideas of puzzles and their accumulation may be found in Merton's distinction between a *chronic crisis*, due to a continuing plurality of orientations, and the *acute crisis* manifested socially and psychologically under specific conditions. 'As distinct from the actual ongoing condition of the discipline, the periodic sense of crisis erupts at moments when sociologists become particularly aware of conspicuous inadequacies of cognitive or practical performance, typically as gauged by heightened aspirations for larger accomplishment'.[18] This seems to describe the contemporary situation. The heritage of 19th- and 20th-century sociology has produced a set of unsolved puzzles, has identified areas of 'specified ignorance', it means 'what is not yet known but needs to be known in order to lay the foundation for still more knowledge'.[19] But it is widely felt that the discipline is not doing enough by way of solving key theoretical problems. Such an attitude can produce various responses, ranging from the ritualistic limitation of cognitive interest to less significant and more readily solvable problems, through a rebellious anti-intellectualism, to the innovative search for better orientations, or at least a creative reformulation of existing orientations.

Merton seems to opt for the last course of action. As we shall see, he contributes to the delimitation and explication of a sociological orientation which is open enough to avoid dogmatism but at the same time definite enough to steer clear of cognitive anarchy. For him, obviously, 'everything does *not* go', and some orientations are better than others.

The focus of sociology

A first approximation to Merton's idea of a cogent sociological orientation is found in his definition of sociology as a discipline: its scope, subject-matter and specific focus. This perspective is internal, characterising the contents of the domain of sociology. Three typical accounts, taken from various periods of his work, deserve extensive quotation, as they exhibit the consistency of his orientation to sociological problems. In 1957, he writes: 'In the main, sociology treats of the social environment, the conditions under which one or another form of social organization comes about, the attributes of organizations and their interrelations, the development of social values and norms, their functions in governing the socially patterned behavior of individuals, and the forces making for changes in social structure'.[20] In 1961, he notes: 'In the large, sociology is engaged in finding out how man's behavior and fate are affected, if not minutely governed, by his place within particular kinds, and changing kinds, of social structure and culture'.[21] And some time before, in 1949, the calling of a sociologist is defined thus: 'the last of the sociologist is that of lucidly presenting claims to logically interconnected and empirically confirmed propositions about the structure of society and its changes, the behavior of man within that structure and the consequences of that behavior'.[22] Thus, to recapitulate, the prime subject-matter of sociology is conceived of as the social structure (or social organisation) and it is to be studied in its multiple and varied aspects; historically genetic (how it came to be), as well as functional (how it affects behaviour); static (how it operates), as well as dynamic (how it changes). In this first approximation, *the focus on social structure* already appears as the defining trait of sociology.

This becomes the more evident when we see how Merton handles the problem of demarcation, the problem of delimiting sociology from related disciplines. The second approximation, as a complementary perspective, is external. It no longer centres on the contents but rather on the boundaries, especially the frontiers, of what is proposed as the domain of sociology. In true Durkheimian fashion, Merton is most concerned to demarcate sociology from psychology. It will be noted that this effort *does not* deteriorate into an anti-psychological crusade. Thus, in 1950 Merton observes: 'This is not to say that the sociological orientation is necessarily "superior" to the psychological, or that it is necessarily at odds with it. But it *is* different'.[23] And in another place he adds: 'however much these distinctive problems differ, they are complementary. . . . Psychological and sociological approaches to a particular problem *prove to be* complementary'.[24]

Though Merton avoids radical antipsychologism, he is far from accepting the opposite extreme of psychological reductionism. He maintains that social phenomena and processes cannot be reduced to (or derived from) individual behaviour; social properties and regularities are not deducible from psychological concepts or laws. As he puts it in colourful style: 'The history of social thought is strewn with the corpses of those who have tried, in their theory, to make the hazardous leap from human nature to particular forms of social conduct'.[25]

What then is the crux of the difference dividing those two complementary and equally legitimate perspectives: the sociological and the psychological? It is the question of the *aspects of phenomena* that are taken for granted or conversely, taken as problematic. For the psychologist, the socio-structural aspect is *given*, and the individual aspect, *problematic*. For the sociologist, the opposite holds: 'the analytical focus is upon the structure of the environment, with the attributes and psychological processes of individuals being regarded as given and not within the theoretical competence of the sociologist to analyze'.[26] The focus on social structure is once again reaffirmed, this time from an indirect, external perspective.

This interpretation of Merton's orientation finds ample corroboration in his concrete substantive analyses. Discussing the problem of 'sociological ambivalence', he observes: 'Unlike the psychological orientation, the sociological one focuses on the ways in which ambivalence comes to be built into the structure of social statuses and roles'.[27] Or in a more concrete application of this idea: 'ambivalence in the help-seeker is not the professional's fault, nor is it the result of an individual's insensitivity or lack of imagination; it is essentially built into the structure of uncertainty within which professional and client must interact'.[28] Studying 'socially expected durations', Merton strictly distinguishes 'individual expectations of durations' (of certain kinds of relationships, collectivities, institutions) from 'structural or institutionalized durations' – taking the latter as the proper subject-matter for sociological analysis.[29] In the research on deviance, he proposes to apply distinct terms for the 'anomic state of individuals' and the 'anomic state of the social system'. The first is termed 'anomia' (after Leo Srole), the second is termed 'anomie'. And then he indicates his prime concern: 'The first thing to note about the sociological concept of anomie is that it is sociological. Anomie refers to a property of a social system, not to the state of mind of this or that individual within the system'.[30] Other examples will be adduced as we move to the analysis of Merton's conception of society in chapters 6 and 7.

The characterisation of sociology as a discipline defined by a focus on social structure allows us to hazard a conjecture concerning Merton's ontological creed. He evidently perceives society as a reality *sui generis*, possessing specific properties and displaying specific regularities, emergent with respect to the properties and regularities of individual human beings. The social reality is *superindividual* (as it is fundamentally novel in relation to individuals) but it is not *supraindividual* (since it is not independent of individuals). The structure involves people and their actions but it is something more than an aggregate of people and activities. It may be called the interindividual reality, since it is produced by varied relationships among pluralities of individuals or it may be called systemic reality, as it results in various social wholes consisting of individuals bound together by networks of interrelations. Such an ontological conception, which may be described as 'structural realism' or 'sociological structuralism',[31] avoids the pitfall of reification, typical of metaphysical holism. It also avoids the atomisation of social reality that is found in the various forms of theoretical individualism. Building on such an ontological foundation, Merton has developed two specific sociological orientations, functional analysis and structural analysis. After examining them separately at first, I shall argue that they are not separate, independent approaches, but rather two complementary sides of a single unified orientation.

Functional analysis

Perhaps no other sociological orientation has been so widely and so hotly disputed as functional analysis. From its roots in the nineteenth century, through the classic formulations of social anthropologists, it reached its peak in sociology during the period after World War II, coming closer than any other orientation to the position of a dominant paradigm or widely accepted orthodoxy. Martindale is correct in saying that 'Most primary theoretical and methodological debates in postwar social science have centered on functionalism and alternatives to it'.[32]

The assessments of functionalism range from total acceptance to total rejection. For some it has been taken as synonymous with a scientific approach to society. Kingsley Davis was maintaining this in 1959: 'It thus appears that the most agreed-upon traits of functionalism are those broadly characterizing scientific analysis in general'.[33] For others, functionalism is the antithesis of a scientific approach to society, since is said to shun the explanatory or theoretical aims of science. Homans expresses this challenge: 'If a theory is an explanation, the functionalists in sociology, were, on the evidence, not successful. Perhaps they could not have been successful; at any rate they were not. The trouble with their theory was not that it was wrong, but that it was not a theory'.[34] It is only recently, in the 70s and 80s that the debate over functionalism loses its vigour, largely replaced by other foci of theoretical concern. Two witnesses give almost identical testimony: 'The debate over the merits and shortcomings of functionalism, which overshadowed most theoretical discussions in sociology and anthropology in the 1950s and 1960s, today appears spent'.[35] 'Although structural – functional analysis is still one of the most significant orientations, impressionistically it no longer seems to occupy the dominant position it did in the late fifties and the sixties'.[36] But on the other hand, as Parsons puts it, it would be a 'slight exaggeration' to claim that functionalism is dead.[37] At most, it is an early, orthodox version of functional analysis which is widely and justly rejected. A developed form of the functional orientation, rid of earlier dogmatic assumptions, opened to other orientations, and enriched by new ideas, provides a basis for sound sociological interpretation. Of that version of functional analysis, I am ready to conclude with Merton that it is 'presently the most promising, though not the only, theoretical orientation to a wide range of problems in human society'.[38]

In the long and controversial career of functional analysis, Merton has been playing a central part. His has been a double role. He helped to bring functional analysis to the fore and raise it to the plane of a theoretical orthodoxy and, at the same time, he helped bring about the demise of its canonical form, introducing a radically new and modified formula of functional analysis. This may qualify as a self-exemplifying case of his idea of the *selective and critical cumulation* of scientific knowledge.

Contemporary commentators refer to Merton's version of functional analysis as 'neofunctionalism', 'empirical functionalism', 'dynamic functionalism'. The crucial novelty of his developing position has involved a three-fold shift of focus: first, from the level of results to the level of method; second, from the rationalistic, abstract, or scholastic approach to a more empirical, middle-range perspective; and third, from a static to a dynamic image of society.

In the course of its prolonged development, functional analysis became a differentiated, heterogenous body of thought. As Nagel aptly observes, 'The label of functionalism covers a variety of distinct (though in some cases, closely related) conceptions'.[39] Some authors emphasise its status as a social theory, in the full meaning of a propositional system designed to explain certain aspects of social reality. An example: the functional theory of stratification by Davis and Moore.[40] Others explicitly qualify their results as 'conceptual schemes', 'generalised systems of theoretical categories', 'conceptual frames of reference'. The works of Parsons above all, as well as Levy, Easton, Loomises and many others provide examples.[41] In both cases, the focus is on the results of sociological research.

Merton chooses a different emphasis. He joins those who refer to functional analysis as a 'methodological orientation', an 'analytic method', a 'research strategy'. In a word, he concurs in the view treating functional analysis pre-eminently as a method of sociological inquiry. For Merton functional analysis provides a strategy of theory-construction; a set of heuristic as well as validating directives, defining a particular way of interpreting and organising sociological data into gradually more and more comprehensive theoretical structures. It is a means toward his overriding goals: the codification, consolidation and cumulation of sociological theory. This character of Merton's functional orientation is aptly noticed by Parsons who describes it as theoretical methodology: 'he [Merton] clearly made a major contribution to the understanding and clarification of the theoretical methodology of what he, I think quite appropriately called "functional analysis" '.[42]

A second specific trait of Merton's brand of functionalism is its empirical bent. In his early, 1948, critique of Parsons, he questioned the undue abstractness and comprehensiveness of 'master conceptual schemes'; 'The basic theory, so-called, runs so far ahead of confirmed special theories as to remain a program rather than a *consolidation* of these theories'.[43] The main weakness of these master conceptual schemes is their scant relation to systematic empirical evidence: as systems of categories they are in a large part not testable, being founded on self-contained and often tautologous premises. Instead, he proposes: 'Complete sociological systems, as in their days complete systems of medical theory or of chemical theory, must give way to less imposing but more adequate sets of limited theory'.[44] The early Merton thus provides a first formulation of his programme for middle range theory, conceived of as a way of overcoming the weaknesses of all-embracing systems of theorising set forth all at once. Thus, even before his exposition of functional analysis in the first edition of *Social Theory and Social Structure* 'Merton begins to direct functional analysis from concern with total systems toward an emphasis on how different patterns of social organization within more inclusive social systems are created, maintained and changed, not only by the requisites of the total system but also by interaction among socio-cultural items within systemic wholes. . . . He is stressing the need for an alternative form of functional analysis in which there is less concern with total systems and abstract statements of system requisites. Instead, to build "theories of the middle range" it is necessary to focus attention on the mutual and varied consequences of specified system parts for each other and for systemic wholes'.[45]

The third and by far the most significant departure of Merton's functional orientation is *the shift from a static towards a dynamic image of society*. Here, the critical revision of the whole functionalist tradition is carried out quite self-consciously, producing a theoretical orientation free from certain weaknesses of earlier formulations: 'Merton's functionalism is very different both from the "classical" functionalism of Comte's and Spencer's sociology and Malinowski's and Radcliffe-Brown's cultural anthropology, and from Parsons' functional structuralism'.[46] It is possible to trace the ways through which Merton modifies and transforms the functionalist heritage.

He begins by identifying the 'central orientation of functionalism' as 'the practice of interpreting data by establishing their consequences for larger structures in which they are implicated'.[47] Functions constitute a subclass of such consequences. These are the consequences which are in turn causally relevant to the state of the system in which the particular structure is located. Functional analysis involves the search for functions. Such a general formulation covers all brands of functional analysis and does not raise any problems. But the trouble begins when functionalists proceed to make it more concrete by introducing further theoretical commitments. This is precisely the case with the anthropological forefathers of functionalism. Merton identifies five 'postulates' of that functionalism which he finds unacceptable. Giving the grounds for his rejection of these postulates, he goes on to his positive proposals, thus giving rise to a dynamic, empirically oriented neo-functional analysis.

The first is the postulate of the 'functional unity of society'.[48] It assumes that the 'standardized social activities or cultural items are functional for the entire social and cultural system'.[49] This would be the case only if the system were completely homogenous, uniform and perfectly integrated. But this is not the general case. 'The degree of integration', writes Merton, 'is an empirical variable, changing for the same society from time to time and differing among various societies. That all human societies must have *some* degree of integration is a matter of definition – and begs the question. But not all societies have that *high* degree of integration in which *every* culturally standardized activity or belief is functional for the society as a whole and uniformly functional for the people living in it'.[50] Barbano puts a heavy emphasis on this point: 'let it be said once and for all that for Merton this question of "integration" is purely and simply one of possible degrees, which does not imply anything with regard to one (or more than one) requirement or need of integration'.[51]

The assumption of full societal integration must therefore be replaced by alternative assumptions. The first of these, which I have identified as the assumption of disunity[52] claims that one and the same element may have different functions with respect to different subsystems of the system of which it is a part. In Merton's terms, 'It is necessary to consider a *range* of units for which the item has designated consequences: individuals in diverse statuses, subgroups, the larger social system and culture systems'.[53] The second assumption refers to the more specific possibility that functions fulfilled by various structural components for various social units may have different vectors, some may be positive functions contributing to its 'adjustment or adaptation', while others may be dysfunctions, 'those observed consequences which lessen the adaptation or adjustment of the system'.[54] Accordingly, this can be designated as the assumption of dysfunctions. In Merton's words, this assumption 'curbs any inadvertent or deliberate tendency in functional sociology to reinstate the philosophy that everything in society works for "harmony" and "the good" '.[55] In an even more specific case, the same item may be both functional and dysfunctional with respect to various social subsystems. This assumption can be distinguished from the preceding as 'functional ambivalence'.[56]

To deal with the situations described by alternative set of assumptions Merton introduced the notion of 'net balance of functional consequences'.[57] The net balance is taken as contingent, empirically variable and requiring concrete assessment in each concrete case. It is worth noticing that the concept can be utilised in two ways. The first is examined by Merton when he speaks of the 'net balance of the aggregate of consequences', referring to the balance of functional and dysfunctional consequences for the system as a whole (or some subsystem thereof). The unit of computation is here *the system*, not a part of it (an item fulfilling those functions or dysfunctions). A second application of the concept is also possible. In this, the unit of assessment is *a part of the system* (an item analysed) and not the whole, and net balance of its consequences for the system – functional and dysfunctional – could be treated as a measure of its total functionality or dysfunctionality.[58]

The second postulate of the traditional functionalism which Merton rejects is described as 'universal functionalism'. It holds that 'all . . . social and cultural items fulfill sociological functions'.[59] This assumption implies an image of society in which there are no dispensable or irrelevant elements, no 'fifth wheels', so to say. This assumption of early anthropological functionalism is only a step away from the assumption that whatever is, is necessary, else, it would not exist. But this is not tenable empirically. As Merton put it: 'although any item of culture or social structure *may* have functions, it is premature to hold unequivocally that every such item *must* be functional'.[60] Thus an opposed assumption, which I call 'specific functionality'[61] must allow for 'the empirical possibility of non-functional consequences, which are simply irrelevant to the system under consideration'.[62]

Continuing his questioning of the problematic assumptions of traditional functionalism, Merton squeezes two quite distinct situations under the heading of 'the postulate of indispensability'. Since they merit separate discussion, I split that postulate into two.[63] In rejecting the postulate in its first meaning, Merton focuses on the alleged indispensability of particular cultural or social forms for fulfilling a particular function in a social system. This assumption claims, in effect, that a given particular element constitutes a necessary condition for attaining a preferred state of the system; in other words, it is being held that without this element the preferred state of the system could neither be attained nor maintained. This calls up an image of society in which all its elements (institutions, norms, values, modes of social action, etc.) are essential to the society and can be modified or replaced, only by subverting its continued existence. In effect, such an assumption disposes of a most interesting feature of human society, the infinite variety and variability of its institutions, ways of life, customs, values, norms of behaviour etc., as a subject for empirical, comparative research.

Merton proposes an alternative assumption which he considers 'a basic theorem of functional analysis'.[64] This he states in emphatic italics: *'Just as the same item may have multiple functions, so may the same function be diversely fulfilled by alternative items'*.[65] The concepts of 'functional alternatives' or 'functional equivalents' or 'functional substitutes' are introduced to cover that empirical possibility. Merton provides an instructive example in the new introduction to his doctoral dissertation: 'The historically concrete movement of Puritanism is not being put forward as a prerequisite to the substantial thrust of English science in that time; other functionally equivalent ideological movements could have served to provide the emerging science with widely acknowledged claims to legitimacy. . . . The interpretation in this study . . . does not presuppose that only Puritanism could have served that function. As it *happened*, Puritanism provided major (not exclusive) support in that historical time and place. But that does not make it indispensable. However, and this requires emphasis, neither does this functional conception convert Puritanism into something epiphenomenal and inconsequential. It, rather than conceivable functional alternatives, happened to advance the institutionalization of science by providing a substantial basis for its legitimacy'.[66]

It would seem that such a concept might be better described as 'structural alternatives' (equivalents or substitutes).[67] In fact Merton's related notion of 'structural constraint' would make the proposed terminological usage fully congruent. Structural constraint limits the class of structural alternatives that can emerge and operate consequentially. The empirical range of possible structural alternatives is determined by particular features of the particular society, by its internal constitution as well as by external, environmental circumstances.[68] Whether described as functional or structural alternatives, the central idea of alternatives has important implications for sociological inquiry. It directs attention to the *great variability of structural arrangements* that can fulfill the same function while having differing other consequences. Thus, it alerts the research worker to the wide range of possible cultural and historical diversity. In cases where an expected social structure is absent in a particular society, it mandates a search for structural alternatives. In this way, it helps disclose the hidden functions of other institutions or structures in the society. And where a particular expected structure is present in a society, the concept directs a search for particular factors to explain the absence of feasible alternatives.

The fourth postulate of traditional functionalism rejected by Merton is closely related, since it also involves the assumption of indispensability. In this case, with reference to certain kinds of functions fulfilled in the social system: 'it is assumed that there are certain *functions* which are indispensable in the sense that, unless they are performed, the society (or group or individual) will not persist'.[69] This postulate implies that there are some indispensable states or conditions for the system to exist. Merton refers to these assumed indispensable states as 'functional requirements', 'functional prerequisites' or 'functional needs'.[70] He notes that lists of such needs have been proposed by functional sociologists and anthropologists from Malinowski to Parsons, but seems uneasy about the concept. He had remarked in the early public discussion of theory with Parsons that 'the concept of "functional needs" (or prerequisites) . . . is at present one of the cloudiest and least articulated concepts in the entire panorama of functional conceptions'.[71] Somewhat later, he extends this criticism: 'this remains one of the cloudiest and empirically most debatable concepts in functional theory. As utilized by sociologists, the concept of functional requirements tends to be tautological or *ex post facto*; it tends . . . to be confined to the conditions of "survival" of a given system'.[72]

The notions of 'survival', 'persistence', or 'existence' of societies provide little empirical meaning to the concept of requirements. 'I wonder', says Lehman, 'if there are clear criteria of existence with regard to societies. . . . If it is not clear, whether the same society still exists (say, after certain very significant changes have occurred), then it cannot be clear whether some item has effects which contribute to the society's existence'.[73] The notion of functional requirements seems to be an unfortunate legacy of the organic analogy which underlay much of functionalist thinking. It is obviously parallel to the concept of organic needs. But 'where individual needs can be clearly identified, as they can in the case of biological needs, function statements of this type are probably more satisfactory scientific statements than in the case where the reference is to a poorly specified social structure'.[74] Were Merton following his own hints, he would perhaps have rejected the notion of requirements *in toto* and reserved the concept of functional alternatives (substitutes, equivalents) precisely for those situations in which certain kinds of functions can be realised instead of others, neither of them constituting a necessary prerequisite.[75] Or he would even go further to admit – with Sjoberg – that functional requirements of the same system may be mutually contradictory.[76] As will be seen, his vacillation on this point is directly related to another ambiguity concerning the overall goal of functional analysis; providing descriptive, interpretative accounts, or full-fledged explanations of social phenomena.

The fifth postulate of traditional functionalism is not identified explicitly, but can be readily inferred from the context of Merton's critical discussion along with his positive proposals. I describe this as the postulate of transparent functions. It assumes that people are commonly aware of the functions served by their own actions, social institutions or other elements of the social system. It is based on the 'inadvertent confusion, often found in the sociological literature, between conscious *motivations* for social behavior and its *objective consequences*'.[77] As Merton also observes: 'concepts of subjective disposition are often and erroneously merged with the related, but different, concepts of objective consequences of attitude, belief and behavior'.[78] Such an assumption is unacceptable on empirical grounds as well: it runs against the obvious facts of social life encoded by such expressions as 'side-effects', 'unanticipated consequences', 'unintended consequences' and so on. It involves simplified and, one might say, unduly optimistic picture of society. As Merton points out emphatically: 'It need not be assumed . . . that the *motives* for entering into marriage ("love", "personal reasons") are identical with the *functions* served by families (socialization of the child). Again, it need not be assumed that the *reasons* advanced by people for their behavior ("we act for personal reasons") are one and the same as the observed consequences of these patterns of behavior. The subjective disposition may coincide with the objective consequence, but again, it may not. The two vary independently'.[79] In human society, what one wants to achieve sometimes has little or nothing to do with what one's activity actually achieves.

Thus, in its extreme form the postulate must be replaced by an alternative assumption, based on a set of closely related distinctions. To begin with, functions are to be understood as objective consequences. But not all objective consequences, of course, are functions. Functions, as we recall, are the objective consequences which make for 'adjustment or adaptation' of a social system or specified unit within it. Objective consequences may become exposed to human awareness, either of those who brought them about or of other people. The same is true of those qualified consequences known as functions. They may be the subject of human awareness or remain outside of human consciousness. Merton formulates it in his famous dichotomy of manifest and latent functions: 'Manifest functions are those objective consequences contributing to the adjustment or adaptation of the system which are intended and recognized by the participants in the system; Latent functions, correlatively, being those which are neither intended nor recognized'.[80]

The main objection one can raise against the foregoing distinction has to do with the ambiguity of *intention* and *recognition*. As Campbell observes: 'although Merton treats intention and recognition as if they were synonymous, they can and clearly do vary independently of each other'.[81] The human awareness has various modalities. To intend something is to have a disposition or wish to bring it about, by one's own actions. Note that intention need not be, though of course may be, conscious. And in turn, recognition may take the form of anticipation, predicting correctly some outcome brought about by one's own action, or the form of being aware of such an outcome after the fact, when it has occurred. Perhaps it would be useful to introduce two dichotomies instead of one; to retain the manifest-latent distinction to refer to the dimension of recognition (or anticipation), introducing the new pair of terms: intended and unintended, for the dimension of intention.[82] In the words of Spiro: 'If manifest functions are those consequences of role performance which are recognized by the members of society, latent functions are those consequences which – whether intended or unintended – are not recognized. That the paradox of an intended but unrecognized function is apparent rather than real, becomes clear when one considers that motives may be unconscious as well as conscious'.[83]

It is interesting to note that Merton was aware of most of these points in his discussion of 'unanticipated consequences of purposive social action', preceding the essay on 'manifest and latent functions' by several years. At that early article he emphasised that 'unforeseen consequences should not be identified with consequences which are necessarily undesirable (from the standpoint of the actor)'. In the same vein he noticed 'those cases where apparently unintended consequences are *ex post facto* declared to have been intended'.[84] It is all the more surprising that those fine-grained points are somehow forgotten and the relevant distinctions fused, when he comes to propose the oversimplified dichotomy of manifest and latent functions.

In spite of the weakness described above, the distinction itself has had very significant implications for sociological inquiry. As Merton put it: 'armed with the concept of latent function, the sociologist extends his inquiry in those very directions which promise most for the theoretic development of the discipline. He examines the familiar (or planned) social practice to ascertain the latent, and hence generally unrecognized functions (as well, of course, as the manifest functions)'.[85] Escaping the danger of assuming that people are commonly and uniformly aware of social functions, Merton's emphasis on latent functions opens up the problematic areas inaccessible to common-sense.

Neo-functionalism

Rejecting the five postulates of traditional functionalism, Merton arrives at his own, highly original approach, codified in the famous 'paradigm for functional analysis'. Its novelty has been widely recognised. Manis and Meltzer remark that 'Merton's position is scarcely doctrinaire functionalism'.[86] Giddens observes that 'Merton's account, it is clear enough, is one of the most liberal versions of functionalism'.[87] And Merton himself has suggested that 'in functional theory, stripped of those traditional postulates which have fenced it in and often made it little more than a latter-day rationalization of existing practices, sociology has one beginning of a systematic and empirically relevant mode of analysis'.[88]

Owing to its unorthodox nature when introduced in the late 1940s, Merton's account of functional analysis is not vulnerable to most of the criticism typically directed toward the functionalist orientation in sociology. As Giddens observes: Merton 'anticipates and in some degree attempts to meet criticisms of functionalism that later became focal to the debate; such as that functionalist schemes allow no mode of approaching problems of conflict, power and so on'.[89] By reviewing such typical criticism, we can appraise its relevance for Merton's neo-functionalism.

We begin with the claim of teleology or finalism. Some critics read functionalist accounts as asserting that some elements of the system appear or persist *because* they serve certain functions. This type of functional explanation, where the (present) existence of some pattern, norm, role or other item in the social system is explained by its (obviously – future) beneficial consequences for the wider system to which it belongs – raises considerable difficulties. As Homans formulated the common doubts: 'Suppose that a particular institution were good (functional) for a society. But what produced the fit between the institution and the goal of that society?'.[90] In other words: what kinds of mechanism can link the *later goals* (preferred states of the system) with the existence or persistence of *earlier means* (specified components of the system)? This question must be met by those who formulate functional explanations by means of functional laws of the form: a given institution (or other element) appears or survives in the system as a device for meeting the exigencies of the system.

Merton formulates such laws and consequently functional explanations, but surprisingly seldom compared to other uses he makes of functional analysis. Here are some of those *rare* examples of functional laws. Discussing the role of 'political machines' or 'bossism' in American political system, Merton makes a characteristic statement: 'the functional deficiencies of the official structure *generate* an alternative (unofficial) structure *to fulfill* existing needs somewhat more effectively. Whatever its specific historical origins, the political machine persists as an apparatus *for satisfying* otherwise unfulfilled needs of diverse groups of population' [italics mine].[91] Discussing the ambivalence of the social role of the physician, Merton and Elinor Barber delineate the set of norms and counter-norms, as alternating guidelines in the course of evolving behaviour, and claim: 'This alternation of subroles *evolves* as a social device *for* helping people in designated statuses to cope with the contingencies they face in trying to fulfill their functions' [italics mine].[92] Analysing patterns of friendship, Merton and Lazarsfeld observe that each type of social structure has a typical corresponding degree of homophily (friendship forming between people 'of the same kind', as opposed to heterophily when friends are chosen among those of 'differing kind'): 'The task then becomes that of discovering whether, in accord with the hypothesis, marked departures from this level of homophily produce dysfunctional consequences for the social structure which *tend to return* the system of interpersonal relations to the previous level' [italics mine].[93] Finally, analysing the evolution of the professional ethos, Merton notes: 'the expertise and privileged position of professionals confer authority, power, and prestige that can be readily utilized in their own interest rather than their clients' interest. Normative constraints *are designed* as a counterpoise to such structurally induced temptations for the exploitation of clients' [italics mine].[94] The big question in all those examples is the nature of the causal mechanism bringing the analysed institutions about.

Theoretically speaking, three approaches to this question are conceivable. One mechanism of such functional determination of evolving social structures can be described as rational. Those who propose this mechanism assume that the members of a society have full and adequate knowledge of the social goals, or functional requirements (needs) of the system, as well as the idea of the best means to achieve them, and then they purposefully create, introduce or support requisite means (by introducing certain norms, creating certain institutions etc.). This kind of deliberate modification of normative structure (or wider: of social structure) is a mechanism which of course holds only for manifest functions in the full, restrictive sense of the term. But even in this case, the unfounded additional assumption must be made: namely that intention and recognition is equivalent to action. Homans seems justified in his reservations: 'We do doubt that intelligent recognition that a certain institution would be good for a society is ever sufficient – though it may be necessary – condition for its adoption. If it were, the history of human society would be happier than we observe it to be'.[95]

It must be admitted that Merton never commits himself to those dubious assumptions necessary for the adoption of rational mechanism. Nevertheless, there are two passages where he seems to approach the position resembling the one described above. Look again at the pattern of homophily studied by Merton and Lazarsfeld. They observe: 'Local communities disturbed by what is often described as "snobbery" can be taken to exemplify the type-case in which a degree of status-homophily culturally defined as "excessive" releases social forces which may affect the frequency and character of friendships. Such *counteractions* are often observed in the direct and expressive forms of *arranging* for "get-togethers" among those of differing status'.[96] In other words, communities *recognise* the detrimental effects of homophily in terms of status (choice of friends only among status-equals), and *deliberately organise* encounters crossing the status lines. Such 'get-togethers' can then be legitimately explained by their functions for the community, without the risk of teleology. Similarly, professional codes and controls seem sometimes considered by Merton as purposefully introduced to curb possible abuses of professional's advantages over clients.[97] If this is the case, then the existence of such codes can be legitimately explained by their functions for the clients without the risk of teleology. But those cases seem of marginal interest to Merton, because of his main focus on latent, rather than manifest functions. And in the case of latent functions the rational mechanism surely cannot work.

Another possible mechanism of functional determination is evolutionary: positing diversely originating structures subjected to the principles of random mutation and social selection in the form of witting or unwitting responses to the differential consequences of those structures for the persistence of the social system. As an effect of this mechanism only such societies are believed to persist in which the institutions conducive to persistence *happened to appear*, whereas the other societies perish. In the long run, the goals or requirements of the system come to be correlated – in a sufficient if not necessarily optimal measure – with the actually existing structural arrangements. Many authors have called attention to the fallacies inherent in evolutionary arguments.[98] Merton is certainly aware of them.

And yet, he often seems to come close to invoking evolutionary mechanism, especially in dealing with the more complex domain of latent functions; 'unconsciously evolved devices' for meeting requirements of the system. For example, in the case of the political machine: 'In this *struggle* between alternative structures for fulfilling nominally same function of providing aid and support to those who need it, it is clearly the machine politician who is *better integrated* with the groups which he serves than the impersonal, professionalized, socially distant and legally constrained welfare worker' [italics mine].[99] Similarly, with respect to business: 'These "needs" of business, as presently constituted, are not adequately provided for by conventional and culturally approved social structures; *consequently*, the extra-legal but more-or-less efficient organization of the political machine *comes to provide* these services' [italics mine].[100] In other words, the political machine exists because it serves the requirements (needs) of specific sectors of the society; workers and business at the same time. This explanation is faultless and non-teleological, but only if the dubious evolutionary assumptions are accepted.

It may be conjectured that Merton would be most sympathetic to the solution to the finalism dilemma proposed by Ernest Nagel[101] and Carl Hempel;[102] this invoking the assumptions of directive-organisation or self-regulation of a social system. I base this supposition on Merton's numerous references to *feed-back mechanisms*, *causal loops* etc., as well as on his endorsement of Stinchcombe's discussion of functional analysis clearly informed by such notions.[103] But there is not enough evidence to say whether he accepts or not all those quite rigorous and again often empirically dubious assumptions that go with the principles of directive-organisation or self-regulation.

The whole point however is that in order to be valuable and valid, the functional analysis *need not purport to provide explanations* of social phenomena. I believe that functional explanation, so difficult to disentangle from the traps of teleologism, is *not* central to Merton's functional analysis. It seems to me that at those moments when Merton formulates functional laws and functional explanations, he is haunted by the ghosts of Malinowski, Radcliffe-Brown and the earlier tradition of functionalism, which he has skilfully attempted to overcome. Were he consistent, he would abandon the attempt at functional explanation, focusing rather on *functional interpretation*; the identification of functions and dysfunctions, manifest and latent – and the account of their 'net balance' for specified social systems, or for specified elements of such systems. This in itself is of immense cognitive importance. And this is in fact what he does most extensively, applying functional analysis in many domains of social life; the recognition of accomplishment in science,[104] silent majorities in organisations,[105] social control in the medical profession,[106] the differing visibility of various social problems,[107] deviant adaptations,[108] bureaucratic personality,[109] democratic structure in voluntary associations,[110] conflict, deviant behaviour and reward-system in science[111] and so on through a long list.

Others share my reading of Merton's chief intention. For example, Barbano observes: 'For Merton, functional analysis is not so much a model of explanation as an interpretative scheme'.[112] Turner expresses a like opinion: 'Merton recognized . . . that the net balance of consequences does not reveal the cause of an item. This must be undertaken in a separate causal analysis, although Merton did not give great emphasis to this fact'.[113] If this reading of Merton is correct, the charge of teleology or finalism does not hold, except for the marginal and rare cases when he commits himself to functional explanations, thus remaining still in the orbit of traditional functionalism with all its inherent weaknesses. I agree with Barbano that if one thinks of Merton as the father of neo-functionalism (dynamic functionalism, empirical functionalism); obviously the orientation that dominates his theoretical work, 'nothing teleological, totalistic or holistic can be traced in Merton's functionalism; here we do not have a whole determining teleologically the development of the functions and life of the parts, but a structural context, structural connections and tensions, susceptible of differential analysis'.[114] Merton does formulate sociological explanations, but they are *not functional*. Rather, they are fully legitimate and valid *structural explanations*, as we shall see later on in this chapter. But let us stay for a moment with other criticisms directed against Merton's functional analysis.

The one, perhaps the most common, accuses Merton's neo-functionalism of the bias of wholly static analysis. It has been raised among others by such authors as: Dahrendorf,[115] Homans,[116] Buckley,[117] and Lockwood.[118] The import of that criticism is not so much the inability of functionalism to incorporate social change as such but rather its alleged inability to incorporate a specific type of change: endogenous, internally generated change. Obviously, there is not much place for analysing the intrasystemic sources of change, so long as the postulates of functional unity, universal functionalism, and functional indispensability (in both forms) are accepted. But the whole thrust of Merton's critique of traditional functionalism fully explicated in the 'paradigm for functional analysis' in 1949 (it means some two decades *before* the attack of his critics), leads precisely to putting social system in motion. In his neo-functionalist image, social systems are seen as *pervaded by strains, tensions, contradictions, conflicts*, constantly undermining the consensus or equilibrium and *producing social change*. The assumptions of disunity, dysfunctions, functional ambivalence, structural and functional alternatives – which we have discussed – clearly entail a dynamic view of society. As Merton states in his 1949 'Paradigm': 'We have noted that functional analysts *tend* to focus on the statics of social structure and to neglect the study of structural change. This emphasis upon statics is not, however, *inherent* in the theory of functional analysis. . . . This practice, useful at the time it was first introduced into anthropology, has disadvantageously persisted in the work of some functional sociologists'. And here comes the most important claim: 'The concept of dysfunction, which implies the concept of stress, strain and tension on the structural level, provides an analytical approach to the study of dynamics and change'.[119] He concludes in that early formulation: 'I am concerned primarily with extending the theory of functional analysis to deal with problems of social and cultural change'.[120] What can be more straightforward than this? Giddens emphatically summarises the matter: 'Critics of functionalism have not infrequently asserted that it cannot supply a theory of conflict, or of social change. This is easily shown to be mistaken'.[121]

Finally, a criticism that became particularly characteristic for the wave of militant anti-functionalism of the seventies, holds that functionalism is inherently and necessarily conservative, or even reactionary. In fact, this type of criticism was prominent enough in the thirties and the forties, for Merton to have a section in the 1949 'Paradigm' entitled: 'Functional Analysis as Ideology' followed by a thorough discussion of the issue. He says: 'The fact that functional analysis can be seen by some as inherently conservative and by others as inherently radical suggests that it may be *inherently* neither one nor the other. It suggests that functional analysis may involve no *intrinsic* ideological commitments although, like other forms of sociological analysis, it can be infused with any one of wide ranging ideological values'.[122] And expands this thought as follows: 'To the extent that functional analysis focuses wholly on functional consequences, it leans toward an ultraconservative ideology; to the extent that it focuses wholly on dysfunctional consequences, it leans toward an ultra-radical utopia. "In essence", it is neither one nor the other'.[123] Stinchcombe makes the same point: 'The conservative cast of functional theory is not logically necessary'.[124]

And again, Parsons almost echoes the rejection of criticism as invalid: 'The status of functional analysis is entirely independent of any ideological implications in the usual sense. In particular, it has nothing to do with political conservatism or a defense of the status quo'.[125]

So much for Merton's mode of functional analysis. A quarter-century after the publication of the paradigm for functional analysis, Merton writes an important paper 'Structural Analysis in Sociology'[126] which presents a correlative sociological orientation summarised in the form of 'Fourteen Stipulations for Structural Analysis'. Some commentators have taken this as a radical break with functional analysis, as the formulation of a radically new approach. This is the position taken, for example, by Barbano who states that this involves an emancipation of structural analysis from functional analysis: 'structural analysis has recently grown further and further apart from it, and in fact has now established itself as a distinct branch of sociological analysis, critical of the concept of function and functionalism in general'.[127] Others – with whom I am in agreement – regard structural analysis as a natural outgrowth of functional analysis, complementing or supplementing it, but not at all supplanting or rejecting it. Merton's own position is explicit: 'The orientation is that variant of functional analysis in sociology which has evolved, over the years, into a distinct mode of structural analysis'.[128] Here, it is enough to notice the congruent ideas of structural analysis which remain salient to functional analysis: first, the delimitation of the subject-matter of functional analysis as the *patterned*, persisting or recurrent, in a word, structural components of society;[129] second, the concept of structural constraints as limiting the variability and range of possible functional alternatives;[130] third, the concept of structural context as directing and canalising the source of social change, when dysfunctions, strains and tensions accumulate in sufficient degree.[131] There is no opposition of Merton, the functionalist, to Merton, the structuralist. The two theoretical orientations have been consolidated into one.

Structural analysis

Barbano is probably right in saying that 'if any one discipline can lay special claim to use the word "structure", it is sociology'.[132] From the days of Comte, the notion of social structure has been an idea crucial in sociological thinking. Indeed, sociologists, such as Peter Blau, argue that the focus on social structure defines sociology as such.[133]

The perennial interest of sociology in social structure has, of course, nothing to do with the relatively recent 'structuralist revolution' in the humanities (linguistics, social anthropology, ethnology, art criticism etc.). *'Sociological structuralisms'* of Comte, Spencer, Marx, Simmel, Durkheim up to Merton's structural analysis are distinct from the *'logical-linguistic structuralisms'* of de Saussure, Lévi-Strauss, Piaget and many another. Blau's comment is much in point: 'I think it more appropriate to consider him [Merton] a structural theorist, not in the special sense in which Lévi-Strauss's followers use the term, but in the distinctly sociological sense of structural analysis, in the tradition of Durkheim and Radcliffe-Brown'.[134] Merton himself has been quite explicit on this point: 'the basic ideas of structural analysis in sociology long antedated the composite intellectual and social movement known as "structuralism" '.[135]

The main tenet of sociological structuralism is summed up aptly by Bottomore and Nisbet: 'we shall hold to a simple but accurate and historically justifiable definition of structuralism as it is found in sociological and social-anthropological writing: "The relation is more important than the parts" '.[136] This represents the common core of the varieties of the structural approach. But the notion of social structure evidently comprises something more. Consider some current definitions of a social structure in the sociological literature:

(1) 'organization of relationships',[137]
(2) 'definable articulation, an ordered arrangement of parts',[138]
(3) 'consistent, more or less persistent regularities',[139]
(4) 'pattern, i.e. an observable uniformity of action or operation',[140]
(5) 'essential, deep, underlying conditions',[141]
(6) 'characteristic more fundamental than other more superficial characteristics',[142]
(7) 'the arrangement of the parts which controls much of the variance in the phenomena',[143]
(8) 'relations among groups and individuals that find expression in their behavior'.[144]

A *generic concept of social structure* can be derived from those definitions and specified in terms of four definitional criteria:

- relations, relationships, interdependencies (emphasised in definitions 1 and 2),
- regularity, pattern, invariance, repetition, persistence (emphasised in definitions 3 and 4),
- fundamental, essential, hidden, deep dimension (emphasised in definitions 5 and 6), and
- determining, influencing, constraining, controlling impact with respect to empirical, observable phenomena (behaviours) (emphasised in definitions 7 and 8).

The concept of social structure is clearly crucial in Merton's sociology. One of the four pervasive themes underlying his work has been identified precisely as a structuralist theme. It is not by chance that his major book is entitled *Social Theory and Social Structure*. Nor that in 1961 the Loomises entitle their chapter: 'Robert K. Merton as a structural analyst'.[145] Nor that Wallace takes Merton to represent one brand of 'structuralism' among the three he singles out.[146] It is also symptomatic that the two *Festchriften* in honour of Merton, prepared by his onetime students, friends, and associates include the term 'social structure' in their titles: *The Idea of Social Structure*,[147] and *Science and Social Structure*.[148] Reflecting on his own intellectual development, Merton confirms those indicators: 'By the mid-1950s my own research program, as distinct from that of the local thought-collective of which I was a member, had shifted from a monographic focus on particular sets of empirical sociological questions to a renewed focus on problems in structural sociology'.[149] It is worthwhile to look more closely at the meaning of that concept in Merton's work, basic to what Goode has called a 'newer, more sophisticated form of structuralism'.[150]

Merton's generic idea of the social structure includes the definitional criteria we have instituted. The focus on *relations* is clear from at least the early characterisation of social structure formulated in 1949, long before the 'structuralist revolution' or 'structuralist infatuation':[151] 'by social structure is meant that organized set of social relationships in which members of the society or group are variously implicated';[152] as well as in the later work, as when he claims that: 'the structure of status-sets and role-sets provides a basic form of interdependence in society'.[153] The emphasis on the *patterned* character of relations is one of the central themes pervading Merton's work, and the term 'patterned', a qualifier he is particularly fond of. As Lazarsfeld noted, 'Throughout his writings, this is probably the technical term he uses most often'.[154] In a formulation which approximates an explicit definition of social structure, this aspect is placed in the front: 'The patterned arrangement of role-sets, status-sets and status-sequences can be held to comprise the social structure'.[155] In the context of concrete structural analysis, he refers to structure as 'institutionally patterned relations' between individuals or social roles.[156]

The third constitutive criterion of social structure – the idea of a deep, hidden, *underlying level* (corresponding to the idea of latent functions in functional analysis) has only recently been explicitly incorporated in Merton's structural analysis, and this seems to be the only aspect of his approach directly influenced by 'logical-linguistic structuralism'. Merton states it himself: 'It is analytically useful to distinguish between manifest and latent levels of social structure . . . (with the aside that structuralism as set forth in other disciplines – for example by Jakobson, Lévi-Strauss, and Chomsky – finds it essential to distinguish "surface" from "deep" structures)'.[157]

But perhaps most important for Merton's notion of social structure is the fourth criterion, the idea of *constraining* or *facilitating* influences exerted by social structure on actual social phenomena (behaviours, beliefs, attitudes, motivations, etc.). 'Behavior is a result not merely of personal qualities', Merton was writing in 1957, 'but of these in interaction with the patterned situations in which the individual behaves. It is these social contexts which greatly affect the extent to which the capacities of individuals are actually realized'.[158] The concept of 'structural context' and especially 'structural constraint', as limiting the effective field of action appears in the early 'paradigm for functional analysis': 'The interdependence of the elements of a social structure limits the effective possibilities of change or functional alternatives. The concept of structural constraint corresponds, in the area of social structure, to Goldenweiser's "principle of limited possibilities" in a broader sphere. Failure to recognize the relevance of interdependence and attendant structural restraint leads to utopian thought'.[159] The same idea reappears in the straightforward and generalised formulation: 'I assume that the structure constrains individuals variously situated within it to develop cultural emphases, social behaviour patterns and psychological bents'.[160]

The most famous application of the idea is found as early as 1938, in Merton's theory of deviance where the main explanatory condition is defined as one in which 'the social structure rigorously restricts or completely closes access to approved modes of reaching [culturally extolled] goals *for a considerable part of the same population*'.[161] Another early example, in 1948, long before the time of 'affirmative action' legislation, is the analysis of structural limits of legal reform: 'Whether a law providing for equitable access to jobs will in fact produce this result depends not only on the law itself as on the rest of the social structure. The law is a small, though important, part of the whole'.[162]

But the structural context is not conceived only in negative terms, as a *limiting constraint*, but also as a positive influence, *facilitating*, encouraging, stimulating certain choices by actors or agents: 'the social structure strains the cultural values, making action in accord with them readily possible for those occupying certain statuses within the society and difficult or impossible for others. . . . The social structure acts as a barrier or as an open door to the acting out of cultural mandates'.[163]

Applications of this notion in Merton's concrete analyses are legion. One example is the study of 'institutionalized altruism', where this relatively infrequent pattern of behaviour is found to be produced in specific structural contexts: 'Institutionalized altruism is the special form of altruism in which structural arrangements, notably the distribution of rewards and penalties, promote behavior that is beneficial to others. [In this situation] alternatives of action are weighted by social structure to increase the rate at which individuals choose altruistic actions beyond what it would otherwise be'.[164] Another example is in the analysis of 'sociological ambivalence' as deriving from specific social structures; Merton and Elinor Barber propose to find out 'how and to what extent ambivalence comes to be built into the very structure of social relations', and more specifically, to study 'the processes through which social structures generate the circumstances in which ambivalence is embedded in particular statuses and status-sets together with their associated social roles'.[165]

Apart from the *generic notion* of the social structure, certain properties distinguish Merton's *specific notion* of it. First of all, Merton's idea of social structure is synthetising since it is clearly informed by all four criteria – and also complex and multidimensional. This property is variously manifested. Social structure covers a plurality of components, elements, items shaped into various kinds of structures. As Barbano puts it: 'Merton's analysis of social structure does not postulate holisitic social entities but pluralistic social structures'.[166] These pluralistic components are structurally varied: statuses, roles, role-sets, status-sets, status-occupants, status-distributions, opportunity-structures, control-structures, norms, norm-sets, values, institutions, collectivities, groups, organisations, etc. These components cohere on various levels: micro-level and macro-level, the cultural or normative level and the social or opportunities level. Members of the society are variously aware in gradation of the workings of the social structure, ranging from the thoroughly latent to the fully manifest. In a geometric metaphor, in Merton's conception, social structure can be represented by a three-dimensional spatial model, like a molecule, in which single atoms are caught in the multidimensional network of interlinkages, rather than by a diagram on a single plane.

Another property of Merton's idea of social structure is the emphasis on asymmetrical relationships: conflicts, contradictions, strains, tensions, ambivalences. As Merton puts it: 'It is fundamental, not incidental to the paradigm of structural analysis that *social structures generate social conflict* by being differentiated, in historically differing extent and kind, into interlocking arrays of social statuses, strata, organizations, and communities that have their own and therefore potentially conflicting as well as common interests and values'.[167] A special case is found in the concept of 'sociological ambivalence' which holds that 'normative structures do not have unified norm-sets'; rather, ambivalence is built into those structures 'in the form of incompatible patterned expectations and a "dynamic alternation of norms and counter-norms" in social roles'.[168]

Finally, Merton's conception of social structure holds it to be auto-dynamic, producing endogenous pressures toward its own transformation: '*social structures generate both changes within the structure and changes of the structure* and . . . these types of change come about through cumulatively patterned choices in behavior and the amplification of dysfunctional consequences resulting from certain kinds of strains, conflicts, and contradictions in the differentiated social structure'.[169]

Resting on such a concept of social structure, the term 'structural analysis' can have two distinct meanings: the analysis *of* social structures or analysis *with reference* to social structures. The first meaning is unspecific, as it covers every kind of sociological analysis which by definition must treat some components of society or some of their interrelations. It is only the second meaning which identifies the sociological orientation properly known as 'sociological structuralism'. This requires structural analysis to examine any sociologically interesting unit from the perspective of its location in a larger structural context, with particular emphasis on the constraining or facilitating influences of this context on the state and transformation of the unit. Thus, if the focus is on individual members of society engaging in a social activity, the aspect of interest to a sociologist is their location in a structural network: in a ritual or ceremony, for example, a 'description of the participants (and on-lookers) is in *structural terms*, that is, in terms of locating these people in their inter-connected social statuses . . . in terms of role, status, group affiliation and the interrelations among these'.[170] To paraphrase Merton's characterisation of functional analysis, one may say that the central orientation of structural analysis is the practice of interpreting data by establishing their determinants in the larger structures in which they are implicated.

In this case 'interpreting data' may well mean not only identifying, describing, but also explaining data. Structural explanations are in principle valid in form, free from the risk of finalism or teleology, since they do not refer to any succeeding events or states of the social system, but rather to conditions preceding, or at most concurrent with the problematic phenomena. In such structural explanations the phenomenon is explained by invoking *structural laws*, it means uniformities of constraining or facilitating consequences of certain locations in the social structure plus specifying the *structural conditions* which establish the fact that a problematic phenomenon is so located. In this sense, it can be conjectured that all of Merton's explanations of social phenomena (even those which are labelled as functional explanations) are ultimately structural. That accords with Blau's observation that 'the structural nature of Merton's explanatory principles is apparent in his substantive theoretical writings'.[171]

For example, even in Merton's early functional writings, when he attempts to explain the phenomenon of structurally induced deviance, he searches for the ways in which 'some *social structures exert a definite pressure upon certain persons in the society to engage in non-conforming rather than conforming conduct*'.[172] The famous and influential theory of 'Anomie and Deviation' (presented first in the 1938 article 'Social Structure and Anomie') is for me a prime example of structural analysis (and not, as most commentators believe, of functional analysis). Here, the explanation of differential rates of deviance rests on locating various types of deviants in differing planes of the social structure, such that some are subjected to structural cross-pressures. Some of these pressures originate in the normative structure, directing people toward certain goals; others originate in the opportunity structure, blocking their access to the legitimate means for seeking these goals. Deviant adaptation is a to-be-expected outcome of such a situation; thus, it is explained structurally in the full sense of the concept of explanation. As Moore puts it: 'it goes beyond a mere recognition of the propensity to sin and identifies society as an instigator of sin'.[173]

Combining functional and structural analysis

Functional analysis specifies the *consequences* of a social phenomenon for its differentiated structural context; structural analysis searches for the *determinants* of the phenomenon in its structural context. Obviously, both orientations refer to the different sides of the same coin: they scrutinise two vectors of the same relationship, between a social phenomenon and its structural context. They are mutually complementary. Blau recognises this complementarity quite clearly: 'the functional paradigm is in effect a structural paradigm, which accounts for observable social patterns in terms of the structural conditions that give rise to them, except that it supplements this analysis of antecedents by stressing the importance of tracing the functional and dysfunctional consequences of these patterns'.[174]

The same point has been brilliantly grasped by Stinchcombe in his reconstruction of Merton's theoretical logic, or as he calls it 'the paradigm behind the paradigms in Merton's work on social structure'.[175] The *structural aspect* of the paradigm describes the mechanisms by which the set of alternative possibilities for action becomes delimited and differentiated for each kind of structure, and for each position within that structure. The *functional aspect* focuses on the mechanisms through which each of the alternative action-possibilities produces institutional consequences, significant for the structure as a whole or any segments thereof. Merton's explanatory interest rests on *patterned choices* within designated structural and functional conditions, this providing the mediating link between structural pressures and functional outcomes. In Stinchcombe's words: 'the core process that Merton conceives as central to social structure is the choice between socially structured alternatives'.[176] And further: 'the core variable to be explained is different rates of choice in different social positions in a structure, or in different structures, between these institutionally consequential alternatives'.[177]

In Stinchcombe's reconstruction, the basic causal process goes from 'structural forces to institutionally consequential choices, and thence to institutional patterns'.[178] He refers to Merton's 'recasting of the nature of functional analysis' by drawing upon the notion of feedback or what came to be known even later as 'causal loops'. Two kinds of causal loops are distinguished in Stinchcombe's account: one through which 'institutional consequences of action act back to shape the nature of the alternatives that people are posed with',[179] and another, through which the repetition of certain choices shapes the permanent tendencies of the 'social character' amplifying the chances for similar choices in the future (or in other words, producing the 'systematic biographical patterning of choices'[180]). As Stinchcombe puts it: 'Repetitive situational adaptations form character'.[181]

He goes on to dissect the processes of structural pressure into two distinct mechanisms: one which operates, so-to-say, *from the outside* of the choosing agent, setting the range of alternatives open to him and the other which operates *from the inside*, by shaping the motivations for particular choices among available alternatives. 'Externally constraining social facts have to get into people's mind in order to constrain them'.[182] This 'structural induction of motives' is realised by means of four sub-processes: 'socialization into a culture, reward systems, self-affirmation in a social role, and structurally induced needs'.[183]

An excellent example of combined functional and structural approach is to be found in the Merton–Lazarsfeld study of friendship formation. The authors focus on the pattern of homophily (i.e., by way of reminder, the choice of friends from people who are like oneself in some designated respect). A large part of the analysis is functional, an inquiry into 'the consequences of the same relations for those directly involved in them and for the larger group at particular times'.[184] Merton goes on: 'On this plane of functional sociology, it is the problem of discovering the processes through which different degrees of homophily become functionally appropriate or inappropriate for different types of environing social structure'.[185] But equal attention is devoted to structural considerations, the contexts inhibiting or facilitating the occurrence of homophily. The social structure (mainly status differentiation in the community) and the cultural or normative structure are discussed separately. And finally the study states the necessity of searching for *feedbacks* or *causal loops*: 'tracing the processes through which different degrees of homophily within designated types of social structure and culture produce functional and dysfunctional consequences which in turn react to affect the patterns of friendship'.[186]

The third dimension: temporal analysis

As we have seen Merton focuses on the operation of structural pressures on indicated elements of society and the functional contribution of elements to social structure. Thus far, this takes the existence of those structures for granted, as given. But it is, of course, also of interest to inquire how the social structures *originate in the first place*, and how they subsequently evolve, or develop. In other words, to complete the picture one must study the processes of morphogenesis: the production and reproduction of social structures.[187] This requires functional and structural analyses to be supplemented with a third approach, which I will describe as temporal analysis.

In various places of Merton's work there are signs of clear recognition of the importance of temporal dimension as well as hunches about solution of this problem. I claim that there is a rudimentary (often implicit) temporal orientation in Merton's analyses, which seems to be growing in importance as his work proceeds. From the early analysis of 'social time' in a paper written together with Sorokin,[188] to the recent memorial piece written in honour of Lewis Coser on 'socially expected durations',[189] Merton indicates awareness and implications of 'the important sociological commonplace that all manner of social structures have their temporal contexts',[190] and refers to 'the perspective of historical sociology, that past and present contexts of those structures constrain or facilitate their development in certain rather than other directions'.[191]

Put most generally, a temporal orientation requires treating the present state of affairs as a phase in a continuous time-sequence, the *accumulated outcome* of past processes, and the *embedded potentials* for future process. In this theoretical perspective, the present state of affairs is seen as endowed with a historical coefficient; its character depends on the location in the historical sequence, the nature of preceding events and the pool of possible subsequent events. The crucial implication of this perspective is that superficially identical or similar situations may turn out to be quite different in their meaning and consequences, depending on their place in a historical sequence. The factor of time, of 'age' enters not as an ordering device, not in the sense of 'dating', but as inherent, ontological, causally significant dimension of the situation.

Thus, a temporal analysis of a present social reality can take two directions: retrospective − looking back and reconstructing the causal chain leading to present conditions (one may speak here of genetic analysis) and prospective, projecting future developments regarded as potentially inherent in present conditions (one speaks of futurological analysis).

In this general sense, temporal analysis is not restricted to the level of macro-structures; it is equally relevant with respect to mezzo-structures and micro-structures. In the case of macro-structures − societies, nations, economies, political systems etc. − it comes closest to what is actually being done by historians; especially the theoretically oriented historian of the modern brand. But the same logic applies to mezzo-structures: collectivities, groups, communities − which also have specific, time-bound, sequential fates. To distinguish this from grand 'History', one might perhaps use the term 'chronicle'. Finally, a historical coefficient is obviously present on the level of micro-structures: of social actions, interactions, relations. 'Career' and 'biography' are terms often used in this connection.

Merton's explicit acknowledgement of a temporal orientation is clear in his article from the late 1950s: 'it is possible to distinguish between a theory which deals only with the responses of individuals to culturally-induced stresses . . . and a theory which deals also with *the effects of the aggregated and sometimes socially organized responses upon the normative structure itself*'.[192] Consequently, he emphasises the need for temporal analysis, the study of morphogenesis, alongside with structural (and presumably functional) analysis: 'sociologists have never lost sight of the principle that social relations are sustained by social processes . . . It is clear . . . that the observed patterns can in turn be conceived as the resultants of social interaction, as process rather than product'.[193]

But his actual applications of such perspective focus – in line with his general theoretical and empirical interests – on the micro-structural and at most mezzo-structural level. For example, he notices the relevance of personal 'biography' for present conduct: 'not only his current status but also his past history of statuses affect the present and future behavior of the individual'.[194] And, in a more metaphorical vein: 'Just as the new convert is more royalist than the king, so the ex-royalist is more republican than the *citoyen*, born and bred'.[195] The importance of the past course of group-development on its present functioning is also noticed: 'the problem of the ways in which the past histories of large aggregates of pairs affect the probable course of their social relationships'.[196] We find an early clear recognition of time-location as a significant variable in studying individual acts and interactions as well as human groups: 'the same act will have quite different consequences according to the phase of the system of social interaction in which it occurs . . . The same act has different probabilities of occurring and different social and psychological consequences when it does occur, depending upon the phase in the system of social interaction'.[197] And in another connection: 'The actual "age" of a group is a property which presumably affects other properties of the group: its flexibility, relative standing, system of normative controls etc.'.[198]

There is an important article that sets forth particularly clear analysis of the temporal dimension of a social phenomenon. I refer again to the study of friendship as a social process, with correlative analyses by Merton and Lazarsfeld. In this inquiry, the explicit choice of a *processual perspective* leads the authors toward a temporal (genetic) analysis *par excellence*. The observable, structural patterns are seen as a result of morphogenesis: 'By selective and adjustive processes in friendship we mean patterned sequences of social interaction between friends in which each phase generates and regulates the subsequent phase in such a manner as to give rise to the observed patterns of friendship between people of designated kinds'.[199] The forms of friendship are examined in terms of patterned sequence: 'friendships are in fact continually in process of change – some being only in the early stages of formation, others long and firmly established, and still others, for one reason or another, being well along toward dissolution. Static observations, made at a given instant, tempt one to drop this obvious fact from view. We must form a picture or a model of the dynamic processes, both social and psychological, of which the observed patterns of friendship are merely resultants'.[200] The genetic perspective allows us to see that even identical expressions of friendship differ depending on the history of the relationship: 'will disagreeing friends who have exhibited both friendship and disagreement in the past differ, in their future patterns, from disagreeing friends who previously agreed? There is reason to believe that they will'.[201]

However, even in this concrete, empirical study, informed by the genetic perspective, there is a significant gap: no explicit account is given of the mechanisms through which the past sequence affects present state of affairs. Some hint of this mechanism is found, perhaps, in Merton's concept of the 'accumulation of advantages and disadvantages' which has proved fruitful in the sociology of science.[202] Merton moves toward generalising this concept in his paradigm for structural analysis: 'On the macro-level, the social distributions (i.e., the concentration and dispersion) of authority, power, influence, and prestige comprise structures of social control that change historically, partly through processes of 'accumulation of advantage and disadvantage' accruing to people occupying diverse stratified positions in that structure (subject to processes of feedback under conditions still poorly understood)'.[203] Still, this solution is at most partial and not fully explored. We shall have occasion to return to this concept, but the problem remains: *how* does the past influence the present; *how* does a social or cultural heritage limit or direct subsequent conduct; *how* is the collective memory produced; *how* the collective (social) learning proceeds? The problem becomes more and more difficult when one moves from the level of individual biography to the level of group-chronicle or social history.

So far I have documented Merton's utilisation of genetic analysis. But in his most recent work, he does take up the other side of the temporal orientation, focusing on the ways in which *the future is embedded in the present*. His main concept for dealing with this aspect of social reality, 'a prime temporal component of social structures and interpersonal relations' is that of 'socially expected durations'.[204] He emphasises that this concept 'focuses on time future, on the social framework of prospective durations'.[205] But at the same time, it refers to present structural arrangements, it designates 'a consequential property of social structures of every kind: of groups and organizations, of social statuses and role-sets, and of social relationships'.[206] Merton's recent, full definition runs this way: 'Socially expected durations – hereafter, SED or SEDs for short – are socially prescribed or collectively patterned expectations about temporal durations embedded in social structures of various kinds: for example, the length of time that individuals are institutionally permitted to occupy particular statuses (such as an office in an organization or membership in a group); the assumed probable durations of diverse kinds of social relationships (such as friendship or a professional–client relation); and the patterned and therefore anticipated longevity of individual occupants of statuses, of groups, and of organizations'.[207] He strongly emphasises the structural quality of SEDs as collective and patterned (normative): 'Such structurally defined durations were not expectations which individuals *happened* to have; they were, rather, normatively prescribed and, in varying degrees, authoritatively enforced durations'.[208]

Such shared, patterned, normatively prescribed expectations of the future course of events inherent in present social structure significantly influence current behaviour and processes. For example: interpersonal relationships categorised as *Gemeinschaft* relations, such as acquaintanceship and marriage have diverse currently structural properties owing to quite different expectations of their continuation: 'marriage, which even in these days of growing serial monogamy, is normatively defined as presumptively "permanent or having an indefinitely extended duration" will both generate and tolerate heavier loads of hostility as well as affection than relations, such as acquaintanceship, which are defined as temporary. As a result, the enduring relationship accumulates a greater stock of ambivalence'.[209] Another example of the current effect of SEDs is the 'lame-duck pattern' – the case of the 'incumbent of a social position which is to be vacated at a specified time in the comparatively near future'.[210] The anticipatory behaviour of both the incumbents of such positions and of their role-partners and associates is significantly influenced by the temporal perspective.

It is a fair guess that Merton will pay growing attention to the temporal dimension of social life, perhaps arriving at a third paradigm – along with the paradigms for functional analysis and structural analysis – this one for temporal analysis.[211] This is needed to give his sociological orientation more rounded form by simultaneously taking functional, structural and temporal aspects of social phenomena into systematic account. And this would signify a fulfilment of the legacy of his two self-acknowledged masters, not alone Durkheim but also Marx.

6
On Social Structure

Early in his career, Merton observed: 'We have many concepts but fewer confirmed theories; many points of view, but few theorems; many "approaches" but few arrivals. Perhaps some further change in emphasis would be all to the good'.[1] In the chapters to come we shall see how he heeds his own advice. Here, we leave the level of Merton's approaches, and focus on his arrivals, the substantive claims about the subject-matter of sociology developed through his specific methodology and theoretical orientation. Having studied his ideas about science and sociology, it is high time to find out what he thinks about society. Apart from its intrinsic interest, an endeavour of this kind should bring a bonus. As biblical wisdom has it: by their fruits you shall know them. An appraisal of Merton's substantive results will provide an indirect clue to the value of his method and approach. To the extent that the arrival is successful, it suggests that the road was well-chosen.

Merton does not present a substantive image of society in systematic fashion. Instead of sustained, unified exposition, he chooses the method of selecting particular problems and elucidating them in a detailed and thorough manner. The result: islands of enlightenment dispersed here and there in a sea of twilight, and occasional darkness. This has led some commentators to claim that Merton's theory is not systematic. Since one fundamental assumption of this book is precisely the reverse – namely that there *is* a system of theory in Merton's work, or to put it metaphorically, that there is an underlying logic or pattern in the mosaic of his theoretical contributions – I shall try to identify and clarify this system, logic and pattern.

That objective cannot be reached through the detached reporting or literal summarising of Merton's ideas. It requires considerable licence on the part of the analyst. He must supply the links between various components of the image of society and rearrange them to produce a coherent whole. This is the job of synthetic reconstruction. Furthermore, he must sometimes choose among the multiple formulations of the same idea, the one to be taken as the most fundamental. Merton is a persistent scholar; he begins with a hunch, develops it a little and then returns to it many times, often after many years, elaborating, modifying and testing the crucial idea. I shall abstract from those twisting roads to sociological wisdom and, as a rule, adopt the ideas in their final shape, assuming that in this case the latest word *is* the best word.[2] All this imposes a job of critical selection.

The reconstructive and selective input of the analyst is evident already in the ordering of the chapters to come. I shall first present my interpretation of the anatomy of society described in Merton's work; its components, aspects, dimensions and their intricate interrelations. I shall then outline the dynamics of society; the sources and mechanisms of social change as Merton conceives them. And finally, I shall sketch Merton's image of the agents ultimately responsible for the operation and transformation of society – human beings and their actions.

Anatomy of social structure

Attempting to reconstruct the complex, differentiated and heterogenous whole described as human society, I shall be guided by one main concern: to specify and rigorously distinguish its various levels, dimensions and aspects from the point of view of their ontological nature. As this is *not* Merton's main concern, I shall have to depart at some points from his literal statements, suggesting some reinterpretation of his categories or terminological usages. The justification for such a procedure will be found both in Merton's explicit pronouncements concerning the structural orientation, and in several implicit hints dispersed throughout his work.

The crucial idea underlying my interpretation comes down to a double distinction: first, the distinction between social structure and social life; and second, the distinction between three aspects of social status and three dimensions of social structure – normative, opportunity and ideal.

The notion of social structure, explicated in the preceding chapter, implies a basic duality. If structure is seen as a network of interrelations, there must be something on which it is predicated. If structure is seen as a pattern, there must be something subjected to patterning. If structure is seen as something hidden, deep, underlying, there obviously must be something on the surface under which it is hidden. And if structure is seen as determining, constraining, and facilitating, there must be something which is determined, constrained, or facilitated. Merton never gives a name to that complementary dimension of social reality. I shall therefore refer to it by the term he uses in presumably similar sense in one of his empirical studies,[3] the neutral, common-sense term, 'social life'. Thus, as a first approximation, the social reality may be represented as a two-tier edifice, consisting of social structure and social life.

The status of the two dimensions differs in fundamental ontological respects. Social structure refers to *abstract* properties and relations, which can only be inferred, assumed, posited. Social life refers to *concrete*, actual phenomena, which can be observed, empirically identified, asserted. The social structure refers to an inter-individual (if not super-individual) reality, shared by a plurality of people, and is, in this sense, objective. Social life refers ultimately to the actual conduct of human individuals (in isolation or in collectivities), their actions and interactions, always full of subjective, idiosyncratic components. To grasp the intuitive distinction more fully, compare the relationship described as love with the kiss; the social role of a dentist and extracting the tooth; the norms of etiquette and eating at Maxim's; class interest and going on strike. The two levels must be characterised separately. Only then can they be recombined by establishing the nature of the links that bind them together. I begin with the level of social structure.

Merton's core idea, fully congruent with his structural orientation, is to consider human individuals as *structurally located*, anchored in the network of social relationships. The structural location of a person is described as his or her social status; an identifiable 'position in a social system occupied by designated individuals'.[4] A doctor, a student, a housewife, a father – are examples of statuses. Each social status, considered as the central building-block of a social structure, has three distinct aspects. Attached to it is a patterned set of social (shared) expectations concerning the proper behaviour of any incumbent. This is a normative aspect of a status, grasped by Merton's important concept of a 'role-set': 'that complement of role relationships which persons have by virtue of occupying a particular social status'.[5] Similarly, each social status has an attached set of 'life-chances', options, resources, facilities available to the incumbents. This is an opportunity-aspect of a status.[6] Finally, each status has an attached set of patterned beliefs, ideas, creeds typically held by any incumbent. This is an ideal aspect of a status.

Merton's pervasive preoccupation is with the plurality, differentiation and heterogeneity of the social structure: 'even the seemingly simple social structure is extremely complex'.[7] This leads him to the significant observation that individuals inexorably occupy *multiple*, rather than single statuses, and to the related concept of 'status-set': 'the complement of social statuses of an individual'.[8] This concept refers to the particular moment in time; it is static in nature. Introducing the time dimension Merton supplements the analysis with the dynamic concept of a 'status-sequence'. 'Considered as changing in the course of time, the succession of statuses occurring with sufficient frequency as to be socially patterned will be designated as a *status-sequence*, as in the case, for example, of the statuses successively occupied by a medical student, intern, resident, and independent medical practitioner'.[9]

Utilising those notions Merton formulates the definition of the social structure: 'The patterned arrangements of role-sets, status-sets and status-sequences can be held to comprise the social structure'.[10]

This definition seems to me to be biased in the normative direction, as it singles out the role aspect of the social status. Merton does not elaborate on the other two aspects: the aspects of opportunities and ideas associated with a status. Perhaps, by analogy, it would be possible to extend his analysis of opportunity aspect by introducing a notion of opportunity-set, the complement of opportunities linked in a patterned way to a status-set; as well as his analysis of the ideal aspect by introducing a notion of ideology, a patterned network of ideas and beliefs. But this would lead me too far from Merton.

Instead, I propose to change a perspective and analyse social structure in abstraction from the individuals occupying statuses and performing roles. We shall focus on the social structure *per se*, as a skeleton of the social world, trying to identify its dimensions and components. Such analysis will be complementary to the image presented so far.

In one of his earliest analytic efforts, Merton distinguished the concept of cultural structure from that of social structure in the narrow sense; 'the salient environment of individuals can be usefully thought of as involving the cultural structure, on the one hand, and the social structure, on the other'.[11] The definitions follow: 'cultural structure may be defined as that organized set of normative values governing behavior which is common to members of a designated society or group. And by social structure is meant that organized set of social relationships in which members of the society or group are variously implicated'.[12] Both categories have been elaborated and modified in later work. Cultural structure comes to be characterised exclusively in normative terms. In certain specific contexts, it is replaced by the notion of 'normative subculture' understood as 'a body of shared and transmitted ideas, values, and standards toward which members of the profession are expected to orient their behavior'.[13] Similarly, the idea of social structure in the narrow sense is gradually enriched with the help of the notion of opportunity-structure. As early as the second edition of *Social Theory and Social Structure*, Merton suggests that this notion may be useful. He alludes to a 'still loosely utilized but important concept of what Weber called "life-chances" in the opportunity-structure'.[14] This concept is crucial to the developing theory of anomie and deviation. The definition, clearly informed by anomie-theory runs as follows: 'opportunity structure [is] the location of people in the social structure that affects the probability of their moving toward culturally emphasized goals in ways that are normatively approved'.[15] The concept has wider applications. Merton refers in various contexts to 'socially structured capacities',[16] 'socially structured opportunities',[17] 'socially restricted opportunities',[18] 'the structure of opportunity', 'the facilities provided by a social position',[19] 'social-structural differences in ease or difficulty of role-performance',[20] 'differential advantage deriving from the current arrangements',[21] 'vested interests'[22] etc. It seems justified to assume that he comes to differentiate between the normative and opportunity dimensions of the social structure.

But in various places in his work, a third dimension appears as well. In one place he refers to the 'state of the public mind' or 'prevalent outlook';[23] at another, he speaks of perspective and outlook as 'a product of social position';[24] at still another he introduces 'the basic distinctions between attitudes and overt behavior, and between publicly affirmed and privately held attitudes'.[25] Finally, he clearly indicates that norms and values are conceived of as different from beliefs *about* norms and values typically shared in a society. Referring to racial and ethnic inequities, he makes the significant statement: 'It is a relation not between two variables; official creed, and private practice, but between three: first, the cultural creed honored in cultural tradition and partly enacted into law [normative structure?], second, the beliefs and attitudes of individuals regarding the principles of the creed; and third, the actual practices of individuals with reference to it [social life?]'.[26] These distinctions seem to refer to the domain of social consciousness, as structural, not psychological dimension; the public, shared, patterned beliefs, creeds, appraisals, expectations rather than private, individual, idiosyncratic convictions. Although Merton does not introduce a separate term to refer to this domain, I shall designate it, in neutral fashion, as 'the ideal structure'.

Thus, the anatomy of the social structure is to be represented as the combination of three dimensions: normative structure, opportunity-structure and ideal structure. Each is clearly of different ontological nature. And each deserves more thorough study.

The most extensive analysis refers to normative structure, which for Merton seems to constitute the core of social structure. The normative bias is visible again, this time from the abstract perspective. In fact, in the standard, textbook expositions of Merton's image of social structure with its emphasis on the notion of role-set, there is sometimes an imputation of normative reductionism. In my reading, Merton is far from that, and normative structure – even though commanding the major share of his attention – is only one dimension of his complex and differentiated concept of social structure.

The normative structure is a network that binds together several and varied components. Those components seem to be of three orders. The first-order components may be thought of as a sort of ultimate units or atoms on which the structure is based. These first-order components of the normative structure can be distinguished according to the phases of action they regulate. They are conceived of as 'analytically separable although they merge in concrete situations', and are designated as 'culturally defined goals' and 'institutional norms'.[27] To simplify the discussion, I shall refer to them as values and norms, respectively.

Values are understood as the prescribed, expected, legitimate goals of activity: 'objectives for all or for diversely located members of the society . . . the things "worth striving for" '.[28] The Loomises grasp the crucial property of values as *shared* and *objectified*: 'To the degree that it is shared by sizeable numbers of people as a basis for interaction it becomes an institutionalized goal and as such becomes part of the social structure'.[29] And they go on to note with reference to norms: 'To the degree that they become definitions of expected behavior in social interaction they are institutionalized as parts of the social structure'.[30] Thus, norms are understood as the prescribed, expected, legitimate courses of activity, indicating the right means to given ends. They are, in Merton's words, 'the morally binding expectations of appropriate behavior prevailingly held by those subject to the institution',[31] 'technically and morally allowable patterns of behavior indicating what is prescribed, preferred, permitted, or proscribed'.[32] Merton adopts the standard typology of norms originating in Sumner's work: 'Groups and organizations differ in the extent to which they exercise control through expressly formulated rules (law); through less definitely formulated but definitely patterned expectations of behavior which are reinforced by sentiment and supporting moral doctrine (mores); and through routinized, often habitual but less strongly affective, expectations (folkways)'.[33]

Those basic elements cluster into second-order components, metaphorically speaking, the molecules. Again there are two kinds, distinguished according to the principles of their constitution and construction: roles and institutions. As concerns the concept of a role, Merton makes a crucial analytic step separating the *normative dimension* (which belongs to the social structure), and the *behavioural dimension* (which belongs to what I am describing as social life). Since he is taking the concept of a role from Linton who meant by it 'the behavioral enacting of the patterned expectations attributed to . . . position',[34] Merton sometimes seems to retain the behavioural dimension as intrinsic to a role. But one can see that later he tends to reserve the term exclusively for the normative dimension. He says at one place, for example, 'From the perspective of sociological ambivalence, we see a social role as a dynamic organization of norms and counter-norms';[35] and at another, he identifies social role with 'culturally defined expectations'.[36] In the purely normative sense, as a component of the normative structure, the role appears as a cluster of norms and values prescribing the behaviour of an actor *vis-à-vis* each of the typical partners of his social position (the 'alters', as Parsons would put it). In other words, it is a set of shared expectations of behaviour in relation to various kinds of people with whom one is related by virtue of occupying a particular position (status). Thus, the role of a physician toward a patient, the role of a teacher toward a student, the role of a husband toward a wife.

The concept of institution is undoubtedly conceived of by Merton in normative terms, even though its precise definition is not given. But I find strong corroboration of imputing to him the usage suggested for example by Kingsley Davis, in which it signifies the cluster of norms and values integrated around a major societal function or domain of social life.[37] The family, religion, economy, polity, education, science – are cases in point. For example, Merton emphasises its normative core when he introduces the idea of science as, in one aspect, an institution: 'Like other institutions, science has its corpus of shared and transmitted ideas, values and standards designed to govern the behavior of those connected with the institution'.[38]

Finally, the most complex, the third-order components of a normative structure arise by clustering the elementary entities. In this connection, Merton introduces the fruitful idea of a role set. He starts by observing that 'a particular social status involves, not a single associated role, but an array of associated roles'.[39] Thus, the single status of a student entails roles relating the status-occupant to teachers, student peers and superiors, administrators, schools nurses, etc.; the single status of a physician entails roles relating him to patients, fellow doctors, nurses, technicians, hospital administrators, social workers, medical insurance companies, etc; the single status of a daughter entails roles relating her at least to a mother and father, and to sisters, brothers, grandparents, and more remote relatives, as the case might be. Merton rejects the prior notion (for example typical of Linton) that each social position or status involves a *single* role and emphasises the analytical and ontological importance of noting that it involves *a set* of roles: 'This fact of structure can be registered by a distinctive term, role-set, by which I mean that complement of role relationships which persons have by virtue of occupying a particular social status'.[40]

Merton notes that the role-partners (the 'alters') related to each social status, themselves differ significantly with respect to other status dimensions: He proceeds to observe that the status occupant having a role-set involves 'the structural circumstance' that their 'role partners . . . are differently located in the social structures. As a result, these others have, in some measure, values, [interests, ideas] and moral expectations differing from those held by the occupant of the status in question . . . [This constitutes] a structural source of instability in the role-set'.[41] An important elaboration of that point was carried out by Peter Blau. His concept of 'status complements' deals with the internal composition of the collectivities of role partners which stand in a specific role relationship to an individual, or briefly: 'the composition of alters who stand in a specific role-relation to egos. Egos are all incumbents of a given status'.[42] The degree and kinds of variation in the status-complement significantly affect role relations. Two kinds of variation are distinguished: horizontal differentiation is called 'social heterogeneity' (example: the division of labour), and vertical differentiation, 'status inequality' (example: variations in power or reputation).[43] Those varying dimensions of differentiation Blau describes as 'parameters of social structure', and illustrates their empirical validity in analysis of the academic status where they serve to identify the 'status complements' of faculty members, students, researchers, technicians etc., and their bearing on the respective social role of a scholar.

Note that the concept of a role-set relates to a single status. Further structural complexity arises from the basic structural fact that individuals invariably occupy multiple statuses, often in 'differing institutional spheres' (example: father, husband, physician, Catholic, Social Democrat, head of School Board, member of tennis club), 'each of the statuses in turn having its distinctive role-set'.[44] Merton refers to this situation with the term status-set. It should be emphasised though that here the concept of status-set is applied only in one of its aspects – the normative one – and signifies the complex cluster of role-sets cohering around a set of social statuses held by an individual at the same time. Merton puts great emphasis on the complexity and heterogeneity of status-sets and treats it as a basic variable in status-set analysis. And adding a dynamic dimension, he proposes to study the patterned sequences of role-sets and status-sets (clusters of role-sets).[45]

The concept of a status-set (in its normative aspect) is very powerful analytically. Unfortunately, so far Merton has not developed the detailed analysis of status-set in his printed work. There are only some dispersed hints in *Social Theory and Social Structure*,[46] and some selected points in the 1970 paper on 'Insiders and Outsiders'.[47] Merton developed this topic extensively by means of 'oral publication' in a series of more than 20 lectures in the 1960s and 1970s. He focused then on four analytic problems: the distinction of cross-cutting status-sets and mutually exclusive status-sets; the distinction of dominant, salient and central statuses in status-sets;[48] the process of status- and role-accumulation and decrement; and the process of activation of statuses in status-sets, with emphasis on functionally relevant and functionally irrelevant statuses. Merton's students have at times made use of these oral publications in their work,[49] but one can hope that Merton will put together those insightful analyses in a printed form.

Social institutions – another type of component of the normative structure – also interrelate producing more complex totalities. Merton clearly recognises this, even though he does not pay much attention to those totalities. It is, he says, 'the general sociological premise that the institutional orders coexisting in a society – the family, economy and polity, science, religion and education – are variously interdependent while each still retains a measure of independence'. Such totalities of interdependent, while partly independent, institutions are probably what Merton refers to at places as the 'general cultural systems', or 'institutional complexes'.[50]

Such is the pluralistic and multi-level composition of a normative structure. The second dimension of social structure, the opportunity structure, is not analysed as thoroughly. For that reason, the place of interpretation and conjecture in this account grows. At the most elementary level, each status may be construed as having its own variable scope of opportunities, structurally determined and *independent of the qualities of particular incumbents*. These opportunities include access to resources, facilities, access to legitimate and illegitimate means to action, generalised currencies of social interaction such as influence, power, wealth, knowledge, prestige, etc. The incumbents of a status have vested interests in extending the scope of opportunities associated with that status or at least in keeping it intact. In Merton's words: 'Vested interests oppose any new order which either eliminates or at least makes uncertain their differential advantage deriving from the current arrangements'.[51]

The more complex, second-order components of the opportunity structure may be construed by analogy to Merton's analysis of normative structure. The concepts of 'opportunity-set' and 'opportunity-sequence' could be proposed to deal with the clusters of opportunities associated with a status-set, or a status-sequence, respectively. It would be interesting to see how the variable composition of the total scope of opportunities associated with an individual's status-set (or status-sequence) mutually amplifies, diminishes or even neutralises his actual chances of effectively using them. The idea of congruent, ambivalent or even contradictory vested interests attaching to the same status is also worthy of further elaboration, apart from notions of 'sociological ambivalence' or 'role-conflict', which in my interpretation – as shall be seen – refer exclusively to the normative dimension of social structure.

The most complex, third-order component of the opportunity structure is the stratificational hierarchy. Merton describes it as 'the hierarchic differentiation of statuses',[52] where the basis of differentiation is precisely the variable scope of opportunities of specified type attaching to each status (for example: variable access to wealth, or education, or power, or prestige, etc.). This variety of the notion of opportunity structure is most extensively put to use in his theory of anomie and deviant behaviour. Various social strata or classes are seen as having differential access to legitimate (normatively prescribed) means of reaching goals related to cultural values. For example: 'recourse to legitimate channels for "getting in the money" is limited by a class structure. . . . Of those located in the lower reaches of the social structure, the culture [normative structure] makes incompatible demands. On the one hand, they are asked to orient their conduct toward the prospect of large wealth . . . and on the other, they are largely denied effective opportunities to do so institutionally'.[53]

Opportunities of one kind (say: access to education) which define one stratificational hierarchy are not independent of opportunities of another kind (say: access to power), which define another stratificational hierarchy. In particular social structures, various kinds of opportunities are typically related in patterned fashion: 'populations may be socially stratified in different hierarchies. In ways not too clearly understood, these several hierarchies of stratification are inter-related'.[54] And the potential relations are quite varied: mutually supportive (when being educated helps becoming rich), mutually exclusive (when having power hinders obtaining prestige), or mutually neutral (when having power and acquiring high level of education are independent). Certain types of status provide determining opportunities that in turn provide access to others; while other statuses become secondary, or irrelevant for obtaining access to further opportunities. Thus, wealth as strategic can enlarge access to education, power, prestige etc. Every social structure has typical clusters of various kinds of opportunities, or otherwise put, of various dimensions of stratification. They produce a master, composite hierarchy of opportunities, vested interests, or strata (the term 'class structure' could perhaps be reserved for a synthesised differentiation). The context of such patterned clusters determines actual meaning of each status; it is a different thing to be wealthy in a society where wealth brings prestige and power, and in one where it does not correlate with other dimensions of stratification, not to speak of occasional ones, in which wealth as such gets condemned.[55] An important problematic related to such observations is found in sociological theory in connection with such concepts as 'status inconsistency' or 'status decomposition'. Merton somehow neglects this, perhaps due to his overriding concern with the structures of norms and values rather than opportunities.

We now turn to the third dimension of social structure, which I have described as the ideal structure. This is by far the least explored by Merton. I have argued above that he is clearly aware of the necessity to distinguish the ideal structure from the normative structure and the opportunity-structure, when he indicates that people formulate beliefs *about* norms and values as well as *about* opportunities. The subject-matter – content of beliefs – is obviously not the same, ontologically speaking, as beliefs. They belong to different categories. But that is about as far as it goes. One can only venture conjectures as to how Merton would construct this category.

To begin with, he would certainly relate it to the notion of differentiated positions held by people in society. Beliefs and ideas (as opposed to idiosyncratic, personal convictions) would be taken to belong to the ideal structure if they were *associated in patterned ways with social positions*. They would constitute a sort of typical creed cohering around the various structural locations. This is clearly implied in Merton's analysis of professions: 'We should anticipate that different criteria of effectiveness of professional work would be employed by professionals and their clients, if only as a result of their different statuses with attendant differences in values, knowledge, and interests'.[56] The same is true of intellectuals: 'perspectives and outlook are largely a product of social position. Intellectuals are oriented toward more or less defined social circles and accommodate their interests, attitudes, and objectives to these circles'.[57] Similar hints are to be found in Merton's discussion of bureaucratic structure, where some sentiments, attitudes and rationalisations, such as *esprit de corps*, 'nonlogical pride of craft', 'sense of common destiny', 'domineering attitude', 'belief in serving the people'[58] are seen as providing a typical ideological superstructure of this kind of organisational form.[59]

For Merton, as could be expected, the crucial types of beliefs in the ideal structure are those that refer to social norms and values (one might perhaps say: normative consciousness). Such beliefs are not accidental, individual, but patterned: 'Knowledge of these norms ... does not merely happen to vary empirically among individuals; the availability and extent of such knowledge is also presumably patterned by the group structure'.[60] Two important variables mediate in this process. They are signified by Merton with particular concepts: 'visibility' and 'observability'.[61] Visibility is the property of that which is being observed: in our present discussion norms and values, but also role-performance, marks of social rank etc. Norms and values differ in being widely or narrowly visible, in 'the extent to which moral expectations held by others are known to individual members of the group'.[62] For example, the norm forbidding homicide is more visible than, say, some very specific tax rule. Unlike visibility, observability is a property of social position (status). It focuses on the variable and *structurally patterned access* to information and knowledge of what is going on at various places of the social system; it 'is a name for the extent to which the structure of a social organization provides occasion to those variously located in that structure to perceive the norms obtaining in the organization and the character of role-performance by those manning the organization. It refers to an attribute of social structure, not to perceptions which individuals happen to have'.[63] For example, it has long been observed that the secretary's position in an office or a firm is provided with greater potential for observability, than the position of a boss, not to mention the ordinary employee.

The variable degrees of visibility and observability as well as their variable distributions among differentiated segments of the population, produce significant combined effects in the social consciousness (or in my terminology, in the ideal structure). Two types of patterns are singled out by Merton. They are of basically opposed character. One is described by Floyd Allport's term, 'pluralistic ignorance'; another Merton calls the 'fallacy of unanimity'. Pluralistic ignorance is 'the pattern in which individual members of a group assume that they are virtually alone in holding the social attitudes and expectations they do, all unknowing that others privately share them'.[64] The opposite case of the 'fallacy of unanimity' is described thus: 'Continuous association with like-minded individuals tends to produce the illusion that a large measure of consensus has been achieved in the community at large. The unanimity regarding essential cultural axioms that obtains in these small groups provokes an overestimation of the strength of the movement and of its effective inroads upon the larger population, which does not necessarily share these creedal axioms'.[65]

Reasoning by analogy with Merton's analysis of normative and opportunity structures, one is tempted to reconstruct the internal complexities of the ideal structure. This would entail identifying ideological clusters, or systems associated not only with single positions but with typical bundles of positions – status-sets, social strata, classes (in the sense suggested parenthetically above). But this would lead us too far beyond Merton.

The foregoing sketchy and to a large extent hypothetical account of Merton's image of social structure carries one message: 'The concepts remind us, in the unlikely event that we need to be reminded of this insistent and obstinate fact, that even the seemingly simple social structure is extremely complex'.[66]

For the second main level of social reality, correlative to social structure, which Merton clearly recognises, I have chosen the term 'social life'. Much more self-evident than social structure, it refers to phenomena close to common experience, with concrete, empirically identifiable, directly observable characteristics. Perhaps for this very reason it is normally treated as residual by sociological theorists. In the last analysis social life is simply what actually happens among human beings: what they do, think and want, how they get together and get apart, cooperate and fight, produce and destroy, create and break social bonds, enter and escape from groups and collectivities.

Merton studies social life in three directions. Most attention is devoted to the various types and properties of human aggregates. This involves the basic distinction of three modalities of aggregation: 'social categories', 'social collectivities', and 'social groups'. The definitions run as follows: 'social categories are aggregates of social statuses, the occupants of which are not in social interaction. These have *like* social characteristics – of sex, age, marital condition, income, and so on – but are not necessarily oriented towards a distinctive and *common* body of norms. Having *like* statuses, and consequently *similar* interests and values, social categories can be mobilized into collectivities or into groups'.[67] 'Collectivities [are] people who have a sense of solidarity by virtue of sharing common values [and interests] and who have acquired an attendant sense of moral obligation to fulfill role-expectations. . . . Collectivities are potentials for group-formation'.[68] Finally, 'the sociological concept of a group refers to a number of people who interact with one another in accord with established patterns . . . a number of people having established and characteristic social relations'.[69] Merton's analysis of groups is very extensive; it produces a 'provisional list of group-properties', a catalogue of twenty-six variables for describing social groups.[70] Quite a large part of this has now become a canonical, text-book sociological knowledge.

The second direction of analysis is concerned with the domain of action; human behaviour and particularly the mutually oriented conduct of individuals' social interactions. A familiar example is found in Merton's study of 'local and cosmopolitan influentials' which deals with interpersonal influence and the flow of communication.[71] Perhaps least emphasised, at times only sketched, is the third direction of studying social life – analysis of human personality. One example where this problematic enters the focus of Merton's attention is the important article on 'Bureaucratic Structure and Personality'.[72]

Instructive as they are, Merton's analyses of social life are somehow marginal, residual in relation to the core of his theoretical interest, which is centred on social structure. They are certainly underdeveloped if compared with 'a complex and central methodological status the analysis of social structures (or more briefly, structural analysis) occupies in Merton's scheme of thought'.[73] In general, it may be said that social life is treated by Merton as a category theoretically required as a correlate of social structure but devoid of intrinsic relevance. It is important mainly as the designation of that which is shaped, moulded, constrained or facilitated by social structure, as the object of such structural influences and processes.

Varieties of consensus and dissensus

The components of social structure are variously interrelated. It is, in fact, only the study of those interrelations that reveals the social structure in the proper sense of the term, as a *relational network*. Thus far we have only prepared the ground for such a study, by indicating the set of components on which the social structure is predicated. I now propose my interpretation of the way in which Merton treats the links binding together the components of social structure.

His most extensive analysis is again devoted to the dimension of normative structure. The mutual links of norms, values, roles, institutions, role-sets, status-sets, institutional orders – are studied in detail. The most important feature of Merton's analysis, which sets him apart from traditional functionalists, in his treatment of integration as *problematic and contingent*, not as given. The differing degrees of normative integration span the spectrum, from complete consensus to complete dissensus, with these extreme poles being only analytic possibilities, rarely occurring in empirical reality. And it is striking that, perhaps to counterbalance the bias of 'normative functionalism', Merton focuses his analysis on situations closer to the pole of dissensus. This is the case on every internal level of complexity of the normative structure. I discuss three basic types of normative dissensus which Merton describes under the headings of anomie, sociological ambivalence and role-conflict.

At the most comprehensive level, dealing with the integration of normative components within the framework of a whole society, Merton claims that 'full or substantial consensus in a complex, differentiated society exists for only a limited number of values, interests and derived standards for conduct'.[74] He tends to assume the dominant reality of 'cultural conflict', the far-ranging pluralism, ambivalences, and downright contradictions among normative components of the society. His general image of a society-wide normative structure clearly allows, under specified conditions, for prevailing deregulation of normative standards, a degree of 'normlessness' or a state of anomie. Indicating the significant origins of the concept in Durkheim's seminal work, Merton puts it this way: 'The first thing to note about the sociological concept of anomie is that it is – sociological. Anomie refers to a property of a social system, not to the state of mind of this or that individual within the system. It refers to a breakdown of social standards governing behavior and so also signifies little social cohesion. When a high degree of anomie has set in, the rules governing conduct have lost their savor and their force. Above all else, they are deprived of legitimacy. They do not comprise a social order in which men can confidently put their trust. For there is no longer a widely shared sense within the social system, large or small, of what goes and what does not go, of what is justly allowed by way of behavior and of what is justly prohibited, of what may be legitimately expected of people in the course of social interaction'.[75] I propose to signify this first meaning of the concept by numerical subscript as $Anomie_1$.

A special case of $Anomie_1$ results from incompatibilities between various institutions within an institutional order. For example, in the educational order, the secondary school and the university may to some extent represent the same values and norms, may in this sense be mutually integrated; but they may also affirm quite different and even divergent norms and values (say: the value of conformity at school and the value of originality at the university; the norm of acquiring fact-centered information at school and the norm of independent problem-solving at the university). Similarly, in the political order, the government may affirm autocratic values and the parliament, democratic values; while, in the economic order, the fiscal administration may emphasise norms of planning and the enterprises stress the principles of self-management and 'free markets'. Those examples may suffice to register the general theoretical idea.

Another analytically distinguishable kind of integration and dissensus refers to the link between norms and values regulating the same type of conduct. Again, the level of their integration is not taken as given but as contingent and problematic: 'To say that these two elements, culture goals and institutional norms, operate jointly is not to say that the ranges of alternative behaviors and aims bear some constant relation to one another. The emphasis upon certain goals may vary independently of the degree of emphasis upon institutional means'.[76] Norms may be congruent with values, in the sense that they prescribe behaviour instrumental to the reaching of prescribed goals or incongruent with values, in the sense that the prescribed behaviour does not serve to attain those goals, indeed may interfere with their attainment. In the latter situation, to conform to the norms means losing out in reaching the goal while if one retains the goal one must turn to the use of normatively *proscribed* (but technically more efficient) practices. Merton's example is taken from the domain of sport: 'in competitive athletics, when the aim of victory is shorn of its institutional trappings and success becomes construed as "winning the game" rather than "winning under the rules of the game", a premium is implicitly set upon the use of illegitimate but technically efficient means. The star of the opposing football team is surreptitiously slugged; the wrestler incapacitates his opponent through ingenious but illicit techniques'.[77] More up-dated illustrations could include drug-taking by competitors, or the financial under-cover machinations prejudging the score typical for some professional sports. It is not by chance that a special prize instituted by UNESCO rewards for outstanding cases of fair-play; something which at least in sports was presumably taken for granted.

Merton addresses various modalities of incongruence between norms and values in his theory of anomie, endowing the term with the second meaning, as distinct from simple 'normlessness', and referring rather to the disjunction in the 'norm-value' pairings. I shall signify this concept as Anomie$_2$. The polar forms of such disjunction include the virtual atrophy of either values or norms within a pair. A less extreme form occurs when 'the original purposes are forgotten and ritualistic adherence to institutionally prescribed conduct becomes virtually obsessive'.[78] The conduct of over-zealous bureaucrats, or religious bigots provide fitting examples. And there is the opposite form characterised by an over-emphasis upon goals: 'the range of alternative procedures is limited only by technical rather than institutional considerations. Any and all devices which promise attainment of the all-important goal would be permitted in this hypothetical polar case'.[79] The domain of business, pervaded by the overwhelming drive toward profits and economic success, provides numerous illustrations.

The most extended and famous analysis examines one more type of incongruence: the dissociation between normative structure and opportunity structure, described as a condition of anomie, in the third meaning of that Durkheimian term. I shall refer to that concept of anomie as Anomie$_3$.

Merton believes that the full coordination of norms-values and opportunities is the exception rather than the rule. He refers somewhat nostalgically to 'those happy circumstances in which moral obligation and self-interest coincide and fuse',[80] and elsewhere maintains that 'considerations of morality and expediency rarely coincide'.[81] A more frequent condition is rather 'the disjunction between culturally prescribed aspirations and socially structured avenues for realizing these aspirations (what one of us has long described as the "opportunity structure"). It is neither cultural conflict nor social conflict, but a contradiction between the cultural structure and the social structure'.[82] And it is precisely this *disjunction* that is meant by Anomie$_3$: 'Anomie is then conceived as a breakdown in the cultural structure,[83] occurring particularly when there is an acute disjunction between the cultural norms and goals and the socially structured capacities of members of the group to act in accord with them. ... It is the conflict between cultural goals and the availability of using institutional means – whatever the character of the goals – which produces a strain toward anomie'.[84] It will be noted that Anomie$_3$ is, strictly speaking, a particular case of the dissociation or lack of fit between normative structure and opportunity structure. It occurs when access to opportunities somehow lags behind values and norms enjoining that action to be directed toward indicated goals.[85] The opposite case, which Merton does not analyse, would occur when norms and values lag behind opportunities actually open to people, unjustifiably blocking their realisation for all or some; in a word, by frustrating their vested interests. Example: anachronistic or obsolete laws, rules of etiquette etc.

The last type of inter-level dissociation, treated more casually and in large measure implicitly, obtains between the normative structure and the ideal structure, particularly that fragment of the latter which includes *belief about* norms and values, roles and institutions. In studying ethnic discrimination, Merton suggests: 'Once we substitute these three variables of cultural ideal, belief, and actual practice for the customary distinction between the two variables of cultural ideals and actual practices, the entire formulation of the problem becomes changed'.[86] He then mentions the possibility of interest here: 'so far as beliefs of individuals are concerned, we can identify two types: those who genuinely believe in the [official] creed and those who do not (although some of these may, on public or ceremonial occasions, profess adherence to its principles)'.[87] Such beliefs, treated here still as if they were psychological, individual phenomena can be conceived of as patterned in a society and consequently as structural phenomena. Structural ideas about normative order are generally covered by the term 'legitimacy' (in one of its meanings). Thus the shared, widespread *withdrawal of legitimacy* from the normative structure must be treated as a state of ideal structure, not reducible to personal convictions held by this or that individual. At one place, Merton seems to introduce what I propose as a fourth concept of anomie, when he refers to the dissociation between normative consciousness (the fragment of the ideal structure) and the normative structure: 'appreciable numbers of people become estranged from a society that promises them in principle what they are denied in reality. And this withdrawal of allegiance from one or another part of prevailing social standards is what we mean, in the end, by anomie'.[88] This variety of the concept of anomie I wish to signify as Anomie$_4$.

Leaving for a time the problematics of anomie, I am moving to the second major type of normative dissensus that falls under Merton's idea of 'sociological ambivalence'. This refers to the relationship between normative standards constituting a single social role. In Merton's usage of the term 'role', treated as a component of the main structural unit, the 'role-set', a single role designates the relationship of an incumbent of social position (status) to one kind of role-partner, drawn from among the circle of such partners in the role-set (for example: it regulates the behaviour of a physician *vis-à-vis* his patient; or a scholar *vis-à-vis* his peers; or a husband *vis-à-vis* his wife). Merton evidently considers this type of integration as extremely significant, and as in previous cases he focuses on the analysis of conditions where such integration is unstable or absent. The term 'sociological ambivalence' is applied to such social situations in the first of its two meanings: 'In its most restricted sense, sociological ambivalence refers to incompatible normative expectations incorporated in a single role of a single social status (for example, the therapist role of the physician as distinct from other roles of his or her status as researcher, administrator, professional colleague, participant in the professional association, etc.)'.[89] In a later contribution, the definition is elucidated further: 'The core type of sociological ambivalence stems from the socially patterned situation in which incompatible behaviors, attitudes, or values are simultaneously expected by one person in the course of one relationship'.[90] I signify this concept as Sociological Ambivalence$_1$.

The roots of sociological ambivalence are identified by Merton and Elinor Barber in these terms: 'From the perspective of sociological ambivalence, we see a social role as a dynamic organization of norms and counter-norms'.[91] Applying the idea to the medical profession, Merton claims: 'for each norm there tends to be at least one coordinate norm which is, if not inconsistent with the other, at least sufficiently different as to make it difficult for . . . the physician to live up to both'.[92] One case in point is 'detached concern', a composite which combines two patently opposed norms, instrumental impersonality and compassionate concern: 'Physicians must be emotionally detached in their attitudes toward patients. *But*: They must avoid becoming callous through excessive detachment, and should have compassionate concern for the patient'.[93] Another patterned ambivalence is the following: 'Physicians must provide adequate and unhurried medical care for each patient. *But*: They should not allow any patient to usurp so much of their limited time as to have this be at the expense of other patients'.[94] Altogether, Merton lists twenty similar ambivalences inherent in the physician's social role.

Another application of the idea is found in Merton's study of 'the ambivalence of organizational leaders'.[95] This returns to Veblen's notion of 'trained incapacity' which Merton put to use in his study of 'bureaucratic structure and personality' three decades before. In this usage, 'trained incapacity' is defined as 'a state of affairs in which one's abilities come to function as inadequacies. Recurrent actions based upon training, skills and experiences that have been successfully applied in the past result in inappropriate responses *under changed conditions*'.⁹⁶ Another patterned ambivalence in the leadership role is expressed by the famous paradox phrased by one of the heroes of the French Revolution: 'I must follow them; I am their leader'. Here, two norms are at odds: the one requiring of leaders to *represent* or reflect the aspirations, goals and wishes of those they lead and the other, requiring them precisely *to lead*, to set aspirations and goals for them. In another recent context, Vanessa Merton together with her father Robert Merton and Elinor Barber develop the theme of sociological ambivalence, tracing it in the relationship of help-seekers and help-givers. The authors conclude that 'the normative structure of helping relationships in general creates conflict, because the apparent role-requirement of dependency and need is so antithetical to the culturally reinforced self-image of autonomy, responsibility, and competence most adults feel obliged to maintain. Yet adopting a stance of dependency can be quite functional for obtaining the desired – and at the same time, perhaps resented – assistance'.⁹⁷ As the authors put it: 'helpers need to be helpful at least as much as the helpless need to be helped', yet in 'unnerving' fashion, it seems that 'the less helpless the client, the less helpful the professional can be'.⁹⁸

Normative dissensus obtains not only between the norms and values (expectations) within a single role, but also between such norms and values within a social institution. Here as elsewhere, *malintegration is the rule rather than exception*: 'A major characteristic of social institutions is that they tend to be patterned in terms of potentially conflicting pairs of norms'.⁹⁹ Once again Merton uses the concept of 'sociological ambivalence', this time in its second meaning: 'sociological ambivalence is imbedded in social institutions generally'.¹⁰⁰ I shall describe it as Sociological Ambivalence$_2$. His analysis of the 'ambivalence of scientists' provides a case in point: 'In saying that the social institution of science is malintegrated, I mean that it incorporates potentially incompatible values'.¹⁰¹ Thus the value set upon originality, leading to a focus on establishing one's priority in scientific discoveries is in tension with the value of humility, indicating one's indebtedness to predecessors and contemporaries; the norm of organised scepticism, calling for the meticulous checking and cross-checking of results is in tension with the norm of 'communism' calling for results to be made public knowledge without delayed publication. Merton records a variety of ambivalences in the ethos of science.

The institution of marriage provides another domain subject to sociological ambivalence. Thus, the romantic complex and taboos on intermarriage provide incongruent principles for the choice of marriage partners. They 'make for some instability and lack of consensus in appraising certain interclass marriages that may be disapproved in terms of the endogamous norms but praised in terms of romanticism'.[102]

A final illustration can be drawn from the operation of bureaucracy, where the norms presenting standard, impersonal, routine treatment of clients' problems may block solutions in individual cases thus running counter to norms of efficiency: 'Since functionaries minimize personal relations and resort to categorization, the peculiarities of individual cases are often ignored'.[103] This leads to a paradox. 'The very elements which conduce toward efficiency in general produce inefficiency in specific instances'.[104] Nor does simply restoring elements of personal concern with clients provide an easy solution: 'Since the group is oriented toward secondary norms of impersonality, any failure to conform to these norms will arouse antagonism from those who have identified themselves with the legitimacy of these rules. Hence, the substitution of personal for impersonal treatment within the structure is met with widespread disapproval and is characterised by such epithets as graft, favoritism, nepotism, apple-polishing, etc.'.[105] Sociological ambivalence produces a basic and not fully resolvable dilemma.

We move now to the most complex level of normative structure which Merton focused on, and discuss the type of normative dissensus that he describes as role-conflict. This concept has two distinct meanings. A specific kind of integration obtains between distinct roles within a role-set. The normative standards defining appropriate relationships with some role-partners are not always coordinated with the standards defining relationships with other role-partners. A polar case of integration appears in 'those special circumstances in which all those in the role-set have the same values and same role-expectations'.[106] But this, Merton maintains, is 'a special and, perhaps historically rare, situation'.[107] Thus, he focuses instead on the uncoordinated condition described as 'role-conflict' or more structurally, 'conflict of roles in the role-set'. I shall refer to this concept as Role Conflict$_1$.

In significant degree, such conflict derives from the structural fact that various role partners of an individual occupying certain social position are typically located in various places of the social structure, with differing values and interests. Consequently, they will tend to make different and often *incompatible normative demands* of the individual.[108] Consider, for example, the precarious position of a university professor subjected to conflicting demands from students, academic colleagues, administrative staff, the senate, educational authorities at the local and central level and so on. Generalising this case, one can say with Merton that 'particularly in highly differentiated societies, the role-partners are drawn from diverse social statuses with, to some degree, correspondingly different social values. To the extent that this obtains, the characteristic situation should be one of disorder, rather than of relative order'.[109] This differs patently from the situation described earlier as 'sociological ambivalence': 'The strain resulting from the incompatibilities of simultaneously held multiple roles [in Merton's sense of the set of roles associated with a single social status]',[110] say the Loomises, 'is to be distinguished from that which is imposed by conflicting expectations of the single role [in Merton's sense of the segment of the role-set]'.[111] Thus, to repeat, the Role Conflict$_1$ signifies a strain *within* a role-set.

A different kind of normative integration or conflict obtains between role-sets accruing to the various statuses in an individual's status-set. The phenomenon of a status-set with its multiple role-sets which are relevant for the same individual, implies the contingent possibility of their mutual coordination or conversely, the lack of such coordination. Merton focuses on the latter case, which is also usually described as 'role conflict', or more structurally 'conflict *between* role-sets'. I shall signify this concept as a Role Conflict$_2$. It is well illustrated by the frequent predicament of the husband who is also a father, businessman, politician, stamp-collector, golfer, Mason and Baptist, and so is subject to the different and sometimes contradictory expectations (demands) associated with those multiple positions (statuses comprising his status-set). The more complex and differentiated a society, the more complex and heterogenous are individuals' status-sets, and the more probability for conflicts among respective role-sets. Such conflicts 'confront the occupants of these statuses with distinctly different degrees of difficulty in organizing their role-activities'.[112]

The eight kinds of normative dissensus which have been

distinguished above with categories of anomie, sociological ambivalence and role-conflict exhibit Merton's analytical sensitivity to the problems of contradictions, conflicts, strains and tensions in the social structure. His image of the social structure is far removed from the harmonious, perfectly integrated picture based on the postulate of consensus adopted by the anthropological ancestors of functionalism.

Modalities of behavioural adaptations

In true Durkheimian style, Merton puts great emphasis on theoretical problems of structural determination. One readily detects in many of his substantive studies analyses of the *constraining or facilitating influence* of social structures on the realities of social life. He analyses, for example, structurally induced rates of intermarriage,[113] structurally generated competition among faculty members in medical schools,[114] structurally determined styles of influentials,[115] structural limitations upon professional control,[116] structurally generated ethnic discrimination,[117] structurally produced social disorganisation,[118] structurally induced deviant behaviours,[119] and so on.

Merton's approach to the problem of structural determination has two important theoretical characteristics. First, he treats the effects of social structure upon social life as the synthetic, combined product of pressures originating on *various structural levels*, not as the product of a single type of structure. It is the entire social structure, as unique totality of norms, opportunities and ideas, which shapes the concrete course of social life. In that totality, the crucial, primary, ever-present level is normative structure. But its impact is qualified, modified, or catalysed by characteristics of the two other structures. By ignoring this essential point, one can easily follow in the footsteps of Chapman and ascribe a one-sided 'ideological stigma' to Merton: 'Only where the cultural element is exalted above the personal and social elements of the generic model as a "scientific" (utopian) model of social reality, could Merton's ideological stigma appear and remain unchallenged for twenty years'.[120] Second, Merton considers structural determination in its prime sense as structures *setting limits* to or *putting bounds* on the range of probable and feasible *human choices*. He does not conceive of such determination as a direct one-to-one implementation of social structure in the concreteness of social life through the imprinting of that structure on behaviour, personality, or collectivity formations of individuals. Thus, structural determination is simply *the delimitation of range of possible choice*. Only recall Stinchcombe's revealing observation: 'the core process that Merton conceives as central to social structure is the choice between socially structured alternatives'.[121] To mistake Merton's position for a crude structural determinism (or, in particular, a normative or cultural determinism) leads to the kind of unfounded criticism found in Chapman, who sees in Merton's work 'a permanent domination of the person and other forms of social action by a single cultural construct elevated to the place of deity and given total defining power over social thought and action'.[122]

Merton's actual theoretical orientation toward the structural determination in social life, is clearly seen in his analysis of conforming and deviant behaviour. There he *begins* with the normative dimension. He distinguishes conforming behaviour, understood as abiding by socially defined relevant normative standards, and deviant behaviour, understood as violating such normative standards. He focuses most attention on patterns of deviant behaviour as theoretically significant. As Cuzzort and King observe: 'Deviant behavior presents a critical problem to those who accept a sociological perspective. The problem is this. On the one hand the sociologist is well aware that society and culture have an almost crushing capacity to induce conformity on the part of the individual. On the other hand, innovation does exist. The directives of the culture may be challenged or modified. How can deviation occur within a system which has so much power to prevent it?'[123] The reasons for people choosing one or another modality cannot be explained by reference to the normative structure itself. It requires taking the other dimensions of social structure into systematic account. The behaviour is not a mere embodiment of social norms. In the words of Rose Laub Coser: 'Merton has stood Durkheim on his head; rather than having the individual confronted with ready-made social norms that are external, coming down *in toto*, so to speak, for Merton individuals have to find their own orientations among multiple, incompatible, contradictory norms. The individual solutions are not arbitrary, to be sure; they are available in the social structure'.[124] But to account for the choices made among the structurally available solutions, the analysis must include other dimensions of the social structure, the opportunity structure and the ideal structure. Merton adopts 'the theoretic orientation of the functional analyst who considers socially deviant behavior just as much a product of social structure as conformist behavior'.[125] Proceeding further on this road, he searches for structural preconditions of the fact that people variously relate their behaviour to binding rules: some conform and some deviate while all conform at times and deviate at times.

The proposed solution appears in the famous theory of anomie (in the sense of $Anomie_3$ – to be exact). Deviant behaviour is seen as the normal, to-be-expected effect of a social structure in which there obtains a dissociation between the dimension of norms-cum-values and the dimension of opportunities. 'It is, indeed, my central hypothesis', Merton states, 'that aberrant behavior may be regarded sociologically as a symptom of dissociation between culturally prescribed aspirations and socially structured avenues for reaching these aspirations'.[126] An in another context expands: 'It is the conflict between culturally accepted values and the socially structured difficulties in living up to these values which exerts pressure toward deviant behavior and disruption of the normative system'.[127]

Two types of example make these abstract formulations more concrete. One refers to a particular society, another to a specific domain of social life. Merton maintains that in contemporary American society 'It is when a system of cultural values extols, virtually above all else, certain common success-goals for the population at large while the social structure rigorously restricts or completely closes access to approved modes of reaching these goals for a considerable part of the same population, that deviant behavior ensues on a large scale'.[128] And in the particular domain of science, he carefully analyses cases of 'deviant behavior in response to a discrepancy between the enormous emphasis in the culture of science upon original discovery and the actual difficulty many scientists experience in making an original discovery. In this situation of stress, all manner of adaptive behaviors are called into play, some of these being far beyond the mores of science'.[129]

But deviant behaviour is not all of a piece. It covers a wide variety of empirical cases. On the basis of the distinction between values (specifically, 'culture goals') and norms (specifically, 'institutionalized means'), Merton construes his well-known 'typology of the modes of individual adaptation'.[130] The rationale of the typology is strikingly simple: people may conform or deviate either in relation to *norms*, in relation to *values*, or in relation to *both*. If they conform to the culturally valued goals but deviate from the institutionalised norms, the mode of their behaviour is described by the neutral term 'innovation'.[131] (Examples: delinquency, but also the behaviour of innovators in various areas of life.) If they deviate from valued goals but conform to norms, the mode of behaviour is 'ritualism'. (Examples: overly zealous bureaucratic behaviour, religious compulsiveness.) If they deviate from both values and norms without instituting viable normative alternatives, 'retreatism' emerges. (Examples: the behaviour of vagabonds, outcasts, some forms of psychotic behaviour.) Finally, if they deviate from both valued goals and institutional norms, but propose alternative normative solutions, this is the case of 'rebellion'. (Examples: dissent, heresy, revolutionary action.) The typology is summed up by means of a diagram:[132]

Modes of adaptation	Culture goals	Institutionalised means
I. Conformity	+	+
II. Innovation	+	−
III. Ritualism	−	+
IV. Retreatism	−	−
V. Rebellion	±	±

where (+) means acceptance, (−) rejection and (±) replacement.

In order to explain the differential rates of each of those possible behavioural responses, as they occur in various groups, collectivities, classes, or societies, Merton draws upon other levels of social structure, the opportunity structure and the ideal structure.

In the opportunity structure, he focuses on a specific kind of opportunity: access to legitimate (normatively prescribed or at least acceptable) means for reaching goals set by dominant values. Such access is normally correlated with the amount of wealth, power, prestige etc. possessed by the individuals, or to put it otherwise, it varies with the position held by individuals (or groups, or collectivities) in any type of status-connected stratification. The prime dimension of this variation is the socio-economic (or 'class') position, but Merton takes into account other dimensions as well – ethnic, racial, religious etc. In general, he puts forward the following hypothesis: 'although we know from many sources that the official crime statistics uniformly showing higher rates in the lower strata are far from complete or reliable, it appears from our analysis that the greatest pressures toward deviation are exerted upon the lower strata'.[133] It is so precisely because lower strata have most restricted access to various legitimate means, while the general values of society, cutting across stratificational divisions, hold out the attainment of similar dominant (generic) goals, in kind, if not always in amount.[134] 'Several researches have shown that specialized areas of vice and crime constitute a "normal" response to a situation where the cultural emphasis upon pecuniary success has been absorbed, but where there is little access to conventional and legitimate means for becoming successful'.[135]

The aspiration levels and opportunity structure typically found in urban settings tend to produce strong pressures toward deviation. Merton refers to a 'towering structure of opportunity': 'the opportunity-structure reaches substantially higher in the city than elsewhere in the society. And whatever the nature of rewards – fame, lofty status, power, money, association with elites – these are extended in the city, particularly in the metropolitan colossus'.[136] But the variable access to those great opportunities remains limited, always far smaller than the number of aspirants attracted there by the vision of success. As Merton puts it in adopting the language of Saint Matthew, 'though many are called, comparatively few can be chosen', and the 'towering structure of opportunity . . . excites great expectations, not easily relinquished, and so condemns many to that kind of bitter disappointment that leads to despairing retreat or aberrant ritualism or, on occasion, to open rebellion'.[137] In these structural circumstances, 'almost every form of human aberration is more frequent in the city than the small town or the rapidly constricted farmland'.[138]

The second sphere of significant variables interacting with differentials in opportunities to produce differing rates of deviant behaviour is the ideal structure. Here again, Merton focuses on selected aspects: patterned beliefs about norms and values and patterned beliefs about opportunities. The first take the form of the withdrawing or granting of legitimacy to normative structure or some of its components. The crucial distinction between expedient or opportunistic deviance, manifested only in the behavioural realm and coupled with the acceptance of respective norms and values (example: the thief) and the total deviance based on the self-conscious rejection of norms and values (example: the heretic), can be theoretically located only by introducing this additional variable from the domain of ideal structure. The second aspect which refers to the beliefs about the opportunity-structure rather than about the normative structure, takes the form of optimistic or pessimistic appraisals of available means; to put it otherwise, it amounts to variable confidence in the practicality of one's aspirations. The city provides again an instance of the situation which produces over-optimistic appraisals of opportunities and unrealistically elevated aspirations, since 'it is more difficult to reduce hopes when confronted with evidence that others have been able to realize them'.[139]

Variable opportunities and variable beliefs about values, norms and opportunities interact to produce distinct forms of deviation. Thus 'innovation' appears when scarce access to effective legitimate means is accompanied by a general acceptance of normative order skewed toward an emphasis on values. This is the case when 'the sacrosanct goal virtually consecrates the means', and 'the avenues available for moving toward this goal are largely limited by the class structure to those of deviant behavior',[140] resulting in choosing or contriving of illegitimate, but expedient means. 'Ritualism' occurs when available but ineffective legitimate means are accompanied by the acceptance of normative order, skewed toward an emphasis on norms. 'It involves the abandoning or scaling down of the lofty cultural goals' while 'one continues to abide almost compulsively by institutional norms'.[141] Legitimate means are adopted even though they do not help achieve the goals, which recede or are lost sight of. 'Retreatism' appears when both legitimate and illegitimate means to reach goals prove to be inaccessible. The earlier, because of limited access to legitimate opportunities; the latter because of the deep commitment to dominant norms and values which prevents recourse to illegitimate ways.[142] Cloward observes another modality of this situation, one in which attempts at illegitimate procedures also bring failure: 'retreatist adaptations may arise with considerable frequency among those who are failures in both worlds, conventional and illegitimate alike'.[143] A full repudiation of norms and values results and individuals passively withdraw from the social game. Finally, 'rebellion' is generated by the outright repudiation of dominant goals and the inaccessible legitimate means, coupled with an attempt to introduce a new normative order and to realise new goals, by way of new means, legitimated in terms of new values and norms. 'Rebellion . . . involves a genuine transvaluation, where the direct or vicarious experience of frustration leads to full denunciation of previously prized values'.[144]

Merton's theory of anomie has been extremely influential in the study of deviant behaviour for many years. As Cole observes: 'Until the late 1960s, Social Structure and Anomie was probably the dominant theory in the area of deviance'.[145] Even though in the 1970s labelling theory and conflict theory became more salient, Cullen evaluating deviance theories in 1984 writes: 'Merton's perspective still occupies a central position in the field'.[146] It still commands a considerable army of followers, some of whom are applying it in empirical research and some of whom have elaborated and extended the theory in various respects. The extensions have to do with the three dimensions of social structure treated as providing structural contexts of deviance.

Thus, in his theory of delinquent subcultures, Cohen developed Merton's idea that normative structures have a pluralistic character, and that the notions of conformity and deviance are therefore always relative to the structural frame of reference.[147] As Merton observed: 'conformity to norms of an out-group is thus equivalent to what is ordinarily called nonconformity, that is, nonconformity to the norms of the in-group'.[148] Certain normative structures commonly viewed as pathological from the perspective of the wider society may be wholly accepted from the perspective of a group of delinquents. For them, their delinquency is simply conformity with their particular 'delinquent subculture' and is reinforced by interaction with significant peers. The deviant adaptation is shown to be not so much an individual response as a collective response, amplified by group-bonds and loyalties among the deviants. In referring to Cohen's contribution, Merton notes that 'one must presumably look to the social interaction among these likeminded deviants who mutually reinforce their deviant attitudes and behavior which, in the theory, result from the more or less common situation in which they find themselves'.[149]

Dubin proposed another extension of the analysis of normative structure. He proposes more fine-grained distinctions of the normative components toward which people orient their behaviour. Leaving the category of values (specifically: 'cultural goals') intact, he distinguishes two subcategories of norms: 'institutional norms' and 'institutional means'. The norms are more general, valid for the society at large and setting wide limits of acceptable behaviour. The means are more specific, valid for particular institutions in the society, and prescribing a concrete repertoire of ways in which general norms are to be implemented in each institutional setting. Dubin states that 'Institutional norms set the limits between which the institutional means are prescribed – the limits of legitimate behaviors in a particular institution. Beyond the norms lie illegitimate behaviors'.[150] For example, 'innovation' may signify the replacement of 'institutional norms' (Merton's original meaning), the replacement of 'institutional means' alone, or the replacement of both norms and means. Dubin calls these different situations 'normative invention', 'operating invention' and 'institutional invention' respectively. Similar distinctions are applied to all of Merton's forms of adaptation.[151]

A significant addition to the analysis of opportunity structure has been made by Cloward[152] and by Cloward and Ohlin.[153] They attempt to consolidate Merton's theory of anomie with criminological theory of 'differential association' represented by E. Sutherland. They indicate that Merton focused on differentials in access to *legitimate* means, taking access to illegitimate (deviant) means for granted, as if they were freely and commonly accessible. But, drawing upon Sutherland's conceptions Cloward observes: 'the availability of *illegitimate means* . . . is controlled by various criteria in the same manner that has long been ascribed to conventional means. Both systems of opportunity are (1) limited, rather than infinitely available, and (2) differentially available depending on the location of persons in the social structure'.[154] The motivation to employ criminal methods is not the same as actually committing crime. To commit crimes with any regularity one does best to learn something of effective techniques. To steal something (and not to be caught) one must not only want to do it, but also, preferably, should know *how* and should place oneself in conducive circumstances. This observation leads Cloward and Ohlin to introduce fine-grained distinction of 'learning structures' and 'opportunity structures' in the narrow sense: 'When we employ the term "means", whether legitimate or illegitimate, at least two things are implied: first, that there are appropriate learning environments for the acquisition of the values and skills associated with the performance of a particular role; and second, that the individual has opportunities to discharge the role once he has been prepared. The term subsumes, therefore, both learning structures and opportunity structures'.[155] By analogy to Sutherland's idea of 'differential association', they propose the concept of 'differential opportunity structures'; the variable balance of opportunities to employ legitimate and illegitimate means.[156] Merton sees the importance of those extensions to his theory, as they introduce 'strategic new variables for the analysis of the social and cultural contexts that, by hypothesis, give rise to varying rates of deviant behavior'.[157]

Finally, extensions of the analysis of ideal structure are proposed by Harary and Dubin. The earlier observes that the granting or withdrawal of legitimacy to norms and values may have several forms. In particular 'one must be careful to distinguish between a relationship of indifference and a relationship which is negative, such as rejection'.[158] In effect, there are three 'valences' of attitudes towards goals, as well as means: acceptance, rejection and indifference. Dubin, following a similar logic explicates a distinction implicit in Merton's analysis. He observes that the withdrawal of legitimacy, or simply a rejection of norms and values is not of a piece. He proposes to distinguish the active rejection, implying the seeking of normative alternatives and the passive rejection expressed in purely behavioural, extra-normative accommodations. Merton's categories of innovation and rebellion represent active rejection, whereas ritualism and retreatism represent passive rejection.[159]

So much for Merton's theory of anomie. He provides a less complex but instructive case of the structural influence on behaviour in the form of what he calls 'institutionalized altruism'. The sociological problem is to account for the structural basis of altruistic actions, by which is meant 'behavior which benefits others at the expense of the benefactor. By expense, we mean only that the yield to the benefactors is less in the short run than if they not engaged in altruistic behavior'.[160] Merton goes on to observe that institutionalised altruism 'focuses attention on alternatives of action that are weighted by social structures to increase the rate at which individuals choose altruistic actions beyond what it would otherwise be (if based wholly upon human nature, prior socialization, or other dispositional tendencies)'.[161] Psychological explanations will not do. 'The will, or for that matter, goodwill, cannot be turned on and off like a faucet. Social intelligence and goodwill are themselves *products* of distinct social forces', as he remarked in a much earlier paper.[162]

In applying structural explanation to the case of altruism, Merton identifies institutionalised altruism as 'the special form of altruism in which structural arrangements, notably the distribution of rewards and penalties, promote behavior that is beneficial to others. . . . Where altruism has been institutionalized, we expect an increase in the kinds of behavior benefiting others, whether the benefactor's motives are altruistic or egoistic'.[163] It will be noted that the concept of institutionalisation is used here in a specific sense of a particular *mode of coordination* between the normative structure and the opportunity-structure. The Loomises observe: 'The concept of institutionalization as used by Merton is important . . . because as a process it bridges the cultural and social planes'.[164] Stinchcombe elaborates this notion of institutionalisation in his interpretation of Merton: 'The attachment of specified rewards . . . or punishments . . . to the structured bundles among which people must choose, by specific social structures . . . determines the motivational potential attached to the bundles. As these structurings of choice change . . . the rates of choice change'.[165]

Merton's analysis of the phenomenon of institutionalised altruism focuses on one social sector, the professions. He argues not that 'professional men and women largely engage in such [altruistic] behavior' but only that 'it occurs more frequently than would be the case in the absence of the designated institutional arrangements'.[166] The arrangements are found, first of all, in the normative structure or ethos of the professions, with its emphasis on the value of helping along with the correlative norm of altruism. The value and norm are built into professional roles. But the existence of norms and values does not suffice. Additional structural arrangements in the opportunity structure and additional widespread and shared beliefs in the ideal structure are required to account for the occurrence of altruistic acts on the scale in which it occurs compared with other types of occupations.[167] The opportunity structure, in effect, leads professionals to develop vested interests in altruistic conduct: 'The institutional arrangements of the professions tend to make it a matter of self-interest for individual practitioners to act altruistically. . . . The collective effort is to devise arrangements such that, in the long run, the exploitation of clients is counter-productive for attaining self-interested ends'.[168] Those arrangements – of course not always efficient – take the form of specific rewards and sanctions distributed in the professional communities as well as by clients themselves. Such mechanisms of social control modify the balance of gratifications obtained by professionals. 'Under such circumstances, there is no zero-sum relationship between altruism and reward: putting clients' interests first becomes the institutionally prescribed means for moving toward practitioners' own ends, beyond altruism itself'.[169] This tendency is reinforced by transformations of the ideal structure – the increasing public concern with professions and the emergence of patterned belief that, as Everett Hughes put it, 'everyone has a right to education, health, and to those other kinds of increase of life which [Herbert] Spencer had said it was the function of professions to provide'.[170] Those beliefs provide rationalisations for the operation of social control; they justify the rewarding of altruistic acts and the punishing of exploitative acts. The combined structural contexts – the normative, opportunity and ideal – work to produce higher levels of altruistic actions in the practice of the professions, *than would occur in their absence*, and presumably higher than in occupations lacking those arrangements.

Moulding personality

Social structure exerts significant influence not only on what people do, their actions, but also on what they think and want. As Rose Laub Coser puts it: 'not only behavior but the thinking process itself would seem to be related to the nature of social relationships'.[171] This is the second dimension of social life shaped by structural contexts. Merton's structural analysis of course assumes that human individuals are complex products of social influences and not alone of immanent, psychological processes. What people have in common with others largely results from identifiable characteristics of the social structures in which they coexist; sociologically speaking, what distinguishes each of us as a unique individuality largely results from one's particular location in the structural network. The idea of primacy of social structure over individual personality is linked with Durkheim's theory. And the idea of a differentiated impact of specific structural configurations as responsible for idiosyncratic personalities, is linked with Simmel's study of 'social types'. Merton is emphatic on both points: 'the individuality of human beings can be sociologically derived from social differentiation and not only psychologically derived from intrapsychic processes. Thus, the greater the number and variety of group affiliations and statuses distributed among individuals in a society, the smaller, on the average, the number of individuals having precisely the same social configuration'.[172] As Rose Laub Coser later put it more succinctly: 'The combination of multiple identifications makes the person unique'.[173]

The coordination of social structure and personality is a basic functional requirement: 'The efficacy of social structure depends ultimately upon infusing group participants with appropriate attitudes and sentiments'.[174] Such 'infusion' viewed from the external perspective of social structure is contained in the concept of socialisation; viewed from the internal perspective of personality, in the concept of internalisation.

Merton defines socialisation as 'the process through which individuals are inducted into their culture'.[175] From the perspective of individuals it 'designates the processes by which people selectively acquire the values and attitudes, the interests, skills, and knowledge – in short, the culture – current in the groups of which they are, or seek to become, a member. It refers to the learning of social roles'.[176] The emphasis on culture in this context seems unwarranted both in terms of the wider logic of Merton's structural analysis, where opportunity structures and ideal structures are taken into account together with normative structures (cultural elements), and in terms of his own illustrations where he consistently deals with the acquisition of 'interests' and 'knowledge', and not only 'values' and 'behavioral patterns'. It would seem more consistent to define socialisation simply as – more or less efficient, and more or less persistent – mapping of the *entire social structure* – norms, opportunities and beliefs – on the personalities of human individuals. Then, for analytic reasons one could perhaps distinguish normative socialisation from pragmatic socialisation and cognitive socialisation.

Merton's most extensive discussion of the process of socialisation is found in the study of medical education. He states that we are still far from grounded and detailed knowledge in this area: 'the social and psychological processes through which socialization comes about, so that different individuals in the same group variously assimilate the established culture, have become, only in recent years, the object of methodical and sustained inquiry'.[177] His own image of those processes can be summed up in three points. First, the main mechanism of socialisation is conceived, in Meadian fashion, as interaction with 'significant others': 'students acquire the values which will be basic to their professional way of life in the course of their social interaction with others in the school, exchanging experiences and ideas with peers, and observing and evaluating the behavior of their instructors'.[178] Second, and following from this, one must distinguish 'direct learning through didactic teaching' from less conspicuous but perhaps even more important 'indirect learning, in which attitudes, values and behavior patterns are acquired as by-products of contact with instructors and peers, patients, and other members of the health team'.[179] Therefore, concepts of 'educational environment',[180] 'climates of value and the organization of relations between students',[181] and the like become crucial for analysis. Third, since socialisation is a process continuing permanently throughout the life-course, the study of early induction into social structure should not preempt the study of 'adult socialization'.[182]

More specific considerations are found in Merton's famous study of bureaucratic personality, where he examines social structure in terms of its effects rather than attendant processes. The bureaucratic structure, defined along Weberian lines, is shown to produce personality traits that work counter to its avowed goals. To analyse this phenomenon, he draws, as we have noted, upon Veblen's concept of 'trained incapacity', which Merton defines as 'that state of affairs in which one's [trained] abilities function as inadequacies or blind spots'.[183] More specifically, bureaucrats develop patterns of ritualistic overconformity to institutional means: bureaucratic discipline leads to 'a transference of the sentiments from the *aims* of the organization onto the particular details of behavior required by the rules. Adherence to the rules, originally conceived as a means, becomes transformed into an end-in-itself; there occurs the familiar process of *displacement of goals* whereby an "instrumental value becomes a terminal value" '.[184] The extreme embodiment of the resulting inflexibility is 'the bureaucratic virtuoso, who never forgets a single rule binding his action and hence is unable to assist many of his clients'.[185]

Merton thus supplements Weber's analysis of the functions of bureaucracy by focusing on its dysfunctions. He analyses the process leading to these dysfunctional patterns in four points: '(1) An effective bureaucracy demands reliability of response and strict devotion to regulation, (2) Such devotion to the rules leads to their transformation into absolutes; they are no longer conceived as relative to a set of purposes. (3) This interferes with ready adaptation under special conditions not clearly envisaged by those who drew up the general rules. (4) Thus, the very elements which conduce toward efficiency in general produce inefficiency in specific instances'.[186] Stinchcombe extends Merton's analysis by indicating the positive feed-back loop between bureaucratic structure and bureaucratic personalities, a vicious cycle of growing bureaucratisation: 'Repetitive situational adaptations form character. Thus, the timidity and narrow-mindedness of a bureaucracy are not only maintained because the situations that produce timidity and narrowness are continuously present. They are also maintained because over time the people in them become timid and narrow'.[187]

Accepting Merton's general account of the process, Cohen challenges his diagnosis concerning results. On empirical grounds he argues that inefficiency of bureaucracy is as often due to excessive flexibility and voluntaristic modifications of policies, as to inflexibility, or rigidity in rule-following. He observes that 'flexibility in itself does not necessarily decrease the dysfunctional aspects of bureaucracy'.[188] All depends on the goals of bureaucratic organisation and the expectations of significant, and differentiated, publics. Although Cohen's criticism is valid for certain cases, Merton's analysis remains an excellent account of mechanisms through which specific structural configurations shape the organisational personalities of incumbents. His study should not be read as an exhaustive characterisation of bureaucracy in all its forms, but rather as a case study of mechanisms and processes through which social structure forms organisational personality and character.

Thus far social structures serving to shape personality have been treated as if they were homogenous, consensual, harmonious and consistent. But Merton's overriding preoccupation with heterogenous structures that incorporate dissensus, disharmony and inconsistencies, must also find expression in this present problematics. It can be expected on theoretical ground that he would centre on ways in which the schizoid quality of social structure with its dissociation of normative and opportunity levels (Anomie$_3$) as well as disregulation or normlessness at the normative level (Anomie$_1$, Anomie$_2$) produce parallel schizoid dissociation in human personality and character. And in his later work, he does take up the study of 'anomie and anomia', the generation of *anomic personalities* by *anomic social systems*. 'To prevent conceptual confusion', he suggests, 'different terms are required to distinguish between the anomic state of individuals and the anomic state of the social system, for though the two are variously connected, they are nevertheless distinct'.[189] Those whose personalities reflect *anomie* pervading a social structure are said, after Leo Srole, to exhibit *anomia*, and are designated as anomics. They perceive society as unpredictable and lacking order, themselves as devoid of guidance, leadership or the support of associates, and their goals as receding into oblivion. Merton systematically examines modes of relationship between the proportions of anomics in a society, the modalities of their individual behaviour and the occurrence of anomie as a *structural property of a social system*. He sets forth a design of inquiry which 'simultaneously presents variables dealing with (1) types of collectivities: their degree of anomie, (2) types of individuals, exhibiting anomia or not, (3) patterns of social relations: sustained association with individuals of like or differing kind and, within each of these three types of contexts, (4) rates of deviant (or reciprocally, of conforming) behavior'. Without attempting to examine this in detail, we do note the basic conclusion that 'anomie, anomia and deviant behavior become mutually reinforcing, unless counteracting mechanisms of social control are called into play'.[190]

Another type of case in which conflict-ridden social structure leads to psychological imbalance, following up the Merton-Barber theory of 'sociological ambivalence' is thoroughly analysed by Janis. He adopts the proposal to distinguish 'sociological ambivalence' as a structural condition, embedded in social structure, and 'psychological ambivalence' as 'the experienced tendency of individuals to be pulled in psychologically opposed directions, as love and hate for the same person, acceptance and rejection, affirmation and denial'.[191] Merton and Barber conjectured that 'individuals in a status or status-set that has a large measure of incompatibility in its social definition will tend to develop personal tendencies toward contradictory feelings, beliefs, and behavior'.[192] Janis takes off from that and traces this process in detail in the relationships of 'health-care professionals' and their patients, particularly with reference to the ambivalence of 'detached concern' built into the ethos of the medical profession. He concludes: 'A "double focus" on sociological and psychological aspects, as recommended by Merton, is essential for a comprehensive analysis of the causes and consequences of ambivalence, which could eventually lead to an integrated "psycho-social theory" '.[193]

The cases of anomie and sociological ambivalence serve to illustrate the disruptive impact of conflictual social structures on individual personalities; one may say, the *personal dysfunctions* of such structures. But this is not a full formulation. Under indicated conditions, heterogeneous, pluralistic, and conflict-ridden social structures can also benefit personality; they have *personal functions*. Merton treats the complexity of social structures as *contributing* to the individual autonomy in at least three contexts. Examining the phenomenon of differing composition of members of role-sets, he observes that 'the power-structure of role sets is often such that the status-occupant more nearly has autonomy than would be the case if this structure of competing powers did not obtain'.[194] He goes on, almost in Meadian terms, to show how the complexity of role-sets facilitates the 'taking the role of the other' by individual incumbents. He locates the development of structurally induced empathy: 'The extent to which empathy obtains among the members of a society is in part a function of the underlying social structure. For those who are in the role-sets of the individual subjected to conflicting status-obligations are in turn occupants of multiple statuses, formerly or presently, actually or potentially, subject to similar stresses. This structural circumstance at least facilitates the development of empathy'.[195] And finally, in a specific analysis of status-sets in relation to cognitive perspectives and 'social epistemology', Merton points out that occupying both 'Insider' and 'Outsider' statuses simultaneously makes for creative interchange of ideas and a more adequate grasp of social reality: 'In structural terms, we are all, of course, both "Insiders" and "Outsiders", members of some groups and, sometimes derivatively, not of others; occupants of certain statuses which thereby exclude us from occupying other cognate statuses. . . . Insider and Outsider perspectives can converge through reciprocal adoption of ideas and the developing of complementary and overlapping foci of attention in the formulation of scientific problems. . . . There can develop trade-offs between the distinctive strengths and weaknesses of Insider and Outsider perspectives that enlarge the chances for sound and relevant understanding of social life'.[196]

These implications of Merton's theory have been picked up and developed by Rose Laub Coser.[197] Her crucial hypothesis states that individual autonomy in modern society is possible and induced precisely *because of* the complexity, heterogeneity and incompatibility of various components of modern social structure: 'the multiplicity of expectations faced by the modern individual, incompatible or contradictory as they may be, or rather precisely because they are, makes role articulation possible in a more self-conscious manner than if there were no such multiplicity'.[198] Under such conditions, individuals are encouraged or even made to develop reflexive, innovative, flexible, self-directing, non-parochial, relativistic perspectives and attitudes. After a scrutiny of relevant empirical data she concludes: 'Complex role-sets and differentiated roles are not alienating restrictions on individuality; they are its basic structural precondition'.[199] This is one more of the ways in which social structure moulds personalities and characters, and consequently the whole of social life.

7

On Social Processes

To say that society is always in motion is a commonplace. No one seriously doubts it. Significant differences in theoretical perspectives arise only when the quality of that motion is taken as problematic and analysed in detail. Then, several distinctions appear as crucial. One refers to the *locus of change*. In some perspectives it is perceived as occurring in the domain of social life, in others, in the domain of social structure. Another distinction refers to the *scope of change*. At times it is treated as immanent, closed within the boundaries of the analysed domain, or, to put it briefly, as 'change in'; at other times, as transcendental, producing major transformations of the analysed domain, or, to put it briefly, as 'change of'.[1] And finally is the distinction that refers to the *origins of change*. For some, they are found outside of analysed domain, and the change is then treated as exogenous; for others, they are located inside the domain, and the change is treated as endogenous.[2]

The theoretical positions opting for the first alternative in each of the foregoing pairs can be justifiably described as static. There are various degrees of a static orientation. The most extreme excludes any consideration of the change in the domain of social structure, focusing wholly on changes in social life, in human behaviour, social interactions, group-formations and dissolutions, the crystallisation of attitudes, the shaping of personalities etc. A weaker form of the static orientation considers structural change, but only of the immanent sort – change in social structures but not change of structures. The weakest version does take into account changes of structures but treats these only as exogenous, as deriving solely from external sources while fully excluding the possibility of endogenous change.

In contrast, a dynamic theoretical standpoint is here construed as one that considers changes both in social life and in social structures, treating them as not only immanent *changes in* but also as transcendental *changes of* these structures and recognising both their exogenous and endogenous sources. The strongest version of the dynamic perspective – one might say the dynamic position *par excellence* – is characterised by a dominant theoretical focus on endogenous changes of the social structure with a relative neglect of both structural changes of the other types and changes in social life.[3]

In this chapter I shall argue that *the image of society underlying Merton's social theory is dynamic* in the precise sense explicated. Occasional accounts of Merton's sociology as static in orientation are groundless. As Loomis and Loomis noted long ago, Merton is 'irrevocably committed to a study of the dynamics of social change no less than to the stabilities of social structures'.[4] That interest pervades all of Merton's work, from the earliest period when he dealt with historical changes of religion and science, of society and culture in 17th-century England to his most recent studies of change in 'socially expected durations'.[5] As the Loomises go on to say: 'In view of the contemporary accent on social change . . . it is instructive to note the early attention devoted thereto by Merton and to be sensitized to its pervasive presence in his works'.[6]

Structure, conflict and change

The notion of social change in Merton's theory is clearly associated with two other concepts; of social structure and of social conflict. Merton's enduring focus on the social structure has been the leitmotif of the entire preceding analysis. In light of what has been noted in the two preceding chapters, which document his theoretical perspective as a 'sociological structuralist', it is hardly surprising to find that the type of change to which he devotes most attention is *structural change*. This concept has a double meaning. Structural change$_1$ designates change pertaining to the social structure as distinct from social life. Structural change$_2$ designates change originating in the social structure (as distinct from extrastructural sources located in social life, or natural events). Of the four analytic categories resulting from the logically possible combinations of these distinctions, Merton's focus is placed in the first, the purely structural category centred on *structurally produced change in and of social structures*. He also gives some but less consideration to the mixed structural categories: structurally induced change in social life and extrastructurally induced change in and of social structures. He does not deal with the non-structural category of changes in social life caused by extra-structural sources which are regarded as *ad hoc*, accidental, irregular, unpatterned and, therefore, as outside his theoretical net.

The significance of structurally induced social conflict and kindred notions in Merton's analysis of society has been examined at length in the preceding chapter. Varieties of conflict were there distinguished and his interest in each kind of conflict illustrated by many examples. This focus was stated as early as the first appearance of *Social Theory and Social Structure* in 1949. At that time Merton – the functionalist – was saying: 'The key concept bridging the gap between statics and dynamics in functional theory is that of strain, tension, contradiction, or discrepancy between the component elements of social and cultural structure. Such strains may be dysfunctional for the social system in its then existing form; they may also be instrumental in leading to changes in that system. In any case, they exert pressure for change'.[7] It becomes even more pronounced in the 1975 paradigm for structural analysis: 'it is fundamental, not incidental, to the paradigm of structural analysis that *social structures generate social conflict* by being differentiated, in historically differing extent and kind, into interlocking arrays of social statuses, strata, organizations, and communities that have their own and therefore potentially conflicting as well as common interests and values'. And he goes on to explain: 'social conflict cannot occur without a clash of values, norms, or interests variously shared by each of the social formations that are in conflict. . . . It is precisely that kind of socially patterned differentiation of interests and values that leads structural analysis to hold that social conflict is not mere happenstance but is rooted in social structure'.[8]

In the light of this type of formulation in Merton's early, intervening and late writings, it seems odd to have some commentators attribute a static orientation to him. But others have noted that 'It is precisely the contradictions and incompatibilities in social life that have been the focus of Merton's work. Merton stands in a long tradition, from Vico to Hegel and Marx, that stresses conflict and contradiction in society. . . . He has attempted to *specify* and *locate* disjunctions, contradictions, and conflicts within the social structure . . . Merton's model of social structure sensitizes the analyst to the presence of conflicts and contradictions'.[9]

The notion of conflict enters into dynamic analysis only to the extent that the sources and the consequences of conflict and change are specified in detail. Merton focuses on *conflictual change*. This concept also has a double meaning: 'conflictual' may signify 'conflict-generated', or 'conflict-effecting'. Conflictual change$_1$ designates change produced by conflict (as opposed to other possible sources). Conflictual change$_2$ designates change producing conflict (as opposed to other structural effects, such as equilibrium). Merton's interest centres almost entirely on conflictual change in the 'pure' sense, combining both meanings, the *change produced by conflict and the change reproducing conflict in the social structure*. But he also devotes attention to one of the 'mixed' categories, namely, conflict-generated change that under specified conditions brings about consensus and consonance rather than always reproducing conflict.[10]

Combining both emphases typically found in Merton's dynamic analysis – the focus on structure and the focus on conflict – we can formulate and synthesise his theoretical orientation to social and cultural change. His main preoccupation is with structural changes generated by and reproducing structural conflict.

The basic typology of structural changes is implicit in the foregoing discussion. Merton puts it emphatically and explicitly in italics: '*social structures generate both change within the structure and change of the structure.*'[11] The first type of changes involves the 'functioning' or 'operation' of society. These consist in ongoing adaptive processes which reproduce specified states of a social structure, or at least keep them within the limits which give that structure its identity. The second type of changes involves the 'transformation' of society. This consists of the processes that disrupt the existing structure and create a basically new one in its place. They may be referred to as 'morphogenetic'.[12] The first type of change brings about the *reproduction of an old social order*; the second type of change brings about the *production of a new social order*. We now consider how Merton construes both types of changes and both types of related social processes.

Adaptive processes

The general conception of adaptive processes is this: structural conflict brings about reactions that tend to reduce or to eliminate structural conflict. It involves *compensatory mechanisms* founded on the logic of negative feed-back in cybernetics. These mechanisms operate either spontaneously, as Merton says 'unwittingly', or in a planned, purposeful way, in Merton's terms 'by design'.[13]

I shall refer to the first as latent dynamics, and to the second as manifest dynamics of adaptive processes. The distinction is basically analytic. Both kinds of dynamics can coincide in the same concrete process and they can imperceptibly overlap. For example, manifest dynamics may produce unintended and unrecognised consequences and switch on the latent dynamics; latent dynamics may become recognised, accepted and purposefully utilised, switching on manifest dynamics.[14] For simplicity, though, each type is discussed separately.

An extensive example of the first kind – latent dynamics – is provided by Merton's analysis of the articulation of roles in the role-set and of the social dynamics of adaptation in status-sets.[15] As will be recalled, the concepts of role-set and status-set constitute the crux of Merton's image of the social structure. Various types of conflicts are shown to derive from the complexity – plurality and differentiation of components – of the social structure, and in turn, to constitute the 'structural sources of instability' in the social structure. The important question, then, is the processes through which the role conflicts within the role-set and conflicts among role-sets within the status-set can be coped with. For, obviously, some individuals under the cross-fire of incongruent normative expectations do manage to cope while others do not. But those individual, idiosyncratic adaptations do not interest Merton. Rather, he seeks to find the structural arrangements that provide the social mechanisms for the reduction or elimination of structural strains. For Merton, these 'mechanisms' (distinctive kinds of social processes) do not appear out of nowhere, as teleologically posited, but derive from specified potentialities of social structure. Referring to the role-set, he observes that 'the notion of role-set . . . raises the general problem of identifying the social mechanisms which serve to articulate the expectations of those in the role-set so that the occupant of a status is confronted with less conflict than would obtain if these mechanisms were not at work'.[16] In like fashion he observes that status-sets differ in degrees of complexity, with some involving structurally numerous and diverse statuses while others have few and fairly homogenous statuses. He goes on to note that 'Counteracting such difficulties which are potentially involved in complex status-sets are several types of social processes'.[17]

All such mechanisms and processes are, of course, treated as *contingent*, and this in a double sense. First, they need not work out automatically but *require decisions*, structurally facilitated, by organised collectives. And second, they need not to be ultimately efficient; structurally induced social conflicts are never wholly eliminated. As Merton states expressly: 'even when these mechanisms are at work, they may not, in particular cases, prove sufficient to reduce the conflict of expectations below the level required for the social structure to operate with substantial efficiency'.[18] The limiting case is when the social mechanisms themselves 'break down so that structurally established role-sets do not remain relatively stabilized'.[19] Then, the change of the structure will normally ensue. This will be discussed in the next section devoted to morphogenetic processes. For a moment though, let us stay with the cases when social mechanisms do operate to bring about adaptive results.

Merton analyses six social mechanisms which are structurally available for copying with conflict in the role-set. It is first observed that various partners in the role-set are *differentially involved in the relationship* with a focal person, and consequently address demands and expectations toward that person with differing intensity. For example; structurally, a physician faces more and stronger demands from patients, colleagues and hospital administrators than, say, from ambulance drivers or X-ray technicians. And conversely, for him, the expectations of patients, colleagues and hospital administrators are more significant than those of the technical personnel. Thus, he can cope with the possible role-conflict by paying selective attention to the expectations originating in his role-set, with stronger emphasis on the expectations and demands of 'more significant' others. Merton puts it in general terms: 'What holds for the particular case . . . holds for the occupants of any other status: the impact upon them of diverse expectations of appropriate behavior among those in their role-set can be structurally mitigated by differentials of involvement in the relationship among those constituting their role-set'.[20]

A second structural pattern provides a comparable mechanism. The various partners in a role-set have *differential power* with respect to a focal person, owing to the fact that their social positions are located on different levels of power-hierarchies. 'As a consequence of social stratification', Merton observes, 'the members of a role-set are not apt to be equally powerful in shaping the behavior of status occupants'.[21] Note that differentiated power is not conceived as mainly given or accidental, but rather as patterned, in brief – as structural. It does not refer to the hypothetical case of a patient, who happens to be the President, and therefore, in absolute terms, has more power for the time over the physician who treats him, that other patients, colleagues, nurses and hospital administrators put together. Rather, it refers to the *structural circumstance* that the directors of hospitals have more enduring power over interns than, say, have patients or nurses. The necessity to subject oneself to the expectations of those more powerful in the individual's role-set works to resolve the role-conflict, if not the personality conflict or at least justifies one's conformity to some and not other expectations.

Third, role-partners have unequal opportunities for monitoring the performance of the focal person. The 'observability' of his behaviour by those in his role-set holding different positions is structurally patterned: 'To the extent that the social structure insulates an individual from having his activities known to members of his role-set, he is not uniformly subject to competing pressures'.[22] Specific structural arrangements provide such insulation. the institution of 'privileged information' and 'confidential communication' typical of various professions serves as one example. Merton believes that in some measure and in some situations, ' "privacy" is not merely a personal predilection; it is an important functional requirement for the effective operation of social structure'.[23]

A fourth mechanism involves enlarging observability among partners of the role-set of the conflicting and mutually incompatible expectations addressed to the focal person. Pressures on that person are reduced as various role-partners become aware of his insoluble predicament: 'when it becomes plain that the demands of some are in full contradiction with the demands of others, it becomes, in part, the task of members of the role-set, rather than that of the status-occupant to resolve these contradictions either by a struggle for exclusive power or by some degree of compromise'.[24] That process of contention shifts the nature of the structurally induced conflict among those competing for a larger share of his loyalty, obedience, etc. 'The status-occupant, originally at the focus of the conflict, virtually becomes a more or less influential bystander whose function it is to highlight the conflicting demands by members of his role-set and to make it a problem for them, rather than for him, to resolve *their* contradictory demands'.[25]

A fifth mechanism derives from the structural basis of mutual support among those experiencing similar predicaments of role-conflict. As Merton explains: 'The actual and potential experience of confronting conflicting role-expectations among those in one's own role-set is to this extent common to occupants of the status. . . . Such conflicts of role-expectations become patterned and shared by occupants of the same social status'.[26] Typical structural arrangements called forth by this mechanism are trade unions, professional associations, professional codes, etc., which 'constitute social formations designed to counter the power of the role-set; of being, not merely amenable to these demands, but of helping to shape them'.[27]

Finally, a sixth social mechanism, the most radical of all, is identified: this involves abridging the role-set, eliminating some of the roles which make it up. This can take the form of an individual adaptation; a person who cannot endure conflicting pressure breaks off the relationship with certain role-partners, or leaves the status altogether, thus escaping from its entire role-set. Of course, the status-occupant *is not free* to break off certain relationships, or to escape a status at will, but is always structurally constrained: 'this mode of adaptation is possible only under special and limited conditions. It can be effectively utilized only in those circumstances where it is still possible for the status-occupant to perform his other roles, without the support of those with whom he has discontinued relations. Otherwise put, this requires that the remaining relationships in the role-set are not substantially damaged by this device'.[28] Compare the case of a person breaking with a circle of friends, with that of a spy or a soldier deserting his allegiances.

But the case which should interest Merton most, in line with his structural approach, is not the one when 'the individual goes, and the social structure remains',[29] but rather one in which the structure of the role-set as a whole is changed by eliminating some types of relationships with some types of partners. The manager who fires all the industrial psychologists in the plant and decides not to employ any other, liquidating the respective positions in his staff, may serve as an illustration. He radically resolves his role-conflict, deriving from their expertise, demands and 'unrealistic' proposals; even though it does not help him much in solving the social conflicts or human relations problems in his plant. Of course, the structural limitations of this possibility are still more stringent than in the preceding case. It requires a large share of power, of the kind which has been referred to in sociological literature as 'meta-power',[30] to reshape the structure of the role-set. In fact, this is already a case bordering on the processes of morphogenesis rather than adaptation.

Turning to a higher level of structural complexity, Merton addresses the issue of conflicts arising from the divergent expectations attached not to the role-set of a single social position, but to the multiple positions occupied by each individual: 'Complex status-sets not only make for some form of liaison between subsystems in a society; they confront the occupants of these statuses with distinctly different degrees of difficulty in organizing their role-activities'.[31] Social structures evolve social mechanisms for counteracting these difficulties. They are largely analogous to mechanisms operating in role-sets.

To begin with, the 'social perception of competing obligations entailed in status-sets serves to cushion and to modify the demands and expectations by members of the role-sets associated with some of these statuses'.[32] Example: death in immediate family temporarily exempts an employee from role-obligations to the employer. Second, there may develop a patterned consensus in the ideal structure defining the relative importance of various positions. 'To the extent that there is a *prior* consensus on the relative 'importance' of conflicting status-obligations, this reduces the internal conflict of decision by those occupying these statuses and eases the accommodation on the part of those involved in their role-sets'.[33] For example, if the dominant culture puts heavier emphasis on professional obligations than family obligations, it makes it easier for the professional to neglect the family, and for the family to reconcile itself with such neglect. Third, the fact that the cross-pressures of multiple statuses is a universal human experience facilitates structurally induced, *patterned empathy* among those having demanding expectations of others. The boss can understand the predicament of a newly-wed employee, because he still remembers the demands on his time (and energy) made by his own wife. Fourth, with repeated patterns of such conflicts between various statuses, meta-norms, or 'standards of priority'[34] emerge to help regulate patterned choices among status-obligations in these typical situations of conflict. 'Friends come first', would be an example of such a meta-norm typical for some cultures. Finally, the fact that an individual acquires the conflicting statuses not simultaneously but in biographical sequence means that they are not combined at random. A process of *self-selection* guided by the criterion of congruence, and not only social selection operates: 'In terms of the value-orientations already developed, people reject certain statuses which they could achieve, because they find them repugnant, and select other prospective statuses, because they find them congenial'.[35] Consider the improbable case of a Christian Scientist physician or a Quaker general. One can add that *selective recruitment* to various positions acts in the same direction, demanding from potential incumbents specific value-orientations, skills or competences. Example: graduates of an art academy are not likely to become professional soldiers and will hardly be admitted to West Point Military Academy, in the unlikely event that they apply. As a result of these processes of self- and social selection, the status-set is less conflictual at any given moment *than it would be*, if a random selection of statuses obtained.[36]

Goode provides an interesting continuation and extension of Merton's analysis, looking at the same problem not so much from the point of view of structural mechanisms involved but rather from the perspective of an individual who is likely 'to face a wide, distracting, and sometimes conflicting array of role obligations. . . . He cannot meet all these demands to the satisfaction of all the persons who are part of his total role network'.[37] As a result, the individual experiences 'role strain' and faces the psychological necessity to reduce it to some managable proportions. Goode also enumerates strategies available to the individual. Some aim at reorganising the 'total role network' of an individual, some at striking the best 'role-bargains' within the existing network. In the first group of strategies, Goode includes: 'the "compartmentalization" of role relations when their inconsistency is ignored; the "delegation" when some role behavior is left to others; the "elimination" of role-relationships, when a person resigns from them;[38] the "extension" of role-relations in order to excuse inefficient performance in all the roles or to facilitate the better performance of preferred ones; the raising of "barriers against intrusion", when partners are prevented or discouraged from initiating or continuing certain role relationships'.[39] A second group of strategies include methods of setting the 'role price', that is arriving at 'the level of performance which the individual finally decides upon',[40] within a role network.

A structural point of view reappears in Goode's basically interactionist or 'exchange' perspective, when he recognises the structural context in which individuals cope with role-strain, and attempt to strike role-bargains. That context constrains choices limiting the field of possible reactions and encouraging certain options among those which are possible: 'It is to the individual's interest in attempting to reduce his role strain to demand as much as he can and perform as little, but since this is also true of others, there are limits on how advantageous a role bargain he can make'.[41]

Goode states: 'Several of our mechanisms are paralleled by Merton's'.[42] There is a common logic underlying their conceptions: individual adaptations become shared, objectified, and institutionalised in the social structure; from private evasions to role strain, the process leads to structurally embedded evasions from role (and status) conflicts, and ultimately to structural mechanisms available in the social structure itself, of the type discussed by Merton. Such an imputed causal process would fit the category of 'unwitting' or spontaneous adaptations which gradually evolve from the 'bottom' of the multiplicity of repeated patterns, individual actions and interactions. This seems to be both Merton's and Goode's image.

Sometimes it is conceivable to interpret the adaptive process also as a purposeful, planned effort to introduce structural arrangements alleviating or eliminating conflicts, strains and tensions. Even in the illustrative case of role conflicts, compensating structural arrangements are often introduced *by design*, enacted rather than evolved, whether at the level of industrial plant, bureaucratic organisation, or state administration. This would of course be the more so in other types of compensating or adaptive changes: for example, restoring equilibrium after an acute social or political crisis, counteracting outbreaks of violence, curbing a demographic explosion, etc. Quite a large share of adaptive changes in contemporary societies is due to the pursuit of specified policies; the introduction of structural set-ups which are planned rather than spontaneous, instituted rather than institutionalised. Analysis of such purposive adaptive processes would certainly unravel further ways of adaptive modification of social structure. Yet, Merton seems to be much more interested in the latent than the deliberate mechanisms, except insofar as deliberate policy enactments result in unanticipated or unintended consequences or both.

Structure-building

Adaptive processes cover only a part of social dynamics. Changes *in* social structure reducing inefficiency, conflicts, strains and tensions from what they would otherwise be, must be distinguished from the changes *of* social structure which transform it significantly or produce new structural arrangements. These are described as morphogenetic (or structure-building) processes.

The distinction between the two is, as usual, only analytic. The empirical difference between these types of processes is by no means clear-cut. Adaptive and morphogenetic processes often merge; there is often a degree of overlap. There are, in particular, two types of situations in which adaptive processes imperceptibly turn into morphogenetic processes. The first, already hinted at, occurs when adaptive mechanisms *fail to operate at all adequately*. Then the conflicts, stresses and tensions which are not curbed lead to the breakdown of the structure; its de-structuration and a subsequent re-structuration. Extreme inefficiency of adaptations tends to bring about morphogenesis. There is probably some threshold beyond which this effect occurs; up to that threshold 'social systems are forced to limp along with that measure of ineffectiveness and inefficiency which is often tolerated'.[43] The second type of effect occurs when adaptive mechanisms *operate rather 'too' efficiently*. The accumulation of many new structural arrangements introduced, often on the *ad hoc* basis, to stabilise the system, may pass a threshold beyond which the structure loses its identity and turns into a new one. The large number of changes *within* the structure in effect produce a change *of* the structure. What was intended as adaptation gives rise to morphogenesis. Keeping these empirical border-line cases in mind, I shall focus on the analysis of pure morphogenetic processes.

In taking up the issue of morphogenesis, I begin by noting that Merton departs in important respects from the Durkheimian tradition. He does so by systematic attention to the neglected, reverse side of the Durkheimian implication: 'social facts→ human conduct'. As has often been noticed, Durkheim tended to take the existence of social structure for granted, as something *given* in terms of which human conduct can be explained. The sources of social structures remained largely unproblematic. A theory of morphogenesis, in contrast, takes this as problematic, and starts to study not alone the ways in which social structure moulds individuals and their actions, but also the ways in which individuals through their actions mould social structure. Merton has contributed to that evolving theory.

In Merton's theoretical orientation, the general scheme of morphogenetic process can be condensed as follows: under conditions still little understood, structural conflict brings about transformations of social structure up to the point when a new structure emerges and the structural conflict is reproduced in a new form. The basic logic underlying the process is that of amplification rather than counteraction, or, to put it differently, positive rather than negative feed-back.[44] Again, the mechanism may be either latent, 'unwitting', not purposefully designed, or manifest, purposeful and planned. Mixed cases are the rule rather than exception in social reality. Both kinds of dynamics, latent and manifest can coincide in the single process, following parallel courses or interacting in specified ways. The latent dynamics may become recognised in varying degree, and become manifest dynamics, or the manifest dynamics may produce unintended consequences, thus involving latent dynamics. A major type is the reproduction of conflict in a social structure created by design, through almost never intended consequences. I write 'almost never', only to leave room for cases in which social reformers or revolutionaries intentionally attempt to build or deepen conflicts in social structure, counting on a resulting disruption of the structure over the long run. But even in such cases, the sought-for long-run outcomes of their efforts, in the utopian societies of the future, do not provide a place for indigenous conflicts. When such conflicts inevitably reassert themselves in new form, such architects of the future are apt to be much surprised and dismayed.[45]

Similarly as in the case of adaptive processes, Merton appears to be biased in attending to the latent dynamics of morphogenesis, occasionally taking into account the emerging recognition or acceptance of latent consequences of purposive action. Pure, manifest dynamics, the purposeful creation of social structure on the basis of a preconceived plan (say, by means of legal reforms), does not receive nearly the same amount of attention.

Merton singles out two general mechanisms of morphogenesis. The first may be described as the *mechanism of accumulated dysfunctions*; the second, the *mechanism of accumulated innovations*. Both shall be discussed presently.

From the time of his functional writings in the 1930s and 40s, Merton was adamant in linking the concept of dysfunction with issues of social change: 'By focusing on dysfunctions as well as on functions, this mode of analysis can assess not only the bases of social stability but also the potential sources of social change. . . . The concept of dysfunction, which implies the concept of strain, stress and tension on the structural level, provides an analytical approach to the study of dynamics and change'.[46] Coupled with the idea of the 'net balance of the aggregate of consequences',[47] the concept of dysfunction allows for the conjecture that 'when *the net balance of the aggregate of consequences* of an existing social structure is clearly dysfunctional, there develops a strong and insistent pressure for change'.[48] And another concept present already in the 'paradigm for functional analysis', that of 'structural context'[49] is utilised to help explain in principle, not only the tendency toward change, produced by the dysfunctional net balance, but also the specific directions such change may take. Merton puts it in a form of a 'basic query': 'To what extent does knowledge of the structural context permit the sociologist to anticipate the most probable directions of social change?'.[50]

Keeping in mind the various meanings of the concept of dysfunction, embodying the idea of differentiation and relativisation of consequences of a social pattern, depending on the frame of reference adopted, one may suggest four modalities of the dynamic mechanism based on the accumulation of dysfunctions. First is the situation when certain structural elements are dysfunctional for a social system as a whole, or some of its core segments. For example, the unrestrained pattern of egoistic hedonism if sufficiently widespread may lead to the disruption of the social system. The larger the number of such dysfunctional elements, and the more dysfunctional each of them, the more likely is the system to break down. Second is the case when some elements are basically functional for a social system, but have some additional, dysfunctional side-effects. For example, the competitive success orientation may be beneficial for the economy, but at the same time may lead to the neglect of family life and consequent breakdown of family structure. The question now becomes that of the *relative* weight of the accumulated dysfunctional side-effects which, passing over a hypothetical threshold outbalance functional outcomes and lead to institutional breakdown and 'basic social change' in the form of replacement of structure. A third and, in Merton's conception, basic and empirically frequent case obtains when certain structures are *functional for certain groups or strata in the society and dysfunctional for others*. Examples: private enterprise, progressive taxation, social security, apartheid, affirmative action, etc. The net outcome – toward stability or toward change – is then determined by the *comparative power* of the diverse groups and strata beneficially or adversely affected by those patterned social arrangements. As groups or strata dysfunctionally affected attain sufficient power, they are likely to introduce structural changes. Finally, a fourth type occurs when some structural elements are functional for certain subsystems (i.e. meet certain functional requirements) and dysfunctional for other subsystems (i.e. preclude other functional requirements). For example, traditional mores or *Gemeinschaft* forms of collectivities, certainly beneficial for the integration of society may often stand in the way of economic modernisation, thus becoming dysfunctional for the economic subsystem. The pressure for change here depends on the complex set of historical circumstances determining the relative functional significance of the subsystems dysfunctionally affected (or requirements blocked). If the dysfunctions touch the subsystems of a strategic, core significance in a given historical situation, structural change is likely. Merton sums up mechanism of morphogenesis, covering the four types of situations I have singled out, in these words: 'the accumulation of dysfunctions in a social system is often the prelude to concerted social change that may bring the system closer to the values that enjoy the respect of members of the society'.[51]

The alternative mechanism of morphogenesis is the accumulation of innovations. In line with Merton's overriding orientation, the notion of innovation is accorded a structural meaning; it is only the *structural innovation* that counts. This qualification means not only that it has *structural consequences*, which are adopted and embedded in a structure, involve structural change. It also means that the innovation has *structural origins*, either in the sense that it is induced by social structure (as in his anomie theory) or in the sense that the innovation is catalysed by social structure, encountering conducive structural conditions, falling on 'fertile soil', so to say (as in the analysis of multiples in scientific discovery, or more generally, the role of great innovators in history).

Keeping in mind that social structure is here construed in elaboration of Merton's conception as consisting of three analytical dimensions (normative structure, opportunity structure and ideal structure), we assume that structural innovations occur within each dimension; originating in each and bringing about transformations in each. The analytically pure cases in which the occurrence, origins and consequences relate to the same dimension of structure can be terminologically distinguished. Thus, 'the institutionalization of norms and values' is taken to refer to morphogenesis in the normative dimension, 'the crystallization of interests and life-chances', to morphogenesis in the dimension of opportunity-structure, and 'the articulation of beliefs', to morphogenesis in the dimension of ideal structure. As usual, the concrete social reality is not so simple. We find combined cases when the process of morphogenesis is initiated within one structural dimension, proceeds at another one, and brings effects in the third one. For example, an economic reform (introduced by means of legal regulations) starts in the normative structure, produces restructuration of opportunities (interests, life chances) of various groups, strata or classes, and fundamentally modifies the belief systems (ideologies, doctrines) shared by large segments of society.

Understandably enough, not all these modalities of morphogenesis are given equal attention in Merton's analysis. One selective bias, which we have noted, favours the latent dynamics of morphogenetic process to the neglect of manifest dynamics. Another bias entails dominant focus on normative morphogenesis, the change of normative structures, with less attention devoted to changes of opportunity structures, and almost none to the changes of ideal structures. Merton's account of one type of social change – *crescive normative change* – is therefore the most developed, paradigmatic case of his approach to the processes of morphogenesis. It can be traced to the important concept of 'institutionalized evasions of institutional rules' which he proposed in the late 1930s in lectures at Harvard and developed in print in 1940s. It is also found in his theory of anomie, when among the modes of adaptations, he includes the creative responses of innovation, and particularly – rebellion. This image of crescive normative change calls for discussion in more detail. I shall attempt to introduce the full meaning of complex Merton's concepts through several analytic steps.

To begin with, by normative change is understood the change of components of the normative structure: norms, values, roles, institutions, institutional complexes. For the sake of simplicity, I shall speak of the change of norms but all that will be said applies equally to the other normative elements. Crescive normative change is understood as a change originating in the domain of behaviour and evolving to reach the normative domain.

The change of norms by this route presupposes a normative deviation as a sort of prelude. As Bierstedt observes: 'some deviations from an old structure are almost certainly part of the process of creating a new one'.[53] But deviations are not of a piece. This crucial category requires precise definition. Merton has put it this way: 'An adaptation is described as deviant (and not invidiously so) when behavior departs from what is required by cultural goals, or by institutional norms, or by both'.[54] Deviance should not be confused with merely idiosyncratic conduct; one must 'distinguish new forms of behavior that are well within the range of the institutionally prescribed or allowed and new forms that are outside this range. Following the useful terminology of Florence Kluckhohn, the first of these can be described as "variant" behavior and only the second as "deviant" '.[55]

Merton distinguishes two major forms of deviance in the proper sense: the nonconforming behaviour and the aberrant behaviour. They differ in several respects. First, nonconformity is *public*, aberrant behaviour *private*: 'nonconformers announce their dissent publicly; they do not try to hide their departures from social norms. Political or religious dissenters insist on making their dissent known to as many as will look or listen; aberrant criminals seek to avoid the limelight of public scrutiny'.[56] Second, nonconformity involves the *withdrawal of legitimacy* from current norms, aberrant behaviour is accompanied by *according legitimacy* to norms: 'Nonconformers challenge the legitimacy of social norms they reject, or at least challenge their applicability to certain kinds of situations. . . . Aberrants, in contrast, acknowledge the legitimacy of the norms they violate but consider such violation expedient or expressive of their state of mind'.[57] Third, nonconformity is positive, *constructive*, aberrant behaviour is merely *negativistic*: 'nonconformers aim to change the norms they are denying in practice. They want to replace what they believe to be morally suspect norms with ones having a sound moral basis. Aberrants, in contrast, try primarily to escape the sanctioning force of existing norms, without proposing substitutes for them'.[58]

Nonconforming behaviour and aberrant behaviour initiate two different paths of normative morphogenesis; with different stages and internal mechanisms. One may be called the *morphogenesis via normative innovation*, another – *morphogenesis via norm evasion*. I will trace the causal sequences, beginning with the latter case.

Morphogenesis via norm evasion starts from incidents of aberrant behaviour by individuals who find the norms too demanding for them, even though generally legitimate. As Jacobson defines it: 'A norm evasion . . . is a special subtype of norm violations in that it is deliberate as well as devious'.[59] For example, the thief does not question the legitimacy of the fifth commandment; will be outraged if something is stolen *from him*, and not particularly surprised if caught and sentenced. The structural origins of such behaviour are traced, as we remember, to the condition of Anomie$_3$ – discrepancy between the normative structure and opportunity-structure: 'The dominant pressure leads toward the gradual attenuation of legitimate, but by and large ineffectual, strivings and the increasing use of illegitimate, but more or less effective, expedients'.[60] This point is emphasised by the Loomises: 'As a source of social change Merton regards of prime importance the strains and tensions between the cultural expectations and social realities'.[61]

Some part of evasions from norms remain fully private, invisible, undetected – and therefore *socially inconsequential*. But when evasions become more widespread, undertaken by a plurality of individuals, the public awareness is apt to be awakened. Their more and more frequent occurrence may become widely recognised, even though the concrete villains are not identified. When they *do* become identified, the examples of particularly skilful evaders may become the subject of public lore, often tainted with envy. As Merton observes: 'Those successful rogues – successful as this is measured by the criteria of their significant reference groups – become prototypes for others in their environment who, initially less vulnerable and less alienated, now no longer keep to the rules they once regarded as legitimate'.[62]

The occurrence of common incentives to evasion among the large collectivities of individuals coupled with the widespread belief that 'everybody does it' and the tendency to imitate successful evaders – account for the patterning of evasions; their regular and repeatable character. In the Harvard lectures of 1938–39 Merton was already distinguishing between 'institutionalized evasions of institutional rules' and 'illicit and non-institutional evasions'.[63] The latter term describes precisely the case discussed presently, which Robin Williams has extended as 'patterned evasion' and defined as a situation 'where a publicly accepted norm is covertly violated on a large scale, with the tacit acceptance or even approval of the same society or group, at least as long as the violation is concealed'.[64] Tax evasions, cheating on examinations, petty theft in business firms, avoidance of customs duties and currency controls, provide familiar examples. The occurrence of patterned evasions brings us closer to the actual normative morphogenesis. But note that here the norms are *still accorded legitimacy*.

The most crucial phase comes when, as Merton puts it, 'A mounting frequency of deviant but "successful" behavior tends to lessen and, as an extreme potentiality, to eliminate the legitimacy of the institutional norms for others in the system'.[65] It is only now that his early concept of 'institutionalized evasions' fully applies. 'Evasions of institutional rules are themselves institutionalized when they are (1) patterned in fairly well-defined types; (2) adopted by substantial numbers of people rather than being scattered subterfuges independently and privately arrived at; (3) organized in the form of a fairly elaborate social machinery made up of tacitly cooperating participants, including those who are socially charged with implementing the rules; and (4) rarely punished and when they are, punished in largely symbolic forms that serve primarily to reaffirm the sanctity of the rules'.[66] Institutionalisation in this sense is more than the mere patterning, since it involves not only repetition or regularity of behaviour but the *granting of a degree of legitimacy*, widespread acceptance or even positive sanctioning to evasive behaviour. The structural sources of institutionalised evasions are traced again to the dissociations and strains between normative domain and other dimensions of social structure as well as of social life: 'The pattern [of institutionalized evasions of institutional norms] develops whenever the laws governing a political jurisdiction or the formal rules governing an organization have lagged behind the changing interests, values, and wants of a substantial part of the underlying population. For a time, the evasions make the law tolerable'.[67] An excellent example of institutionalised evasions is elaborated by Merton in the case of certain kinds of divorce procedures. He observes: 'they are patterned in a few well-defined types; they are adopted by a majority of men and women seeking divorce rather than being scattered subterfuges privately and independently arrived at; to be effective, the evasions require an elaborate social machinery made up of tacitly cooperating clients, lawyers, judges, trained connivers and specialized creators of make-believe evidence of adultery; the evasive practices are widely known to depart from the letter and spirit of the law but . . . they are nevertheless condoned by officers of the court charged with implementing the law; and finally, the evasions are rarely punished, and when they are, they provide largely ceremonial occasions for reaffirming the sanctity of the law. These, then, are truly institutionalized evasions'.[68]

There are some concrete modalities of the phase of institutionalised evasions. Two of them are explicitly noted by Merton; the third, by Jacobsen. The first is norm erosion. This occurs when evaded *norms are long established and traditional* in the normative structure, but no longer congruent with current realities: 'the pattern of institutionalized evasions develops when practical exigencies confronting the group or collectivity (or significantly large parts of them) require adaptive behavior which is at odds with long-standing norms, sentiments, and practices. . . . The norms and sentiments are for a time ostensibly retained intact, while tacitly recognized departures from them become progressively accepted in their own right'.[69] The second modality is norm resistance. In contrast to the case of norm erosion, these norms being evaded are *new*, freshly introduced 'from above', and departing from established ways of acting. It occurs 'when newly-imposed requirements for behavior are at odds with these deep-rooted norms, sentiments, and practices. The newly-imposed institutional demands are in fact evaded while the slowly-changing norms and sentiments continue to govern actual behavior'.[70] A good example is the commonly encountered resistance to social reforms, as in the case of Prohibition or civil rights legislation. A third modality involves norm substitution. This occurs when the old norm remains in force but widespread evasion acquires tentative legitimacy through the scale and long tradition of its occurrence. As Jacobsen explains: 'Patterned evasions may acquire partial legitimacy by sheer longevity, and become a tradition by default. When this happens, the norm itself does not change, but the evasion gains a measure of legitimacy from "benign neglect" '.[71] Thus 'non-smoking' prohibitions in public places are generally ignored since 'no one seemed to object to it till now',[72] but these become operative when violations are strongly protested in public. Merton seems to refer to this type of situation when he observes: 'Institutionalized evasions, it appears, tend to persist only so long as they are kept tacit. This means that "everyone knows" of the evasions in his private capacity but this severally known fact is not dramatically and repeatedly called to collective attention'.[73]

These successive types of institutionalised evasions lead to the final phase of a morphogenetic process: the introduction of new norms by authorities or attaining by evasions the status of sanctioned norms, fully legitimised and embedded in a new normative structure. Thus, referring to the notoriously large-scale evasions of obsolete divorce laws, Merton observes: 'should public testimony to these institutionalized evasions repeatedly occur, bringing out into the open the full extent of the gap between the principles of the law and the frequency of circumventory practices, this would also exert powerful pressure in its way for change of the law'.[74] This closes a cycle of morphogenesis, and of course opens a new one, as new norms inevitably begin to be evaded, at least by some members of society, and the process of normative change starts to operate again.

It is regrettable that the phenomenon of institutionalised evasions and its place in morphogenetic change have not been explored more thoroughly. Merton seemed to promise further inquiry in this direction as early as 1949: 'This is a complicated phase of change in social structure which requires far more detailed examination than is suitable here'.[75] Some thirty years later he acknowledged, with only slight exaggeration: 'practically no one has picked up the notion of "institutionalized evasions of institutional norms". I happen to believe that this represents a collective oversight of a basic sociological idea. But since I myself have not put anything in print on the subject for a good many years, the fault sits squarely on my doorstep'.[76]

Another major mechanism of normative change operates through normative innovation rather than norm evasion. Here, the norm is denied legitimacy from the beginning, and rejective behaviour (nonconformity) diverging from the norm is open. Merton locates this type of response to Anomie$_3$ as 'rebellion'. He describes this mode of adaptation in the following way: 'This adaptation leads men outside the environing social structure to envisage and seek to bring into being a new, that is to say, a greatly modified social structure. It presupposes alienation from reigning goals and standards. These come to be regarded as purely arbitrary. And the arbitrary is precisely that which can neither exact allegiance nor possess legitimacy, for it might as well be otherwise. . . . Rebellion . . . involves a genuine transvaluation, where the direct or vicarious experience of frustration leads to full denunciation of previously prized values'.[77]

Merton suggests that the vehicle of the normative change of this type is an 'organized movement for rebellion'[78] or a 'revolutionary group'.[79] But the internal dynamics of social movements is given only limited attention. One can therefore only venture a conjecture about Merton's possible image of the morphogenetic process in form of normative innovation by analogy with his account of institutionalised evasions. Such a reconstruction will be supported by Merton's dispersed observations or implicit hints.

The Loomises summarise the process in these terms: 'The modes of nonconforming adaptation . . . are in reality non-modal alternatives employed by the minority, which may in time supplant the conforming adaptations, and are likely to do so to the degree that they are functionally superior for greater numbers of the population than presently employed behavior patterns'.[80] A more concrete conception of the process begins with the *precipitation of change*. This occurs when certain individuals react in a rebellious fashion to the structural strain produced by anomie. Some nonconformers 'challenge the legitimacy of social norms they reject, or at least challenge their applicability to certain kinds of situations'.[81] Their dissent may remain private, fully idiosyncratic, and the attempts to publicise it may fail all along the line (either because of the inherent weakness of the message, or the efficient insulation and defence of the established structure). In order to become structurally consequential normative innovations have to be widely disseminated and acquire a 'monopoly of imagination'.[82] This can be thought of as a *filtering of social change*. Merton seems to assume that, under definable conditions, the chief criterion of selection between initially accepted and rejected (or simply, ignored) innovations is their *functional significance* for the society (or group): 'Under certain conditions, public nonconformity can have the manifest and latent functions of changing standards of conduct and values which have become dysfunctional for the group'.[83] Elsewhere he notes: 'Some (unknown) degree of deviation from current norms is probably functional for the basic goals of all groups. A certain degree of "innovation", for example may result in the formation of new institutionalized patterns of behavior which are more adaptive than the old in making for realization of primary goals'.[84] With the initial acceptance, or the take-off of innovation the *phase of dissemination* begins. New normative arrangements obtain widening support among the members of society. As Merton observes: 'Nonconformers can appeal to the tacit recognition by others of discrepancies between the prized values and the social reality. They thus have at least the prospect of obtaining the assent of other, initially less critical and venturesome, members of society whose ambivalence toward the current social structure can be drawn upon for support'.[85] Finally, one notes the *accommodation of change* in which various components of the normative structure, both new and old, attain some degree of congruence, at least for the time being. This would close a cycle of normative morphogenesis and open the next one, when some individuals inevitably rebel anew against the modified normative structure.[86]

In examining the process of normative change both through normative evasion and normative innovations, Merton emphasises structural constraints and facilitations, as one would expect from his structural orientation. But of course behind every evasion, there is the *evader*, and behind every innovation, the *innovator*. Some individuals have to exhibit requisite personal propensities: innovativeness, creativeness, imagination, intellectual and personal courage etc. in order to change the normative structure.

When structurally conducive circumstances do or do not obtain, probabilities of mobilising these individual traits differ accordingly. Thus, neither individual creativeness nor structural conduciveness alone is enough. They must coincide. Among several indications that Merton recognises this *complementarity of structural and psychological factors*, one may point to his study of scientific discovery as a specific type of innovation. Here he rejects both the 'great man theory', claiming exclusive significance for individual genius in major discovery and the 'environmental determination theory', asserting the inevitability of discoveries under certain cultural and social circumstances. Instead, on the basis of a study of multiple and single discoveries in science, he opts for an intermediate position 'in which an enlarged sociological theory can take account both of the environmental determination of discovery while still providing for great variability in the intellectual stature of individual scientists . . . [The theory rejects] the false disjunction between the social determination of scientific discovery and the role of genius or "great man" in science'.[87]

So much for what I have described as normative morphogenesis; change of the normative structure. This is clearly the most important level of structural change for Merton. The Loomises correctly note: 'The concept of institutionalization as an ongoing process by which non-conforming behavior, to the degree that it is actively superior, gradually supplants the old institutions to be in turn institutionalized as conforming behavior is a key process responsible for social change'.[88] Merton pays much less attention to the two other levels of morphogenesis: change of opportunity-structure and change of ideal structure. I shall have therefore to exercise considerable licence in my interpretation.

It seems to me that the core mechanism of change in the domain of opportunity-structure is described by Merton's important idea of 'accumulation of advantage and disadvantage'. He used it originally in the study of science, referring to it as the Matthew principle, or 'Matthew effect', in explicit association with the fragment of the Gospel according to St Matthew: 'For unto every one that hath shall be given, and he shall have abundance: but from him that hath not shall be taken away even that which he hath'.[89] Merton has examined this principle intensively as it works in the reward system of science. Studying cases of collaboration and of independent multiple discoveries he observes that 'eminent scientists get disproportionately great credit for their contributions to science while relatively unknown scientists tend to get disproportionately little credit for comparable contributions'.[90] As early as 1942, and later in 1968 he hints that the idea can be *generalised*: 'the principle of cumulative advantage operates in many systems of social stratification to produce the same result: the rich get richer at a rate that makes the poor become relatively poorer'.[91] Finally, in 1975, Merton generalises the concept and introduces it as one of the major stipulations in his 'paradigm for structural analysis': 'on the macro-level, the social distributions (i.e. the concentration and dispersion) of authority, power, influence, and prestige comprise structures of social control that change historically, partly through processes of "accumulation of advantage and disadvantage" accruing to people occupying diverse stratified positions in that structure (subject to processes of feedback under conditions still poorly understood)'.[92] 'Cumulation of advantage' is a self-amplifying process in which initial differences in 'access to the opportunity-structure in a given field of activity' allow for some individuals to acquire 'successively enlarged opportunities to advance' their work and 'the rewards that go with it'.[93] Thus, the selective accumulation of advantages just as in the correlative process, initial disadvantages in access to opportunity structures, produce crescive structural changes, leading in effect to highly stratified and eventually polarised distribution of life-chances, interests and the like. This can then be mitigated or countered only by the enacted and enforced redistribution of opportunities. Merton is quite clear that he conceives of this mechanism as widely applicable: '*Mutatis mutandis*, cumulative advantages accrue for organizations and institutions as they do for individuals, subject to countervailing forces that dampen exponential cumulation'.[94]

Turning to the third level of morphogenetic process – change of the ideal structure – it must be noted that its crescive, latent variety escapes Merton's attention. The problems of *social learning* (as distinct from *individual learning*); cumulation of societal self-awareness, encoding of experiences in 'social memory' – so important for the post-Durkheimian tradition – have not, so far, been extensively studied by him. To some extent he compensates for this selective omission when dealing with the enacted, manifest variety of morphogenetic change. I turn to this now.

In general, the consideration of purposeful, planned, enacted structural change is linked with the study of *power*. The phenomenon of power has not received full treatment in Merton's theory. It is certainly one of the lacunae in his theoretical system. I have linked this with his relative de-emphasising of Weberian tradition. And similar observations are made by other commentators. The Loomises observe: 'The concepts treated under controlling, i.e. power, decision making . . . receive relatively less attention from Merton'.[95] Stinchcombe echoes this appraisal: 'Merton has not systematically analyzed power systems and their implications'.[96] In his definitions of power and authority, Merton does not go far beyond the tenets of classical conceptions. Power is defined as 'the varying capacity of a group to enforce its collective decisions upon (a) its members, and (b) its social environment'.[97] Or, more precisely: 'By power . . . is meant nothing more than the observable and predictable capacity for imposing one's own will in a social action, even against the resistance of others taking part in that action'.[98] Finally, authority is understood as 'the power of control which derives from an acknowledged status, inheres in the office and not in the particular person who performs the official role'.[99] These concepts are used in the study of role-sets and status-sets, and then Merton proves his ability to identify new problems and aspects of social structure and social action (as for example, the predicament of the individual confronted by conflicting demands on the part of the members of the role-set, themselves differing in power).[100] But this is not sufficient to deal with the enacted social change. Here I simply outline the direction in which one could go beyond Merton in studying this process.

The creation or transformation of social structure in purposeful, planned, enacted manner is obviously tantamount to the exercise of power (or authority). But a peculiar form of power is involved. Its referent, the object of control, is not the conduct of social members, but the *structural framework of their conduct*; not the course of the social game, but the *rules and conditions of the game*. The concepts of 'meta-power' and 'relational control' proposed by Baumgartner, Buckley, Burns and others are directly relevant here: 'Human actors deliberately try to alter the existing matrix of action possibilities, outcomes, and orientations within which social action occurs. We refer to the exercise of such "meta-power" as relational control, that is, control over social relationships and structures, which we distinguish from power within a given structure'.[101]

The ability to introduce and enforce the changes of social structure may be analytically conceived in three categories, depending on the dimension of social structure subjected to control. Political power is basically the ability to change norms (laws), values, roles and institutions – briefly, the normative structure. Economic power is basically the ability to change opportunities and life-chances, redistribute rewards and penalties, modify vested interests – briefly, to transform the opportunity structure. Finally, ideological power is basically the ability to change shared and dominant beliefs, creeds, outlooks, ideas, doctrines – briefly, the ideal structure. Each of these forms of power and related structural changes would have to be studied in close detail to unravel the mechanisms of enacted, purposeful social transformations.

The only aspect of enacted change that Merton picks out for more thorough scrutiny is the exercise of *ideological power* in modifying the ideal structures. This is studied under the headings of mass persuasion, propaganda and interpersonal influence. But even here, he approaches the issue only indirectly, since his focus, in this exceptional case, is on the social-psychological rather than structural level. He studies the mechanisms and techniques of shaping beliefs and opinions of individuals. There is quite a long logical step from that to the analysis of social consciousness (ideal structure) and its origins (morphogenesis). But at least, it is a beginning.

For Merton, the generic socio-psychological category seems to be the influence (or more precisely, the influence on opinions). It has two variants: mass persuasion (and its special form: propaganda) is a subtype of influence flowing from some centre, so-to-say 'from above', and typically transmitted by mass-media; interpersonal influence, on the contrary, flows from the partners of individuals in their interactional networks, and typically utilises direct communication. The earlier is a vertical influence; the latter a horizontal influence. Merton makes the distinction explicitly: 'Influence through mass media is patently not the same as interpersonal influence'.[102]

The processes of mass persuasion are analysed by Merton in considerable detail, on the basis of an empirical case-study of an extremely successful war-bond campaign in World War II.[103] Here Merton, the empirical researcher, is at his best. Perhaps the most revealing point in the study has to do with the larger social context of mass persuasion. The general social situation, prevailing 'climate of opinion', the directions and tendencies of earlier persuasive appeals, encoded in collective memory are shown decisively to co-determine the effective mass persuasion. More specific form of mass persuasion – propaganda – is taken up as the subject for a series of empirical studies carried out with Paul Lazarsfeld and Patricia Kendall. Propaganda is defined as 'any and all sets of symbols which influence opinion, belief or action on issues regarded by the community as controversial'.[104] Analysing the effectiveness of propaganda, Merton typically identifies paradoxical, of course unintended, cases of its countereffectiveness, 'boomerang effects'[105] or 'boomerang responses': 'Under certain conditions . . . people respond to propaganda in a fashion opposite to that intended by the author'.[106] This phenomenon is more common than one might expect. 'All media', Merton asserts, 'are richly endowed with boomerangs. Unintended responses may arise in any case where one group tries to impress another with the need for acting or thinking along certain specified lines'.[107] Several types of boomerang effects are distinguished and studied in detail, including the most general one, 'propaganditis' which signifies a common distrust of any message, defined – correctly or mistakenly – as propaganda.[108]

Processes of interpersonal influence are traced in an empirical research in the local community of Rovere. Interpersonal influence is conceived of as 'the direct interaction of persons in so far as this affects the future behavior or attitude of participants (such that this differs from what it would have been in the absence of interaction)'.[109] The study was centred on discovering *which kinds of individuals* exercise *what kind of influence* in the course of interaction, direct and mediated. It first attempted to identify 'influentials', those who exercised more influence than others of seemingly like social kind. It went on to examine the sources of influence. It tackled the problem of the 'avenues to' various kinds of interpersonal influence and the further problem 'who is influential for whom?' (or are these relationships wholly random?). Finally it began to identify the problem and to propose provisional findings with regards to the spheres of influence – single or few in contrast to many.

The most important result of Merton's study is the discovery of two patterns of interpersonal influence, local and cosmopolitan.

The first aspect of the difference relates to those who exert the influence – the *typical orientations* or attitudes of 'influentials' or Lazarsfeld's 'opinion leaders'. 'By a local', Merton states, 'I mean one who is largely oriented to his organization or immediate community that dominates his interests, concerns, and values. By a cosmopolitan, I mean one who is oriented toward the larger social world beyond his immediate organization or community, with extended interests, concerns, and values'.[110] In the community Merton studied, for the local influential 'Rovere is essentially his world', whereas the cosmopolitan influential 'resides in Rovere but lives in the Great Society'.[111] The second aspect involves the *differing bases* of their influence. For the local influentials, 'their influence rests on an elaborate network of personal relationships. . . . The influence of local influentials rests not so much on what they know but on whom they know',[112] while for the cosmopolitan influentials, the opposite holds. A third aspect of the distinction relates to the *wants of the influenced* which can be satisfied by each type of influential: 'It appears that the cosmopolitan influential has a following because he knows; the local influential, because he understands. The one is sought out for his specialized skills and experience; the other for his intimate appreciation of intangible but effectively significant details'.[113] A fourth aspect has to do with the *scope of influence.* 'Monomorphic influentials' exert 'influence in one rather narrowly defined area'; they are the 'experts in a limited field'. In contrast, 'polymorphic influentials' exert 'interpersonal influence in a variety of (sometimes seemingly unrelated) spheres'.[114] Merton finds that 'the locals are the more likely to be polymorphic and the cosmopolitans, monomorphic'.[115]

Those concepts and analytical observations, insightful and fruitful,[116] provide only a beginning of a systematic account of morphogenesis at the level of ideal structure. In the further study of this problem the vast area of education, understood as the intended, purposeful shaping of social consciousness, and the rich results of educational sociology, will have to be brought into the picture.

Behind the stage: action and agent

Social processes, whether adaptive or morphogenetic, whether resulting in the smooth operation of society or in its transformation, are carried out *through the actions* of human beings. Behind social processes, there are always some acting individuals or collectivities. Merton is too sophisticated to fall into the trap of sociological reification. He recognises that the ultimate moving force and the carrier of social dynamics cannot be anything else but people. And the direction and course of social dynamics can only depend on what people do, on human choices. As Stinchcombe reads Merton: 'There is, to be sure, consistent attention to the fact that people have to do all social actions. . . . Externally constraining social facts have to get into people's minds in order to constrain them. But people are clever about getting what they want out of a constraining social structure'.[117]

Merton does not provide a systematic and explicit theory of social action, in the style of Weber, Pareto, Znaniecki, or Parsons. This has led some hasty readers of his work to claim that he has no theory of action at all. Thus Bierstedt states: 'It merits attention, however, that there is so little of Parsons in Merton. . . . Nor can one discover in Merton any face of a voluntaristic theory of action. In fact, action is not a category in Merton'.[118] Similarly, Campbell traces the sources of ambiguity in the categories of manifest and latent functions precisely to the underdeveloped status of Merton's theory of action.[119]

It is undoubtedly true that the structural side of the equation which some adopt, 'structure versus action', is closer to Merton's heart. In the subject index to *Social Theory and Social Structure* there is virtually no reference to 'social action', whereas there are twenty-four references to 'social structure'. But there is a partly implicit and necessarily selective account of the category of action that can be reconstructed from Merton's work. This supplements his structural ideas and roots them firmly in the ultimate ontological substratum of the social world, the conduct of its members.

Merton starts from a *voluntaristic image of action*, conceiving it in terms of 'means-ends' scheme. As he put it in one of his earliest papers (in 1936): 'In considering purposive action, we are concerned with "conduct" as distinct from "behavior", that is, with action that involves motives and consequently a choice between alternatives'.[120] Non-instrumental types of action seem to be at the margin of his focus. Rational quality of action is seen as relative to the perspective of the actor; or more precisely to his normative and cognitive framework – *preferences* and *knowledge*. Merton counterposes such relative, or subjective rationality to the absolute or objective rationality: 'Above all, it must not be inferred that purposive action implies "rationality" of human action (that persons always use the *objectively most adequate* means for the attainment of their end)'.[121] I think Merton would accept the definition of rational action, in the sense of subjective rationality, as such in which the choices taken by an individual fall within the area delimited on the one hand by his scale of values and norms, and on the other hand, by his appraisal of the conditions in which he finds himself, including the situation as well as his own potentials for action. To put it metaphorically, the subjective rationality provides the gate through which the external social structure enters human heads. The normative structure is reflected in personal preferences, constrains and facilitates the selection of goals and means; the opportunity structure and the ideal structure are reflected in the personal knowledge, they constrain and facilitate the appraisal of actual conditions and potential possibilities.

Human action has two important properties; it is subjective and it is reflexive. The *subjective coefficient* of every action is rooted in the fact that individuals act in terms of their normative and cognitive beliefs: 'we respond not only to the objective features of a situation, but also, and at times primarily, to the meaning this situation has for us'.[122] The objective situation is subjectively appraised by acting individuals. Two mechanisms, through which human subjectivity affirms itself mediate between the situation and action. They are: *the interpretation* by means of the 'definition of a situation', and *the relativisation*, by means of the 'frame of reference'.

The first mechanism – that of interpretation – is elucidated in what Merton described in the latter 1930s as 'the Thomas theorem'. He regards it as a 'theorem basic to the social sciences' or even 'probably the single most consequential sentence ever put in print by an American sociologist'.[123] The theorem as set forth by W. I. Thomas reads: 'If men define situations as real, they are real in their consequences'.[124] Its important emphasis on the *objective consequences of human subjectivity* should not blind one to the purely objective processes operating in social life, independently of human awareness. Merton emphatically notes that the reverse of the Thomas theorem does not hold. It is not true that 'If men do *not* define situations as real, they are not real in their consequences'.[125] To avoid the fallacy of total subjectivism Merton proposes a counterpart to the Thomas theorem: 'And if men do *not* define real situations as real, they are nevertheless real in their consequences'.[126] The Thomas theorem indicates the peculiar human potential of extending reality by means of independent causal power of interpretation, imagination, projection. It does not presuppose the insulation of individuals from the impact of reality.

It seems that the Thomas theorem has a double relevance: for the issue of subjectivity and for the issue of reflexivity. For present purposes (as I am focusing on the issue of subjectivity) it simply holds that people act on the basis of their subjective perceptions of the situation, whether those perceptions are adequate or inadequate. So far as the origins of action are concerned, the distinction between true and false interpretations is simply irrelevant. People do what they *think* is best under the circumstances (subjectively rational) whether this is so or not. This partial meaning of the Thomas theorem may be grasped by such an extended paraphrase: 'If men define situations as real, they are real in their impact *on their own decisions to act*'. I shall present another paraphrase when we come to the issue of reflexivity, and the second partial meaning of the theorem.

A second mechanism through which the subjective factor connecting social structure with human action affirms itself is the process of relativisation. It is in his work on reference groups that Merton deals with it most extensively. Hyman's term 'reference group' is rather misleading because, of course, it is a human action rather than a human collectivity of a certain type which is in the focus of attention. What Merton (and earlier, Hyman) in fact studies is the behaviour in terms of some, subjectively selected frame of reference; 'reference group behaviour' means not so much the behaviour *of* reference groups, but rather human behaviour *in terms of* particular frames of reference supplied by the groups, but also by reference individuals, statuses, 'role models',[127] 'culture heroes', 'reference idols',[128] etc. What is central to the idea of 'reference group' is then clearly the idea of *reference* (i.e. relativisation), and not the idea of group. It covers 'those processes of evaluation and self-appraisal in which the individual takes the values or standards of other individuals and groups as a comparative frame of reference'.[129] As Shibutani observes: 'When used in this manner, the concept of reference group points more to a psychological phenomenon than to an objectively existing group of men; it refers to an organization of the actor's experience'.[130]

Similar point is made by Pollis: 'If a noticeable gain is to be made via the reference group construct, it should be defined at the social psychological level of analysis. That is, it should be a construct designed to explain an individual's behaviour as that behavior is related to the individual's significant socio-cultural worlds'.[131]

Merton's theory of reference groups, one of the most developed theories of the middle range, attempts to explain why individuals select certain frames of reference and not others, some sociocultural worlds and not others, why they identify with some groups and individuals and not others. It also attempts to trace the consequences (functions) of those choices for the wider society. Both the origins and consequences of the selection are *referred to the social structure*, and thus, in one sense, reference-group theory is another exemplification of Merton's structural orientation. But the behavioural phenomenon itself, though structurally constrained and structurally consequential, is of course non-structural in character; it is located in the domain of human action.

Merton emphasises the fact that individuals borrow their frames of reference, orientation, or perspective, from the groups they consider significant. The reference groups from which they take normative orientation, which set and maintain standards for them, are of what Kelley described as a 'normative type'.[132] Those from which one takes cognitive orientation, which provide the frame of comparison, relative to which the individual evaluates himself and others – are of Kelley's 'comparative type'.[133] Merton has noted: 'The two types are only analytically distinct, since the same reference group can of course serve both functions'.[134]

The orientations of an individual may be shaped by his reference groups positively, or in the negative way (*a rébours*). The individual may identify himself with the group and *emulate its standards*, normative or cognitive. But he may also abhor the group and *defy its standards* to the extent that he is constrained not to act in the ways the group demands or even to act in patently opposed ways. As Merton puts it: 'The positive type involves motivated assimilation of the norms of the group or the standards of the group as a basis for self-appraisal; the negative type involves motivated rejection, i.e. not merely non-acceptance of norms but the formation of counter-norms'.[135]

An individual of course often selects the group to which he or she *actually belongs*, as a reference group. For a long time sociologists have taken it as a given that membership groups are the sources of individuals' acquired ideas, beliefs, values, norms, etc. Else, what is meant by education or socialisation. But tucked away in this age-old transparently clear assumption was the further tacit premise that these were acquired only from groups of which one was actually a part. As it turns out, the theoretically more interesting case is the derivation of normative or cognitive orientation from a group to which one *does not actually belong*. As Merton observes: 'Men frequently orient themselves to groups other than their own in shaping their behavior and evaluations, and it is the problems centered about this fact of orientation to non-membership groups that constitute the distinctive concern of reference group theory'.[136] One process through which non-membership groups shape individuals' orientations is labelled by Merton as 'anticipatory socialization': 'the acquisition of values and orientations found in statuses and groups in which one is not yet engaged but which one is likely to enter'.[137]

The fact that an individual may attach his or her loyalties both to membership groups and non-membership groups, coupled with the notorious plurality of group-affiliations of individuals, further enlarged by group-affiliations which one seeks – provide conditions for conflicts among one's frames of reference; one's normative and cognitive orientations. As Shibutani points out: 'each person internalizes several perspectives, and this occasionally gives rise to embarrassing dilemmas which call for systematic study'.[138] Following the letter of Merton's analysis, as well as its spirit – the pervasive concern with conflict, contradictions, strains, and tensions characteristic for the human condition – Pollis builds a typology of 'reference group conflicts'. There are four, particularly interesting categories. One is a 'membership group – reference group conflict', where the individual is expected to behave in certain ways by the group to which he actually belongs, but derives his different standards of conduct from the reference group with which he subjectively identifies.[139] To put it metaphorically, his body is here, his soul elsewhere. Example: a bank clerk who dreams of becoming a rock star. Another is the 'reference group – reference group conflict', where an individual subjectively identifies with two or more reference groups, neither of which he actually belongs to, and all of which impose different standards.[140] An example: a student who cannot decide whether to become a baseball professional player or an attorney. His soul is torn, to put it metaphorically. The third category covers a combination: 'membership cum reference group versus pure reference (non-membership) group', when an individual belongs to one group with which he strongly identifies (participates with his body and soul, so to say), but at the same time identifies with some other group to which he aspires to belong.[141] Example: a committed scholar, who would also like to become a jazz musician. The fourth category covers a conflict of two groups, both of which are membership groups and at the same time reference groups for an individual, but demand contradictory attitudes or behaviours. This case is typically dealt with in the analyses of conflicts within the status-sets. Example: a devoted father pursuing a professional career, and feeling guilty both when he stays after hours in his office, and when he plays with the kids at home.

The concepts of reference group in the narrow sense (non-membership group) and of anticipatory socialisation, systematically identify the force of *patterned subjectivity* in human action. They describe the situations in which individuals subject themselves to the dictates of groups to which they do not (objectively) belong and which therefore would have no grip on them, save for their subjective identification. The social structure constrains or facilitates their actions only because they have, in effect, submitted themselves to structural influence. They themselves have chosen the drummer to whose beat they march or the audiences in front of whom they perform.

But there is another important characteristic of human action. Along with its subjectivity, human action has the attribute of *reflexivity*. And here the next implication of the Thomas theorem has strong relevance. This may perhaps be grasped by another, extended paraphrase of the statement: 'If men define situations as real, they are real in the consequences of their actions *on the situations themselves*'. As we have noted earlier, people act on the basis of their definitions of situations, according to their interpretations of conditions but those actions – *whether based on sound or unsound perceptions* – bring about tangible results in the objective world. Whether the action was based on a correct or incorrect, an appropriate or inappropriate interpretation does not affect the actual consequences once the action is taken. In particular, *the consequences of action may react on the situation of action*. It may happen that action taken on the basis of a wrong appraisal of the situation will so modify the situation that the initial (false) appraisal will seemingly become right. Or else it may happen that action taken on the basis of a correct appraisal of the situation will so modify the situation that the initial (correct) appraisal will turn out to be seemingly wrong. This is the *puzzle of reflexivity*, one which Merton confronted early in his career in dealing with the mechanisms of 'self-defeating predictions' in 1936 and of the 'self-fulfilling prophecy' in 1948.[142] The concepts and the terms have become widely diffused, in vernacular and not alone in sociology. Many variants of the terms have since appeared: 'self-destroying prophecies', 'self-frustrating predictions', 'self-confirming prophecies' and the like.

The core common to both concepts is the recognition that, as Stinchcombe put it: 'Information on what is going to happen puts a future-oriented animal such as man into a different choice situation'.[143] In Merton's early formulation, 'self-defeating prediction' refers to the pattern in which 'public predictions of future social developments are frequently not sustained precisely because the prediction has become a new element in the concrete situation, thus tending to change the initial course of developments'.[144] Thus, he suggests that Marx's prediction of the increasing misery of the masses, has evoked countermeasures such as unionism, the socialist movement etc. and thus contributed to the emergence of welfare capitalism, curbing the tendency toward immiseration. In contrast, the 'self-fulfilling prophecy is, in the beginning, a false definition of the situation evoking behavior which makes the originally false conception come true. . . . The initially fallacious expectation makes for a seemingly confirmed outcome'.[145] And more concretely: 'In that pattern, an initially false but widely shared prediction, expectation, or belief is fulfilled in practice not because it was at the outset true, but because enough people took it to be true and, by acting accordingly, produced the outcome that would otherwise not have occurred'.[146] Merton's example: blacks in the United States were believed after World War I to be unfit for unionism, they were excluded from unions and therefore jobs, and many indeed did become strikebreakers. To generalise from this example: 'The specious validity of the self-fulfilling prophecy perpetuates a reign of error. For the prophet will cite the actual course of events as proof that he was right from the beginning'.[147]

These examples indicate that the phenomenon of reflexivity covers a wide and heterogeneous array of cases. At one extreme, there is the *private* self-fulfilling prophecy of an individual concerning the success or failure of his own action. Common wisdom notes that a belief in success contributes to actual success for it mobilises persistent, determined, purposeful actions. And nothing guarantees failure better than expectation of failure, for it effectively paralyses the requisite actions. But these are of course not always the case since individual personality traits significantly intervene. For some, too strong a conviction of future success can lead to slackened effort, just as moderate anxiety about failure can effectively mobilise action. An excellent example of such private self-fulfilling prophecies is found in the sociology of science. Thus, in their study of age and aging in science, Zuckerman and Merton note the mechanism of the personally induced self-fulfilling prophecy as scientists approaching an age at which their research potential is bound to decay assume increasing administrative and teaching duties in what amounts to a 'preemptive' shift of roles.[148] In effect, these scientists indeed slow down or halt their research activities.

A little more complex is the case of prediction formulated about an individual's action by some significant others, rather than by oneself. Normally, though not unexceptionally, the opposite self-defeating mechanism will operate. Hearing from his significant others: 'you will certainly succeed' an individual may slow down his efforts, repose in glory with the highly probable consequence of failure. And hearing: 'you are bound to fail' he may mobilise energies and resources, finally to succeed. Again, some personality traits, and perhaps particularly the initial level of the individual's self-appraisal, will become an intervening variable, and may basically change the direction of the process. It also becomes more complex if the appraisals of others referring to an individual are influenced by institutionalised or other authoritative judgments. As Merton noted in his 1960 paper ' "Recognition" and "Excellence": instructive ambiguity:' 'if the teachers, inspecting our Iowa scores and our aptitude test figures and comparing our record with that of our age-peers conclude that we are run-of-the-mine and *treat us accordingly*, then they lead us to become what they think we are'.[149]

An extensive socio-psychological research carried under the heading of 'interpersonal expectancy effects' has introduced, with cumulatively growing sophistication and rigour, experimental designs that move on to specify the intervening mechanisms, conditions, limitations of this fundamental regularity.[150]

Of course, to be causally effective *public* prediction must be communicated to individuals (more specifically, perceived and believed by them). An interesting and widely studied example is the effect of election-predictions on voting behaviour, and consequently upon election-results. Buck has introduced the concept of 'dissemination status' to deal with variable knowledge of the prediction among members of groups or collectivities.[151] A certain level of dissemination must be reached before a sufficient number of group members become sufficiently affected in their actions to switch on the mechanism of reflexity. As Merton put it: 'prophecies become self-fulfilling only when the prophet has acquired wide credibility'.[152]

Still further along the continuum of complexity, we encounter codified creeds, ideologies or doctrines held by groups or societies that influence their actions in self-fulfilling or self-defeating ways. Here prophecies shift from 'private' to 'structural' or 'institutionalised' level (become 'system-induced' rather than 'personally-induced'). This is because codified and sanctioned creeds turn into persistent *institutionalised arrangements*. The fundamental theoretical point – germane to theory as it is to policy – is that institutionalised arrangements based on faulty beliefs can perpetuate self-fulfilling prophecies on a massive scale.

Finally, at the extreme end of the continuum we find a situation when the theories, or the whole theoretical systems proposed by the social sciences have self-fulfilling or self-destroying effects. It is indeed the most baffling case, when some of the supposedly true theories turn out to be false, by virtue of massive actions informed by (or undertaken in the name of) those very theories. Or else, when supposedly true theories may turn out to be true, by virtue of actions taken by the masses of their committed followers. This raises some fundamental epistemological questions concerning the validity of social-scientific theories in general. As Friedrichs puts it: 'Of critical import in the social and behavioral science alone is the fact that the very discovery of an order in the realm of the social must inevitably, by the very grammar that adheres to social or behavioral research, act to some degree as a new and unique element in the stream of empirical events that make up human interaction'.[153] Two of epistemological issues require further intensive inquiry: whether the mechanism of reflexivity is indeed *peculiar* to the social domain and whether it is in principle impossible to take the impact of theory on social practice into account at the initial stage of its formulation, so as to *incorporate the requisite, compensating provisos* in its text.[154] Perhaps a good theory in the social sciences must do so to be truly predictive.

But this would lead us too far from Merton. One trusts that he will address these and related issues himself. Recently he confessed: 'the book "Self-Fulfilling Prophecy" is still among the foremost in the queue of work-to-be-done'.[155]

This array of considerations have taken human action as having both subjective and reflexive aspects. As Giddens sums it up: 'action – and reflexivity – has to be regarded as central to any comprehensive attempt to provide a theoretical explanation of human social life. At the same time, it is of the first importance to avoid the relapse into subjectivism that would attend an abandonment of the concept of structure'.[156] As we have seen, Merton has repeatedly noted the hazards of such 'total subjectivism' while recognising that human action has a *subjective component* and focusing on the constraining or facilitating role of the social structure. Thus, a certain apparent, but only *apparent*, duality or strain appears in his theory. Approached from the internal perspective, human action seems based on *free choice* and has constructive potentials with respect to the social structure. Approached from the external perspective, human action seems to be pervasively influenced, moulded, *constrained* by the social structure, itself treated as given. This duality was recognised by Stinchcombe: 'The core process that Merton conceives as central to social structure is the choice between socially structured alternatives'.[157] Who, then, is a human agent: an *active creator* of social structures or a *passive slave* of structural demands; the subject or object of social processes; the producer or product of social reality?

Merton's answer is evidently found in passages such as these: '. . . this sociological perspective has the scientifically extraneous but humanly solid merit of leaving a substantial place for people-making-their-future-history while avoiding the utopianism-that-beguiles by recognizing that the degrees of freedom people have in that task are variously and sometimes severely limited by the objective conditions set by nature, society, and culture'.[158] And therefore 'although a theory of social structure includes the prime concept of social constraint, this does not require us "to bring man back in" for the sufficient reason that (so-to-say) "man has been there right along" '.[159]

Man is free, but only partly so. He is *partly free from structural determination*, as the complex, pluralistic and conflictual composition of social structure always leaves him some relative autonomy; and as the mechanisms of socialisation and social control do leave him some leeway from structural demands. He is *partly free to influence social structure* and his choices may make a difference, as they take part in a sequence of morphogenesis. Such can be the rephrasing of Merton's position on the first part of the issue.

Correlatively, social structure is causally effective with respect to individuals, but also only in part. It constrains and facilitates human actions by *delimiting the field of possible alternatives*, and sometimes encouraging the choice of particular alternatives within the field. But it never narrows down to a single option: 'social constraints imposed by the routines of social status and roles which limit and pattern the range of choices still allow for differentiated individual choice, albeit with different psychic costs and gains'.[160] And also social structure is partly independent of human agents. To some extent it is distributively given to each even though it is collectively produced by all (though not in the same measure). Thus, it is *insulated to some degree from the impact of any one individual*. This is, in brief, Merton's position on the second part of the issue.

Merton's theory seems to grasp the fundamental dialectics of human existence: *the interplay of the social and individual aspects of people*. Through such dialectics, people are social yet retain their identity; and society, though ultimately produced by people, remains a superindividual reality. People are subjects and also objects of social processes; producers but also products of social structures; creators but also embodiments of the society. Merton often recognises the similarity of his two-sided standpoint to Marx's often quoted formulation: 'Men make their own history but they do not make it just as they please. They do not make it under circumstances chosen by themselves, but under circumstances found, given and transmitted from the past'.[161]

Such a position allows Merton to escape the dangers of both total objectivism and total subjectivism (or what he derogatively refers to as 'sociological Berkeleyanism'). As he puts it: 'It is one thing to maintain, with Weber, Thomas, and the other giants of sociology, that to understand human action requires us to attend systematically to its subjective component: what people perceive, feel, believe and want. But it is quite another thing to exaggerate the sound idea by maintaining that action is nothing but subjective'.[162] Once again, Merton's predilection for the middle way and 'golden-mean' proves to be sound and fruitful.

8
A Modern Sociological Classic

Now that the work of Robert K. Merton has been reviewed, interpreted and systematised in topical order – according to the main problem-areas of his concern – it is time to return to another perspective; to dig deeper under the surface and to summarise the pervasive emphases, foci, and leitmotifs of his sociology. In this final chapter I abandon the topical order and adopt a *thematic order*.

It was Gerald Holton who invented the idea of 'thematic analysis' and the concept of 'themata' as useful tools in the study of science. I adopt this conception though only in a loose, general manner without the rigour of Holton's thorough study.[1] It is perhaps not accidental that Merton himself takes interest in the notion of 'thematic analysis'. In his interpretation of this important contribution, he observes: ' "thematic analysis" . . . assumes underlying elements in the concepts, methods, propositions, and hypotheses advanced in scientific work. These elements function as themes that motivate or constrain the individual scientist in his cognitive formulations and consolidate or polarize the cognitive judgments appearing in the community of scientists'.[2] And then Merton defines the central concept: 'The themata of scientific knowledge are tacit cognitive imageries and preferences for or commitments to certain kinds of concepts, certain kinds of methods, certain kinds of evidence, and certain forms of solutions to deep questions and engaging puzzles'.[3]

The concept of themata can be applied in various ways. Certain themes can be found to characterise periods in the development of scientific discipline. In this usage, the concept comes fairly close to Kuhn's notion of a 'paradigm'. They can also be identified as typical for certain communities of scholars. In this usage, the concept seems to coincide with Fleck's idea of 'thought-styles' and 'thought-collectives'. A third application refers to the work of an individual scholar which can be characterised by specific themes or by a unique configuration of themes. As Merton explains: 'Some scientists, especially the pathbreakers, have their distinctive configuration of themes. These configurations, I take it, make up much of the styles of thought that characterize many scientists and uniquely identify scientists of utmost consequence'.[4]

It is precisely this last application of thematic analysis that is most relevant to my discussion. I shall try to identify the *tacit themes and thematic configurations* in Merton's work. Only at this level of analysis can we understand Merton's impact, influence and following. Something in the deep structure of his intellectual mosaic – apart from the brightness of each stone – must make it so appealing to so many. Merton is right in noting, in accord with Holton, that 'if we do not perceive the basic themata in a scientific work, we cannot understand well enough what makes it important, the reasons for its distinctive reception, and, not least what is "sacred" enough in it to withstand disappointing delays in confirmation or to survive seeming disconfirmation'.[5] And this observation is most relevant for his own work.

Reading and re-reading Merton's books, articles and minor publications, as well as outlines, proofs, correspondence and various background materials, I have come to identify four pervasive leitmotifs or themes. The first is most general, it cuts across the dimensions and levels of his inquiries, relates to all the topics he takes up and defines his unique style of thinking. This I have chosen to call the *classicist theme*. The second pervades his image of scientific, and particularly of sociological, method. This I have called the *cognitivist theme*. The third underlies his sociological orientation towards a most varied subject-matter – science, society, social process – this being the *structuralist theme*. And the fourth characterises his substantive image of social reality, his reading of social structure and social processes. After Louis Schneider, I call it the *ironic theme*. This final chapter traces and illustrates the four themes in some detail by drawing on our earlier acquaintance with Merton's ideas.

The classicist theme

Were I asked to give the most concise characterisation of Merton's thought, I would put it in three words: *balance*, *system*, and *discipline*. Through obvious association with the terminology of art-history the combination of those three traits deserves a name of classicist theme.

Whatever part of Merton's work one reads, one finds a striking preoccupation with the *intermediate formulations* and a persistent avoidance of extreme, dogmatic, one-sided points of view. In that Aristotelian tradition of the 'golden-mean', Merton is always trying to develop a balanced, multi-dimensional view of the matters under study. 'It seems improbable', he observes of various theoretical orientations in sociology, 'that the angels of light are all on one side and the angels of darkness, all on the other'.[5] And this intellectual persuasion is directed toward every subject-matter he tackles. Consider only a list of typical illustrations from his various interests, which have been examined in the topical chapters.

Analysing science, Merton attempts to find balanced, intermediate solutions to numerous riddles. In addressing its epistemological foundations, he opposes the ideas of radical relativism as well as the notion of thought as only a passive reflection of objective reality. He opts for a 'triadic' epistemology; affirming the existence of an objective reality, but also allowing for the sociological mediation of 'thought collectives' in developing cognitive representations of reality. So, too, he is equally opposed to the continuing rather than provisional separation of reason and experience, rational and empirical cognition, both indispensable for attaining reliable knowledge of that reality. Science stands on two legs, theoretical and empirical. It is crippled when either of those is long missing. With regard to scholarly roles, the same persuasion is expressed in his protest against a radical opposition of theoreticians and researchers, with an effort at a personal synthesis of both. As he puts it: 'The stereotype of the social theorist high in the empyrean of pure ideas uncontaminated by mundane facts is fast becoming no less outmoded than the stereotype of the social researcher equipped with questionnaire and pencil and hot on the chase of the isolated and meaningless statistics'.[6] And turning to the justification of the scientific enterprise, Merton rejects an opposition of truth and practical relevance as necessarily *competing criteria*; of pure and applied research as unrelated areas of scientific effort; and of scholasticism and narrow utilitarianism as research ideologies. For him, as for Whitehead, science is 'the river with two sources, cognitive and practical. Neither can long be separated from the other. Or in his own words: 'Some scientists, both by temperament and capacity, are no doubt better suited to the exclusive pursuit of one or the other of these paths of inquiry [theoretical and applied]; some may move back and forth between both paths; and a few may manage to tread a path bordered on one side by the theoretical and on the other by the practical or applied. This last path is, in the main, the one I have followed in these essays'.[7] Finally reflecting on the overall history of science, he rejects both unilinear cumulativism or incrementalism, and the notion of radical scientific revolutions, as alone adequate formulations of scientific development. Knowledge is cumulative, but *selectively* cumulative and far from any unilinear progress; it is revolutionary, but always in some *continuity* with the past.

Similar intermediate orientations are encountered in Merton's account of sociological method. Perhaps the most apparent example is his opposition to purely abstract, conceptual schemes, 'grand theory', to use Mills' apt phrase,[8] as well as to narrowly empirical fact-finding. This gave rise to the seminal ideas of 'middle-range theory' and 'middle-range problems', as directions strategic for the development of sociology. Here, on the middle level, 'two-way traffic' between social theory and empirical research is held to produce optimum results. Another case-in-point is his rejecting a dichotomy of quantitative–qualitative analysis, and an effort to utilise both in mutually fertile combination. As Manis and Meltzer see it: 'while Merton's work has been predominantly qualitative and interpretative, he has often drawn upon, and strongly favored, data, concepts, and theories with clearly quantitative implications'.[9] Similarly, in adapting Weber's solution to the riddle of the place of valuations in sociology, Merton rejects, like Weber, both extreme standpoints: extreme *axiologism*, which treats valuations as inevitable and even fruitful in various phases of inquiry and extreme *neutralism*, which posits a complete separation of science from the domain of values. Instead he accepts the inevitability of valuations at the phase of problem-selection, but banishes them from all other stages of inquiry. Finally, in opting for 'disciplined eclecticism' and 'theoretical pluralism' in the selection of theories, he rejects with equal force any form of theoretical *monism* and any form of theoretical *anarchism*. There is no ultimate, single, complete theory of society, but it does not imply that all hypotheses are equally plausible; some theories happen to be better than others.

On the level of sociological orientation, Merton's attempt to strike the golden mean also appears evident throughout. Most generally, in his rejection of total *subjectivism* ('sociological Berkeleyanism') as well as total *objectivism* (simplistic behaviorism),[10] in favour of their balanced synthesis; where it is recognised that social phenomena have subjective aspects, but they do not reduce to the meanings or symbols, being intersubjectively shared, persistent and – at least to some degree – given for each human individual. Merton is also opposed to a one-sided *synchronic* (or static) approach, from which the dimension of time is missing, just as he is opposed to an exclusively *diachronic* perspective which sees human society only in its aspect of temporal succession and change. The image of social structure in the process of ongoing patterned change avoids the pitfalls of both extreme positions. Similarly, in his approach to larger historical processes, Merton rejects both the narrow *idealistic* interpretation in which only beliefs, ideas, creeds and values seem to count, and the narrow *materialist* interpretation, in which the economic substructure is alone the determinant. He opts for the combination of both elements in their mutual interplay as the valid mode of explanation of historical processes.

Finally, in Merton's substantive image of society one also finds several facets clearly reflecting his predilection for intermediate positions. Thus, he rejects an 'oversocialised image of man' as a *passive product* of social constraints and also rejects the idea that man is *totally free*, wholly independent of the social milieu. Man as socially constrained but partly autonomous; socially moulded but capable of retaining a distinct identity appears as an image informed by both perspectives but liberated from the one-sidedness of each. In his view of human action, Merton avoids pure *voluntarism* by treating action as constrained and limited but also avoids *determinism*, by treating the field of action as consisting of multiple patterned alternatives or possibilities of choice. The image of human choice, within structurally set context of possibilities, combines fruitful elements drawn from the extreme standpoints. In analysing social structure, Merton, likewise, avoids the trap of an 'overintegrated image of society', which is *harmonious* and fully equilibrated and escapes the opposite danger of seeing it as only *conflictual*. In Barbano's appraisal: 'Merton undoubtedly represents the more advanced stream of sociology which does not necessarily see "virtue" only in integration and social conformity, nor yet only beyond the pale of the society we live in'.[11] He treats both 'faces of society'[12] as complementary and equally real.

All this epitomises the central component of Merton's classicist theme. As Turner aptly describes this aspect: 'Merton has occupied a unique position in sociological theorizing. His tempered and reasoned statements have repeatedly resolved intellectually stagnating controversies in the field'. He goes on to refer to 'Merton's seemingly charismatic capacity to "resolve" issues'.[13]

Another component of the classicist theme is the pervasive *attempt to order and systematise* intellectual issues. This is what Coser refers to as the Cartesian aspect of Merton's thought.[14] This emphasis was obvious in his early statement of goals as 'the consolidation of theory and research and codification of theory and method'.[15] It has appeared time and again in his later work, when he was applying his device then described as 'paradigms' to order concepts, methods and orientations in various spheres. It appears also in his predilection for typologies, classifications, enumerations and taxonomies. Relevant in this connection is the ease with which it becomes possible in his conceptual scheme to move between the concrete and the general, relating facts and abstractions, finding concrete implications of embodiments of general phenomena, and indicating general implications of concrete events. As Garfield put it: 'He is a special kind of scientist: forever reminding us of the forest, while describing it tree by tree'.[16]

Yet another component of the classicist theme is the *intellectual discipline* to which Merton subjects the various phases of his work. The self-conscious, critical use of rules and methodological canons in the process of research and theory-construction: what he almost obsessively refers to as 'disciplined inquiry' – is coupled with great attention given to the clarity, simplicity, consistency and elegance in the formulation of ideas. As Coser has observed: 'Merton, much like Simmel before him, delights in the elegant display of ideas. One has the impression that often, for Merton, systematization is undertaken for the sake of elegance; there is a esthetic quality to it'.[17]

The classicist theme defines Merton's thought-style as a whole. The remaining themes relate to particular segments of his work.

The cognitivist theme

Were I to characterise in a few words Merton's thinking about scientific, and particularly sociological, method, I would emphasise the *search for knowledge, enlightenment, understanding* of reality; briefly, human cognition. Hence, the term 'cognitivist theme'.

Cognitive goals of science are equally relevant in the domain of social and natural disciplines. Merton believes that sociology can and should be a full-fledged member of the family of sciences. General standards of evidence, explanation, prediction, or briefly – the canons of scientific method – have been set by the natural sciences, and therefore sociology, an immature an underdeveloped discipline, should attempt to match those standards as much as possible. It should strive for logical coherence, empirical validity (confirmation and falsifiability) and in effect explanatory and predictive power, even though it is still far from the levels found in the best developed sciences of nature. But in principle, and at the core the sciences – whether social or natural – are one: 'the logical structure of experiment . . . does not differ in physics or chemistry or psychology. . . . Nor do the near-substitutes for experiment – controlled observation, comparative study and the method of "discerning" – differ in their logical structure in anthropology, sociology or biology'.[18] Thus with allowance for some divergences; obviously extensive at the level of *scientific procedures*, but also touching the level of *general canons* (e.g. the different logic of prediction owing to the mechanism of self-fulfilling and self-defeating prophecies appearing only in the social domain, or different patterns of selective cumulation in social and natural disciplines), Merton accepts in principle the thesis of the unity of the sciences.

He also accepts the ideal of the categorical (i.e. non-normative) science. It should study what *is* and not what *should be* the case, and therefore strive to eliminate valuations, prescriptive or proscriptive judgments, programmatic statements from its results: 'As sociologists, emphatically not as citizens, students of social problems neither exhort nor denounce, neither advocate nor reject'.[19] Here Merton clearly underplays the difference in this respect between the social and natural sciences. In his view both should purge normative components from their theories.

With all the reservations concerning ultimate practical relevance of scientific results, Merton seems to believe in the primacy of purely cognitive goals of science. Such a primacy is a matter of logic; it stems from the necessary status of pure, categorical knowledge as a premise in deducing scientifically grounded, rational practical directives or policies. His case for science is therefore cognitivistic rather than utilitarian.

The ultimate test for science is the recourse to empirically observable reality. Merton's strong *commitment to facts, data, empirical results* led Coser to speak of the Baconian aspect of his thought: 'openness to all the multiple facets of objective phenomena "out there" '.[20] The confrontation of results with objectively existing reality is – for Merton – the ultimate criterion of validity for scientific claims. Empirical research provides the decisive, crucial test of theoretical ideas. Science springs from experiment and disciplined, controlled observation, and returns to experiment and observation to check its truthfulness. But it must be emphasised that Merton is far from any notion of 'naked facts'. As early as 1941 he was declaring the idea of *interpreted nature of facts*: 'an explicit conceptual outfit, a part of theory, is necessary even for fruitful discoveries of fact', and then criticised the results of various studies on intermarriage: 'the fact-finders, so-called, have not assembled and classified *relevant* facts and . . . this inadequacy is tied up with their neglect of a coherent theoretical system in terms of which relevance of facts might be determined'.[21] He puts it even more forcefully a little later: 'it is perhaps unnecessary to reiterate the axiom that one's concepts *do* determine the inclusion or exclusion of data, that, despite the etymology of the term, *data* are not "given" but are "contrived" with the inevitable help of concepts'.[22] This idea can be traced in many other places in Merton's work. He clearly recognises that, as one likes to say these days, facts are 'theory-laden'; they do not speak for themselves.

Human cognition, in Merton's view, does progress. The fact is that 'today's astronomers may actually have a more solid, more sweeping, and more exacting knowledge of the sun, moon, planets, and stars than did Aristachos of Samos or even Ptolemy, . . . today's demographers just might have a deeper and broader understanding of the dynamics of population change than, say, the 17th-century William Petty or even the early 19th-century Thomas Malthus'.[23] And from the more sociological perspective of scientific community 'the severest test of truly cumulative knowledge is that run-of-the-mill minds can solve problems today which great minds could not begin to solve earlier. An undergraduate student of mathematics [today] knows how to identify and solve problems which defied the best powers [or even never came to the minds] of a Leibniz, Newton or Cauchy'.[24] It does not mean that science is always linearly, inevitably cumulative; at most it is 'selectively cumulative' and allows for regressions, false starts, blind alleys etc. But with these reservations we know *more* now than we knew before.

Merton's emphasis on the unity of science, categorical nature of science, cognitive goals of science, factual basis of science and scientific progress, has led some commentators to the imputation of a straightforward positivistic creed. Manis and Meltzer refer to 'Merton's positivist-inclined theorizing', and claim that 'Merton's position has been largely on the side of the positivists – if Stouffer and Lazarsfeld may be labeled so'.[25] Lundberg himself referred to Merton's early work as 'fully compatible with, and contributing to, the positions and programs advocated, as far as I know, by any informed behaviorist or "neopositivist" including myself'.[26] I find these imputations unjustified. As I have attempted to document, Merton's ideas *depart far from the extremes of positivist tradition*, and this label cannot be ascribed to him in any meaningful sense, except as the empty, derogatory catch-all phrase. If one necessarily needed general categories under which Merton's work could be classified, Barber's use of the term 'pragmatism' would be more founded. Taking this word in a restricted meaning, not to be mixed up with the full doctrine of Pragmatism, he correctly ascribes to Merton 'a philosophical position of pragmatism (note the small "p") which assumes and then takes for granted that the social world can be known, and can be known to a desired degree of objectivity, validity, and usability by scholars conforming to scientific standards and methods that have produced such knowledge about the physical and biological aspects of the world. Such a philosophical position is obviously a prerequisite to the sociological enterprise'.[27]

The structuralist theme

If I were asked again to describe in the shortest way Merton's scientific, and more specifically, sociological orientation, I would refer to the idea of *configurations*, *patterns* and *structures* that he unravels in every domain of his interest. Hence, the term 'structuralist theme'.[28]

Merton's structuralism is variously expressed. First, through a strongly anti-reductionist and, one may say 'sociologistic' position. He conceives social reality – in Durkheimian fashion – as a reality *sui generis*, theoretically distinct though empirically interconnected with psychological reality.[29] He identifies himself with leitmotif of sociology: 'a basic commonality amid this diversity of theoretical outlook in the form of an anti-reductionist perspective on the emergent properties of social structure'.[30] Thus, sociological ambivalence is not the same as psychological ambivalence: 'they are on different planes of phenomenal reality, on different planes of conceptualization, on different planes of causation and consequences'.[31] Similarly, anomie is not the same as personal anomia: 'The first thing to note about the sociological concept of anomie is that it is – sociological. Anomie refers to a property of a social system, not to the state of mind of this or that individual within the system'.[32] Institutional altruism, a principle of social organisation, is not the same as altruistic attitudes: 'From the sociological perspective, it need not be the case that individual members of a profession are uniformly motivated by altruistic sentiments, although such motivation makes it easier to live up to this aspect of the professional commitment'.[33] The structurally determined visibility of rules, norms, values or role-performances is not the same as individual perception: 'From the standpoint of sociological theory, visibility is the counterpart in social structure of what, from the standpoint of psychological theory, is social perception'.[34] Ambivalence in the professional role is not the same as the psychological stresses experienced by professionals: 'We are examining sources of ambivalence that are patterned into the professional role. We are not referring to the idiosyncratic frustration that can be assigned to the particular personality of this or that professional, this or that client'.[35] 'Organized scepticism' is not the same as personal doubt: 'this sociological concept of "institutionalized vigilance" does not refer to the personal scepticism of this or that individual but to the normative and socially organized exercise of critical judgment that is integrated with the reward-system of science and scholarship'.[36]

Many more examples of Merton's persistent and rigorous delimitation of sociological and psychological focus could be adduced. Giddens grasps the core of Merton's approach: 'whatever the limitations of functionalism . . . it always placed in the forefront problems of institutional organization, and was firmly opposed to subjectivism in social theory. I believe this emphasis still to be necessary, indeed all the more urgent in view of the upsurge of subjectivism and relativism that has accompanied the waning influence of functionalist notions in the social sciences'.[37]

Another expression of the structuralist theme is the emphasis on structural roots, structural determinants, structural conditions, the structural context of every social phenomenon. As I have had many occasions to point out, this is perhaps Merton's most salient trade-mark. Whatever phenomenon he studies, the focus is on the *constraining* and *facilitating* impacts of social structure. As Lazarsfeld observes: 'For many students, his sociology has an appeal [of the kind] that emanates from psychoanalysis. In the latter, people are pushed around *from within* by unconscious motives and to discover them is fascinating. Now it turns out that people are also pushed around *from without*, and here [also] they do not know about it. To learn that the patterned social structure accomplishes it all is equally stunning – and deservedly so'.[38] Be it deviation or conformity, friendship or hostility, patterns of discovery or priority disputes in science, medical treatment or personal influence, ethnic prejudice or patterns of intermarriage, propaganda or medical education – Merton's focus is always on the constraints and stimuli embedded in the structural context and the mechanisms through which those structural determinants affect actual conduct. Peter Blau perceives this point most clearly: 'Even when Merton examines human choices on the microsociological level, he is concerned with the structural constraints that affect these choices and thus with social conduct, not with the psychological processes underlying them. On the macrosociological level, he similarly focuses on the effects of some social factors on others'.[39]

Yet another expression of the structuralist theme is the persistent focus on the *structural (institutional, standardised, patterned) consequences* of social phenomena. In the words of Turner: 'For Merton, the unique feature of functional analysis is the concern with consequences of a part for other social parts or a social whole'.[40] The concept of function (and correlatively – dysfunction), so central to Merton's sociology, signifies a structural effect making for (or reducing) 'the adaptation or adjustment of a given system'.[41] Similarly, the more general notion of structural consequences includes various types of impact of social phenomena on the structural contexts in which they occur.

What is also most symptomatic for Merton's structuralist bent is his particular interest in hidden, underlying, 'deep' levels of social reality. Note his emphasis on particular sorts of functions and consequences, namely, *latent* functions and *unanticipated* consequences. It is precisely the unintended and unrecognised functions, and more generally the unintended and unanticipated consequences of purposive actions that he takes as central to sociological inquiry: 'It is suggested that the *distinctive* intellectual contributions of the sociologist are found primarily in the study of unintended consequences (among which are latent functions) of social practices, as well as in the study of anticipated consequences (among which are manifest functions)'.[42] Cuzzort and King go as far as to entitle their entire chapter on Merton: 'The Unanticipated Consequences of Human Actions' and claim that 'Merton increasingly became interested in the idea of the unanticipated consequences of social action until, eventually, it formed one of the most resonant underlying themes of his work'.[43] Equally symptomatic is his emphasis on latent social problems – 'conditions that are . . . at odds with values of the society but are not generally recognized as being so'.[44] Merton amply fulfils his own mandate, tracing the unanticipated, unintended and unrecognised consequences of human conduct in various domains of social life, be it political system, or the institution of science, or the family, or ideology, and many others.

My emphasis on Merton's structuralist orientation may seem to contradict common appraisals in which his *functional analysis* is rather brought to the fore. As I have argued *in extenso*, this contradiction is apparent rather than real. Merton's functional analysis and structural analysis are not opposed but clearly *complementary* aspects of his overall orientation; they represent various phases in the development of the same approach to social reality. Already in Merton's functionalist phase, he explicitly resorts to structuralist argumentation when he attempts to put functional analysis into explanatory use. For example, his early article on 'Social Structure and Anomie' often, mistakenly, cited as a prime illustration of functional analysis is in fact a structural explanation *par excellence*, insofar as it derives various forms of deviant adaptation from varied configurations of social structure (signified as anomie). Any time that Merton tries to *explain* social institutions, patterns, forms of social organisation, and not only to *identify* their functions for other institutions or wider social wholes, he inadvertently invokes structural constraints or facilitations. This is why I believe that structural focus must be considered as primary in his sociology, and in a sense subsuming his functionalist persuasion.

The theme of irony

I turn finally to the substantive image of society emerging from Merton's work. Is there an underlying, pervasive theme? Can one find a leitmotif in so many analyses of diverse social phenomena? It seems so. And the key concepts are *complexity* and *paradox*.

Clearly, the human world appears to Merton as a difficult place in which to live, one far removed from a simple, tranquil, harmonious utopia. At the same time, it appears as a challenging world, in which nothing is wholly predetermined and everything is in some degree contingent, constantly requiring choices and decisions. The torment of uncertainty, the agony of ambivalence, the fright of normlessness, the cross-pressures of roles and statuses, the risk of defeat – all those impediments in the human drama also provide human life with meaning, taste and flavour. As Campbell observes: 'Merton's enduring concern has been with the study of the complex and paradoxical character of human conduct'.[45]

In Merton's social world, the reigning theme seems to be – *irony*. Louis Schneider couched his 'minimum definition of irony' in terms of 'the element of the unexpected or unintended in combination with the element of incongruity. . . . As well as incongruity, irony suggests ambiguity and paradox . . .',[46] and he observed that in social science the role of irony is to draw attention to shocking (or 'mocking') *discrepancies between intentions and consequences*, goals and realities. As Weinstein comments: 'Viewed in this light, the similarities between irony, dialectic, and latent functions and dysfunctions are obvious – as, perhaps, are some of the differences as well'.[47] It is not accidental that Schneider chose to deal with 'Ironic Perspective' in his contribution to the 1975 Merton's *Festschrift*. He emphasised 'the notion of strong affinity of structural–functional analysis with ironic perspective' and added that 'the affinity of functionalist outlook and irony . . . is decidedly more evident in that variant of the outlook that has interested Merton than it is in the variant that has been developed by Parsons'.[48] Merton fully acknowledges this diagnosis. In a letter to Schneider he wrote: 'Your decision to write on ironic perspective [for the Festschrift] was itself a symbolic statement, one that unites our joint pasts and, if you'll allow me to say, our joint styles of thought'.[49]

In accord with Schneider's hunch,[50] I refer to the leitmotif underlying Merton's view of social life as the ironic theme. In my interpretation it entails a focus on distinct attributes of society: *complexity*, *contradiction*, *relativity*, *circularity*, and *paradox*. Each of these five parameters of the human condition requires discussion and illustration.

Merton's social world is exceedingly complex. One is reminded of Comte's notion of *'complication superieure'*. The complexity has several roots. It results from the plurality of social components, whether individuals, roles, statuses, groups, etc. It derives also from the heterogeneity of those components; multiple and varied forms and levels at which social components coalesce; be it institutions, roles, role-sets, status-sets, stratification systems, institutional orders, groups, categories, societies, cultures etc. Further, it results from the reciprocity of social processes interlinking various components, both of the same type and of different types, within the same type and within different types, on the same level and across levels.[51] Finally, it results from the unique location of every individual in this utterly complex and diversified social network, with a consequent plurality of perspectives, frames of reference, definitions of situation, 'social worlds', linked with cross-cutting, overlapping or conflicting loyalties, attachments and identifications.

Merton's social world is also torn by innumerable contradictions, ambivalences, conflicts, strains and tensions. These are a normal, typical, permanent condition at all levels of the social structure. As the extensive typology of such contradictions has been given in chapter seven, it hardly requires repetition here. But one point does require reiteration to contrast with mistaken accounts of Merton's position: his is a *conflictual image* of society *par excellence*, as distant as can be from the image of a harmonious utopia pervaded by consensus and equilibrium. Lewis Coser is right: 'Merton's analytical strategies are characterized, *inter alia*, by his close attention to contradictions and conflicts within global structures, to ambivalences in the motivation of actors, and to ambiguities in the perceptual field to which they orient themselves. Merton's actors face role and status-sets with often contradictory expectations and are continuously navigating between them. . . . The Mertonian world is a universe of warring gods'.[52]

For Merton, the human condition is *relative*, and that in multiple senses. Generally, the underlying common idea is that every expression of human activity or thinking not only has intrinsic significance but obtains much of its meaning from the structural context in which it appears. Thus, there is a *structural* relativity, with respect to a normative structure, or the network of groups or social statuses in which individuals are located. Merton emphasises this type of relativity most of all in his discussion of deviance and conformity: what counts as deviance in one group is an act of conformity in another; what counts as deviance with respect to one norm is an act of conformity with respect to counter-norms. As he puts it: 'conformity to norms of an out-group is thus equivalent to what is ordinarily called nonconformity, that is, nonconformity to the norms of the in-group. . . . one group's renegade may be another group's convert'.[53] The concept of reference groups – so important for Merton – has one of its analytic strengths precisely in this connection. There is, further, a *historical* relativity of all things human. The meaning and significance of the same acts depend on their location in a time-sequence of acts and their historical context. On the one hand, such meaning is determined by the earlier sequence of a chain of events – one may say the unique 'biography' or 'career' of the process. Examining reference-group behaviour, Merton points out that the actual choice of reference groups depends on the preceding life-history of the individual (e.g. whether he is downwardly mobile, upwardly mobile or stationary in his class position). The self-selection of roles and statuses is also shown to depend on the earlier status-sequence (or role-sequence) of the individual.[54] On the other hand, the meaning of human acts is determined by the wider historical context. Again, referring to the issues of conformity and deviance, Merton emphasises that the deviant of yesterday often becomes the standard-bearer of today, or tomorrow. In his words: 'In the history of every society, presumably, some of its culture heroes have been regarded as heroic precisely because they have had the courage and the vision to depart from norms then obtaining in the group. As we all know, the rebel, revolutionary, nonconformist, individualist, heretic, renegade of an earlier time is often the culture hero of today'.[55] Finally, there is a social subjective relativity inasmuch as people appraise their own and others' conduct in terms of normative or comparative frames of reference. The notion of relative deprivation, as used by Merton, covers this aspect of the matter most pointedly. Merton's extensive analyses of reference-groups – and their normative as well as comparative varieties – manifest his awareness of the subjective relativity of social life. His almost obsessive references to 'the Thomas theorem' point in the same direction.

Merton treats social processes as *circular* or *cyclical*. The sequences of compensation or amplification are shown to operate through the mechanisms of latent, unwitting dynamics and through the mediation of consciousness, the manifest dynamics. The first is exemplified by the concept of the latent cumulation of advantages or disadvantages, as in the special case of 'the Matthew effect' or by the mutual enhancement of loyalties, attachments and consensus on values, leading to homophily in friendship-formation. Stinchcombe calls such sequences 'the social magnification processes' and treats them as characteristic foci of Merton's attention.[56] A prime type of a social magnification process is the self-fulfilling prophecy (or self-destroying prophecy), when shared expectations of a future trend become a crucial factor in bringing it about (or preventing it). A special case of circular processes are the cyclical sequences eventually reproducing the initial state of affairs in basically unchanged form after a series of transformations. An instance of such a cycle is the reintroduction of contradictions, conflicts and strains in the social structure, after processes of change, initiated precisely by the pressure of similar contradictions. As Merton puts it: 'no major change in social structure occurs without the danger of temporarily increased conflict'.[57] Or more generally: 'owing to the systemic interdependence among parts of the social structure, organizational efforts to cope with one set of problems will introduce new ones'.[58] Another example is the cycle of anomie and deviance. In this, the structural condition of anomie brings about deviant responses; those in turn produce feelings of vulnerability, uncertainty and loss of guidance at the personal level, the widespread experience of anomia. When this becomes sufficiently common, it produces an anomic social climate, contributing to the perpetuation and enhancement of the anomic structure.[59] Thus, the aggregate effects of human acts, brought about by anomie, feed back on the initial condition of the social structure and make it even more grave. The vicious cycle of anomie and deviance is instituted as 'anomie, anomia, and mounting rates of deviant behavior become mutually reinforcing'.[60]

The ultimate aspect of the ironic theme is *the pervasiveness of paradox in human life*. Merton has a penchant for uncovering paradoxes. Their discovery seems to give particular satisfaction to his playful intellect. Consider only a few of the paradoxes described in his work. The most familiar of these is perhaps the one situated in the theory of anomie: 'the structure of society and culture, ordinarily thought of as operating to produce patterned behavior in rough accord with social norms could, under designated conditions, operate to produce deviant behavior (both aberrant and nonconforming)'.[61] A related and interesting paradox is the so-called anomia of success. This stems only in part from ever-growing, insatiable aspirations of those who are successful. An important social mechanism is also in operation: 'Social pressures do not easily permit those who have climbed the rugged mountains of success to remain content; there is no rest for the weary. . . . More and more is expected of these men by others and this creates its own measure of stress. Less often than one might believe, is there room for repose at the top'.[62] The notion of unexpected consequences is of course pregnant with paradoxes. Merton maintains that 'basic to sociology is the premise that, in the course of social interaction men create new conditions that were not part of their intent. Short-run rationality produces long-run irrationality'.[63] Or more specifically: 'the very elements which conduce toward efficiency in general produce inefficiency in specific instances'.[64] An instructive subtype is identified in the Veblenian 'trained incapacity': 'the very soundness of training for the past leads to maladaptations in the present'.[65] Another paradox is located in Merton's frequent analyses of *'displacement of goals'* in various spheres of social life: 'activities originally conceived as instrumental are transmuted into self-contained practices, lacking further objectives'.[66] Specific, concrete cases of this pattern, considered by Merton as central, occur in bureaucratic structure where 'the organizational means become transformed into ends-in-themselves and displace the principal goals of the organization';[67] or in scientific communities where the institutionalised goal of achieving significant originality and being rewarded by recognition on the part of scientist-peers is displaced by a prime concern with recognition at any cost, ranging from cooking fraudulent data to publishing at great length in the thought that quantity may achieve recognition. In the theory of propaganda we find another famous paradox, the early notion of the 'boomerang effect': 'Under certain conditions . . . people respond to propaganda in a fashion opposite to that intended by the author'.[68] Or more generally: under specifiable conditions 'what you say may be understood in a fashion quite opposed to what you had intended'.[69] There is the paradoxical pattern of 'pseudo-Gemeinschaft', when autotelic values are cynically utilised as instruments of control or manipulation. An example is provided by 'subtle methods of salesmanship in which there is the feigning of personal concern with the client in order to manipulate him the better'.[70] Other paradoxes are inherent in the execution of professional roles. For example, owing to the normative ambivalences embedded in such roles, the 'auxiliatropic paradox' emerges: 'The challenging paradox for sociological theorists is that entirely legitimate, role-prescribed, and presumably functional, professional conduct may lead to resentment and distrust and produce profound ambivalence in the help-seeker'.[71] Or more briefly: 'It is as difficult to seek help as to provide it'.[72]

Many more places can be found, where Merton traces and identifies the intricacies, contradictions, ambivalences and paradoxes of human fate. It may well be one of the most important insights that he contributes to sociological imagination.

The classicist synthesis of classical sociology

Four themes underlying the thought and writings of Robert K. Merton have been singled out, defined and illustrated. It is evident that the four are not of a piece in terms of their logical status. The first – the classicist theme – is of a different order; it defines Merton's pervasive style, his typical approach to issues and problems, while the others – the cognitivist theme, the structuralist theme, and the ironic theme – define the ways in which he conceives of specific spheres of inquiry: sociological method, sociological orientation and the ontology of social reality. Thus, the classicist theme is a sort of 'meta-theme', whereas the others are first-order themes.

It does not require much reflection to see that those first-order themes are strikingly *congenial with leitmotifs of the nineteenth century* and its classical sociological heritage. The cognitivist theme clearly epitomises the quest to turn social thought or social lore into a science; to give it a warranted intellectual and institutional legitimacy akin to that enjoyed by the study of nature. From Comte, through Marx, Spencer to Durkheim and Pareto, this has been an obsessive preoccupation of the classical sociologists. Merton picks up this thread and in his considerations on sociological method specifies his own, modified understanding of scientific cognition and positive science.

The structuralist theme manifests another concern of the 19th-century masters: the quest to turn sociology into a distinct discipline, to provide it with an *intellectual and institutional identity*, by drawing a line of demarcation between it and the natural–scientific as well as other social-scientific disciplines. Again, from Comte, Spencer, through Simmel to Durkheim, the efforts to define a uniquely sociological perspective are superabundant. Here, too, Merton follows in the steps of the masters, and in his discussion of 'sociological orientations' affirms the *sui-generis* uniqueness of both the sociologically defined subject-matter and the particular ways of its study.

The theme of irony is in the tradition of those masters who clearly perceived the *contingent, problematic nature of the social order*; its enormous complexity, immanent tensions, strains, inconsistencies, and consequently the predicaments of human beings having to find their place in, and to cope with their social environment. From Comte's *'complication superieure'* through Marx's 'dialectics' to Simmel's analysis of social conflict, such an image of society is strongly rooted in 19th-century thinking. Starting from it, Merton moves a long way forward; clarifying, codifying and enriching earlier conceptions.

It is the main claim of this interpretation, that by bringing together the three themes – the cognitivist, the structuralist, and the ironic – *Merton synthetises and extends the classical sociological tradition*. The value of this synthesis results from the orientation he takes toward the classical heritage. It is here that the meta-theme of his thought – the classicist theme – provides the foundation for bringing together but also pushing forward the achievements of predecessors.

The classicist theme leads him to cut away part of classical heritage; to remove biases, absolutisms, and dogmatisms. Through that approach, Merton attains balanced, intermediate positions on various traditional issues, unravels entangled premises to reach their rational core, unmuddles the muddle of sociological controversies. This allows him also to introduce a further measure of order and systematisation in the classical heritage. Merton's determined effort to clarify, codify, consolidate, and organise disparate pieces of sociological wisdom results in a mosaic that is rewarding aesthetically as well as intellectually. In short, the classicist orientation subjects the classical heritage to further 'disciplined inquiry', a methodologically self-conscious confrontation with empirical evidence, and logically self-conscious determination of its internal coherence. The synthesis becomes much more than a summary of earlier ideas; it results in their selective and critical reformulation and cumulation.

But all this would not account, yet, for the significance and impact of Merton's synthesis, were it not for its truly *creative quality*. At virtually every point he tackles, some novel concepts, insights, ideas are added to the classical heritage. He not only clarifies, systematises, reformulates the work of the masters; he also modifies and transforms it. The entire content of this book provides evidence and grounds for such claim.

Perhaps Merton's most important service to the development of contemporary sociology is *the vindication of the classical heritage*, so needed in view of certain destructive, premature challenges. He shows with new vigour that the ideas of the 19th-century masters are not exhausted or dead. In his work, paradigms of classical thought gain new vitality, as they are shown to be fruitful; both in the explanatory sense, as means of accounting for large areas of social experience and for solving the puzzles confronting men and women in their social life; and in the heuristic sense, as means of raising new questions and suggesting new puzzles for solution.

An important, and only seemingly paradoxical, function of Merton's synthesis is to indicate directions of inquiry that will eventually elaborate and overcome it. Its systematic and lucid quality enables us not only to perceive past and current knowledge but also 'the various sorts of failure: intelligent errors and unintelligent ones, noetically induced and organizationally induced foci of interest and blind spots in inquiry, promising lands abandoned and garden-paths long explored, scientific contributions ignored or neglected by contemporaries, . . . serendipity lost'[73] – to put it in Merton's characteristic prose. Ultimately, it leads toward mapping further domains of 'specified ignorance': 'what is not yet known but needs to be known in order to lay the foundation for still more knowledge'.[74] It is precisely here that the past and future of science meet.

Various domains of such 'specified ignorance' have been identified in Merton's work. Some of these omissions reflect inherent weaknesses of the sociological tradition; others result from Merton's selective foci. Whichever the case, his work brings the bonus of clearly *suggesting the need for more thorough studies* in several directions. First, the theory of human agents within the social context; the model of personality, the theory of motivation, the conceptualisation of needs, attitudes etc. Second, the theory of human action within the structural constraints and facilitations; of its anatomy, sequential course, social determinants and social functions. Third, the political dimension of social life; the theory of power and authority, as factors pervading all domains and levels of social structure and social change. Fourth, the macro-sociology of classes, nations, ethnic groups, social stratification and social mobility. Fifth, the theory of social process and social development; of overall transformations of social systems in the long durations of historical time. *Agent, action, power, classes, and history* – those concepts define agenda of concern for anybody who would like to round out the Merton synthesis, and fill in the lacunae. For such an effort his own sociological orientations, conceptual elaborations, and theoretical propositions provide a fruitful means and promising avenues.

But what about the long-run perspective, in which the entire classicist synthesis of classical sociology will perhaps have to be overcome, giving way to some radically new and comprehensive paradigm of sociological thinking? Will there appear such a paradigm? Will sociology pass through a veritable scientific revolution? Probably. But most certainly not as a result of negativistic rejection of earlier theory[75] or through the arrogant *fiat* of self-appointed discoverers of ultimate truths.[76] Rather, thanks to the disciplined, systematic, selective, critical, and creative *continuation* of that which is worthwhile in the classical heritage of sociological wisdom.

The way to strive for the better sociology of the future is to stand firmly and confidently on the shoulders of sociological giants: such as those of Merton.

Notes and References

Preface

1. First edition, 1949; second edition, 1957; revised and enlarged edition, 1968 (New York; The Free Press). Translated into: French, Italian, Japanese, Spanish, Hebrew, Portuguese, Polish, Hungarian, Serbo-Croatian, Chinese and German (in part).
2. *Webster's New World Dictionary of the American Language* (Cleveland, 1959: The World Publishing Company), p. 1678.
3. Dated 15 May 1970 (mimeographed).

Chapter 1

1. Merton, STSS, p. 70.
2. Merton, 1975a, p. 335.
3. This strategy is 'unorthodox' only in the social sciences. After all, probably 95 per cent of all the scientific work in the world is published in the form of articles; much less so, of course, in the humanities and with the social sciences somewhere in between the natural sciences and the humanities.
4. Bell, 1980, p. 13.
5. Merton, *On the Shoulders of Giants: A Shandean Postscript*, a Vicennial Edition (New York, 1985: Harcourt Brace Jovanovich). First published in 1965.
6. Merton, *Sociology of Science; An Episodic Memoir* (Carbondale, 1979: Southern Illinois University Press).
7. First edition: 1938.
8. Bierstedt, 1981, p. 486.
9. Ibid., pp. 495 and 487–8.
10. Loomis and Loomis, 1961, p. 246.
11. The term is introduced by C. W. Mills, 1959.
12. Stinchcombe, 1975, pp. 26–27. See also Boudon, 1977: 'there is more systematic and general theory in Merton's work than he himself has ever confessed' (p. 1356).
13. Bierstedt, 1981, p. 488.
14. Lazarsfeld, 1975, p. 61.
15. Stinchcombe, 1975, p. 30.
16. He certainly shares Toulmin's conviction that 'a scientist who fails to criticize and change his concepts, where the collective goals of his discipline require it, offends against the "duties" of his scientific "station", as much as a somnolent night-watchman or an insubordinate soldier' (as quoted in Merton, 1984b, p. 282).

17. Reflecting on his friendship with late Louis Schneider, Merton admits: 'We were both addicted to oral publication, continually and sometimes for years revising our thoughts in lectures before putting them into print' (Merton, 1984c, p. xxxv). He calls it a 'pattern of delayed print'. Sometimes even in his own appraisal this strategy of avoiding premature publication appears – *post facto* – as too rigorous. In a recent conversation he brought to my attention the titles of four books which 'should have been published', even though at the time he did not feel completely satisfied with their content.
18. Merton, STSE, p. xxix. This sentence reads: 'On the basis of the foregoing study, it may not be too much to conclude that the cultural soil of seventeenth-century England was peculiarly fertile for the growth and spread of science'.
19. As Boudon puts it: 'the best way to honor [important] work is to extract the sometimes latent though obsessive main intuitions responsible for the importance of the work' (1977, p. 1356).
20. When substantially significant for the clarity of interpretation, I inform the reader of the original dates of publication of articles or essays, later collected in separate volumes.
21. See: Popper, 1976, pp. 180–93.
22. In fact I shall venture, at times, to take up the challenge of elaboration myself. Attempting to remain faithful to Merton's implicit intentions and the overall spirit of his analysis, I shall suggest some new distinctions, concepts and hypotheses.
23. This term introduced by Merton in a 1963 article (as reprinted in SRPP, ch. 8), will be discussed in more detail in chapter 4 of this book.
24. On those other faces of Merton, see Morton M. Hunt, 'How Does It Come To Be So? Profile of Robert K. Merton', in: *New Yorker*, 28 January, 1961.

Chapter 2

1. See M. W. Miles, 'Bibliography – Robert K. Merton, 1934–1975', in L. A. Coser (ed), *The Idea of Social Structure; Papers in Honor of Robert K. Merton* (New York, 1975: Harcourt Brace Jovanovich), pp. 497–522; and a supplement 'Publications since 1975' compiled by M. W. Miles (mimeographed).
2. Znaniecki, 1940.
3. Znaniecki subdivides the crucial category of 'Scholars' in the following way (as summarised by Merton, SOS, pp. 42–3):
   (1) Sacred scholar: perpetuates sacred truths through exact and fruitful reproduction of their symbolic expressions . . .
   (2) Secular scholar: with the following subtypes:
      (a) discoverer of truth . . .
      (b) systematizer . . .
      (c) contributor . . .
      (d) fighter for truth . . .

(e) disseminator of knowledge . . .
   1. populariser . . .
   2. educating teacher'.
4. Merton, SOS, p. 43.
5. Merton (with Lazarsfeld), 1954, p. 18.
6. Ibid. pp. 18–19.
7. Zuckerman and Merton, in: Merton, SOS, p. 520.
8. Ibid., p. 520.
9. It is striking how often the terms 'pattern' and 'structure', in their various forms, appear and reappear in Merton's analyses of society. This has been noted by Lazarsfeld, 1975, p. 57, among others.
10. Merton, STSS, pp. vii–viii.
11. Ibid., p. xiv.
12. Merton evidently suffers from perfectionism, coupled with an incessant, not always satisfied drive toward a better and wider understanding of things social. At the age of seventy-four he envisages 'about seventy articles still to be written' and complains that excessive self-criticism has kept him from publishing four books (one of them awaiting already eight years for his decision to print). (In a private communication to me) Quite recently he put forward something he calls a 'self-emancipation proclamation': 'I resolved, quite firmly, not again to commit myself to writing a paper for: a symposium (no matter how meritorious that symposium might be), to delivering a lecture (no matter how enticing an occasion that might be), to preparing a paper to be read at a national or international conference (no matter how significant that occasion might be), write a review (no matter how enticing the book) . . . and so on and on through the varieties of *ad hoc* scholarly commitments one makes as a matter of course . . . I have my own program of scholarly work and I do not want to be deflected from it'. (In a letter to Nico Stehr, dated 23 Dec., 1983). A year later comments on the effects of his proclamation: 'I have found this to be a soul-satisfying guideline, one that has led to my doing more writing that I find reasonably satisfying than in any equivalent period before' (Letter to R. Turner dated 17 July, 1984) In a letter to me dated 22 April, 1984, he refers to six extensive projects on his immediate agenda: 'the queue of matters clamoring for publication in print [as distinct from oral publication] is forbiddingly long'.
13. Quoted in Merton, 1980, p. 31.
14. Merton, STSS, p. 70.
15. Ibid., p. 616.
16. Ibid., p. 68.
17. Merton, 1985, p. 5.
18. In Merton's study there is a sort of symbolic audience of his 'significant others' – the collection of photographs of famous scholars, teachers, intellectuals on a wall in front of his desk: Whitehead, Freud, Thomas, Henderson, Sarton, Sorokin, Stouffer, Kroeber, Polanyi, Parsons, Gini, Szilard, Knopf, Lipchitz and three photographs of Lazarsfeld.

19. Merton, SA, p. 86.
20. It is characteristic that for many of the multiple foreign translations of STSS, Merton adduces special introductions which relate to the sociological tradition of the given country. For example, in the Polish edition of 1982 carefully traces his relationships with such representatives, old and young, of Polish sociology as Malinowski, Znaniecki, Ossowski, Ossowska, Malewski, Podgórecki, Nowak – and even the present author.
21. Merton, SOS, p. 374.
22. Bierstedt, 1981, pp. 466–7. See also: Manis and Meltzer, 1974, p. 1.
23. Turner, 1978, p. 91.
24. Garfield, 1977, p. 5.
25. Manis and Meltzer, 1974, p. 9.
26. Garfield, 1980, p. 61.
27. Blau, 1975a, p. 136.
28. Lazarsfeld, 1975, p. 60.
29. Bierstedt, 1981, p. 486.
30. Garfield, 1980, p. 71.
31. Manis and Meltzer, 1974, p. 5.
32. Coser, 1975, p. 85.
33. Stinchcombe, 1975, p. 11.
34. Garfield, 1980, p. 64.
35. Ibid., p. 65.
36. Ibid., p. 71.
37. Oromaner, 1970, p. 324.
38. Ibid., p. 329. But note that Merton himself warns: 'citation counts cannot be responsibly taken as the controlling basis for appraisals of individual performance. At best, they are ancillary to detailed judgments by informed peers'. Merton, 1979, p. 10.
39. Translated into: French, Italian, Japanese, Spanish, Hebrew, Portuguese, Polish, Hungarian, Yugoslavian (Serbo-Croatian), Chinese and German (in part).
40. Manis and Meltzer, 1974, p. 4.
41. Merton, STSS, p. ix.
42. Bierstedt, 1981, p. 461.
43. Hodges Persell, 1984, pp. 362–363.
44. Merton, 1980, p. 3.
45. Manis and Meltzer, 1974, p. 4.
46. Coser, in: Coser and Nisbet, 1975, p. 8.
47. Caplovitz, 1977, pp. 146 and 145. Merton himself says: 'During the past 55 years, the files lead to an estimate of approximately 200 book-manuscripts and about ten times that number of article-length manuscripts' (in a letter to the author, 5 Feb., 1985).
48. Letter to Eugene Garfield, dated 2 Aug., 1983.
49. In a letter to the author dated 22 April, 1984.
50. Cole and Zuckerman, 1975, p. 164.
51. Merton, STSS, p. 446.
52. Donoghue, 1981. See also: Donoghue, 1985.

53. Merton, OTSOG, p. 9.
54. Ibid., p. 178.
55. Ibid., p. 43.
56. In a letter to the author dated 5 Feb., 1985.
57. Merton, OTSOG, p. 45.
58. Merton, STSS, p. 35.
59. Taken out of context this aphorism has been sometimes misunderstood as a call to bury intellectual ancestors in perpetual oblivion. Such a striking misconstruction can be found in Levine, 1981, p. 60: 'Sociologists seemed driven to avoid the classics, following with apparently fanatic devotion the injunction suggested by the Whiteheadian epigraph to R. K. Merton's widely influential book of essays first published in 1949. . .'. It seems that the aphorism has been picked up in this mistaken meaning by the sociological 'Now-generation'. In a letter to Helmut Wagner, dated 12 March, 1983, Merton explains: 'Whitehead was remarking on the costs of excessive authority in the development of thought and criticising the substitution of commentary on old works for new work. . . . Whitehead's own lifelong interest in the predecessors of his contemporary thought, to say nothing of my own deep interest in the genesis and development of sociological ideas, might have signaled that we were scarcely calling for a studied ignorance of pathmakers and their work'.
60. Merton, STSS, p. 31.
61. Ibid., p. 332.
62. Merton, OTSOG, p. 163. Zuckerman, 1977a, p. 88 perceives this spurious dilemma of continuity and originality: 'the seeming paradox that norms of science call for both conformity and nonconformity is of course no paradox at all. The approved form of conformity is to the cognitive standards of what is defined as constituting scientific work while the approved form of nonconformity involves original contributions that advance upon previous claims to knowledge by denying their validity . . .'.
63. Recently Merton has come upon a new term in his beloved Oxford English Dictionary: 'the putamen', to refer to such core, fundamental ideas.
64. Merton, OTSOG, p. 45.
65. Merton, STSS, p. 587.
66. Coser, in: Coser and Nisbet, 1975, p. 4.
67. Note that there is not a single piece in his prolific bibliography of purely expository or historical research on this or that thinker, no one's 'intellectual portrait', or the like.
68. Coser, 1975, p. 97.
69. Stinchcombe, 1975, p. 14.
70. Coser, 1975, p. 87.
71. Ibid., p. 97.
72. Merton, STSS, p. xiii.
73. Ibid., p. 63.

74. Ibid., p. 68. See also: Merton, 1983a, p. 124.
75. See: Merton, 1934.
76. Barbano, 1968, p. 82.
77. Coser, 1975, p. 88.
78. Edition Plón, Paris, 1965.
79. Giddens, 1977, p. 97.
80. Barbano, 1968, p. 82.
81. Merton, SOS, pp. 216–17.
82. Merton, 1982a, p. 917.
83. Merton, SSEM, p. 11.
84. Coser, in: Coser and Nisbet, 1975, p. 7.
85. Gouldner, 1973, p. x. Affinity with Marx is also emphasised by Boudon, 1976, p. 1357.
86. Bierstedt, 1981, p. 498. I understand Bierstedt here as referring to the influence of Marx on American thinkers; the reception of his ideas in American sociology.
87. Merton, SOS, p. 102.
88. Merton, SSEM, p. 8.
89. Merton, 1983a, p. 124.
90. Merton (with Lazarsfeld), 1954, p. 36.
91. Merton, STSS, pp. 373–374.
92. Merton, STSS, p. 352.
93. Ibid., pp. 342, 346.
94. Merton himself takes an exception to such an appraisal: 'Others might say that the debt to Weber is considerable. Witness the doctoral dissertation with its hypothesis of the connections of ascetic Protestantism to the early days of modern science. . . . Again, the consequential and explicit departure from the Weber model of bureaucracy to focus on the dysfunctions and other unanticipated consequences of aspects of bureaucratic structure. . . . I believe that other, more scattered influences of Weber can also be found'. (In a letter to the author dated 22 April, 1984).
95. Merton, 1983a, p. 124.
96. Merton, SA, pp. 147–53.
97. Merton, STSS, p. 250. Though one must admit that the emphasis on the dysfunctions of bureaucracy is an original and significant modification of Weber.
98. Merton, 1983a, p. 124.
99. Ibid., pp. 123–125.
100. Those designations are not used by Merton himself, but rather by commentators and critics of his work.
101. Merton, 1982b, p. 8.
102. Merton, 1984f, p. 1.
103. Ibid., p. 5.
104. Ibid., pp. 9–30.
105. 'Sociological Aspects of Invention, Discovery and Scientific Theories'. In P. A. Sorokin, *Social and Cultural Dynamics*, 4 vols (New York 1937: American Book Company), pp. 125–80 and 439–76.

106. Sorokin, 1966, pp. 451–2.
107. Ibid., p. 452.
108. Merton quotes this in 1984f, p. 28.
109. Merton, 1980, p. 70.
110. See Merton, 1945.
111. Merton, 1980, p. 70.
112. Parsons, 1975, p. 67.
113. Ibid., p. 80.
114. An informal account of this intimate relationship, as seen by Lazarsfeld, is given in his contribution to Merton's 'Festschrift' of 1975, pp. 35–66.
115. Coser, 1975, p. 87.
116. Merton says: 'I am wholly persuaded that neologisms (new words) are essential to register new perceptions, conceptions, and phenomena if only to ease ready reference'. (Letter to William Golden, dated 23 December, 1984, p. 3).
117. A good example is the term self-fulfilling prophecy (and its counterpart, the self-defeating prophecy) used extensively in everyday language and political discourse. 'I recall', writes Merton, with his characteristic irony, 'the mixed feelings with which I read in President Nixon's budget message of 1971 that he counted on his optimistic forecast for the economy becoming, the language is his, 'a self-fulfilling prophecy'. I cherished the promised outcome but was minded to inform the President that prophecies that become self-fulfilling do so only when the prophet has wide credibility'. (In a letter to William Golden, dated 23 December, 1984, p. 11).
118. The full definition and characterisation of 'obliteration by incorporation' runs as follows: 'the obliteration of the source of ideas, methods, or findings by their incorporation in currently accepted knowledge. In the course of this hypothesized process, the number of explicit references to the original work declines in the papers and books making use of it. Users and consequently transmitters of that knowledge are so thoroughly familiar with its origins that they assume this to be true of their readers as well. Preferring not to insult their readers' knowledgeability, they no longer refer to the original source. And since many of us tend to attribute a significant idea or formulation to the author who introduced us to it, the altogether innocent transmitter sometimes becomes identified as the originator. In the successive transmissions of ideas, repeated use may erase all but immediately antecedent versions, thus producing an historical palimpsest in which the source of those ideas is obliterated'. (Merton, 1979, p. 9)
119. An excellent example of this is Veblenian concept of 'trained incapacity'.
120. Supplements to *Oxford English Dictionary*, volumes 1–3, credit at least 10 word-coinages explicitly to Merton. These are: dysfunction, local and cosmopolitan influentials, latent function, manifest function, opinionnaire, out-grouper, retreatism, retreatist, ritualist, role-set.

121. Reflecting on his early work and explaining why he used the term 'ethnic' instead of 'racial' in the article of 1940 ('Fact and Factitiousness in Ethnic Opinionnaires', *American Sociological Review*, 5 (1), Feb., pp. 13–28), Merton says that even then he 'was quite evidently persuaded that the particular words one used to designate concepts went far toward influencing thought' (In a letter to William Golden, dated 23 December, 1984, p. 5).
122. Lazarsfeld, 1975, p. 43.
123. Bierstedt, 1981, p. 445.
124. Barnes and Dolby, 1970, p. 3.
125. *The Student-Physician: Introductory Studies in the Sociology of Medical Education* (edited with George G. Reader and Patricia L. Kendall). (Cambridge 1957: Harvard University Press).
126. Merton, SRPP, p. 156.
127. Cole, 1975, p. 175.
128. See: *Mass Persuasion* (with Marjorie Fiske and Alberta Curtis) (New York 1946: Harper & Brothers).
129. Hyman, 1975, p. 265.

Chapter 3

1. The concept of the 'image of science' is discussed extensively by Yehuda Elkana. See for example: Elkana, 1981, pp. 15–19 (he uses the term 'image of knowledge'). See also Lepenies, 1981, pp. 245–61.
2. See: Merton, STSE, and Merton, 1984a.
3. Merton, SOS, p. 217.
4. Ibid., p. 39.
5. Merton, STSE, p. xvii.
6. Ibid., p. ix.
7. Merton, SSEM, p. 75.
8. The term is not Merton's; I borrow it from Hall, 1963.
9. J. W. Nett, as quoted in Hall, 1963, pp. 9–10.
10. Hall, 1963, p. 10.
11. Ibid., p. 11.
12. Merton, SOS, p. 11.
13. Merton, OTSOG, p. 134.
14. Merton, SOS, p. 102.
15. Ibid., p. 40. Note that the term 'paradigm' is used by Merton in a sense different from that proposed much later by T. S. Kuhn. For Merton it means simply a systematic exposition or codification of concepts, assumptions, problems in a given domain of inquiry. For more on the history of the usage of the concept see Toulmin, 1972, pp. 106–7.
16. Ibid., p. 47.
17. Merton, 1983a, p. 126.
18. Merton, STSS, p. 495.
19. Merton, SSEM, p. 112.
20. Merton, STSS, p. 552.

21. Ibid., p. 552, ref. 14.
22. Ibid., p. 585.
23. Merton, STSE, p. vii.
24. Cole, Zuckerman, 1975, pp. 160–2.
25. Merton, SSEM, p. 19.
26. A good example of this interaction is provided by Zuckerman's study of deviance in science, where she explicitly intends to 'provide occasions highlighting certain aspects of deviant behavior generally', and more precisely to detect 'how far does the special case of deviant behavior in science illuminate the various theoretical perspectives on deviant behavior – conflict theory, differential association theory, and anomie-and-opportunity-structure theory'. Zuckerman, 1977a, pp. 89–90.
27. Merton, SSEM, p. 22.
28. Merton, STSE, p. xi.
29. Merton, STSS, p. 661.
30. Ezrahi, 1980, pp. 45 and 48.
31. Some branches of science in medieval Europe could provide a fitting illustration. But the phenomenon is by no means unknown in modern science.
32. Cole, 1975, p. 176.
33. Mulkay, 1980, p. 118.
34. Merton, SA, p. 32.
35. Merton, SOS, p. 134.
36. Ibid., p. 136.
37. Ibid., p. 328.
38. Merton, SSEM, p. 22.
39. Merton, SOS, p. 258. In a letter to D. A. Hollinger whose paper "The Defense of Democracy and Robert K. Merton's Formulation of the Scientific Ethos" (1983) suggested a link between a notion of the scientific ethos and the historical experiences of Nazi Germany, Merton reports that his concern with the fate of science under the Nazi regime gave birth to his initial explication and persistent interest in the scientific ethos: 'I have no doubt that at the time my focus on the institutional structure of science was reinforced, if not evoked, by the political discourse of the Nazi period' (letter dated 19 May, 1983).
40. Merton, SOS, p. 260.
41. See: Milosz, 1953.
42. Merton, SOS, pp. 264–265.
43. Ibid., p. 266.
44. Ibid., p. 254.
45. As quoted in Ezrahi, 1980, p. 45.
46. Merton, SOS, p. 269.
47. Merton, STSS, p. 588.
48. Mulkay, 1980, p. 111.
49. Merton, SRPP, p. 5. See also: Merton, STSS, p. 595, ref. 16.
50. Merton, STSS, p. 605.
51. Ibid., p. 607.

52. See Merton's theory of anomie discussed in chapter 6 and 7 for another application of this distinction.
53. Merton, SRPP, p. 214.
54. Merton, STSS, p. 586.
55. Merton, SOS, p. 302.
56. Ibid., p. 323.
57. Merton, 1959, p. 181.
58. Merton, SRPP, p. 214.
59. Merton, STSS (1957 edn), p. 544.
60. Merton, STSS, p. 607.
61. Merton, SRPP, p. 256.
62. Such a rephrasing of the term was suggested by Bernard Barber, 1952. It is consistently used by Patel, 1975.
63. Merton, STSS, p. 610.
64. Merton, SOS, p. 302.
65. Ibid., p. 339.
66. Ibid., p. 614.
67. Merton, STSE, pp. 220–1. Note that as early as 1938 Merton was maintaining that 'rules of evidence in science' are related to the historical and social context and that making the case for a scientific claim is a social process.
68. Merton, 1980, pp. 18–19.
69. Merton, 1984c, p. xxxiii and OTSOG, p. 204.
70. Merton, 1984a, p. 1102. Zuckerman insightfully observes that 'the norm of [organized] scepticism is organized in a double sense. First, it provides moral justification for the conspicuously pragmatic practice of having some peers assigned the task of critically assessing the adequacy of scientific claims. And second, the norm is reinforced by the reward system of science which confers peer recognition on the scientists who identify flaws in the work of others along with the recognition that comes with contributions of their own'. Zuckerman, 1977a, p. 91.
71. But precisely because of that, it had a strong didactic impact on shaping the ideology of science in America. In a letter to Merton dated 13 May, 1983, the historian D. A. Hollinger asserts: 'In the history of that ideology, your formulation of the scientific ethos played a role very much like the role played in the history of ideas about the American West by Frederick Jackson Turner's "frontier thesis" '.
72. Merton, SA, p. 35.
73. Ibid., p. 33.
74. Ibid., pp. 18 and 17.
75. Mitroff, 1974, p. 590.
76. Merton, SA, pp. 8 and 18.
77. Mulkay, 1980, p. 124. More specifically: 'In applying rules to specific acts, further variable processes of reasoning are typically involved which are in no way specified in the rules themselves. . . . We should not assume that any norm can have a simple literal meaning

independent of the contexts in which it is applied' (p. 112). And further: 'The processes of interpretation which accompany the application of these rules are highly variable and they appear to depend partly on participants' subtle judgments about various aspects of the social world of science' (p. 121).
78. As is clearly implied, for example, at several places in Broad and Wade 1983.
79. Merton, SA, p. 40.
80. This is an obvious allusion to Wrong's famous article: 'The Oversocialized Conception of Man in Modern Sociology', 1961.
81. Barnes and Dolby, 1970, p. 13.
82. Mitroff, 1974, p. 587.
83. Merton, SOS, p. 321.
84. Merton, 1984d.
85. Merton, SOS, p. 323. It is interesting to note that in the case of science, the hypothesis of anomie and variable opportunity structure does not fully fit the existing empirical evidence. After a thorough scrutiny of the detected cases of deviance in science, Zuckerman concludes: '. . . our review of the evidence does not find the hypothesized differences in deviant behavior among scientists having differential access to opportunity for scientific achievement. Neither Kammerer, Summerlin, nor the other scientists we have noted engaging in deviance were shut off from such access. . .'. Zuckerman, 1977a, p. 131.
86. Merton, 1984d.
87. Merton, SOS, pp. 309–21.
88. Merton, 1984d.
89. Zuckerman, 1977a, p. 110.
90. Ibid., p. 113.
91. Babbage, 1830, as quoted in Merton 1984d.
92. Zuckerman, 1977a, p. 117.
93. Ibid., p. 119.
94. Ibid., pp. 119–121.
95. Ibid., p. 98.
96. Ibid., p. 131.
97. Ibid., p. 131.
98. Barnes and Dolby, 1970, p. 7.
99. Ibid., p. 16.
100. Merton, 1980, p. 19. This corresponds more or less to the system of social control in Zuckerman's terminology.
101. This is one of Merton's leitmotifs, already present in STSE, p. 219.
102. Merton, SOS, p. 311.
103. Merton, SA, p. 45.
104. Merton, 1980, p. 19.
105. Merton, SOS, p. 450.
106. Ibid., pp. 439–459.
107. In a letter to the author dated 22 April, 1984, p. 6.
108. Merton, OTSOG, p. 219.

109. In a letter to Laura Nader dated 24 December, 1978, p. 3., Merton lists a long bibliography of that misattribution.
110. Merton, STSS, pp. 27–28. Merton's concept of 'obliteration by incorporation' (OBI) has proved fruitful and influential. See: Cole and Zuckerman, 1975; Cole, 1975; Garfield, 1975; Zuckerman, 1977b.
111. Letter to Laura Nader, dated 24 December, 1978, p. 8.
112. Merton, SOS, pp. 298–301.
113. Ibid., pp. 439–440.
114. Zuckerman, 1977a, pp. 125–128.
115. Merton, SOS, p. 446.
116. Ibid., p. 440.
117. Here, he draws chiefly upon the extensive research project, based on interviews with Nobel laureates, which was conducted by Zuckerman (1977b).
118. Merton, SOS, p. 442.
119. Ibid., p. 477.
120. Zuckerman and Merton, 'Age, and Age Structure in Science', in: Merton, SOS, pp. 520–522.
121. Ibid., p. 520.
122. Ibid., pp. 497–559.
123. See de Solla Price, 1961 and 1963. Also: Crane, 1972, and Chubin, 1983. Merton explicitly acknowledges this as a 'cognitive conduit': 'It was Derek J. de Solla Price who, in a brilliant stroke of terminological recoinage, adapted and conceptually extended the seventeenth-century term "invisible college". . .' (Merton, SSEM, p. 5).
124. Merton, SSEM, p. 6.
125. Ibid.
126. See: Fleck, 1979.
127. Merton, 1976, p. 6.
128. Cole and Zuckerman, 1975, p. 150. In a letter to Helmut Wagner dated 12 March, 1983, Merton emphasises his 'deep interest in the genesis and development of sociological ideas' and 'the importance [he] attaches to tracing and trying to understand the diffusion of ideas through historical time as well as cognitive space'.
129. Merton, STSE.
130. Ibid., p. xvii.
131. Ibid., p. ix.
132. Merton, 1984a, p. 1099.
133. Merton, STSE, p. xvi.
134. I have described this constellation earlier as 'scientific mind'.
135. Merton, STSS, p. 589.
136. Merton, STSE, p. xviii.
137. Ibid.
138. Nelson, 1972, p. 206.
139. Merton, STSE, p. xix.
140. Merton, 1984a, p. 1101.
141. Ibid., p. 1095.

142. Patel, 1975, p. 71.
143. Merton, 1984a, p. 1097.
144. Ibid., p. 1092. Two recent examples of continuing dispute are Abraham, 1983; and Becker, 1984.
145. Hall, 1963, p. 13.
146. Tenbruck, 1974, p. 316.
147. Ibid., p. 320.
148. Kearney, 1973.
149. Hall, 1963, p. 4.
150. Ibid., p. 7.
151. Merton, 1984a, p. 1100.
152. Nelson, 1972, p. 210.
153. Ibid., p. 206.
154. Merton, 1936, p. 112.
155. Merton, 1948, p. 164.
156. Merton, 1984a, p. 1107.
157. Merton, 1976, p. 9.
158. Ibid. At a public lecture presented in 1982 at a Temple University Colloquium (Merton, 1982d), he clarifies the issue of progress: 'Speaking of the progress of science in this concrete historical sense means only that the contemporary physical and life sciences can account with more widespread coherence, precision, and often predictability for all the natural phenomena which the ancients tried to account for, and much else besides, including an indefinitely wide range of natural phenomena which were not even detectable' (p. 6). By the way, isn't it symptomatic that he is reluctant to include the social sciences in that image of progress? We detect here another implicit claim for the specific, peculiar nature of the social sciences (in spite of commonality with natural sciences at the level of fundamental scientific canons); namely the different criteria of progress, perhaps more akin to those used in arts and letters.
159. Merton, 1959, p. 177.
160. Merton, SOS, p. 369. The ultimate mechanism of scientific progress is, of course scientific discovery, and its ultimate agent, the discoverer. Merton chooses as a strategic ground for identifying and analysing this aspect of scientific process, the familiar phenomenon of independent, multiple discoveries, or simply 'multiples' as opposed to unique discoveries of 'singletons' (SOS, pp. 343–70). On the basis of extended investigations, he arrives at an insightful hypothesis that recognises the role of genius in science without falling into the trap of an individualistic 'great man theory' of science: 'By conceiving scientific genius sociologically, as one who in his own person represents the functional equivalent of a number and variety of often lesser talents, the theory maintains that the genius plays a distinctive role in advancing science, often accelerating its rate of development and sometimes, by the excess of authority attributed to him, slowing further development' (p. 370). However, the phenomenon of multiples also demonstrates the equally significant role of the social

context, the cognitive and social environment which is ripe or not for particular kinds of discoveries. Recently Merton's theory of 'multiples' has been critically discussed in an important paper by Patinkin (1983).

161. It may be of interest to note that these observations appeared in 1959. I do not at all claim that there was an anticipation of Kuhn's major monograph (1962) in Merton's work. But it is a case of significant consonance of ideas independently reached. Merton asserts the gradual growth of scientific knowledge through recognising that the current doctrines do not allow for newly observed phenomena (Kuhn's 'anomalies'), followed by changes, modifications, further specifications in the current theory (Kuhn's 'normal science'). But he also recognises the alternative mechanism of change when anomalies that accumulate put in question the existing theory, leading to 'replacements' or 'mutations' (Kuhn's 'revolution').

162. Merton, STSS, p. 21.

163. Merton, SOS, p. 8. Merton links this pattern of varying degrees of awareness of the implications of ideas even by their formulators with the long history of priority disputes in science. In a letter to Merton dated 12 December, 1978, the Nobel laureate physicist Chen Ning Yang writes: 'I, myself, was involved in a few disputes of the kind covered by the Whitehead quote. Fortunately, none of them was about any truly major developments. The Yang-Merton correspondence illustrates the 'cognitive conduit' function transmitting ideas that have been previously accorded little attention. Yang writes to request the exact reference to the correlative Whitehead's aphorism which appears in the eipgraph to the numerous printings and translations of Merton's STSS (p. 1): 'Everything of importance has been said before by somebody who did not discover it'.

164. Merton, 1984a, p. 1101.

165. Merton, SOS, p. 403.

166. Phillips, 1974, p. 77.

167. Ibid., p. 60.

168. Ibid., p. 77.

169. See: Mulkay, 1979; Douglas, 1975; Bloor, 1976; Barnes, 1974. For comprehensive reviews of those developments see: Collins, 1983 and Kuklick, 1983.

170. Fleck, 1979. Merton recalls 'the convoluted path taken in helping to turn Fleck's rather idiosyncratic German into reasonably lucid English' (in a letter to the author dated 22 April, 1984).

171. Merton, STSS, pp. 635–6.

172. Merton, 1981a, pp. 5–6.

173. Ibid., p. 6.

174. Ibid., p. 6.

175. Ibid., p. 7.

176. Ibid., p. 6. He refers ironically to 'these times of acute – not disciplined – subjectivism' (in a letter to James F. Short, Jr. dated 23 April, 1981).

177. Ibid., pp. 7–8. This is, Merton says, 'what I have also believed since I lived in the 17th century, with excursions into the 18th and 19th centuries, that facts are not *simply* there; that facts are statements about assumed realities cast in terms of a conceptual scheme...' (in a letter to James F. Short, Jr., dated 23 April, 1981).
178. Merton, 1980, p. 20.
179. Merton, STSS, p. 595.
180. Mitroff, 1974, p. 590.

Chapter 4

1. Bierstedt, 1981, p. 460.
2. Sztompka, 1979a, pp. 6–16.
3. Merton, 1948, p. 165.
4. Merton (with Lazarsfeld), 1954, p. 61.
5. Merton, 1948, p. 165.
6. See Mills, 1959.
7. Merton, 1964, p. 240.
8. Merton, 1961, p. 18.
9. Merton, 1971, p. 191.
10. Merton, STSS, p. 590.
11. Ibid. (1957 edn), p. 49.
12. Ibid. (1968 edn), p. 587.
13. Merton, 1959, p. 177.
14. Merton, STSS, p. 149.
15. Ibid., pp. 149 and 153.
16. Merton, 1964, p. 226.
17. Merton, STSS (1957 edn), p. 13.
18. Merton (with Lazarsfeld), 1954, p. 62.
19. Merton, SOS, p. 344.
20. Merton (with Lazarsfeld), 1954, p. 25.
21. Merton, 1961, p. 22.
22. Merton, SOS, p. 61.
23. Merton, STSS (1957 edn), p. 6.
24. Merton, STSS (1968 edn), p. 47.
25. Merton, STSS (1957 edn), p. 6.
26. Similar solution is elaborated in more detail in my book, Sztompka, 1979a.
27. Merton, STSS (1968 edn), p. viii.
28. Ibid., p. 104.
29. Merton (with Lazarsfeld), 1954, pp. 56–66.
30. Merton, STSS, pp. 140–141.
31. Merton, 1934, p. 543. Evidence that after half a century he still keeps to this anti-positivist persuasion may be found in a recent piece of 'oral publication', his lecture presented to the Temple University Colloquium in 1982 (Merton 1982d). He says: 'I join with our speakers in rejecting that conception of scientific progress which

holds that the growth of what scientists are willing to certify as knowledge proceeds in linear, wholly cumulative fashion, inexorably and through the almost automatic use of something called "the scientific method" (as this is typically described in those many slim volumes bearing that title)' (p. 16).
32. Merton, 1964, p. 241.
33. Merton, SOS, p. 393.
34. As quoted in Merton, SOS, p. 393.
35. D. A. Hollinger claims that 'Merton's formulation of the scientific ethos is . . . an intelligent and revealing artifact of the effort made by a generation of intellectuals to vindicate a set of social values identified with the liberal political tradition' (1983, p. 3). He traces the origins of Merton's idea to the intellectual protest against the political practice of Nazi Germany, and then points out the reasons why the idea of the scientific ethos has got progressively detached from that original context 'in which the practice of sociology and the defense of democracy went comfortably together' (p. 2): 'As the autonomy of science from external influences and demands was increasingly urged and defended . . . it became all the more important that the moral qualities for which science was ostensibly a vehicle be seen as intrinsic to science. . .' (p. 12). In a letter to Nico Stehr dated 19 May, 1983 Merton comments on Hollinger's paper and somewhat reluctantly seems to admit the crucial point: 'It is a rather interesting effort to focus on the conceptual and particularly the historical connections between the ethos of science and the context of democratic values and discourse in the 1930s and 1940s. I find myself rather taken with the principal thesis. . . '. I address this issue more extensively and in a manner different from Merton's in Sztompka, 1979a.
36. Merton, STSS, p. 39.
37. Merton, SOS, p. 14.
38. Merton, 1961, p. 20.
39. Merton (with Lazarsfeld), 1954, pp. 59–60.
40. Merton, SOS, p. 37.
41. Ibid., p. 213.
42. Ibid., p. 323.
43. Merton, 1945. For recent appraisal of Merton's relationship to Popper and Kuhn see Cavanaugh, 1985.
44. Merton, STSS, p. 148.
45. Merton, 1984a, p. 1108.
46. Ibid., p. 1111.
47. Ibid., p. 1109.
48. Merton, SRPP, p. 44.
49. Merton, SOS, p. 257. But in the same paper (written originally in 1938) he manifests a prescient awareness that science may be 'responsible for endowing those engines of human destruction which, it is said, may plunge our civilization into everlasting night and destruction' (pp. 261–2) and goes on to protest against 'a tendency for scientists to assume that social effects of science must be beneficial in the long run.

This article of faith performs the function of providing a rationale for scientific research, but it is manifestly not a statement of fact. It involves the confusion of truth and social utility which is characteristically found in the nonlogical penumbra of science' (p. 263).
50. Merton, SRPP, pp. 217–18.
51. Merton, STSE, p. xxii.
52. For more detailed discussion of this point see Sztompka, 1983. The distinction of 'internal' and 'external' models of practical application is introduced in Sztompka 1979a.
53. Merton, SRPP, p. 17.
54. Merton, 1961, p. 20.
55. Merton, SRPP, p. 50.
56. Ibid., p. 64.
57. Ibid., p. 55.
58. Merton, SA, p. 173.
59. Merton, STSS, p. 624.
60. This is sometimes referred to as a 'clinical approach'.
61. Merton, SRPP, pp. 27–28.
62. Ibid., p. 45.
63. Ibid., p. 48.
64. Merton, STSS, pp. 52–53.
65. Merton, SRPP, p. 218.
66. Ibid., p. 65.
67. Ibid., p. 23.
68. Ibid., p. 22.
69. Ibid., p. 23.
70. See Sztompka, 1973.
71. Merton, SA, p. 112.
72. Merton, SRPP, p. 18.
73. Merton, SOS, p. 90.
74. Merton, SRPP, p. 25.
75. Ibid., p. 33.
76. Merton, STSS, p. ix.
77. Ibid., p. 159 (the first formulation is as early as 1948).
78. Ibid., p. 144.
79. Merton, SRPP, p. 100.
80. Ibid., p. 101.
81. Merton, STSS (1957 edn), p. 20.
82. Merton (with Lazarsfeld), 1954, p. 24.
83. Merton, 1961, p. 19.
84. Merton, 1984b, p. 267.
85. Merton, STSS, p. 146.
86. Merton, STSS, p. 307.
87. Merton, 1959, pp. 184–5.
88. Merton, STSS, p. 169.
89. Merton (with Lazarsfeld), 1954, pp. 58–9.
90. Merton, STSS, p. 169.

91. Merton, SOS, p. 163.
92. Merton, STSE, p. xv.
93. Merton, STSS, p. 153 (this conviction is formulated as early as 1948).
94. Merton (with Sills and Stigler), 1984e.
95. Ibid., p. 331.
96. Merton, STSS p. 152. On the prerequisites of 'precise' qualitative analysis, see Lazarsfeld, 1972.
97. Ibid., p. 279.
98. Merton, SA, p. 222.
99. Merton, STSS, p. 142.
100. Ibid., p. 153.
101. Merton, SA, p. 239.
102. Merton, STSS, p. 157.
103. Ibid.
104. Ibid., p. 158.
105. Ibid., p. 166.
106. Ibid., p. 170.
107. Ibid., p. 2.
108. Ibid., p. 140.
109. Ibid., p. 143.
110. Ibid., p. 150.
111. Ibid., p. 143.
112. Ibid., p. 149.
113. Ibid.
114. Ibid., p. 39.
115. Ibid., p. 143.
116. Ibid., p. 142.
117. Ibid., p. 39.
118. Merton, SRPP, pp. 79–80.
119. Merton, STSS, p. 40.
120. Merton, SRPP, pp. 79–80.
121. Merton, STSS, p. 40.
122. Ibid., p. 39.
123. Ibid., p. 40.
124. Ibid., p. 70.
125. Bierstedt, 1981, pp. 152–3.
126. Merton, STSS, p. 67.
127. Ibid., p. 39.
128. Merton, 1948, p. 165.
129. Merton, STSS, p. 45.
130. Merton, 1948, p. 165.
131. Goode, 1975, p. 73.
132. Merton, STSS, pp. 39–40.
133. Ibid., p. 39.
134. Ibid., pp. 40, 51. See also: Merton, 1948, p. 165.
135. Merton, STSS, p. 51.
136. Weick, 1974, p. 357.
137. Merton, 1948, p. 165.

138. Merton, STSS, pp. 39–40 and 51.
139. See: Sztompka, 1974b.
140. See: Smelser, 1962.
141. See: Allport, 1954.
142. For the applications in archeology, see: Raab, Goodyear, 1984; in biology, see Gould, 1974. And in sociology itself, in the appraisal of George Hillery: 'A large section of sociology has adopted middle range strategy since Merton first proposed this approach. . . . Middle range theory is becoming that which many sociologists are already doing' (Hillery, 1983, p. 2). More specifically, on the applications of the middle-range strategy in the sociology of organisations see: Pinder and Moore, 1980; and in the field of social work, see: Loewenberg, 1984.
143. Eisenstadt, 1980, p. 30.
144. Merton, STSS, p. 68.
145. Ibid., p. 43.
146. Ibid., p. 63.
147. Opp, 1970, p. 247.
148. Ibid., pp. 246 and 250.
149. Ibid., p. 247.
150. Ibid., p. 253.
151. Merton (with Lazarsfeld), 1954, pp. 20–1.
152. See: Kuhn, [1962] 1970. In this case, as different for example from Merton's note on the implications of anomalies in science, the similarity is purely terminological; it does not touch the concept of the 'paradigm', which is quite distinct in Kuhnian and Mertonian usage.
153. Merton, STSS, p. 69.
154. Ibid., p. 70. For the examples of such use see: Rex, 1981, chapter 5: Duke, 1976, pp. 205–13; Cullen and Cullen, 1978. On the use in social anthropology; Firth, 1975, p. 13.
155. Martindale, 1959, p. 78.
156. Ibid., p. 80.
157. Merton, SOS, p. 11–12.
158. Merton, SA, p. 211.
159. Ibid., p. 212.
160. Ibid.
161. Ibid.
162. Merton, 1981, p. v.
163. Ibid., p. i.
164. Blau, 1975b, p. 1.
165. Merton, SRPP, p. 80.
166. Merton, 1981, p. iv.
167. Merton, SA, p. 169.
168. Ibid., p. 142.
169. Merton, SRPP, p. 81.
170. See the elaboration of that idea in 'Social Conflict Over Styles of Sociological Work' (1961), as reprinted in SOS, pp. 47–69.
171. Ibid., p. 44.

172. Ibid., p. 57.
173. See Alexander, 1982, for the explication of the important notion of 'theoretical logic'.

Chapter 5

1. Merton, SA, p. 131.
2. Merton, 1984b, p. 264.
3. He tends to avoid the term 'approach', except in an ironic context.
4. See extensive discussion of these two traditions in Sztompka, 1979.
5. Kuhn, 1970, p. viii.
6. Birnbaum, 1971, p. 108.
7. Merton's initial formulation of similar ideas may be found as early as 1948 in an article 'The Position of Sociological Theory'. Of course I am not making any priority-claim on behalf of Merton. To do it would come too close to the sin of 'adumbrationism' (as Merton calls it) and to illustrate once again the aptness of Whitehead's observation (often quoted by Merton and even used as a motto to STSS): 'Everything of importance has been said before by somebody who did not discover it'.
8. Merton, 1981, p. i.
9. Merton, SA, pp. 109–10.
10. Merton, 1961, p. 20.
11. Merton, 1981, p. i.
12. Merton, SOS, p. 51.
13. Merton, 1971, p. 190.
14. Merton, 1981, p. vii.
15. Merton, SA, p. 116.
16. Ibid., p. 118.
17. Merton, 1971, p. 191.
18. Merton, SA, p. 111.
19. Merton, 1971, p. 191.
20. Merton, SRPP, p. 170.
21. Merton, SA, p. 184.
22. Merton, STSS, p. 70.
23. Ibid., pp. 325–6.
24. Merton, SRPP, pp. 170 and 180.
25. Merton, SOS, p. 290.
26. Merton, SRPP, pp. 169–170.
27. Merton, SA, p. 5.
28. Merton (with Vanessa Merton and Elinor Barber), 1983c, p. 25.
29. Merton, 1984b, pp. 280–1.
30. Merton, 1964, p. 226.
31. See: Bottomore and Nisbet, 1978.
32. Martindale, 1965, p. ix.
33. Davis, 1959, p. 760.
34. Homans, 1964, p. 108.

35. Giddens, 1977, p. 96.
36. Cole, 1975, p. 206.
37. Parsons, 1975, p. 79.
38. Merton, STSS, p. xiv. This opinion is corroborated by citation studies. In a recent study of current textbooks of sociology Wells, 1979, finds that 'Functionalism reached its peak in the 1960–1965 period, but is still cited more frequently and extensively than conflict theory. . . . Clearly, functionalism has not been replaced by the conflict paradigm. Instead, both perspectives are receiving increased attention' (p. 430).
39. Nagel, 1961, p. 522.
40. Davis and Moore, 1945.
41. Parsons, 1951; Levy, 1952; Easton, 1953; Loomis and Loomis, 1961.
42. Parsons, 1975, p. 67.
43. Merton, 1948, p. 165.
44. Ibid., p. 166.
45. Turner, 1978, pp. 72–73 and 75.
46. Barbano, 1968, p. 47.
47. Merton, STSS, pp. 100–1.
48. Ibid., p. 79.
49. Ibid., p. 79.
50. Ibid., p. 81.
51. Barbano, 1968, pp. 69–70.
52. Sztompka, 1974, p. 128.
53. Merton, STSS, p. 106.
54. Ibid., p. 105.
55. Merton, SRPP, p. 85.
56. This is my term, not Merton's.
57. Merton, STSS, p. 105.
58. Ibid., p. 86. It is one thing to say that society X is imbalanced because pervaded by multiple dysfunctions, and it is another thing to say that institution Z is on the whole dysfunctional for the society X. In the first case the judgment is about a social whole (or some subsystem thereof); in the second – about an element of society (an item subjected to functional analysis).
59. Ibid., p. 79.
60. Ibid., p. 85.
61. Sztompka, 1974, p. 82.
62. Merton, STSS, p. 105.
63. The same procedure is adopted by Richter, 1965.
64. Merton, STSS, p. 87.
65. Ibid., pp. 87–8.
66. Merton, STSE, p. xviii.
67. Sztompka, 1974, p. 91.
68. Merton, STSS, p. 106.
69. Ibid., p. 87.
70. Ibid., p. 106.
71. Merton, 1948, p. 166.

72. Merton, STSS, p. 106.
73. Lehman, 1966, p. 275.
74. Ibid., p. 277.
75. The mechanism of sublimation is a good example from the field of psychology (more specifically psychoanalysis).
76. Sjoberg, 1960, pp. 340–341.
77. Merton, STSS, p. 114.
78. Ibid., p. 104.
79. Ibid., pp. 78–79.
80. Merton, STSS, p. 105.
81. Campbell, 1982, p. 34.
82. Similar observations are made by Levy, 1952; Spiro, 1961; Isajiw, 1968; Sztompka, 1961; Giddens, 1976. Zeidenstein, 1979 has added even more subtle distinctions. First, he introduces the dimension of time. In his view the subjective awareness of consequences is a changing quality. Therefore 'there are two other logically possible types of consequences: these which are originally unintended but later recognized (which may be termed unplanned-manifest), and those which are intended but upon their fruition remain unrecognized (planned-latent) by participants in the social system' (p. 458). Second, Zeidenstein differentiates between various degrees of recognition; ignorance is not the same as mistaken diagnosis, and both are not the same as adequate recognition. 'We might expect different modes of behavior from a given set of participants at a given time, depending on whether they are ignorant of consequences, recognize them accurately, or recognize them innaccurately' (p. 459). Finally, he cross-tabulates the typology of manifest and latent functions, with that of functions and dysfunctions. It allows to point out the interesting category of manifest dysfunctions, it means 'acts calculated and accurately recognized as inhibiting the adaptation of a social system' (p. 459). Such acts are often utilised by revolutionaries or *agents provocateur* as a tactical means for raising general unrest and destabilising the system – either for the sake of its future reconstruction or introducing harsh measures against opposition.
83. Spiro, 1961, p. 108.
84. Merton, SA., p. 146.
85. Merton, STSS, p. 120. A critique of this claim is raised by Campbell, 1982, p. 42. He holds that the study of latent functions is typical for all sociology (and not only for functionalist sociology), distinguishing it from various forms of psychological analysis. Thus, selecting latent functions as a particular domain of inquiry is in his view a 'myth'.
86. Manis and Meltzer, 1974, p. 10.
87. Giddens, 1977, p. 121.
88. Merton, STSS, p. 136.
89. Giddens, 1977, p. 98.
90. Homans, 1962, p. 27.
91. Merton, STSS, p. 127.
92. Merton, SA, p. 18.

93. Merton (with Lazarsfeld), 1954, p. 64.
94. Merton, SRPP, p. 117.
95. Homans, 1962, p. 216.
96. Merton (with Lazarsfeld), 1954, p. 65.
97. Merton, SRPP, p. 117.
98. I review the debate in detail in Sztompka, 1974, pp. 143–146.
99. Merton, STSS, p. 129.
100. Ibid., p. 130.
101. See: Nagel, 1956.
102. See: Hempel, 1965.
103. See: Stinchcombe, 1968 and Stinchcombe, 1975. Already in the 1940s Merton attended a number of conferences devoted to the exploration of feedback mechanisms, organised by the Macy Foundation. Others in regular attendance were Margaret Mead, Gregory Bateson, Norbert Wiener, Warren McCullough and many others. This biographical information may add some plausibility to my claim that he would probably choose the third solution to the riddle of finalism.
104. Merton, SOS, pp. 435–436.
105. Merton, SA, p. 99.
106. Merton, SRPP, p. 129.
107. Ibid., p. 61.
108. Merton, STSS, pp. 185–214.
109. Ibid., pp. 249–260.
110. Merton, SA, p. 95.
111. Merton, SOS, p. 321.
112. Barbano, 1968, p. 47.
113. Turner, 1978, p. 101.
114. Barbano, 1968, p. 53.
115. Dahrendorf, 1968.
116. Homans, 1971.
117. Buckley, 1967.
118. Lockwood, 1964.
119. Merton, STSS, p. 107. And in other place: 'By focusing on dysfunctions as well as on functions, this mode of analysis can assess not only the bases of social stability but the potential sources of social change' (p. 94).
120. Ibid., p. 176.
121. Giddens, 1977, p. 119.
122. Merton, STSS, p. 93.
123. Merton, STSS, 1957 ed., p. 40.
124. As quoted in Giddens, 1977, p. 103.
125. Parsons, 1975, p. 73.
126. Reprinted in SA, pp. 109–44.
127. Barbano, 1968, p. 41.
128. Merton, SA, p. ix.
129. Merton, STSS, p. 110.
130. Ibid., p. 107.
131. Ibid., p. 108.

132. Barbano, 1968, p. 41.
133. See Blau, 1974.
134. Blau, 1975a, p. 117.
135. Merton, SA, p. 121.
136. Bottomore and Nisbet, 1978, p. 558.
137. Giddens, 1971, p. 67.
138. Nadel, 1969, p. 7.
139. Blau, 1975b, p. 7.
140. Levy, 1952, p. 57.
141. Allen, 1975, p. 194.
142. Homans, 1975, p. 54.
143. Goode, 1975, p. 74.
144. Blau, 1974, p. 1.
145. Loomis and Loomis, 1961, p. 246.
146. Wallace, 1969, p. 161.
147. Edited by L. A. Coser (New York, 1975: Harcourt Brace Jovanovich).
148. Edited by T. F. Gieryn (New York, 1980: The NY Academy of Sciences).
149. Merton, 1984b, p. 279.
150. Goode, 1975, p. 69.
151. Barbano, 1968, p. 43.
152. Merton, STSS, p. 216.
153. Merton, SA, p. 30.
154. Lazarsfeld, 1975, p. 57.
155. Merton, STSS, p. 424.
156. Merton, SA, p. 21.
157. Ibid., p. 126.
158. Merton, SRPP, p. 174.
159. Merton, STSS, pp. 106–7.
160. Merton, STSS, p. 177.
161. Ibid., p. 200.
162. Merton, SA, p. 209.
163. Merton, STSS, p. 216–17.
164. Merton, SRPP, p. 110.
165. Merton, SA, pp. 4 and 7.
166. Barbano, 1968, p. 45.
167. Merton, SA, pp. 124–125.
168. Ibid., p. 125.
169. Ibid., p. 125.
170. Merton, STSS, pp. 110–111.
171. Blau, 1975a, p. 118.
172. Merton, STSS, p. 186.
173. Moore, 1978, p. 330.
174. Blau, 1975a, p. 118. For similar argument see Karsten, 1983: 'What is a function from one point of view is a structure from another' (p. 189).
175. Stinchcombe, 1975, p. 26.
176. Ibid., p. 12.

177. Ibid., p. 12.
178. Ibid., p. 13.
179. Ibid., p. 13.
180. Ibid., p. 26.
181. Ibid., p. 26.
182. Ibid., p. 16.
183. Ibid., p. 19.
184. Merton (with Lazarsfeld), 1954, p. 58.
185. Ibid., p. 63.
186. Ibid., p. 65.
187. See for example: Buckley, 1967; Giddens, 1979; Touraine, 1977.
188. Merton (with Sorokin), 1937.
189. Merton, 1984b.
190. Merton, 1982c, p. 31.
191. Ibid., p. 32.
192. Merton, STSS, p. 233.
193. Merton (with Lazarsfeld), 1954, p. 24.
194. Merton, STSS, p. 347.
195. Ibid., p. 350.
196. Merton (with Lazarsfeld), 1954, p. 57.
197. Merton, SRPP, pp. 32 and 35.
198. Merton, STSS, p. 366.
199. Merton (with Lazarsfeld), 1954, p. 25.
200. Ibid., p. 29.
201. Ibid., p. 47.
202. The bibliography of articles utilising the concept runs to fifty or so items. See 'Program in the Sociology of Science: Columbia University, 1983' (mimeographed).
203. Merton, SA, p. 124.
204. The concept is introduced for the first time in STSS, 1957 edn, pp. 311–312 (in 1968 edn, pp. 365–6). Recently discussed and elaborated in two papers: Merton, 1982c; and Merton, 1984b.
205. Merton, 1982c, p. 6.
206. Ibid., p. 25.
207. Merton, 1984b, p. 266.
208. Merton, 1982c, p. 22.
209. Ibid., p. 30.
210. Ibid., p. 35. Other similar patterns that he analyses in detail include: deadline pattern, eleventh-hour effect, tenure pattern.
211. Merton reflects on his 'passionate interest in the idea of "socially expected durations" (SEDs) which, I recently discovered, has been in the penumbra of my sociological consciousness for some 40 years and in the intermittent centre for 20. . . . I modestly claim that they [SEDs] are universal, ubiquitous and consequential, and that the sociological understanding of their patterned variety (with appropriately identified parameters), their sources (both of the deliberate and the unplanned kinds, the 'manifest' and 'latent' as it were), their mechanisms (both social and psychological) and their

diverse consequences (both through anticipatory adaptations and after-the-fact adaptations) – that this problematic of SEDs will, in years to come, yield considerable further understanding of sociologically interesting aspects of social phenomena of every kind. As I say, a most modest claim' (in a letter to Ewa Morawska, dated 16 February, 1985, p. 2).

Chapter 6

1. Merton, STSS, p. 52.
2. This is an allusion to the title of Merton's article on 'the fallacy of the latest word' (1984a).
3. See: Merton (with P. S. West and M. Jahoda), *Patterns of Social Life: Explorations in the Sociology of Housing*, two volumes, (New York: Columbia Bureau of Applied Social Research) (mimeographed).
4. Merton, STSS, 1957 edn, p. 368.
5. Ibid., p. 369.
6. This may be called, in line with Merton's occasional usage, the 'rank-aspect' of a social status; as it is precisely the varied scope of opportunities of various kinds (access to wealth, power, prestige etc.) which differentiates (ranks) people in stratificational hierarchies.
7. Merton, STSS, 1957 edn, p. 370.
8. Ibid., p. 370.
9. Ibid., p. 370.
10. Ibid., p. 370.
11. Merton, STSS, p. 216.
12. Ibid., p. 216.
13. Merton, SRPP, p. 180.
14. Merton, STSS, p. 230.
15. Merton, 1964, p. 216.
16. See: Fazey, 1973, p. 418.
17. Merton, STSS, 1957 edn, p. 179.
18. Ibid., p. 179.
19. Merton, 1959, p. 167.
20. Ibid., p. 188.
21. Merton, STSS, p. 255.
22. Ibid., p. 255. Merton writes: 'In periodic lectures ("oral publication") since then [1938], and particularly during the 1950s, I had gone on to develop the notion of "opportunity structures" in some detail' (In a letter to James F. Short, Jr, dated 23 April, 1981, p. 2).
23. Ibid., p. 574.
24. Ibid., p. 268.
25. Merton, 1959, p. 180.
26. Merton, SA, p. 191.
27. Merton, STSS, p. 186.
28. Ibid., p. 186.
29. Loomis and Loomis, 1961, p. 308.

30. Ibid., p. 308.
31. Merton, 1959, p. 178.
32. Merton, SRPP, p. 180.
33. Merton, STSS, p. 373.
34. As quoted in STSS, 1957 edn, p. 368.
35. Merton, SA, p. 17.
36. Metton, STSS, p. 422. See also: Merton, SA, p. 66; Merton, 1959, p. 179.
37. See: K. Davis, *Human Society*.
38. Merton, SA, pp. 32–33.
39. Merton, STSS, p. 423.
40. Ibid., p. 423.
41. Merton, STSS, 1957 edn, p. 370.
42. Blau, 1975a, p. 126.
43. Ibid., p. 131.
44. Merton, STSS, 1957 edn, p. 370.
45. Ibid., p. 370.
46. Ibid., pp. 380–384.
47. As reprinted in Merton, SOS, especially pp. 11–116.
48. As Merton defines: 'Salient status: that status (in person's status-set) to which others primarily respond, which is at the focus of attention in interaction (making only secondary adaptations in their interaction in light of the other statuses in that persons status-set)', 'Dominant status: in case of conflicting obligations between statuses in a status-set, that status to which the other statuses are accomodated (or subordinated)'. 'Central status: that status (in a person's status-set) which constrains the probability of acquiring or dropping other statuses during a person's life-course'. (Outline of lectures entitled: 'Key Concepts of Types of Status in Status-Set' and dated 12 November, 1974, pp. 1–2).
49. For example C. F. Epstein's *Woman's Place: Options and Limits in Professional Careers*, 1970; pp. 87–95.
50. Merton, SRPP, p. 137.
51. Merton, STSS, p. 255.
52. Ibid., p. 369. Merton repeatedly uses the term 'rank' to refer to this variety of opportunity structure.
53. Ibid., pp. 199–200.
54. Ibid., p. 472.
55. USSR in the early period of collectivisation and the campaign against 'kulakhs'; China in the period of Cultural Revolution; Cambodia under the rule of Pol-Pot, provide modern examples.
56. Merton, SA, p. 28.
57. Merton, STSS, p. 268.
58. Ibid., pp. 255 and 237.
59. Imprinting themselves, too, on the personalities of the functionaries.
60. Merton, STSS, p. 391.
61. 'Visibility' is a term of a longstanding usage by American sociologists. 'Observability' is Merton's translation of Simmel's notion of

'übersehbar'. The opposite pole of the correlative variables of visibility and observability is a structurally embedded 'secrecy', typically found, for example, in economic, political and religious bureaucracies (Merton, STSS, p. 400).

62. Merton, 1959, p. 185.
63. Merton, STSS, p. 404.
64. Ibid., p. 431.
65. Merton, SA, p. 194.
66. Merton, STSS, 1957 edn, p. 370.
67. Merton, STSS, p. 353.
68. Ibid., p. 353.
69. Ibid., p. 339.
70. Ibid., pp. 364–380. Valuable observations on the dynamics of group-formation can be found in Merton (with Lazarsfeld), 1054.
71. Merton, STSS, pp. 453–474.
72. Ibid., pp. 249–260.
73. Barbano, 1968, p. 58.
74. Merton, SRPP, p. 53.
75. Merton, 1964, p. 227.
76. Merton, 1938, p. 673.
77. Merton, STSS, 1957 edn, p. 135.
78. Merton, 1938, p. 673.
79. Ibid., p. 673.
80. Merton, SOS, p. 399.
81. Ibid., p. 427.
82. Merton and Elinor Barber, as reprinted in SA, p. 11.
83. Here again, Merton refers to the concept of $Anomie_1$ or $Anomie_2$. If, as I propose to do, one refers to the inter level disjunction described here as $Anomie_3$, then Merton seems to suggest that $Anomie_3$ regularly produces $Anomie_1$ or $Anomie_2$, at the level of normative structure. The large-scale inability of realising cultural goals through normatively legitimate means is taken to make for contradictions, chaos, or 'normlessness' in the cultural sphere.
84. Merton, STSS, pp. 216 and 220.
85. As will be shown later, Merton takes this case to be particularly consequential for the domain of social life, where it tends to generate various forms of social deviation.
86. Merton, SA, p. 192.
87. Ibid., p. 192.
88. Merton, 1964, p. 218. Here, $Anomie_4$ seems to be treated as the outcome of $Anomie_3$.
89. Merton, SA, p. 6.
90. Merton, (with Vanessa Merton and Elinor Barber), 1983c, p. 28.
91. Merton, SA, p. 17.
92. Merton, SRPP, p. 181.
93. Merton, SA, p. 68.
94. Ibid., p. 68.
95. Originally published in 1970; reprinted in SA, pp. 73–89.

96. Merton, SA, pp. 74–75.
97. Merton (with Merton and Barber), 1983c, p. 40.
98. Ibid., p. 22.
99. Merton, SA, p. 33.
100. Ibid., p. 33.
101. Ibid., p. 36.
102. Ibid., p. 227.
103. Merton, STSS, p. 256.
104. Ibid., p. 254.
105. Ibid., p. 258.
106. Ibid., p. 425.
107. Ibid., p. 425.
108. Ibid., p. 424. This was emphasised earlier in our discussion in connection with Blau's concept of 'status complements' and 'parameters of social structure'.
109. Merton, STSS, p. 425.
110. The term 'multiple roles' may have different meaning. As Merton carefully points out: 'It should be plain that the role-set differs from the structural pattern which has long been identified by sociologists as that of "multiple roles". For in established usage, multiple roles refer to the complex of roles associated, not with a *single* status, but with the *various* statuses (often in differing institutional spheres) in which individuals find themselves – the roles, for example, connected with the distinct statuses of teacher, wife, mother, Catholic, Republican and so on. We designate this complement of social statuses of an individual as his status-set, each of the statuses in turn having its distinctive role-set' (Merton, STSS, p. 423).
111. Loomis and Loomis, 1961, p. 286.
112. Merton, STSS, P. 435.
113. Merton, SA, p. 217.
114. Merton (with P. Kendall), 1958, p. 324.
115. Merton, STSS, p. 468.
116. Merton, SRPP, p. 123.
117. Merton, SA, p. 201.
118. Merton, SRPP, pp. 68–70.
119. Merton, STSS, p. 185.
120. Chapman, 1977, p. 18.
121. Stinchcombe, 1975, p. 12.
122. Chapman, 1977, p. 17.
123. Cuzzort and King, 1976, p. 171.
124. Coser, R. L., 1975, p. 239.
125. Merton, STSS, p. 175.
126. Ibid., p. 188.
127. Ibid., pp. 238 and 245.
128. Ibid., p. 200.
129. Merton, SOS, p. 323.
130. Merton, STSS, p. 194 (originally published in 1938). For a most recent appraisal see Kornhauser, 1984, pp. 139–169.

131. There have been periods in English and American history where 'innova' n' was primarily a negative term; more recently, it is apt to be, in many quarters, a positive one. But by and large, it leaves open the question whether the behaviour which departs from normatively approved procedures is positive or negative in terms of valued or disvalued outcomes.
132. Merton, STSS, p. 194.
133. Ibid., p. 198.
134. The amounts of, say, wealth to which people aspire (specific goals) vary by place in the social structure (i.e. by status, such as economic status, political status, religious, ethnic, even age and gender-sex status) while still being oriented toward the generic goal (of wealth), culturally required by the general value of material success.
135. Merton, STSS, p. 199.
136. Merton, 1964, p. 223.
137. Ibid., pp. 223–4.
138. Ibid., p. 222.
139. Ibid., p. 223.
140. Merton, STSS, p. 199.
141. Ibid., pp. 203–4.
142. Ibid., p. 207.
143. Cloward, 1959, p. 578.
144. Merton, STSS, p. 210.
145. Cole, 1975, p. 175.
146. Cullen, 1984, p. 75.
147. Cohen, 1955.
148. Merton, STSS, p. 318.
149. Ibid., p. 233.
150. Dubin, 1959, p. 149.
151. Ibid., pp. 149–164.
152. Cloward, 1959.
153. Cloward and Ohlin, 1960.
154. Cloward, 1959, p. 568.
155. Ibid., p. 568.
156. Ibid., p. 579.
157. Merton, 1959, p. 177.
158. Harary, 1966, p. 694.
159. Dubin, 1959, p. 148.
160. Merton, SRPP, p. 110.
161. Ibid., p. 110.
162. Ibid., p. 253.
163. Ibid., pp. 110–11.
164. Loomis and Loomis, 1961, p. 307.
165. Stinchcombe, 1975, pp. 17–18.
166. Merton, SRPP, p. 112.
167. The theoretical analysis cannot of course determine the absolute rates of such altruistic behaviour – as high or low – but only comparative, relative rates: (1) higher than they would be if the indicated structural

arrangements were absent, and (2) higher than in occupations lacking those arrangements.
168. Merton, SRPP, p. 119.
169. Ibid., p. 120.
170. As quoted in Ibid., p. 114.
171. Coser, R. L., 1975, p. 246.
172. Merton, SOS, p. 115.
173. Coser, R. L., p. 241.
174. Merton, STSS, pp. 252–253.
175. Merton, SRPP, p. 158.
176. Ibid., pp. 186–187.
177. Ibid., p. 187.
178. Ibid., p. 159. Also: STSS, p. 269.
179. Ibid., p. 159.
180. Merton (with P. Kendall), 1958, p. 323.
181. Merton, SRPP, p. 174.
182. Ibid., p. 158.
183. Merton, STSS, p. 252.
184. Ibid., p. 253.
185. Ibid., pp. 253–4.
186. Ibid., p. 254.
187. Stinchcombe, 1975, p. 26.
188. Cohen, 1970, p. 395.
189. Merton, 1964, p. 227.
190. Ibid., p. 237.
191. Merton, SA, p. 6.
192. Ibid., p. 7.
193. Janis, 1980, p. 104.
194. Merton, STSS, p. 428.
195. Ibid., p. 436.
196. Merton, SOS, pp. 113 and 132.
197. Coser, R. L., 1975.
198. Ibid., p. 239.
199. Ibid., p. 239.

Chapter 7

1. Another common, but rather misleading name for this distinction is: quantitative versus qualitative change.
2. Another common term for the latter type is: autodynamic.
3. The strongest version of dynamic standpoint is introduced when an additional, fourth, criterion of change is added; namely whether change is directional or developmental or not. In the Marxist parlance, the only 'true' dynamic position focuses on endogenous, developmental changes of the entire social system.
4. Loomis and Loomis, 1961, p. 315.
5. See Merton, 1982c; and Merton, 1984b.

6. Loomis and Loomis, 1961, p. 314.
7. Merton, STSS, 1949 edn, p. 116; STSS, 1968 edn, p. 176.
8. Merton, SA, pp. 124 and 128.
9. Coser, R. L., 1975, pp. 238–240.
10. This is akin to what L. Coser, one of Merton's early students, described as 'the functions of social conflict'. See Coser, 1956.
11. Merton, SA, p. 125.
12. The term is borrowed from Buckley, 1967.
13. Merton, SA, p. 126.
14. See Sztompka, 1984.
15. Merton, STSS, pp. 425 and 434.
16. Ibid., p. 425.
17. Ibid., p. 435.
18. STSS, 1957 edn, p. 380.
19. Ibid., p. 371.
20. STSS, 1968 edn, p. 426.
21. Ibid., p. 426.
22. Ibid., p. 428.
23. Ibid., p. 429.
24. Ibid., p. 430.
25. Ibid., pp. 430–431.
26. Ibid., p. 432.
27. Ibid., p. 432.
28. Merton, STSS, 1957 edn, p. 379.
29. Ibid., p. 379.
30. Baumgartner et al., 1976.
31. Merton, STSS, 1968 edn, p. 435.
32. Ibid., p. 435.
33. Ibid., p. 436.
34. Ibid., p. 436.
35. Ibid., p. 437.
36. The logic of the thought-experiment or counterfactual conditional thinking seems to underlie much of Merton's theoretical analysis. This enduring passion of Merton's has been noted, for example, by R. L. Coser, 1975, pp. 259–60, n. 12.
37. Goode, 1973, p. 104.
38. This seems to be strictly parallel to Merton's mechanism of 'abridging the role set'.
39. Goode, 1973, pp. 104–106. A very simple device of that type which I am using at this very moment, writing this book, is to disconnect the telephone.
40. Ibid., p. 108.
41. Ibid., p. 119.
42. Ibid., p. 394, ref. 9.
43. Merton, STSS, p. 434.
44. As Maruyama, 1963 calls it: 'the second cybernetics'.
45. As Popper, 1976 puts it: 'Most, if not all, revolutions have produced societies very different from those desired by the revolutionaries.

Here is a problem, and it deserves thought from every serious critic of society'.
46. Merton, STSS, pp. 94 and 107.
47. Ibid., p. 105.
48. Ibid., p. 94.
49. Ibid., p. 106.
50. Ibid., p. 108.
51. Merton, SRPP, p. 89.
52. In the form of 'oral publication' in lectures at Harvard as early as 1938–39, then as a research programme at the Department of Sociology, Tulane University in 1940 (see: Outline of research project dated 13 March, 1940), and in several publications in print, the earliest of which is the 1948 article on 'Discrimination and the American Creed', published originally in MacIver, 1948, pp. 99–126 (later reprinted in Merton, SA, pp. 189–216).
53. Bierstedt, 1981, p. 461.
54. Merton, 1959, p. 178.
55. Ibid., p. 181. Similarly, the 'toleration' of variant behaviour – the scope of allowable concrete implementations of a general norm is to be distinguished from 'factual permissiveness', the passive attitude of social audiences toward behaviour regarded as deviant, and even more from what may be called 'institutionalized permissiveness', the prohibition against the negative sanctioning of deviant behaviour. The latter sense is adopted by Jacobsen who defines permissiveness as 'the institutionalized social climate wherein a person can violate accepted norms in public without incurring sanctions' (Jacobsen, 1979, p. 223).
56. Merton, SRPP, p. 72.
57. Ibid., p. 73.
58. Ibid., p. 73.
59. Jacobsen, 1979, p. 220.
60. Merton, STSS, p. 200.
61. Loomis and Loomis, 1961, p. 316.
62. Merton, 1964, p. 235.
63. As one sees in the outlines of Merton's lectures from that period, as well as the printed examinations in 'Sociology 4' at Harvard, 1939, which includes this question: 'Describe the pattern of the "institutional evasions of institutional rules". In which respects does this pattern differ from illicit and non-institutional evasions? Why is the distinction between institutional and non-institutional evasions drawn?'. One student in that Sociology class was Robin M. Williams, who later developed this problematics substantially.
64. Williams, 1970, pp. 419–420. Similar definition is given by Jacobsen: 'patterned evasion is the widespread and regularly recurring, devious and deliberate violation of an accepted norm, which elicits no perceptible reaction from the social audience' (Jacobsen, 1979, p. 223).
65. Merton, STSS, p. 234.

66. Merton, SRPP, p. 76.
67. Merton, 1963, p. ix.
68. Ibid., pp. ix-x. In response to a query from Chanoch Jacobsen, Merton writes: 'My assumption is that RW [Robin Williams] adopted the more general term "patterned evasion" because he found my term "institutionalized evasion" seemingly too restrictive' (letter dated 23 September, 1979).
69. Merton, STSS, p. 372.
70. Ibid., p. 372.
71. Jacobsen, 1979, p. 226.
72. Ibid., p. 226.
73. Merton, 1963, p. ix.
74. Ibid., p. xi.
75. Merton, STSS, p. 372.
76. In a letter to Hanan Selvin, dated 19 May, 1980.
77. Merton, STSS, pp. 209–210.
78. Ibid., p. 209.
79. Ibid., p. 211.
80. Loomis and Loomis, 1961, p. 316.
81. Merton, SRPP, pp. 72–3.
82. Merton, STSS, p. 211.
83. Ibid., p. 419.
84. Ibid., p. 236.
85. Merton, SRPP, p. 74.
86. An extensive discussion of this sequence is presented in Sztompka, 1985 (in press).
87. Merton, SOS, p. 368.
88. Loomis and Loomis, 1961, p. 309.
89. As quoted by Merton in SOS, p. 445.
90. Ibid., p. 443.
91. Ibid., pp. 253 and 457. Thus one finds a little surprising the observation by Storer in the editorial introduction to the same book that: 'Although Merton does not draw parallels between the reward system of science and those of the economic and political institutions, it is useful to recall [sic!] that they can be drawn – the rich tend to get richer in all three systems. . .' (in SOS, p. 416).
92. Merton, SA, p. 124 (originally published in 1975). Many authors have picked up the topic of 'accumulation of advantage and disadvantage' elaborating it in various directions and in various domains of sociology. Only in the sociology of science the bibliography of direct continuities runs to 47 items (see: 'Program in the Sociology of Science, Columbia University', mimeographed). As one may judge by the title of a forthcoming essay by N. Stehr and V. Meja, they consider this notion as crucial for Merton's structural analysis ('Robert K. Mertons strukturelle Analyse: Die gesellschaftliche Akkumulation von Vorteilen und Nachteilen', in: K. S. Rehberg (Hrsg.), *Gesellschaftstheorien*, Frankfurt am Main: 1985, Suhrkamp Verlag, in press. See also: Allison, Krauze, Long, 1982.

93. Merton, SSEM, p. 89.
94. Ibid., p. 89. Note the striking parallel between this account and the Marxian principle of the growing impoverishment of the proletariat with the resulting polarisation of class structure. See Sztompka, 1979, pp. 311–44.
95. Loomis and Loomis, 1961, p. 293.
96. Stinchcombe, 1975, p. 23.
97. Merton, STSS, p. 178.
98. Ibid., p. 426.
99. Ibid., p. 249.
100. Merton, STSS, 1957 edn, p. 372.
101. Baumgartner et al., 1976, p. 224.
102. Merton, STSS, p. 469, ref. 19.
103. Merton, MP.
104. Merton, STSS, p. 563.
105. Ibid., p. 572. See also: Merton (with Kendall), 1944.
106. Ibid., p. 573.
107. Merton (with Kendall), 1944, p. 1.
108. Ibid., p. 2.
109. Merton, STSS, p. 469. Note again Merton's typical counterfactual *Gedanke-experiment*.
110. Merton, SA, p. 86.
111. Merton, STSS, p. 447.
112. Ibid., p. 454.
113. Ibid., p. 457.
114. Ibid., p. 468.
115. Ibid., p. 468.
116. These concepts (of local and cosmopolitan influentials) have been extensively utilised, and developed in the various social science disciplines.
117. Stinchcombe, 1975, pp. 16–17.
118. Bierstedt, 1981, p. 496.
119. Campbell, 1982, p. 35.
120. Merton, SA, p. 147.
121. Ibid., p. 147.
122. Merton, SRPP, p. 249.
123. Merton, SOS, p. 262; SRPP, p. 248; SOS, p. 262. These 1938, 1948 and 1975 sources indicate his sustained interest in this sociological statement, to which Thomas himself returned only once, quoting the paragraph which it memorably includes during his oral comment on Herbert Blumer's *An Appraisal of Thomas and Znaniecki's The Polish Peasant in Europe and America* (New York, 1939: Social Science Research Council), p. 85. It might be said that Merton served as a 'cognitive conduit' for the 'Thomas theorem'.
124. Merton, SRPP, p. 248.
125. Merton, SA, p. 174.
126. Merton, SA, p. 177.
127. Merton (with Kendall), 1958, p. 349.

128. See: Hyman, 1975.
129. Merton, STSS, p. 288.
130. Shibutani, 1955, p. 563.
131. Pollis, 1968, p. 301.
132. See: Merton, STSS, p. 337.
133. Ibid., p. 337.
134. Ibid., p. 338.
135. Ibid., p. 354.
136. Ibid., p. 288.
137. Ibid., p. 438.
138. Shibutani, 1955, p. 565.
139. Pollis, 1968, p. 303.
140. Ibid., p. 305.
141. Ibid., p. 306.
142. In the articles: 'The Unanticipated Consequences of Purposive Social Action', in: *American Sociological Review*, 1/1936, 894–904; and 'The Self-Fulfilling Prophecy', *Antioch Review*, Summer 1948, 193–210. The first reprinted in SA; the latter in SRPP.
143. Stinchcombe, 1975, p. 21.
144. Merton, SA, p. 154.
145. Merton, SRPP, p. 251.
146. Ibid., p. 103.
147. Ibid., p. 251.
148. Merton, SOS, p. 525.
149. Merton, SOS, p. 428.
150. Rosenthal and Rubin, 1978, review 345 studies of this problem, and there have been hundreds more since. The research on interpersonal expectancy effects in the classroom was spearheaded by the classical Rosenthal-Jacobsen 1968 monograph, *Pygmalion in the Classroom* (New York: Holt, Rinehart & Winston, Inc.).
151. Buck, 1963, pp. 154–155.
152. Merton, SRPP, p. 104.
153. Friedrichs, 1972, p. 266.
154. For more specific discussion see: Grünbaum, 1956; Friedrichs, 1972; Sztompka, 1979; Sztompka, 1983.
155. In a letter to the author dated 22 April, 1984, p. 13.
156. Giddens, 1977, p. 117.
157. Stinchcombe, 1975, p. 12.
158. Merton, SRPP, p. 57.
159. Merton, 1982c, p. 40.
160. Ibid., p. 40.
161. As quoted by Merton, SA, p. 176, ref. 22.
162. Ibid., p. 175.

Chapter 8

1. Holton, 1973. Equally useful for analysis is a somewhat different

concept of 'the central message' recently introduced by Patinkin (see Patinkin, 1983).
2. Merton, 1975a, p. 335.
3. Ibid., p. 335.
4. Ibid., p. 335.
5. Merton, SOS, p. 62.
6. Merton, STSS, p. 156.
7. Merton, SRPP, p. 45.
8. Mills, 1959.
9. Manis and Meltzer, 1974, p. 11.
10. As early as 1948 Merton was emphasising: '*Overt behavioral deviation (or conformity) may signify importantly different situations, depending upon the underlying motivations.* Knowing simply that ethnic discrimination is rife in a community does not therefore point to appropriate lines of social policy. It is necessary to know also the distribution of ethnic prejudices and basic motivations for these prejudices as well' (Merton, SA, p. 197). This important statement clearly reflects his rejection of a simplistic behaviourism (italics in the original).
11. Barbano, 1968, p. 83.
12. The term is Dahrendorf's, 1968.
13. Turner, 1978, p. 91.
14. In Coser and Nisbet, 1975, p. 9.
15. Merton, STSS, pp. vii-viii.
16. Garfield, 1980, p. 61.
17. In Coser and Nisbet, 1975, p. 5.
18. Merton, as quoted in Loomis and Loomis, 1961, p. 253.
19. Merton, SRPP, p. 57.
20. Coser and Nisbet, 1975, p. 9.
21. Merton, 1941, p. 364. Or even earlier in Merton, 1937a, p. 169.
22. Merton, STSS, p. 108n.
23. Merton, 1975a, p. 337.
24. Merton, STSS, p. 27.
25. Manis and Meltzer, 1974, pp. 4 and 7.
26. As quoted in Manis and Meltzer, 1974, pp. 6–7.
27. Barber, 1975, p. 105.
28. As I have gone to great lengths to emphasise in chapters five and six, I have in mind the 'sociological structuralism' going back at least to Marx, Simmel and Durkheim, as distinct from the 'structuralist school' of linguistics, psychology, art-criticism, or Levi-Straussian cultural anthropology. This distinction has been recently redefined by Whitten in this way: '. . . the contrast between structuralist and structural perspectives, which emerged in the late 1940s, has endured. As structural studies created an enormous literature in social anthropology and sociology, structuralism influenced the study of culture and communication in many disciplines, making serious inroads into fields removed from the "social sciences", such as history, music, art, literature, folklore, psychology, and philosophy' (Whitten, 1984, p. 635).

29. But one must guard against treating Merton as a sociological reductionist. He was quite emphatic about his position as early as 1941: 'The theory of social structure *complements* the theory of personal interaction; from a functional standpoint, regularities in the two spheres are mutually implicative' (Merton, 1941, p. 361, italics added). In the words of Lazarsfeld: Merton 'thought of psychology and sociology as complementary and not antithetical . . . he wanted to keep the two separate until he had made up his mind as to how they . . . were to be related' (Lazarsfeld, 1975, p. 51).
30. Merton, 1981, p. ii.
31. Merton, SA, p. 7.
32. Merton, 1964, p. 226.
33. Merton, 1975b, p. 110.
34. Merton, STSS, p. 404.
35. Merton (with Merton and Barber), 1983c, p. 34.
36. In a letter to the author dated 22 April 1984, p. 10.
37. Giddens, 1977, p. 96.
38. Lazarsfeld, 1975, p. 58.
39. Blau, 1975b, p. 16.
40. Turner, 1978, p. 100.
41. Merton, STSS, p. 105.
42. Ibid., p. 120.
43. Cuzzort and King, 1976, p. 177.
44. Merton, SRPP, p. 55.
45. Campbell, 1982, p. 43.
46. Schneider, 1975, pp. 324–325.
47. Weinstein, 1984, p. 124.
48. Schneider, 1984, pp. 233 and 244 ref. 9.
49. Letter to Louis Schneider dated 14 September, 1975.
50. The link between functionalist perspective and ironic theme is also emphasised by Campbell, 1982, p. 43, Cuzzort and King, 1976, p. 175, as well as Bruyn and Matza (see Schneider, 1984, p. 233 and 244 ref. 10).
51. An interesting example of such reciprocity, cutting across various levels of social structure and social life, is reported in Merton's recent work on 'socially expected durations' or SED's: '. . . individually and collectively expected durations [were seen] as strategic, consequential variables that interacted with their behavioral and social consequences for the developing local community. [There emerged] the hypothesis that individual and shared expected durations operated as both independent and dependent variables. They affected and in turn were affected by modes of participation in the organized social life and the interpersonal relations in the community' (Merton, 1984b, p. 275).
52. Coser, 1975, p. 98.
53. Merton, STSS, p. 318.
54. See: Loomis and Loomis, 1961, pp. 285 and 291.
55. Merton, STSS, p. 237.
56. Stinchcombe, 1975, p. 29.

57. Merton, SA, p. 202.
58. Ibid., pp. 93–94.
59. Merton, 1964, pp. 233–4.
60. Ibid., p. 235.
61. Ibid., p. 231.
62. Ibid., p. 221.
63. Merton, 1951, p. 22.
64. Merton, STSS, p. 254.
65. Merton, SA, pp. 74–5.
66. Merton, STSS, pp. 187–8.
67. Merton, SA, p. 102.
68. Merton, STSS, pp. 572–3.
69. Merton (with P. Kendall), 1944, p. 1.
70. Merton, STSS, p. 163.
71. Merton (with Merton and Barber), 1983c, p. 30.
72. Ibid., p. 14.
73. Merton, 1975a, p. 336.
74. Merton, SA, p. 112. See also: STSS, pp. 363 and 471.
75. I have in mind the representatives of the sociological 'now-generation' who reject out-of-hand any ideas older than a decade and who are so fond of the cliché: 'Who now reads Comte?' (or Marx, or Durkheim, or Weber, or Parsons, or – for that matter – Merton). I find their attitude utterly misguided.
76. Enough was written on the 'fads and foibles' of modern sociology (e.g. Sorokin) to require any further comment on the sad case of those who proclaim that theirs is the only and ultimate wisdom.

Bibliography

This is not a bibliography of Merton's published work. It includes only the items actually referred to or quoted in the text. For Merton's bibliography up to 1975 see Mary Wilson Miles, 'The Writings of Robert K. Merton: A Bibliography', in L. A. Coser (ed.), *The Idea of Social Structure: Papers in Honor of R. K. Merton* (New York: Harcourt Brace Jovanovich, 1975), pp. 497–522. There is a Supplement running to 1984, by M. W. Miles (mimeographed).

By Robert K. Merton

Books

Science, Technology and Society in Seventeenth-Century England (New York: Harper & Row, 1970). First published in *Osiris: Studies on the History and Philosophy of Science, and on the History of Learning and Culture* ed. G. Sarton (Bruges; St Catherine Press, 1938), pp. 362–632. Abbreviated in the references as STSE.

Social Theory and Social Structure Enlarged edition (New York: Free Press, 1968). First published in 1949. Revised and enlarged edition published in 1957. Abbreviated in the references as STSS.

On the Shoulders of Giants: A Shandean Postscript, (New York: Harcourt Brace Jovanovich, 1965, The Vicennial Edition, 1985). Abbreviated in the references as OTSOG.

Mass Persuasion: The Social Psychology of a War Bond Drive (with the assistance of Marjorie Fiske and Alberta Curtis) (Westport: Greenwood Press, 1971). First published in 1946. Abbreviated in the references as MP.

The Sociology of Science: Theoretical and Empirical Investigations ed. N. W. Storer (Chicago: University of Chicago Press, 1973). Abbreviated in the references as SOS.

On Theoretical Sociology: Five Essays, Old and New (New York: Free Press, 1967). Abbreviated in the references as OTS.

Sociological Ambivalence and Other Essays (New York: Free Press, 1976). Abbreviated in the references as SA.

Sociology of Science: An Episodic Memoir (Carbondale: Southern Illinois University Press, 1979). Abbreviated in the references as SSEM.

Social Research and the Practicing Professions ed. A. Rosenblatt and T. F. Gieryn (Cambridge, Mass.: Abt Books, 1982). Abbreviated in the references as SRPP.

Articles and other works

1934 'Recent French Sociology' *Social Forces*, 12 (4) May, pp. 537–545.
1936 'Civilization and Culture', *Sociology and Social Research* 21, Nov–Dec., pp. 103–13.
1937a 'Science, Population and Society', *Scientific Monthly* 44, pp. 165–71.
1937b 'Social Time: A Methodological and Functional Analysis' (with Pitirim A. Sorokin), *American Journal of Sociology* 42 (5), pp. 615–29.
1938 'Social Structure and Anomie', *American Sociological Review* 3, pp. 672–82.
1941 'Intermarriage and the Social Structure: Fact and Theory', *Psychiatry* 4, pp. 361–74.
1944 'The Boomerang Response' (with Patricia L. Kendall) *Channels* 21 (7), pp. 1–7.
1945 'Sociological Theory', *American Journal of Sociology* 50, pp. 462–73.
1948 'The Position of Sociological Theory' *American Sociological Review* 13 (2) pp. 164–168.
1954 'Friendship as Social Process: A Substantive and Methodological Analysis', (with Paul F. Lazarsfeld), in: *Freedom and Control in Modern Society* ed. M. Berger, T. Abel, Ch. H. Page (New York: Van Nostrand) pp. 18–66.
1958 'Medical Education as Social Process' (with Patricia L. Kendall) in: *Patients, Physicians and Illness* ed. E. G. Jaco (New York: Free Press) pp. 321–50.
1959 'Social Conformity, Deviation and Opportunity-Structure' *American Sociological Review* 24 (2) pp. 177–89.
1960 'The Mosaic of the Behavioral Sciences' *The Voice of America Forum Lectures* 20. Also appearing in: *The Behavioral Sciences Today* ed. B. Berelson (New York: Basic Books).
1961 'Now the Case for Sociology' *New York Times Magazine* 25 June. Reprinted in: *Sociology; Theories in Conflict* ed. R. S. Denisoff (Belmont, Ca.: Wadsworth), pp. 18–22.
1963 'Foreword', in: *Lawyers and Matrimonial Cases*, by H. J. O'Gorman (Glencoe: Free Press), pp. vii–xiv.
1963a 'Sociological Ambivalence' (with Elinor Barber) in: *Sociological Theory; Values, and Social Change. Essays in Honor of Pitirim A. Sorokin* ed. E. A. Tiryakian (New York: The Free Press) pp. 91–120.
1963b 'Sorokin's Formulations in the Sociology of Science' (with Bernard Barber) in: *Pitirim A. Sorokin in Review* ed. Ph. J. Allen (Durham: Duke University Press) pp. 332–68.
1964 'Anomie, Anomia, and Social Interaction: Contexts of Deviant Behavior' in: *Anomie and Deviant Behavior: Discussion and Critique* ed. M. Clinard (New York: Free Press) pp. 213–42.
1971 'The Precarious Foundations of Detachment in Sociology' in: *The Phenomenon of Sociology* ed. E. A. Tiryakian (New York: Appleton Century Crofts) pp. 188–99.
1972 'Age, Aging and Age Structure in Science' (with H. Zuckerman), in

M. W. Riley et al. (eds) *A Theory of Age Stratification* (New York: Russell Sage Foundation) pp. 292–356. Reprinted in SOS.
1975a 'Thematic Analysis in Science: Notes on Holton's Concept' *Science*, 188, 25 April pp. 335–8.
1975b 'The Uses of Institutionalized Altruism' *Seminar Reports of Columbia University* 3 (6) pp. 105–17.
1979 'Foreword', in: E. Garfield *Citation Indexing: Its Theory and Application in Science, Technology and Humanities* (New York: John Wiley & Sons) pp. vii–xi. Reprinted in: *Current Comments* (Philadelphia: ISI Press) 28, 16 July.
1980a 'On the Oral Transmission of Knowledge', in: *Sociological Traditions from Generation to Generation* ed. R. K. Merton and M. W. Riley (Norwood: Ablex) pp. 1–35.
1980b 'Remembering the Young Talcott Parsons', *The American Sociologist* 15, May pp. 68–71.
1981a 'On Sociological Ways of Thinking about Thinking and Thought', paper presented at the Bicentennial Symposium of American Academy of Arts and Sciences (mimeographed) pp. 1–8.
1981b 'Remarks on Theoretical Pluralism' in: *Continuities in Structural Inquiry*, ed. P. M. Blau and R. K. Merton (London: Sage) pp. i–viii.
1981c 'Our Sociological Vernacular' *Columbia: The Magazine of Columbia University*, November pp. 42–4.
1982a 'Alvin W. Gouldner: Genesis and Growth of a Friendship' *Theory and Society*, 11 pp. 915–38.
1982b 'Wstep' ('Foreword') to the Polish edition of STSS, translated by E. Morawska and J. Wertenstein-Zulawski (Warszawa: Polish Scientific Publishers) pp. 3–19.
1982c 'Socially Expected Durations: A Temporal Component of Social Structure' The ASA Career of Distinguished Scholarship Award Lecture, delivered at San Francisco (mimeographed) pp. 1–57.
1982d 'Progress in Science? A Shapeless Cloud of a Question' The lecture delivered at the Temple University Colloquium in Philadelphia (mimeographed) pp. 1–20.
1983a 'Florian Znaniecki: A Short Reminiscence', *Journal of the History of the Behavioral Sciences* 19, April pp. 123–6.
1983b 'Foreword', in: E. Garfield *Essays of an Information Scientist*, vol. V (Philadelphia: ISI Press) pp. xv–xix.
1983c 'Client Ambivalence in Professional Relationships: The Problem of Seeking Help from Strangers' (with Vanessa Merton and Elinor Barber), in: *New Directions in Helping*, vol. II, ed. B. M. DePaulo et al. (New York: Academic Press) pp. 13–44.
1984a 'The Fallacy of the Latest Word: The Case of "Pietism and Science" ' *American Journal of Sociology* 89 (5) pp. 1091–121.
1984b 'Socially Expected Durations: A Case Study of Concept Formation in Sociology', in: *Conflict and Consensus: A Festschrift for Lewis A. Coser* ed. W. W. Powell and R. Robbins (New York: Free Press) pp. 262–83.
1984c 'Texts, Contexts and Subtexts: An Epistolary Foreword', in: L.

Schneider (ed. J. Weinstein) *The Grammar of Social Relations*, (New Brunswick: Transaction Books) pp. ix–xlv.

1984d 'Scientific Fraud and the Fight to be First', *The Times Literary Supplement* 4257, 2 November.

1984e 'The Kelvin Dictum and Social Science: An Excursion into the History of an Idea' (with David L. Sills and Stephen M. Stigler), *Journal of the History of the Behavioral Sciences*, 20, October pp. 319–31.

1984f 'Remembering George Sarton: Episodic Recollections by an Unruly Apprentice', the lecture delivered at the conference commemorating Sarton's centennial at the University of Ghent (mimeographed).

1985 'Preface to the Vicennial Edition', in: *On the Shoulders of Giants*, new edition (New York: Harcourt Brace Jovanovich). (Quoted from manuscript).

Letters quoted with permission of RKM

To Louis Schneider, dated 14 September 1975
To Paul Samuelson, dated 21 September 1977
To Laura Nader, dated 24 December 1978
To Chen Ning Yang, dated 8 December 1978
To Chanoch Jacobsen, dated 23 September 1979
To Hanan Selvin, dated 19 May 1980
To James F. Short, Jr, dated 23 April 1981
To Helmut R. Wagner, dated 12 March 1983
To Eugene Garfield, dated 2 August 1983
To Piotr Sztompka, dated 6 April 1983
To Nico Stehr, dated 19 May 1983
To Nico Stehr, dated 23 December 1983
To David A. Hollinger, dated 19 May 1983
To Nico Stehr, dated 23 December 1983
To Piotr Sztompka, dated 22 April 1984
To Ralph Turner, dated 17 July 1984
To Piotr Sztompka, dated 12 November 1984
To Piotr Sztompka, dated 26 November 1984
To William T. Golden, dated 23 December 1984
To William T. Golden, dated 25 December 1984
To Piotr Sztompka, dated 29 January 1985
To Piotr Sztompka, dated 5 February 1985
To Ewa Morawska, dated 16 February 1985

Commentaries, criticisms and background

Abraham, G. A. (1983) 'Misunderstanding the Merton Thesis; A Boundary Dispute between History and Sociology', *ISIS*, 74, 368–87.

Alexander, J. C. (1982) *Theoretical Logic in Sociology*, vol. I: *Positivism,*

Presuppositions and Current Controversies (London: Routledge & Kegan Paul).
Allen, V. L. (1975) *Social Analysis* (London: Longman).
Allison, P. D., Krauze, T. K., Long, J. S. (1982) 'Cumulative Advantage and Inequality in Science' *American Sociological Review* 47, pp. 615–25.
Allport, G. W. (1954) *The Nature of Prejudice* (Reading, Mass.: Addison-Wesley).
Babbage, Ch. (1830) *The Decline of Science in England*.
Barbano, F. (1968) 'Social Structures and Social Functions: The Emancipation of Structural Analysis in Sociology' *Inquiry*, 11, pp. 40–84.
Barber, B. (1952) *Science and the Social Order*, (New York: Free Press).
(1975) 'Toward a New View of the Sociology of Knowledge', in: *The Idea of Social Structure: Papers in Honor of Robert K. Merton*, ed. L. A. Coser (New York: Harcourt Brace Jovanovich) pp. 103–16.
Barnes, B. (1974) *Scientific Knowledge and Sociological Theory* (London: Routledge & Kegan Paul).
Barnes, S. B., Dolby, G. R. A. (1970) 'The Scientific Ethos: A Deviant Viewpoint' *European Journal of Sociology* 11, pp. 3–25.
Baumgartner, T., Buckley, W., Burns, T. R., Schuster, P. (1976) 'Meta-power and the Structuring of Social Hierarchies', in: *Power and Control*, ed. T. R. Burns and W. Buckley (London: Sage) pp. 215–88.
Becker, G. (1984) 'Pietism and Science: A Critique of Robert K. Merton's Hypothesis', *American Journal of Sociology* 89 (5) pp. 1065–90.
Bell, D. (1980) *The Winding Passage: Essays and Sociological Journeys 1960–1980* (New York: Basic Books).
Bierstedt, R. (1960) 'Sociology and Humane Learning', *American Sociological Review*, 25 pp. 3–9.
(1981) *American Sociological Theory: A Critical History* (New York: Academic Press).
Birnbaum, N. (1971) 'The Crisis in Marxist Sociology', in: *Radical Sociology*, ed. J. D. Colfax and J. L. Roach (New York: Basic Books) pp. 108–31.
Blau, P. M. (1974) 'Focus on Social Structure', in: The Program of the ASA Convention held in Montreal, pp. 1–2.
(1975a) 'Structural Constraints of Status Complements', in: *The Idea of Social Structure: Papers in Honor of Robert K. Merton*, ed. L. A. Coser (New York: Harcourt Brace Jovanovich) pp. 117–38.
(1975b) 'Parallels and Contrasts in Structural Inquiries', in: *Approaches to the Study of Social Structure*, ed. P. M. Blau (New York: Free Press) pp. 1–20.
Bloor, D. (1976) *Knowledge and Social Imagery* (London: Routledge & Kegan Paul).
Bottomore, T. B., Nisbet, R. (1978) 'Structuralism', in: *History of Sociological Analysis*, ed. T. B. Bottomore and R. Nisbet (New York: Basic Books) pp. 557–98.
Boudon, R. (1977) Review of *The Idea of Social Structure: Papers in Honor of Robert K. Merton*, ed. L. A. Coser (New York: Harcourt Brace Jovanovich, 1975), in: *American Journal of Sociology* 86, pp. 1356–61.

Boulding, K., de Solla Price, D. J., Rosenberg, B. (1966) Review symposium on *On the Shoulders of Giants*, by R. K. Merton (New York: Harcourt Brace & World, 1965), in: *American Sociological Review*, 31 (1) pp. 104–6.

Broad, W., Wade, N. (1983) *Betrayers of the Truth: Fraud and Deceit in the Halls of Science* (New York: Simon and Schuster).

Buck, R. (1963) 'Reflexive Predictions', *Philosophy of Science*, 30 (4) pp. 359–74. Reprinted in *The Nature and Scope of Social Science*, ed. L. I. Krimerman (New York: Appleton Century Crofts, 1969) pp. 153–67.

Buckley, W. (1967) *Sociology and Modern Systems Theory* (Englewood Cliffs: Prentice Hall).

Burns, T., Buckley, W. (eds) (1976) *Power and Control: Social Structures and Their Transformations* (London: Sage).

Campbell, C. (1982) 'A Dubious Distinction? An Inquiry Into the Value and Use of Merton's Concepts of Manifest and Latent Function', *American Sociological Review*, 47 (1), pp. 29–44.

Caplovitz, D. (1977) 'Review Symposium on *The Idea of Social Structure: Papers in Honor of Robert K. Merton*, ed. L. A. Coser', *Contemporary Sociology*, 6 (2) pp. 142–50.

Cavanaugh, M. A. (1985) 'Popper, Merton, and Kuhn on Institutionalization and Change in Science: or the Importance of (not) Being the History Man', in: *Proceedings of the XIII International Congress for the Unity of Sciences* (in press).

Chapman, J. (1977) 'A Critique of Merton's Typology of Modes of Individual Adaptation' *Quarterly Journal of Ideology*, 1, pp. 13–18.

Chubin, D. (1983) *Annotated Bibliography on Invisible Colleges, 1972–1981*, (New York: Garland Publications).

Clinard, M. B. (1958) *Sociology of Deviant Behavior* (New York: Rinehart & Co).

Cloward, R. A. (1959) 'Illegitimate Means, Anomie, and Deviant Behavior' *American Sociological Review*, 24 (April). Reprinted in: *Sociological Theory: A Book of Readings*, II edn, eds L. A. Coser and B. Rosenberg (New York: Macmillan, 1964) pp. 562–82.

Cloward, R. A., Ohlin, L. E. (1960) *Delinquency and Opportunity: A Theory of Delinquent Gangs* (New York: Free Press).

Cohen, A. K. (1955) *Delinquent Boys: The Culture of the Gang* (New York: Free Press).

Cohen, H. (1970) 'Bureaucratic Flexibility: Some Comments on Robert Merton's "Bureaucratic Structure and Personality" ', *British Journal of Sociology*, 21 pp. 390–9.

Cole, J., Zuckerman, H. (1975) 'The Emergence of a Scientific Specialty: The Self-Exemplifying Case of the Sociology of Science', in: *The Idea of Social Structure: Papers in Honor of Robert K. Merton* ed. L. A. Coser (New York: Harcourt Brace Jovanovich) pp. 139–74.

Cole, S. (1975) 'The Growth of Scientific Knowledge: Theories of Deviance as a Case Study' in: *The Idea of Social Structure: Papers in Honor of Robert K. Merton* ed. L. A. Coser (New York: Harcourt Brace Jovanovich) pp. 175–220.

Collins, H. M. (1983) 'The Sociology of Scientific Knowledge: Studies of Contemporary Science' *Annual Review of Sociology*, 9 pp. 265–85.

Coser, L. A. (1956) *The Functions of Social Conflict* (New York: Free Press).

—— (1975) 'Merton's Uses of European Sociological Tradition', in: *The Idea of Social Structure: Papers in Honor of Robert K. Merton*, ed. L. A. Coser (New York: Harcourt Brace Jovanovich) pp. 85–100.

Coser, L. A., Nisbet, R. (1975) 'Merton and the Contemporary Mind', in: *The Idea of Social Structure: Papers in Honor of Robert K. Merton*, ed. L. A. Coser (New York: Harcourt Brace Jovanovich), pp. 3–10.

Coser, L. A., Rosenberg, B. (1964) 'Sociology of Knowledge', in: *Sociological Theory: A Book of Readings*, II edn, eds L. A. Coser and B. Rosenberg (New York: Macmillan) pp. 667–84.

Coser, R. L. (1975) 'Complexity of Roles as a Seedbed of Individual Autonomy', in: *The Idea of Social Structure: Papers in Honor of Robert K. Merton*, ed. L. A. Coser (New York: Harcourt Brace Jovanovich) pp. 237–63.

Crane, D. (1972) *Invisible Colleges: Diffusion of Knowledge in Scientific Communities*, (Chicago: University of Chicago Press).

Cullen, F. T. (1984) *Rethinking Crime and Deviance Theory: The Emergence of a Structuring Tradition* (New York: Rowman and Allanheld Publishers).

Cullen, F. T., Cullen, J. B. (1978) *Toward a Paradigm of Labeling Theory*, (Lincoln: University of Nebraska).

Cuzzort, R. P., King, E. W. (1976) *Humanity and Modern Social Thought*, II edn (Hinsdale: Dryden Press).

Dahrendorf, R. (1958) 'Out of Utopia: Toward a Reorientation of Sociological Analysis', *American Journal of Sociology*, 64 pp. 115–27.

—— (1968) *Essays in the Theory of Society* (Stanford: Stanford University Press).

—— (1980) 'On Representative Activities', in: *Science and Social Structure; A Festschrift for Robert K. Merton*, ed. T. F. Gieryn (New York: N.Y. Academy of Sciences) pp. 15–27.

—— (1981) *Life Chances; Approaches to Social and Political Theory* (Chicago: The University of Chicago Press).

Davis, K. (1959) 'The Myth of Functional Analysis as a Special Method of Sociology and Anthropology', *American Sociological Review*, 24 (Dec.) pp. 757–73.

Davis, K., Moore, W. E. (1945) 'Some Principles of Stratification', *American Sociological Review*, 10, (2) pp. 242–9.

Donoghue, D. (1981) 'I Would Like to Have Written. . .', *The New York Times Book Review*, 6 December.

—— (1985) 'Afterword' to *On the Shoulders of Giants*, Vicennial Edition (New York: Harcourt Brace Jovanovich).

Douglas, M. (1975) *Implicit Meanings*, (London: Routledge & Kegan Paul).

Dubin, R. (1959) 'Deviant Behavior and Social Structure: Continuities in Social Theory', *American Sociological Review*, 24 pp. 147–64.

Duke, J. T. (1976) *Conflict and Power in Social Life*, (Provo, Utah: Brigham Young University Press).
Easton, D. (1953) *The Political System* (New York: Alfred Knopf).
Eisenstadt, S. N. (1980) 'Autonomy of Sociology and Its Emancipatory Dimensions', in: *Science and Social Structure: A Festschrift for Robert K. Merton*, ed. T. F. Gieryn (New York: The N.Y. Academy of Sciences) pp. 28–31.
Elkana, Y. (1980) 'Of Cunning Reason', in: *Science and Social Structure: A Festschrift for Robert K. Merton*, ed. T. F. Gieryn (New York: The N.Y. Academy of Sciences) pp. 32–42.
—— (1981) 'A Programatic Attempt at an Anthropology of Knowledge', in: *Sciences and Cultures: Anthropological and Historical Studies of the Sciences*, eds E. Mendelsohn and Y. Elkana (Dordrecht: Reidel Publishing Company) pp. 1–76.
Epstein, C. F. (1970) *Woman's Place: Options and Limits in Professional Careers* (Berkeley: University of California Press).
Etzioni, A. (1968) *The Active Society* (New York: Free Press).
Ezrahi, Y. (1980) 'Science and the Problem of Authority in Democracy', in: *Science and Social Structure: A Festschrift for Robert K. Merton*, ed. T. F. Gieryn (New York: The N.Y. Academy of Sciences) pp. 43–60.
Fazey, C. (1973) 'Merton, Retreatism and Drug Addiction: The Testing of a Theory', *The Sociological Review*, 31 pp. 417–36.
Firth, R. (1975) 'An Appraisal of Modern Social Anthropology', *Annual Review of Anthropology*, 4.
Fleck, L. (1979) *Genesis and Development of a Scientific Fact*, eds T. J. Trenn and R. K. Merton (Chicago: The University of Chicago Press).
Friedrichs, R. W. (1972) 'Dialectic Sociology: Toward a Resolution of the Current "Crisis" in Western Sociology', British Journal of Sociology, 23 (3) pp. 263–74.
Garfield, E. (1975) 'The "Obliteration Phenomenon" in Science and the Advantage of Being Obliterated', *Current Contents*, 51/52, 22 December pp. 5–7.
—— (1977) 'Robert K. Merton: Among the Giants', *Current Contents*, 28 pp. 5–7.
—— (1979) 'Citation Indexing: The Evolving Grammar of Citation Analysis', *Current Contents*, 28, 16 July pp. 5–6.
—— (1980) 'Citation Measures of the Influence of Robert K. Merton', in: *Science and Social Structure: A Festschrift for Robert K. Merton* ed. T. F. Gieryn (New York: The N.Y. Academy of Sciences) pp. 61–74.
—— (1983a) 'Robert K. Merton – Author and Editor Extraordinaire', part I., *Current Contents*, 39, 26 September pp. 5–7.
—— (1983b) 'Robert K. Merton – Author and Editor Extraordinaire', part II., *Current Contents*, 40, October pp. 5–7.
Giddens, A. (1971) *Capitalism and Modern Social Theory*, (Cambridge: Cambridge University Press).
—— (1977) 'Functionalism: Aprés la Lutte', in: *Studies in Social and Political Theory*, (London: Hutchinson).
—— (1979) *Central Problems in Social Theory* (London: Macmillan Press).

Goode, W. I. (1973) *Explorations in Social Theory* (New York: Oxford University Press).
(1975) 'Homans' and Merton's Structural Approach', in: *Approaches to the Study of Social Structure*, ed. P. M. Blau (New York: Free Press) pp. 66–75.
Gould, S. J. (1974) Review of *Philosophy of Biological Science*, by D. L. Hull, *Science*, 186 pp. 45–46.
Gouldner, A. W. (1959) 'Reciprocity and Autonomy in Functional Theory', in: *Symposium on Sociological Theory*, ed. L. Gross (Evanston: Row & Peterson) pp. 241–70.
(1971) *The Coming Crisis of Western Sociology* (London: Heinemann).
(1973) 'Foreword', in: I. Taylor, P. Walton, J. Young *The New Criminology: For a Social Theory of Deviance*, (London: Routledge & Kegan Paul) pp. ix–xiv.
Grünbaum, A. (1956) 'Historical Determinism, Social Activism, and Predictions in the Social Sciences', *British Journal for the Philosophy of Science*, 7.
Hall, A. R. (1963) 'Merton Revisited or Science and Society in Seventeenth Century', *History of Science: An Annual Review* 2, pp. 1–16.
Harary, F. (1966) 'Merton Revisited: A New Classification for Deviant Behavior' *American Sociological Review* 31 pp. 693–7.
Hesse, M. (1974) *The Structure of Scientific Inference* (London: Macmillan Press).
(1980) 'The Strong Thesis of Sociology of Science', in *Revolutions and Reconstructions in the Philosophy of Science* (Bloomington: Indiana University Press) pp. 29–60.
Hillery, G. A. (1983) 'The President's Page', *The Southern Sociologist*, 14 pp. 2–3.
Hempel, C. G. (1965) 'The Logic of Functional Analysis', in *Aspects of Scientific Explanation*, C. G. Hempel, (New York: The Free Press) pp. 297–330.
Hollinger, D. A. (1983) 'The Defense of Democracy and Robert K. Merton's Formulation of the Scientific Ethos' in: *Knowledge and Society: Studies in the Sociology of Culture Past and Present*, vol. 4, eds R. A. Jones and H. Kuklick (Greenwich: JAI Press Inc.) pp. 1–15.
Holton, G. (1973) *Thematic Origins of Scientific Thought: Keppler to Einstein* (Cambridge, Mass.: Harvard University Press).
Homans, G. C. (1962) *Sentiments and Activities: Essays in Social Science* (New York: Free Press).
(1964) 'Bringing Men Back In', *American Sociological Review*, 29 (5) pp. 809–19. Reprinted in: *Institutions and Social Exchange*, eds H. Turk and R. L. Simpson (Indianapolis: Bobbs Merrill, 1971) pp. 102–16.
(1967) *The Nature of Social Science* (New York: Harcourt Brace & World).
(1975) 'What Do We Mean By Social Structure?', in: *Approaches to the Study of Social Structure*, ed. P. M. Blau (New York: Free Press).
Hyman, H. H. (1975) 'Reference Individuals and Reference Idols', in: *The*

Idea of Social Structure: Papers in Honor of Robert K. Merton, ed. L. A. Coser (New York: Harcourt Brace Jovanovich) pp. 265–82.
Isajiw, W. W. (1968) *Causation and Functionalism in Sociology* (New York: Shocken Books).
Jacobsen, C. (1979) 'Permissiveness and Norm Evasions: Definitions, Relationships and Implications', *Sociology*, May pp. 219–233.
Janis, I. L. (1980) 'An Analysis of Psychological and Sociological Ambivalence: Nonadherence to Courses of Action Prescribed by Health-Care Professionals', in: *Science and Social Structure: A Festschrift for Robert K. Merton*, ed. T. F. Gieryn (New York: The N.Y. Academy of Sciences) pp. 91–110.
Karsten, S. G. (1983) 'Dialectics, Functionalism, and Structuralism in Economic Thought' *The American Journal of Economics and Sociology*, 42 (2), April pp. 179–92.
Kearney, H. F. (1973) 'Merton Revisited', *Science Studies*, 3 pp. 72–78.
Kornhauser, R. R. (1984) *Social Sources of Delinquency; An Appraisal of Analytic Models* (Chicago: The University of Chicago Press).
Kuhn, T. S. ([1962] 1970) *The Structure of Scientific Revolutions*, II edn (Chicago: The University of Chicago Press).
Kuklick, H. (1983) 'The Sociology of Knowledge: Retrospect and Prospect' *Annual Review of Sociology*, vol. 9 pp. 287–310.
Lazarsfeld, P. F. (1972) *Qualitative Analysis: Historical and Critical Essays*, (Boston: Allyn & Bacon).
— (1975) 'Working with Merton', in: *The Idea of Social Structure: Papers in Honor of Robert K. Merton*, ed. L. A. Coser (New York: Harcourt Brace Jovanovich) pp. 35–66.
Lehman, H. (1966) 'R. K. Merton's Concepts of Function and Functionalism', *Inquiry*, 9 pp. 274–83.
Lepenies, W. (1981) 'Anthropological Perspectives in the Sociology of Science', in: *Sciences and Cultures: Anthropological and Historical Studies of the Sciences*, eds E. Mendelsohn and Y. Elkana (Dordrecht: Reidel Publishing Company) pp. 245–261.
Levine, D. L. (1981) 'Sociology's Quest for the Classics: The Case of Simmel', in: *The Future of the Sociological Classics*, ed. B. Rhea (London: George Allen & Unwin).
Levy, M. (1952) *The Structure of Society* (Princeton: Princeton University Press).
Lockwood, D. (1956) 'Some Remarks on the "Social System"', *British Journal of Sociology*, 7 pp. 134–46.
— (1964) 'Social Integration and System Integration', in: *Explorations in Social Change*, eds G. K. Zollschan, W. Hirsch (Boston: Houghton Mifflin) pp. 244–57.
Loewenberg, F. M. (1984) 'Professional Ideology, Middle Range Theories and Knowledge Building for Social Work Practice', *The British Journal of Social Work*, 14 pp. 309–22.
Loomis, C. P., Loomis, Z. K. (1961) *Modern Social Theories: Selected American Writers* (Princeton: Van Nostrand).

Lundberg, G. (1956) 'The Natural Science Trend in Sociology', *American Journal of Sociology*, 61, Nov. pp. 191–202.
MacIver, R. M. (ed.) (1948) *Discrimination and National Welfare* (New York: Harper & Brothers).
Manis, J. C. and Meltzer, B. N. (1974) 'Blumer and Merton: Social Roles and Sociological Theories', *Sociological Focus*, 7 (4) pp. 1–14.
Martindale, D. (1959) 'Sociological Theory and the Ideal Type', in: *Symposium on Sociological Theory*, ed. L. Gross (Evanston: Row & Peterson) pp. 57–91.
(1965) Functionalism in the Social Sciences (Philadelphia: American Academy of Political and Social Sciences).
(1960) *The Nature and Types of Sociological Theory* (Boston: Houghton Mifflin).
(1974) *Sociological Theory and the Problem of Values* (Columbus: Charles Merrill).
Maruyama, M. (1963) 'The Second Cybernetics: Deviation Amplifying Mutual Causal Processes', *American Scientist* 51 pp. 164–179.
Mills, C. W. (1959) *The Sociological Imagination* (London: Oxford University Press).
Milosz, C. (1953) *The Captive Mind* (New York: Alfred Knopf).
Mitroff, I. I. (1974) 'Norms and Counternorms in a Select Group of the Apollo Moon Scientists: A Case Study of the Ambivalence of Scientists', *American Sociological Review*, 39 pp. 579–95.
Moore, W. E. (1963) *Social Change* (Englewood Cliffs: Prentice Hall).
(1978) 'Functionalism', in: *A History of Sociological Analysis*, eds T. B. Bottomore and R. Nisbet (New York: Basic Books) pp. 321–61.
Mulkay, M. J. (1971) *Functionalism, Exchange and Theoretical Strategy* (London: Routledge & Kegan Paul).
(1979) *Science and the Sociology of Knowledge* (London: Allen & Unwin).
(1980) 'Interpretation and the Use of Rules: The Case of the Norms of Science', in: *Science and Social Structure: A Festschrift for Robert K. Merton*, ed. T. F. Gieryn (New York: The N.Y. Academy of Sciences) pp. 111–125.
Nadel, S. F. (1969) *The Theory of Social Structure* (London: Routledge & Kegan Paul).
Nagel, E. (1956) 'A Formalization of Functionalism', in: *Logic Without Metaphysics*, E. Nagel, (New York: The Free Press).
(1961) *The Structure of Science* (New York: Harcourt Brace & World).
Nelson, B. (1972) 'Review Essay' on *Science, Technology and Society in Seventeenth Century England*, by R. K. Merton (New York: Harper & Row, 1970), in: *American Journal of Sociology*, 78 pp. 223–231.
Opp, K. D. (1970) 'Theories of the Middle-Range as a Strategy for the Construction of a General Sociological Theory', *Quality and Quantity*, 4 (2) pp. 243–53.
Oromaner, M. (1970) 'Comparison of Influentials in Contemporary American and British Sociology', *British Journal of Sociology*, 13 pp. 324–32.

Parsons, T. (1948) 'The Position of Sociological Theory', *American Sociological Review*, 13 (2) pp. 156–64.
(1951) *The Social System* (New York: Free Press).
(1975) 'The Present Status of "Structural-Functional" Theory in Sociology', in: *The Idea of Social Structure: Papers in Honor of Robert K. Merton*, ed. L. A. Coser (New York: Harcourt Brace Jovanovich) pp. 67–83.
Patel, P. J. (1975) 'Robert K. Merton's Formulations in Sociology of Science', *Sociological Bulletin*, 24 (1) pp. 55–75.
Patinkin, D. (1983) 'Multiple Discoveries and the Central Message', *American Journal of Sociology*, 89 (2) pp. 302–23.
Persell, C. H. (1984) 'An Interview with Robert K. Merton, *Teaching Sociology* 11 (4) July pp. 355–86.
Phillips, D. L. (1974) 'Epistemology and the Sociology of Knowledge: The Contributions of Mannheim, Mills and Merton', *Theory and Society*, 1 pp. 59–88.
Pinder, C. C., Moore, L. F. (1980) *Middle Range Theory and the Study of Organizations*, (Boston: Martinus Mijhoff).
Pollis, N. P. (1968) 'Reference Group Re-Examined', *British Journal of Sociology*, 19 (3) pp. 300–307.
Popper, K. R. (1976) *Unended Quest: An Intellectual Autobiography* (London: Fontana).
Price, de Solla, D. J. (1961) *Science Since Babylon*, (New Haven: Yale University Press).
(1963) *Little Science, Big Science* (New York: Columbia University Press).
Raab, L. M., Goodyear, A. C. (1984) 'Middle-Range Theory in Archeology: A Critical Review of Origins and Applications', *American Antiquity*, 49 (2) pp. 255–68.
Rex, J. (1981) *Social Conflict; A Conceptual and Theoretical Analysis* (London: Longman)
Richter, M. N. (1965) 'Social Functions and Sociological Explanations', *Sociology and Social Research*, 50 (1).
Riedesel, P. L. (1973) 'The Recent Course of General Theory: An Empirical Investigation', the paper presented at the Annual Meeting of the Midwest Sociological Society (mimeographed).
Rogers, E. M., Bhowmik, D. K. (1970) 'Homophily – Heterophily: Relational Concepts for Communication', *Public Opinion Quarterly*, 34 pp. 523–38.
Rose, G. (1966) 'Anomie and Deviation: A Conceptual Framework for Empirical Studies', *British Journal of Sociology*, 17 (1) pp. 29–45.
Rosenthal, R., Jacobson, L. (1968) *Pygmalion in the Classroom: Teacher Expectation and Pupils' Intellectual Development*, (New York: Holt, Rinehart and Winston, Inc.).
Rosenthal, R., Rubin, D. B. (1978) 'Interpersonal Expectancy Effects: the First 345 Studies', in: *The Behavioral and Brain Sciences*, 3 pp. 377–415.
Schneider, L. (1975) 'Ironic Perspective and Sociological Thought', in: *The Idea of Social Structure: Papers in Honor of Robert K. Merton*, ed. L. A. Coser (New York: Harcourt Brace Jovanovich) pp. 323–337.

(1984) *The Grammar of Social Relations*, ed. J. Weinstein (New Brunswick: Transaction Books).
Schweiker, W. (1968) 'Status Consistency and Merton's Modes of Individual Adaptation', *Sociological Quarterly* 9 pp. 531–9.
Shibutani, T. (1955) 'Reference Groups as Perspectives', *American Journal of Sociology*, 60, May pp. 562–9.
Simon, H. A. (1954) 'Bandwagon and Underdog Effects of Election Predictions', *Public Opinion Quarterly*, 18 pp. 245–53.
Sjoberg, G. (1960) 'Contradictory Functional Requirements and Social Systems', *Journal of Conflict Resolution*, 4 pp. 198–208.
Smelser, N. J. (1962) *Theory of Collective Behavior* (New York: Free Press).
Sorokin, P. A. (1966) *Sociological Theories of Today* (New York: Harper & Row).
Spiro, M. E. (1961) 'Social Systems, Personality, and Functional Analysis', in: *Studying Personality Cross-Culturally*, ed. B. Kaplan (New York: Harper & Row) pp. 93–127.
Stehr, N. (1978) 'The Ethos of Science Revisited: Social and Cognitive Norms', in: *Sociology of Science*, ed. J. Gaston (San Francisco 1978: Jossey Bass) pp. 172–96.
Stigler, S. M. (1980) 'Merton on Multiples, Denied and Affirmed', in: *Science and Social Structure: Festschrift for Robert K. Merton*, ed. T. Gieryn (New York: The N.Y. Academy of Sciences) pp. 143–6.
Stinchcombe, A. L. (1968) *Constructing Social Theories* (New York: Harcourt Brace Jovanovich).
(1975) 'Merton's Theory of Social Structure', in: *The Idea of Social Structure: Papers in Honor of Robert K. Merton*, ed. L. A. Coser (New York: Harcourt Brace Jovanovich) pp. 11–53.
Sztompka, P. (1971) 'The Logic of Functional Analysis in Sociology and Social Anthropology', *Quality and Quantity: European Journal of Methodology*, 5 (2) pp. 369–88.
(1973) *Teoria i wyjasnienie* (Theory and Explanation) (Warszawa: Polish Scientific Publishers).
(1974a) *System and Function: Toward a Theory of Society* (New York: Academic Press).
(1974b) 'O prawach socjologicznych' ('On Sociological Laws'), *Studia Socjologiczne*, 3 pp. 51–86.
(1979a) *Sociological Dilemmas: Toward a Dialectic Paradigm* (New York: Academic Press).
(1979b) 'Marxism, Functionalism, and System Approach', in: *Polish Essays in the Methodology of the Social Sciences*, ed. J. J. Wiatr (Dordrecht: Reidel Publishing Company) pp. 133–156.
(1983) 'Social Development: The Dialectics of Theory and Action' *Reports on Philosophy*, 7 pp. 79–98.
(1984) 'The Global Crisis and the Reflexiveness of the Social System', *The International Journal of Comparative Sociology*, 25 pp. 51–64.
(1985) 'Modalities and Determinants of Structural Change', in: *Approaches to Structural Analysis in Sociology*, eds J. Szmatka, Ch.

Warriner (London: Sage), in press.
Tenbruck, F. H. (1974) 'Max Weber and the Sociology of Science: A Case Reopened', *Zeitschrift für Soziologie*, 3 (3) pp. 312–20.
Toulmin, S. (1972) *Human Understanding* Vol I (Oxford: Clarendon Press).
Touraine, A. (1977) *The Self-Production of Society* (Chicago: The University of Chicago Press).
Turner, J. H. (1978) *The Structure of Sociological Theory*, Revised edition, (Homewood: The Dorsey Press).
Wallace, W. (1969) *Sociological Theory: An Introduction* (London: Heinemann).
Weick, K. E. (1974) 'Middle-Range Theories of Social Systems', *Behavioral Science*, 19 pp. 357–367.
Weinstein, J. (1984) 'Elements of the Sociological Way: Introduction', in: L. Schneider, *The Grammar of Social Relations*, ed. J. Weinstein (New Brunswick: Transaction Books).
Wells, A. (1979) 'Conflict Theory and Functionalism – Introductory Sociology Textbooks, 1928–1976', *Teaching Sociology*, 6 (4) pp. 429–37.
Whitehead, A. N. (1917) *The Organization of Thought* (London: Williams and Norgate).
Whitley, R. D. (1972) 'Black Boxism and the Sociology of Science: A Discussion of Major Developments in the Field', *The Sociological Review Monograph*, 18 pp. 61–91.
Whitten, N. E. Jr. (1984) 'Introduction', in: *American Ethnologist* (special issue on social structure), 11 pp. 635–41.
Williams, R. M. Jr. (1970) *American Society* (New York: Alfred Knopf). First published 1951.
—— (1975) 'Relative Deprivation', in: *The Idea of Social Structure: Papers in Honor of Robert K. Merton*, ed. L. A. Coser (New York: Harcourt Brace Jovanovich) pp. 355–78.
Willie, C. (1973) 'On Merton's Insiders and Outsiders', *American Journal of Sociology*, 79 (2) pp. 1269–72.
Wrong, D. (1961) 'The Oversocialized Conception of Man in Modern Sociology', *American Sociological Review*, 2 pp. 183–93.
Zeidenstein, H. (1979) 'The Consequences of Executive Acts: An Expanded Typology of Merton's Functional Analysis', *Presidential Studies Quarterly*, Fall pp. 457–69.
Znaniecki, F. (1940) *The Social Role of the Man of Knowledge* (New York: Columbia University Press).
Zuckerman, H. (1977a) 'Deviant Behavior and Social Control in Science', in: *Deviance and Social Change*, ed. E. Sagarin (Beverly Hills: Sage) pp. 87–138.
—— (1977b) *Scientific Elite* (New York: Free Press).
Zuckerman, H. and Merton R. K. (1972) 'Age, Aging and Age Structure in Science', in M. W. Riley *et al.* (eds) *A Theory of Age Stratification* (New York: Russell Sage Foundation) pp. 292–356.

Name Index

Abraham, G. A.   304
Alexander, J. C.   304
Allen, V. L.   305
Allison, P. D.   305
Allport, G. W.   62, 110, 171, 305
Aristachos of Samos   247
Aristotle   242

Babbage, Ch.   58, 305
Bacon, F.   91
Barbano, F.   25, 130, 141, 143, 148, 245, 305
Barber, B.   248, 302, 305
Barber, E.   137, 147, 178, 179, 196, 197, 302, 303
Barnes, B.   32, 56, 76, 305
Baumgartner, T.   224, 305
Becker, G.   305
Bell, D.   1, 262n, 305
Bentham, J.   78
Barnard of Chartres   21
Bhowmik, D. K.   312
Bierstedt, R.   2, 14, 15, 17, 26, 32, 81, 106, 215, 262n, 305
Birnbaum, N.   120, 305
Blau, P. M.   15, 116, 144, 150, 166, 250, 305
Bloor, D.   76, 305
Blumer, H.   31
Bottomore, T. B.   144, 305
Boudon, R.   262n, 263n, 305
Boyle, R.   72
Broad, W.   306
Buck, R.   236, 306
Buckley, W.   141, 224
Burke, K.   119
Burns, T.   224, 305, 306

Campbell, C.   135, 228, 252, 306
Caplovitz, D.   19, 306
Cavanaugh, M. A.   306
Chapman, J.   182, 183, 306
Chomsky, N.   146
Chubin, D.   306
Clinard, M. B.   306
Cloward, R. A.   187, 189–90, 306
Cohen, A. K.   188, 306
Cohen, H.   195, 306
Cole, J.   41, 306
Cole, S.   44, 188, 306
Collins, H. M.   307
Comte, A.   80, 92, 129, 144, 253, 258
Condorcet, J. A.   22
Cooley, Ch.H.   22, 306
Coser, L. A.   vi, 16, 24, 30, 153, 245, 247, 307
Coser, R. L.   183, 192, 193, 198, 307
Crane, D.   307
Cullen, F. T.   188, 307
Cullen, J. B.   307
Cuzzort, R. P.   183, 251, 307

Dahrendorf, R.   141, 307
Darwin, Ch.   93, 307
Davis, K.   126, 127, 165, 307
Dewey, J.   49
Dolby, G. R.   32, 56, 305
Donoghue, D.   21, 307
Douglas, M.   76, 307
Dubin, R.   188–9, 190, 307
Duke, J. T.   308
Durkheim, E.   17, 22, 24, 25, 72, 80, 124, 144, 174, 176, 182, 183, 193, 211, 223, 249, 258

Name Index

Easton, D. 127, 308
Einstein, A. 59, 85
Eisenstadt, S. N. 111, 308
Elkana, Y. 308
Epstein, C. F. 308
Etzioni, A. 308
Ezrahi, Y. 43, 308

Fazey, C. 308
Firth, R. 308
Fleck, L. 66, 76, 77, 99, 240, 275n, 308
Friedrichs, R. W. 236, 308

Galileo, G. 22
Garfield, E. 15, 16, 245, 304, 308
Gibbs, W. 85
Giddens, A. ix, x, 25, 136, 137, 142, 237, 250, 308
Giddings, F. H. x
Golden, W. T. 304
Goldenweiser, A. 146
Goode, W. I. 108, 145, 208, 209, 309
Goodyear, A. C. 312
Gould, S. J. 309
Gouldner, A. W. 26, 121, 309
Grunbaum, A. 309

Hall, A. R. 36, 70, 309
Harary, F. 190, 309
Hegel, W. F. 201
Hempel, C. G. 40, 309
Henderson, L. J. 1, 12
Hesse, M. 309
Hillery, G. A. 309
Hobbes, T. 22
Hollinger, D. A. 304, 309
Holton, G. 240, 241, 309
Homans, G. C. 126, 137, 138, 141, 309
Hooke, R. 72
Hughes, E. 192
Hunt, M. M. 263n
Hyman, H. H. 230, 309

Isajiw, W. W. 310

Jacobsen, C. 218, 219, 304, 310
Jacobson, L. 312
Jakobson, R. 146
Janis, I. L. 196, 197, 310

Karsten, S. G. 310
Kearney, H. F. 71, 310
Kelley, H. H. 231
Kelvin, W. 101
Kendall, P. 33, 226
Kennedy, S. x
Kepler, J. 85
King, E. W. 183, 251, 307
Kluckhohn, F. 215
Kornhauser, R. R. 310
Krauze, T. K. 305
Kuhn, T. 113, 120, 121, 122, 240, 310
Kuklick, H. 310

Lakatos, I. 91
Laplace, P. S. 85
Lavoisier, A. L. 83
Lazarsfeld, P. F. 10, 13, 15, 19, 30, 32, 33, 113, 137, 138, 146, 152, 155, 226, 227, 248, 250, 310
Lehman, H. 133, 310
Leibniz, G. W. 58, 248
Lepenies, W. 310
Levine, D. L. 266n, 310
Lévi-Strauss, C. 144, 146
Levy, M. 127, 310
Linton, R. 164, 165
Lockwood, D. 141, 310
Loewenberg, F. M. 310
Long, J. S. 305
Loomis, C. P. 127, 145, 164, 191, 200, 216, 220, 222, 224, 310
Loomis, Z. K. 127, 145, 164, 191, 200, 216, 220, 222, 224, 310
Lundberg, G. A. 248, 311
Lynd, R. 52

MacIver, R. M. 311
Malewski, A. 265n

Name Index

Malinowski, B. 28, 129, 133, 140
Malthus, T. 247
Manis, J. C. 15, 16, 17, 136, 243, 248, 311
Mannheim, K. 37, 38, 46
Martindale, D. 113, 114, 126, 311
Maruyama, M. 311
Marx, K. 25, 26, 37, 38, 144, 201, 238, 258
Mauss, M. 72
Maxwell, J. C. 85, 88
Mead, G. H. 22, 194, 197
Meltzer, B. N. 15, 16, 17, 136, 243, 248, 311
Merton, V. 179
Miles, M. W. x, 263n
Mills, C. W. 82, 243, 311
Milosz, C. 48, 311
Mitroff, I. I. 55, 57, 78, 311
Moore, L. F. 312
Moore, W. E. 127, 150, 307, 311
Morawska, E. 304
Mulkay, M. J. 45, 49, 56, 76, 311

Nadel, S. F. 311
Nader, L. 304
Nagel, E. 127, 140, 311
Needham, J. 72
Nelson, B. 69, 72, 311
Newton, I. 21, 58, 59, 72, 248
Nisbet, R. 144, 305, 307
Nowak, S. 265n

Ohlin, L. E. 189, 190, 306
Opp, K. D. 112, 113, 311
Oromaner, M. 16, 311
Ossowska, M. 265n
Ossowski, S. 265n

Pareto, V. 228, 258
Parsons, T. 3, 17, 28, 29, 80, 108, 127, 128, 129, 133, 143, 165, 228, 253, 312
Patel, P. J. 70, 312
Patinkin, D. 312
Peirce, Ch.S. 91, 99

Persell, C. H. 312
Petty, W. 247
Phillips, D. L. 75, 312
Piaget, J. 144
Pinder, C. C. 312
Planck, M. 85
Podgórecki, A. 265n
Pollis, N. P. 231, 232, 312
Popper, K. R. 6, 12, 91, 312
Price, de Solla D. J. 66, 306, 312
Ptolemy 247

Raab, L. M. 312
Radcliffe-Brown, A. R. 129, 140, 144
Rex, J. 312
Richter, M. N. 312
Riedesel, P. L. 312
Rogers, E. M. 312
Rose, G. 312
Rosenthal, R. 312
Rousseau, J. J. 22
Rubin, D. B. 312

Saint-Simon, H. 22
Samuelson, P. 304
Sarton, G. 28
Saussure de, F. 144
Scheler, M. 37
Schneider, L. 241, 252, 253, 304, 312
Schuster, P. 305
Schweiker, W. 313
Selvin, H. 304
Shibutani, T. 230, 232, 313
Short, J. F. 304
Sills, D. 101
Simmel, G. 22, 27, 144, 193, 245, 258
Simon, H. A. 313
Sjoberg, G. 134, 313
Smelser, N. J. 110, 313
Sorokin, P. A. 28, 29, 153, 313
Spencer, H. 144, 192, 258
Spiro, M. E. 135, 313
Srole, L. 125, 196
Stehr, N. 304, 313

Stigler, S. M. 101, 313
Stinchcombe, A. L. 3, 16, 23, 140, 142, 151, 152, 183, 191, 195, 224, 228, 234, 237, 255, 313
Stouffer, S. 248
Sumner, W. G. 164
Sutherland, E. 189, 190

Tawney, R. H. 67
Tenbruck, F. H. 71, 314
Thomas, W. I. 229, 230, 239
Toulmin, S. 262n, 314
Touraine, A. 314
Trenn, T. 76
Troeltsch, E. 67
Turner, J. H. 14, 141, 245, 250, 314
Turner, R. 304

Veblen, T. 62, 94, 178, 194, 256
Vico, G. 201
Viner, J. 101

Wade, N. 306
Wagner, H. R. 304
Wallace, W. 145, 314
Weber, A. 72, 73
Weber, M. 22, 27, 67, 71, 80, 95, 114, 162, 194, 195, 224, 228, 239, 243
Weick, K. E. 109, 314
Weinstein, J. 252, 314
Wells, A. 314
Whitehead, A. N. 22, 74, 84, 94, 117, 242, 314
Whitley, R. D. 314
Whitten, N. E. 314
Williams, R. M. 217, 314
Willie, C. 314
Wrong, D. 314

Yang, C. N. 275n, 304

Zeidenstein, H. 314
Znaniecki, F. 9, 13, 27, 39, 80, 117, 228, 314
Zuckerman, H. 10, 13, 41, 58, 59, 63, 65, 235, 302, 314

Subject Index

accumulation of advantages and disadvantages   155, 222–3, 255, 295n
action, social   228–37
  means–ends scheme   50, 228
  unanticipated consequences   134, 251
  unintended consequences   69, 134, 251
  voluntaristic model   228–9
adumbrationism   74, 281n
agent, human   237–8
ambivalence, sociological   31, 55, 125, 147–8, 164, 177–80, 196–7, 249
  sociological ambivalence$_1$ 178
  sociological ambivalence$_2$ 179–80
  sociological v. psychological ambivalence   196–7, 249
and–also fallacy   84
anomie   2, 32, 57, 125, 150, 162, 168, 174–7, 184, 196, 249, 256
  anomie$_1$ 174, 289n
  anomie$_2$ 174–6, 289n
  anomie$_3$ 176–7, 184, 216, 220, 289n
  anomie$_4$ 177, 289n
  anomia   125, 196, 249, 256
  anomie and deviation   184–90, 214, 255–6
  anomie in science   51
anomics   196
authority   224
autonomy of science   46
auxiliatropic paradox   257

boomerang effects   226, 257

bureaucratic personality   194–5
bureaucratic structure   2, 170, 180, 194
bureaucratic virtuoso   195
Burke theorem   62, 119

causal loops   140, 151, 152, 195
change, social   142
  change in   66, 149, 199, 202, 210
  change of   66, 149, 199, 202, 210
  conflictual change   202
  dynamic perspective   199–200
  dysfunctions and change   142, 212–13, 284n
  endogenous change v. exogenous change   199
  manifest dynamics v. latent dynamics   203, 211, 255
  structural change   200
civil society   48, 57
classicist theme   4, 5, 7, 20, 22, 27, 241–5, 257, 259
codification   11, 12, 16, 113, 128, 245
cognitive conduit   31, 62, 273n, 275n, 296n
cognitive structure of science   39, 42
cognitivism   51, 107
cognitivist theme   4, 5, 7, 25, 241, 246–8, 257–8
communication system of science   61
communism of science   53
concept-formation   98–102
conceptual elaboration   99–101

Subject Index

conceptual model 106
conceptual ramification 15
conduit function 62
conflict, social 78, 142, 201
  conflictual change 202
  conflictual image of society 37, 148, 173, 182, 196, 201, 253–4
  cultural conflict 174
  role conflict 2, 180–1, 203–7
conformity 183, 185, 254
coterie-science 31
counter-values 51
crisis of sociology 120–3
cryptomnesia 75
culturally defined goals 163
culture *v.* civilization 73

detached concern 178, 197
deviance, social 32, 147, 150, 183, 215, 254
  aberrant behaviour 215–16, 256
  anomie and deviation 184–90, 214, 255–6
  delinquent subcultures 188
  deviations from scientific ethos 56–9, 184, 270n, 272n
  forms of deviation 184–8
  institutionalised evasions of institutional rules 31, 45, 215–20
  nonconformity 215
  patterned evasions 217, 294n
differential association 189
disciplined eclecticism 31, 115–18, 243
disciplined inquiry 12, 82, 87, 113, 245, 259
disinterestedness of science 53
displacement of goals 194, 256
dysfunctions, social 31, 130, 250
  accumulated dysfunctions 212–13
  dysfunctions of bureaucracy 195
  dysfunctions and change 142, 212–13, 284n

manifest *v.* latent dysfunctions 283n

eponymy 31, 63
ethos of science 42, 43, 179
Eureka elation 11
Eureka syndrome 31
externalist approach to science 36

fallacy of compulsive novelty 21
fallacy of dogmatic reiteration 21
fallacy of the latest word 31, 74, 75
fallacy of misplaced concreteness 72, 84
fallacy of unanimity 171
falsificationism 91, 118
feedback 140, 151, 152, 155, 195, 203, 211, 223, 284n
finalism 137–40
five Cs formula 11
focus group 33
focused interview 33
folkways 164
four Ps formula 9, 31, 50, 164
fraud in science 58
freedom of the individual 238
frivolous ignorance 83
function, social 37, 129, 135
  functional alternatives (equivalents, substitutes) 132–4
  functional indispensability 131–2
  functional requirements (needs, prerequisites) 133
  functional unity 129–30
  latent function 31, 135, 139, 251
  manifest function 31, 135, 251
  net balance of functional consequences 130–1, 212
  universal functionalism 131
functional analysis 2, 29, 30, 86, 126–43, 250, 251
  dynamic functionalism 28, 31, 127, 142

functional analysis – *continued*
  empirical functionalism   31, 127
  functional explanation   137, 140
  functional interpretation   140
  functional law   137
  functionalism as conservative   142–3
  neo-functionalism   28, 31, 127, 136–43
  paradigm for functional analysis   136, 141, 146, 212

giants-and-dwarfs metaphor   21–3, 73
golden mean   5, 20, 22, 26, 239, 242
group structure of science   42

heterophily   32, 137
homophily   31, 137, 152

idle curiosity   94
illegitimate means   189–90
image of science   34, 269n
individual autonomy   197–8
influentials   226–7
  cosmopolitan influential   14, 19, 31, 33, 226–7
  local influential   14, 31, 33, 226–7
  monomorphic influential   227
  polymorphic influential   227
in-group   254
innovation   185, 187
  accumulation of innovations   220–1
institution, social   165, 179
institutional complex   167
institutionalisation   72, 191, 217–18, 222
  institutionalisation of norms   214
  institutionalised altruism   31, 147, 190–2, 249
  institutionalised evasions of institutional rules   31, 45, 215–20

institutionalised vigilance   44, 60, 249
integration   129, 130, 173–4, 177
  consensus and dissensus   173–82
internationalisation   193
internalist approach to science   36, 70
interpersonal expectancy effects   236, 297n
interpersonal influence   225–7
invisible colleges   35, 66, 273n
ironic theme   4, 5, 7, 26, 68, 241, 252–7, 258

juvenocracy   31

lame-duck pattern   157
laws   164
legitimacy   177, 186, 215, 216
liberal-democratic order   49, 88, 277n
life-chances   160, 162, 214, 223

macro-environments of science   35
mass communication   33
mass persuasion   225 6
Matthew effect   31, 61, 63, 64, 222, 255
meta-power   207, 224
meta-scientific system   3
method *v*. orientation (approach)   80–1
micro-environments of science   35
middle-range theory   3, 4, 18, 29, 107–13, 128, 231, 243, 280n
mores   164
multiple discoveries   2, 214, 222, 274n, 275n

narrow empiricism   83
norms, institutional   51, 163, 164, 185
  counter-norms   51, 55, 164, 178, 231, 254
  meta-norms   208
  norm erosion   218

Subject Index

norms, institutional – *continued*
  norm resistance 219
  norm substitution 219
  normative structure 163–7, 182
  normative system of
    science 39, 42
nothing–but fallacy 84
now-generation 21, 300n

objectivity 51, 78
obliteration by incorporation
  (OBI) 31, 62, 268n
observability 27, 31, 170, 205,
  288–9n
oral publication 18, 31, 61, 167
oral transmission of
  knowledge 18
organised criticism 54
organised scepticism 31, 44, 54,
  117, 249, 271n
originality 52
originating questions 96
origins of modern science 67–72
out-group 254

palimpsest 62, 268n
paradox 5, 252, 256–7
paradigm 113–15
  Kuhn's sense 120, 240
  Merton's sense 16, 113–15,
    245, 269n
  paradigm for functional
    analysis 136, 141, 146, 212
  paradigm for the sociology of
    knowledge 38
  paradigm for structural
    analysis 143, 223
patterned misunderstandings 31
permissiveness 294n
personality 193, 194, 195
phenomenon of the 41st chair 64
Phoenix phenomenon 31, 70
plagiarism 58, 75
pluralistic ignorance 62, 171
positivism 85–6, 87–8, 248
potentials of elaboration 6
potentials of relevance 6, 31, 92,
  95, 118

poverty of sociology 81
power 204, 205, 207, 213, 224,
  225
practical curiosity 94
praxis 92
problem-formulation 93–8
process, social 199
  adaptive processes 202–10
  circular processes 235, 255
  cyclical processes 255–6
  development 292n
  morphogenetic processes 152,
    154, 155, 202, 207, 210–27
professions 32, 191, 192
progress in science 73, 247–8,
  274n
propaganda 226
propaganditis boomerang 226
proto-concept 99
pseudo-Gemeinschaft 31, 257
puzzles in science 120

quantitative orientation 101

radical epistemological
  relativism 77–8
ratchet effect 64
rationality 228–9
rebellion 185, 188, 220
referee-system in science 63
reference-groups 29, 33, 230–2, 254
  comparative type 231
  negative reference-group 231
  normative type 231
  reference-group behaviour 230
  reference-group conflicts
    232–3
  reference individuals 230
reflexivity 92, 233
relational control 224
relevance 52, 91, 94–5
retreatism 185, 187
reward system of science 63
ritualism 185, 187
roles, social 164–5, 177
  multiple roles 290n
  role-bargains 208
  role-conflict 2, 180–1, 203–7

roles, social – *continued*
  role-set   10, 17, 31, 33, 146, 160, 165–6, 177, 180, 181, 197, 198, 203, 224
  role-strain   208–9
scientific community   13, 39, 45, 60–6
scientific ethos   2, 45, 49, 50–60, 88, 270n, 271n, 277n
scientific mind   45, 49, 50
scientific revolution   74, 113, 120, 260
secrecy   289n
selective accumulation of knowledge   12, 73, 74, 104, 115, 127, 243, 248
self-defeating prediction   234, 235, 246
self-destroying prophecy   234, 255
self-fulfilling prophecy   31, 92, 234, 235, 236, 237, 246, 255, 268n
sensitising ideas   31
serendipity   31, 98
  serendipity pattern   98, 103, 260
serial monogamy   157
social categories   172
social erosion   94
social groups   172
social heterogeneity   166
social life   160, 171–3
social orientation   20
social problems   93
  latent social problems   93, 251
  manifest social problems   93
socialisation   193–4, 232
  adult socialisation   194
  anticipatory socialisation   232–3
  socialisation in science   65
socially expected durations (SEDs)   125, 153, 156–7, 286n, 299n
sociological Berkeleyanism   239, 244
sociological epistemology   38, 75–9
sociological neo-Kantianism   78, 100

sociological orientation   3, 102, 119, 244
sociological problems *v.* social problems   93–4
sociological schools   121
sociological system   3, 158
sociological vernacular   98
sociology   123–5
  sociology *v.* psychology   123–5, 299n
  sociology of knowledge   26, 37–40
  sociology of science   26, 28, 32, 37, 40, 41–5, 75
  sociology of knowledge *v.* sociology of science   37–45
  youthfulness of sociology   84–5, 107
specified ignorance   13, 31, 83, 97, 98, 122, 260
status, social   160
  central status   288n
  dominant status   288n
  salient status   288n
  status-complements   166
  status-inequality   166
  status-sequence   146, 161
  status-set   31, 33, 146, 161, 166–7, 181, 197, 203, 233, 290n
strategic research site   31, 64, 97
structural analysis   31, 115, 143–50, 251
  focus on social structure   123–5, 252
  paradigm for structural analysis   143, 223
  sociological structuralism   31, 126, 144, 149, 200, 298n
  structural explanations   141, 149–50
  structural laws   149
structuralist theme   4, 5, 7, 25, 26, 27, 145, 241, 248–52, 257–8
structure, social   144–7, 159–73, 161–2, 173
  ideal structure   163, 169–71

structure, social – *continued*
  learning structures *v.*
    opportunity structures
    189–90
  normative structure   163–7, 182
  opportunity structure   148, 162,
    167–9, 176, 216, 222–3,
    287n
  parameters of social
    structure   166
  pattern   146, 264n
  social structure and
    personality   193–8
  social structure *v.* cultural
    structure   161–2
  social structure of science   42
  social structure *v.* social
    life   159–60, 183
  structural change   200
  structural constraints   132, 143,
    146, 182, 221, 229, 233,
    238, 250, 252
  structural context   143, 146,
    209, 212, 250, 251
  structural determination   182–4
  structural facilitations   148–9,
    182, 204, 221, 229, 233, 250

technical language *v.* jargon   99
teleologism   137–40
temporal analysis   152–7
thematic analysis   240–1
themes   240–1
theoretical logic   118, 281n
theoretical pluralism   115, 116,
  243

theoretical pluralism *v.*
  theoretical
  fragmentation   121
theory, sociological   89, 104–7
  complementary or contradictory
    theories   116–17
  consolidation of theories   11,
    109, 128, 245
  general theory   3
  grand theory   3, 18, 82, 243
  sociological explanation   89
  theory *v.* research   17, 18
    82–3, 102–7
Thomas theorem   62, 229–30,
  233–4, 255
thought-collective   66, 77, 78,
  122, 240, 242
thought style   77, 78, 240
time   2, 153, 154, 156, 254
totalitarianism and science   47–8
trained incapacity   62, 178, 194,
  256
triadic epistemology   77, 242

unanticipated consequences   134,
  251
unintended consequences   69,
  134, 251
universalism of science   53

values   51, 164, 185
value-relevance   95
variables   100
vested interests   167–8, 176, 191
visibility   27, 61, 170, 249, 288n